Perspectives on Philosophy of Communication

Philosophy/Communication
Ramsey Eric Ramsey, Series Editor

Perspectives on Philosophy of Communication

Edited by Pat Arneson

Purdue University Press
West Lafayette, Indiana

Printed in the United States of America.

ISBN 978-1-55753-431-6
      1-55753-431-4

Library of Congress Cataloging-in-Publication Data
Perspectives on philosophy of communication / edited by Pat Arneson.
    p. cm. -- (Philosophy/communication)
  Includes bibliographical references and index.
  ISBN-13: 978-1-55753-431-6 (alk. paper) 1. Communication--
Philosophy. I. Arneson, Pat, 1961-
  P90.P379 2007
  302.201--dc22

                                      2006026141

J. G. M.

Contents

Acknowledgments

I would like to thank Duquesne University for granting a sabbatic leave that enabled me to pursue work on this project. I am grateful to faculty members in the Department of Communication & Rhetorical Studies for enriching conversation and professional opportunities that have profoundly influenced my scholarship.

The preparation of this book was made possible in part through the generous support of Dean Francesco Cesaro and the McAnulty College & Graduate School of Liberal Arts. Thank you for your support of this project.

My deepest appreciation is extended to the essay authors who generously shared their time and insights about philosophy of communication: Ronald C. Arnett, Leslie A. Baxter, Bettina Bergo, G. Thomas Goodnight, Michael Hyde, Lenore Langsdorf, Richard L. Lanigan, Algis Mickunas, Ramsey Eric Ramsey, and Jessica Sturgess.

Thank you to those who granted permission to reproduce images of philosophers featured in the book: Digne Meller-Marcowicz (Martin Heidegger), Richard Palmer (Hans-Georg Gadamer), Jerome Kohn and the Hannah Arendt Literary Trust (Hannah Arendt), Simone Hansel (Emmanuel Levinas), Suzanne Merleau-Ponty (Maurice Merleau-Ponty), Bruce Jackson (Michel Foucault), Daniel Martino and the Simon Silverman Phenomenology Center at Duquesne University (Maurice Merleau-Ponty), Algis Mickunas (Jean Gebser), Robert Louis Jackson (Mikhail Bakhtin), Frank J. Conahan and the MIT Museum (Roman Jakobson), and Corbis Corporation (Jürgen Habermas and José Ortega y Gasset).

I extend my gratitude to those who generously contributed their time and talents with language translation. This book is better because of your intellectual generosity. Renée Stanton, nos réunions chaque semaine étaient une inspiration. Votre aide avec les photographies des philosophes, de la correspondance multilingue, et de la traduction française des travaux était de valeur inestimable à l'accomplissement de ce projet. Merci. Daniel Aßmus, Ihre Unterstützung beim Erwerb der Photographien und besonders das Aufzeigen von Wegmarken bei den Bibliographien wird hoch geschätzt. Ich bin Ihnen dankbar für Ihre Bereitschaft mich geduldig durch die deutschen Übersetzungen zu leiten. Vielen Dank. Galina Dubrovina, Ваше терпение и внимательность к деталям вдохновляли меня. Я высоко ценю Ваше желание и готовность помочь мне с переводом на русский язык. Ваше жизнелюбие и смех всегда поднимали мне настроение и воодушевляли меня. Большое спасибо за

Вашу помощь и поддержку. A Jill Dishart, me inspiró su entusiasmo para este proyecto. Aprecio mucho su buena voluntad y asistencia con respeto a la traducción en español además de tu curiosidad intelectual. Gracias. Annette Holba, vestri porro term consolation illae exertus eram industrius. Ego sum memor pro vestri scholasticus suffragium quod fulcio meus servo incedo, quod pro vestry probus quod pius suscipio quod dummodo utriusque spiritus quod laxamentum. Gratias ago vos. Eveline Lang, Du verkörperst den philosophischen Geist mit einer Präsenz die inspiriert! Ich bin Dir dankbar für Deine Bereitschaft die mehrsprachigen Bibliografien durchzusehen und für Dein fortlaufendes Interesse an meiner Arbeit über all die Jahre. Vielen Dank!

I would like to thank the students at Duquesne University who make teaching such a wonderful learning experience. I am grateful to students in my philosophy of communication classes for taking part in the discussion of these ideas and urging me to complete work on this project. I would also like to thank my research assistants, Celeste Grayson, Reneé Stanton, and Andrew Bergstrom; James Vota for assistance with images; and Annette Holba for her preliminary reading and ongoing encouragement of this manuscript.

Thank you to Purdue University Press Philosophy/Communication series editor Ramsey Eric Ramsey for including this project in the series. Your thoughtful comments and encouragement have been greatly appreciated. Thanks to Purdue University Press Managing Editor Margaret C. Hunt. Your careful attention to this project and unflagging support has made all the difference. I extend my appreciation to the entire staff at Purdue University Press for their work bringing these ideas to fruition.

Special thanks to Saint Rita of Cascia, patron saint of impossible dreams, and to God, who moved this project forward. Thanks to my friends for your ongoing encouragement and support, and always, my family—you're my heart.

Introduction

Philosophy of Communication: Entering the Conversation

Pat Arneson

The virtue of reading the work of philosophers of communication is that they teach us to think about how we are communicatively situated in the world. The capacity to think critically and consistently, to understand various points of view, is necessary for negotiating one's experience in a postmodern world. This book is offered to readers as an invitation to "think with" philosophers of communication, to consider currents of philosophical discourse in communication studies, and to augment our ways of thinking and "knowing." The chapters are designed to create openings for the reader to pose further questions about the richness and density of our communicative life.

Our intellectual heritage provides ideas that can help us make sense of everyday life. Entrée into this book may be aided by considering ideas that assist in attuning oneself to read philosophy of communication; these include postmodernity, shifting one's understanding of education, and "defining" philosophy of communication. The influential scholars whose work is highlighted in each chapter have responded to some of the same questions we ask about communication. Venturing into philosophy of communication in a postmodern era, one accesses the unsettling of boundaries of communication marked by tensions that are inherent to human interaction.

Postmodernity

Various historical periods (broadly categorized as the antiquity/classical, medieval, renaissance, modern, and postmodern eras) mark changes in the intellectual pursuit of communication. Throughout each historical period, issues at the crossroads of philosophy and communication have been addressed. The philosophers of communication whose work is discussed in this book wrote primarily during the modern historical period, and several witnessed the decline of modernity and concurrent rise of postmodernity. Dennis K. Mumby notes that historical periods embody "different assumptions about the relationships among communication, identity, and knowledge formations."[1] The segmentation of various historical periods is not as "neat and tidy" as would initially appear; various assumptions overlap and extend across the different eras.

While there is no definitive starting point for postmodernism, Stuart Sim asserts that Jean-François Lyotard's 1979 publication of *The Postmodern Condition: A Report on Knowledge* provides "the most powerful expression of postmodernism."[2] The advent of postmodernity, ushered in in part by advances in transportation and communication technologies (compressing time/space), called people to recognize the plurality of narratives that coexist in our global society. This awareness brings forth questions about ethnocentric conceptions of life. In postmodernity, people recognize there is no longer (if there ever was) a common "grand narrative" or "meta-narrative" to which everyone subscribes.[3] Postmodernists are "critical of universalizing theories . . . as well as being anti-authoritarian in their outlook."[4] There is a suspicion and rejection of large narratives. People have an awareness of the numerous conflicting and partial narratives to which one may adhere at differing times. One cannot assume that each individual one comes into contact with will hold similar understandings of the world.

The term "postmodern" resists definition, by virtue of what the term represents—a recognition that individuals live according to different ways of life that are constantly changing in response to additional information and reflection. Norman K. Denzin articulates the breadth of "postmodernism":

> The troublesome oxymoron postmodernism overflows with meaning. It simultaneously refers to a series of historical markers, to the new information technologies in the age of the simulacrum, to the cultural styles and aesthetics which dominate this moment, to the cultural logics that organize work, family, sexuality, race, and class, and most importantly, it references the lived experiences, the personal troubles and the public issues that define life in the late twentieth century. At the level of lived experience postmodernism refers to the attempt by contemporary men, women, and children to get a grip on this doubly modern and postmodern world and make themselves at home in it. The postmodern is everywhere and nowhere. It has no zero point, no fixed essence. It contains all the traces of everything that has come before. Its dominating logic is that of a hybrid, never pure, always paradoxical. It mocks and absorbs historical forms, always having it both ways, always modern and postmodern, nothing escapes its attention. Its logic of use and utility can turn anything from the past into a commodity that is sold, or used to sell a commodity in the present. . . . At the same time, empty seriality is now the bond which unites the audience, and the electronic image is the only sign of reality that counts.[5]

One revelation among postmodernists is that "progress," the driving metaphor of the modern age, is an illusion. Stuart Sim explains, "We see *progress* as linear, with an end, materialistic and having universality associated with it."[6] In an era void of universally shared narratives, the metaphor of progress loses the richness of its entailments and ceases to reverberate through society in the same way it once did. Certainly, aspects of society, including the economic sphere, are still driven by the metaphor of progress, but people are beginning to conceive "progress" differently (e.g., in the movement to "simplify" one's life[7]).

Seyla Benhabib perceives that postmodernity is manifested through a "fractured spirit." She argues there is a "current mood of skepticism . . . based upon an understandable disillusionment" that is destructive to all things essential to the survival of humankind[8] The study of philosophy of communication holds the potential to address this "fractured spirit" (while ever open to the possibility of new and different fractures). The unsettling nature of postmodernity reveals within it opportunities for social change. This includes the opportunity to study multiple viewpoints and cultural recognitions that inform any discussion of human communication—and to consider communication as it shapes these differences—regardless of the question one asks. Calvin O. Schrag claims that "One of the most notable consequences of the advent of postmodernity has been a recognition of the multiplicity of forms of discourse and the heterogeneity of social practices in the affairs of public life."[9] This places communication as central in the postmodern era. Gary Brent Madison expands upon this notion:

> For postmodernism, human understanding is linguistic and interpretive through and through. A good illustration of this is the position defended by philosophical (or phenomenological) hermeneutics. "Why," Hans-Georg Gadamer asked in a famous essay of his, "has the problem of language come to occupy the same central position in current philosophical discussions that the concept of thought, or "thought thinking itself," held in philosophy a century and a half ago?" The answer: "Language is the fundamental mode of operation of our being-in-the-world and the all-embracing form of the constitution of the world." . . . Human linguisticality is accordingly a "universal phenomenon."[10]

Everyone experiences the world through language, used to negotiate one's "situatedness" within the lived world.

Communicators must be mindful in the postmodern age, considerate of ways to better understand connections with others and craft communicative responses. This requires thinking differently about learning and education.

Education as Theoria-Poiesis-Praxis

From the Greek *paideia,* through the Renaissance *studia humanitatis,* to the modern university, the study of rhetoric and communication has played a significant role in education. The compartmentalization of academic disciplines in the university setting artificially segments how one understands and negotiates one's lived experience. One can look to philosophy of communication to think "otherwise" about the educational experience. The postmodern call for a reconfiguration of theoria-poiesis-praxis provides a way to more fully understand the contribution of philosophy of communication for informing one's lived experience.

Philosophy of communication is best understood as a reasoning art. Lenore Langsdorf explains that the reasoning arts recall the time of Socrates when philosophy, poetic, and rhetoric were unified (Greek *paideia*). Following the death of Socrates, Plato advocated the separation of these three disciplines, which was further propelled by Aristotle and the literacy revolution:

> It may well be that philosophy as we have come to know it . . . marked by sophisticated methods of analysis and primarily directed toward demonstrating the truth of propositions or validity of arguments, could only occur within literacy. But poetic and rhetoric, as educational *technai* [useful arts], were also captured by the new technology. As written prose became the genre of communication for education, the rhythms of oral poetic composition that had engaged the bodies and emotions of speakers and hearers were relegated to music and dance, both of which were seen as extra-curricular activities. The curriculum, particularly after cultural change (the "scientific revolution") roughly contemporaneous to another revolution in communication technology (from manuscript writing to mechanical printing) valorized a conception of knowledge as accurate representation of nature. Communication's function was to transmit information arrived at through inductive reasoning from evidence surrendered by nature, or through deduction from general principles or axioms. Given this goal, the creative imaging, sensory and emotional appeal, and potential transformation of audiences that are characteristic of poetic and rhetoric were irrelevant and even unwelcome, since identically repeatable results, regardless of time, place, and personnel (given the requisite training of the latter), were valorized.[11]

Over two thousand years of systematic education has solidified the disparate categories of content we recognize as "philosophy," "poetic," and "rhetoric." Yet in one's everyday life, reasoning works as an integrated and interactive functioning of these areas.

Lenore Langsdorf suggests the instruction of rhetoric, separated from poetic and philosophy, is now experiencing what Richard A. Lanham in *The Electronic Word: Democracy, Technology, and the Arts* called an "extraordinary convergence of social, technological, and theoretical pressures: that, in effect, reverses the literacy revolution that separated the reasoning arts."[12] She cautions that reversing the revolution of literacy does not automatically imply integrated theory, practice, and teaching of the reasoning arts. However, thematizing the suppressed integration opens the possibility for instructional change.[13] Langsdorf identifies the primary social pressure prompting this shift as the "expansion across class lines of the student population during the past century, which confuses the ancient separation between educated elite and general population."[14] For contemporary students, the "normalizing" tradition of the humanities does not "make sense," "perhaps because their everyday (non-classroom) learning and very being has been shaped by other traditions, and by communication technologies other than those of literacy."[15] These and other social and technological pressures have inspired theoretical pressures which are brought to the fore in postmodernism.

Philosophy, poetic, and rhetoric are joined in one's daily experience. Lenore Langsdorf explains, "Once we recognize that we can only interrogate our experience, rather than bypass engagement with the phenomena in order to report how things are apart from it, we see that poetic, in the sense of creative engagement with a cultural scene, rhetorically shapes the content that philosophy analyzes."[16] She draws upon Ernesto Grassi's explication of ingenium: "In contrast to the empiricist tradition that identifies observation of nature and (formal) logical reasoning as the basis of learning, Grassi argues for that basis being in 'ingenious activity': 'The activity of ingenium consists in catching sight of relationships; this 'grasping' is 'the source of creative activity' that develops topics (categories), in terms of which teaching and learning occur."[17] Academic disciplines delimit boundaries on a student's learning, which may hinder one's response to pragmatic questions that require an integration of reasoning arts.

Theoria-Poiesis-Praxis

The separation of the reasoning arts began with Plato and was advanced by Aristotle. Calvin O. Schrag notes that the emergence of modernity further widened the gap between theory and practice,[18] and poiesis was marginalized to the arts. The early separation of reasoning arts privileged philosophy as an area of inquiry.

Lenore Langsdorf explains that philosophers may take several orientations toward investigating any subject matter, including communication: these orientations include attention to the good, being, knowing, doing, and making. These orientations are not necessarily exclusive interests, although philosophers have generally chosen to explore them as separate research specializations. She notes that research and teaching typically are categorized as axiology (the good), epistemology (knowing), or metaphysics (being). Attention to doing (praxis) and making (poiesis) has most often come from outside academic philosophy or as a critique to academic philosophy.[19] While the three areas of theoria, poiesis, and praxis are integrated in the reasoning arts, a brief overview assists in understanding the contribution of each, which are conjoined differently in various philosophies of communication.

Each reasoning art emphasizes a different form of knowledge. Lenore Langsdorf explains that *theoria* displays the kind of knowing called episteme (what is necessarily so) in contrast to doxa (opinion). Episteme is sophia, wisdom, which is the province of philosophy. *Theoria* is not practical and is not productive. "[I]t is concerned with general knowledge, without regard for either its applicability to acting (doing) in particular circumstances or to fabrication (making) particular products. *Theoria* may well inform our knowledge of particular things; but it does not entail any particular knowledge claim or produce its subject matter."[20]

Lenore Langsdorf continues, in contrast to "theoria's strict concern with thinking, praxis is concerned with acting as it is informed by thinking. This 'informing' is a matter . . . of using cognitive procedures intrinsic to theoria—but now in relation to very different subject matter."[21] Praxis displays the kind of knowing called *phronesis*. "[P]hronesis as a mode of reasoning focuses on process rather than product; on human doing and deeds that intrinsically develop in our doing."[22]

Calvin O. Schrag articulates further differences of theoria and praxis. For theoreticians, practice is always in service of theory. This presents two difficulties for praxis. First, "practice, as an application of theory, has to wait upon the determinations of theory for its meaning or intelligibility." Second, "while practice without theory is blind, theory without practice is empty."[23] The subject matter of praxis is the actions in which humans engage as they go about their everyday lives as members of communities. Schrag emphasizes that "Praxis as the manner in which we are engaged in the world and with others has its own insight or understanding prior to any explicit formulation of that understanding. . . . [P]raxis, as I understand it, is always entwined with communication."[24]

For Calvin O. Schrag, communication includes "the manner and style in which messages are conveyed and imparted always against the background of the tightly woven fabric of professional and everyday life, with it shared experiences, participative relationships, joint endeavors, and moral concerns"[25] In Schrag's work on communicative praxis, discourse and action are *about* something, *by* someone, and *for* someone. Communicative praxis "displays a referential moment (about a world of human concerns and social practices), a moment of self-implicature (by a speaker, author, or actor), and a rhetorical moment (directedness to the other)."[26] Communicative praxis is the "amalgam of language and speech, discourse and action 'that textures . . . the space of human endeavoring, exhibiting a striving for an understanding and explanation of the configurations of experience through which such endeavoring passes.'"[27] Schrag "writes of the 'texture' (cf. *textile* and *text*) of communicative praxis to underscore how all its elements are woven together, including everyday speech, the written word, and the 'play and display of meanings' within both perception and human action"[28] In the hermeneutical space of communicative praxis the epistemological subject is decentered and rationality is disseminated into the discursive practices that make up society.[29]

Theoria, praxis, and poiesis each display a different sort of knowing. Poiesis as artifactual *production* (making) is distinguished both from human *action* (doing) and from theoretical *philosophizing* (knowing). Calvin O. Schrag explains that communicative praxis lies "between the theoretical and the practical as they are generally understood."[30] Lenore Langsdorf argues for extending Schrag's concept of communicative praxis to address the significance of poiesis.[31]

If the three modes of knowing were arranged along a continuum from certain to contingent, Lenore Langsdorf notes that techné would occupy the middle position, and the continuum would appear as episteme-techné-phronesis. "It almost seems as though techne is the object of a pulling and tugging from both episteme and praxis: now toward certainty, insofar as techne can be reduced to the sort of replicable methods that characterize science; now toward contingency, insofar as it does not allow of strictly codified methods. Correlatively, poiesis seems pulled at times toward episteme, and at other times toward praxis."[32] This pull "between" episteme and praxis reveals two distinct kinds of making or dimensions within poiesis that are generally not distinguished from one another.[33] "One dimension is the making of things—spatiotemporally existent entities—which are the intrinsic product of poiesis. The second is the constituting of self in performances that may also produce things. The subjectivity that comes into being in the space of communicative praxis is the extrinsic, or transcendent, result of poiesis."[34]

Lenore Langsdorf locates communicative poiesis at the core of the formation of communicative praxis:

> Once we identify the core of this [communicative] process as poiesis rather than praxis, however, and thus recognize that we are concerned with adapting conditions rather than producing things, we are free to use methods other than analysis by composition and division.... [C]onversation—and communication of all sorts—is a brief linguistic hiatus in the going process of action and reflection, doing and making. ... A philosophy of communication that appreciates the function of both poiesis and praxis in mind's emergence understands those responses as rooted in innovative and insightful, and also inherently fallible, processes of generating possibilities for adapting conditions, within the goal of responding to the changing needs of human being.[35]

"[T]he classical notion of poiesis ... [is] in contrast to (but always also, as a moment within) praxis."[36] The convergence of theoria-poiesis-praxis is recalled in postmodernity. Further, as Calvin O. Schrag notes, "One of the most important contributions of postmodernism has been to reinstate rhetoric and communication as native voices in philosophical discourse."[37]

"Defining" Philosophy of Communication

Philosophy of communication both reveals cracks in the smooth surface of scholarship and cracks the smooth surface by tearing open meanings to release new possibilities. As understood in this work, "philosophy of communication" investigates philosophical thought about how humans are communicatively situated in the lived world. Philosophy of communication pertains to the study of ideas used to analyze, describe, and interpret communication as lived experience.

Boundaried tensions are revealed in reading "philosophy of communication." The phrase "philosophy of communication" is the convergence of philosophy with communication. Calvin O. Schrag and David James Miller note the term "convergent" "presupposes something that makes a difference, something that comes between that which comes together." Philosophy of communication examines the "convergence without coincidence" of the two disciplines.[38]

Defining philosophy of communication requires addressing both the areas of communication and philosophy. Drawing from Ramsey Eric Ramsey, "What is communication? Is a bad question because, ultimately, it is . . . unhelpful." Such a question embodies philosophical presuppositions that serve to reify the phenomenon. Such a question considers this vibrant topic to be a static object and directs scholars to look for its "essence." The essence of communication can not be found in a static conception of the phenomenon. Descriptions of communication (and philosophy of communication) must seek to understand the phenomenon in a way that creates space for its fullness.[39]

> Broadly speaking, communication can be thought of as the manner in which persons relate to their social world, to others, and to themselves. Philosophy, again broadly speaking, can be thought of as an intellectual account of the interrelated aspects of the social world. Thinking this way, then, it seems clear that a link between these two fields of study should be strongly forged. Said differently, communication, taken as a human practice, is fundamental for relating with the world, with others, and with ourselves. Because of this there needs to be a rigorous account of how these relations are constituted, and philosophy in general . . . are the means for providing such an analysis.[40]

Philosophy of communication regards the world with a condition of openness and space for possibilities inherent in communication.

Communication enables people to achieve "particular access to the givenness of the world."[41] The interplay of various moments in the communicative process opens up alternate ways of seeing and doing things. As humans, "[w]e are always in language . . . we are in language as we are in-the-world in Heidegger's sense of being-in-the-world."[42] In understanding ourselves as being-in-the-world, "we are always already communally situated, so that . . . communication/community becomes a structural determinate of our being-in-the-world."[43]

Philosophy of communication examines questions related to the nature and function of human communication. Different philosophies of communication provide varying lenses to examine the conditions for, and consequences of, human communication. Ultimately, philosophy of communication looks at the temporal coordinates that "hold together" a given view of the world. The task of philosophy of communication is to articulate the significance of those coordinates for communication with self, other, and society; philosophy of communication "works" to help us enhance our understanding of how communication shapes society and social issues within society. Philosophy of communication, understood as a reasoning art, enables an "innovative, rather than reproductive or representational, understanding of communication"[44] for negotiating oneself in a postmodern world.

Attuning One's Philosophical Spirit

In entering philosophy of communication, it is helpful to take into one's reading a disposition of "philosophical spirit." By this I mean a situated orientation
open to possibility.[45] I invite a hermeneutic reading of the text which recognizes
the relationships of theoria, poiesis, and praxis to collaboratively inform understanding. Calvin O. Schrag reminds us that hermeneutics, as the performance
of interpretation, is at hand "wherever there is speech and action . . . that is at
once an understanding and an expression of meaning through which both self
and world are disclosed."[46] Reading "differently" may require modifying how
one understands language.

Lenore Langsdorf writes that the literacy revolution

> depended upon the eye as much as orality had depended upon the ear.
> Yet the nature of the seen was quite different from the nature of what had
> been heard: principles and maxims were not stated in propositional form,
> quite apart from the lived experiences (ongoing and recalled deeds) that
> had been the medium for epistemic endeavors as well as theoretical and
> moral teaching in oral cultures. Learning became a matter of separating
> mind from sensory involvement in the world, and the philosopher's life of
> conversation with the Forms was extolled as superior to the rhetorician's
> life of conversation with fellow members of the polis. Furthermore, the
> eye engaged in reading does not see the page as it would see the face of
> another who tells of deeds, events, and things. The seeing that occurs in
> reading is quite removed from actually seeing those deeds, events, and
> things about which the rhetor tells. Thus we already have, in Plato, the
> clear and distinct *seeing* of *ideas* that is the distinguishing characteristic
> of good thinking in Descartes.[47]

To read "differently" is to appreciate the adumbrations that reveal and are revealed in poetic creativity of text.

One cannot read in a mechanical manner, considering language to be a
tool at one's disposal. We are always *in* language. We are embedded within language, and language is always at work in our lived experience.[48] Scott McLemee
articulates Hans-Georg Gadamer's perspective: "The world of meanings found
in art, philosophy, and history is far wider and deeper than anything the contemporary interpreter is able to imagine. We are, in effect, a product of that
tradition. Even when arguing with it, we use concepts and language inherited
from tradition."[49]

A reader cannot alter or control his/her reading when one's inquiry is directed at understanding. Lenore Langsdorf notes, "In the midst of this rather
dense multivalence, I 'disclose, discover' what 'would not otherwise have been
noted.'"[50] Irruptive thought may be uncomfortable in its newness, but is not
necessarily discomforting. Edgar Sheffield Brightman expressed, "The spirit
that combines tolerance with conviction, open-mindedness with loyalty, yet

compromises neither, is a mature product of philosophy [of communication] at its best."[51] In reading, one will recognize differences among philosophers' standpoints and orientations. Life is richer when all voices/perspectives find full expression.

Philosophy of communication has the power to change how one orients oneself in the world. Konstantine Boudouris and Takis Poulakos explain that working from a philosophical understanding enables communicators to "interrogate our experience, grasp it in a variety of relations, and speak about it from positions opened up by those relations."[52] Philosophies of communication serve to enrich our understanding of the life process, enabling us to better understand the relationship between communicative content and action.

Ramsey Eric Ramsey notes, "The practice of communication is one powerful manner for disclosing these attendant possibilities of becoming other. It is also a powerful way of explicating for ourselves and other what is blocking these possibilities."[53] There is a restorative nature to the "philosophical spirit." A philosophical spirit injects new meaning into "meaningless" drama and can inspire one to think "differently." Openness to the density of meaning prompts an understanding of the co-extensiveness of self, other, and society in the ongoing construction of the human world. This openness does not, however, invite an "anything goes" interpretation of the ideas that have been carefully and deliberately articulated by philosophers of communication. Features of rigorous hermeneutic inquiry must guide the interpretive process.[54]

With the societal shifts that mark postmodernity, the philosopher's ideas included in this work are even more relevant to understanding communication now than when they were first written. Each philosophical perspective gives shape to discourse and assists us in understanding lived experience and acting constructively with regard to social issues. John C. Kelly recognizes that people ordinarily do not question the everyday "taken-for-granted" world. At times, contrary evidence may force one to realize that some aspect of the given world is not as it was once thought to be. Accepted interpretations may fail to account for a new experience, or the broader society may be persuaded by some of its constituent groups that a new interpretation is better.[55] In this space, philosophy of communication is helpful.

John C. Kelly notes that "To analyze the world of daily life philosophically is to begin to differentiate one's consciousness. That is to say, it is to begin to be aware of and to recognize different forms or modes of human knowing and, consequently, of human communication."[56] As one differentiates one's awareness, previously "invisible" aspects of life become "visible." Living in a postmodern global society requires one to devise means for communication across difference. Calvin O. Schrag explains that "with this travels the tough question What is the *meaning* of communication?"[57] To take up philosophy of communication is to take up the exciting challenges of and within the discipline of human communication/rhetorical studies.

Overview of the Book

This book provides an opportunity to consider the communicative applications of the ideas of various philosophers, yielding the potential to extend the general body of scholarship about human communication. Each chapter includes three sections. First, a biographical sketch of the philosopher of communication provides insight into the historical moment in which the philosopher worked and lived. Second, an invited scholar provides an overview of the contributions each philosopher offers for communication inquiry. Third, a comprehensive bibliography of books, seminars, and lectures in first edition (to the extent possible) along with available English translations is included for each philosopher of communication.

Biographical Sketches

Given the recent controversy surrounding Jean Grondin's biography of Hans-Georg Gadamer,[58] combined with several of the included philosophers' public expressions of dislike for biographies, a reader may question the inclusion of biographical sketches for each featured philosopher of communication. Their inclusion presents the face of the person and claims their biography from the perspective of hermeneutic phenomenology.

In drawing from Hans-Georg Gadamer's work to better write about the philosopher, Scott McLemee recognizes that coming to terms with a philosopher's work is a hermeneutic conversation. One never approaches the world with a blank slate. The process of understanding always begins with some established understanding (prejudice) already in place. Gadamer recognized prejudice as a fact of hermeneutic life that must be accepted before it can be challenged through a "fusion of horizons" between the contemporary interpreter and the cultural tradition. "Tradition, for Gadamer, is one name for the burden of history, for that which we need to confront and think. It is not an authority to which we need to defer."[59] Gadamer had clear misgivings about biography. Scott McLemee cites Jean Grondin: "He [Gadamer] doesn't think you can understand the work out of the person's life. I would say you cannot *reduce* the work to the [person's] life."[60]

I urge readers to interpret this project from a hermeneutic, rather than psychological, perspective. Vernon E. Cronen critiqued the communication discipline's emphasis on psychological interpretations of human communication: "The psychology project replaced the classical rhetorical focus on public action with a strong tendency toward the interiorization of life. The solution to social problems came to be sought at the level of individual 'mind.'"[61] When reading hermeneutically, one cannot project causal motivations to a person's writings (e.g., "because Heidegger was a Nazi that is why"). One can not determine "why" an author wrote as he/she did, short of the writer's articulating his/her authorial intent. John Stewart explains that "understanding is not a matter of achieving a one-to-one correspondence between meaning and author or speaker intent. Cultural, social, and contextual factors are all determinative" in one's writing about the lived world.[62] Gary Brent Madison reminds that "One of the basic tenets of rhetorical (as well as hermeneutical) theory is that no discourse is context-free, or to put it the other way around, that all discourse is 'situated,' originates from out of a specific perspective."[63] While the biographical sketches appear at the beginning of each chapter, they are not to be foregrounded in understanding the philosopher's work: the philosopher's ideas must carry the weight in discussion.

The emphasis in philosophy of communication is on the philosopher's ideas. Calvin O. Schrag shared,

> I am reminded here of the response that we received from Martin Heidegger after setting up the Heidegger circle some thirty or thirty-five years ago. We had planned to discuss Heidegger's approach to technology. So we wrote to him, told him about the existence of the circle, and informed him that we were going to be discussing his approach to technology. We received this very interesting letter from him, telling us that he was touched by the fact that we had an annual meeting devoted to a discussion of his philosophical accomplishments. But he urged us not to talk about his approach, but rather talk about the issue of technology. . . . I am hopeful, in this way, what Friedrich Nietzsche always feared can be avoided, namely becoming a disciple or coming to have disciples.[64]

In addition to Schrag's caution about becoming enamored with a particular individual, there is also the march of time to consider. Many readers may be unfamiliar with events defining the time in which philosophers lived and wrote. Reading the biographical sketches as background information to assist one's hermeneutic interpretation of their work will aid in providing an enriched understanding of the ideas present in each essay.

Essays

Each essay considers the work of a different philosopher, addressing how communication scholarship takes shape under the tutelage of that perspective and providing inspiration for original and important thinking. The essays consider the work of well-recognized philosophers: Martin Heidegger, Hans-Georg Gadamer, Hannah Arendt, Jürgen Habermas, Emmanual Levinas, Maurice Merleau-Ponty, the conjoined work of Roman Jakobson/Maurice Merleau-Ponty/Michel Foucault, Jean Gebser, José Ortega y Gasset, and Mikhail Bakhtin. Different philosophical approaches provide varying understandings in examining the conditions for, and consequences of, communicative praxis.

In considering "where" to begin one's venture, John Stewart cites Calvin O. Schrag: "the philosopher searching for a proper 'starting point' can no longer begin from an unassailable axiom or unimpeachable epistemological principle, but must rather ponder how best to enter the ongoing conversation in such a way that its primary themes, directions, and misdirections can be noted and described."[65] One considers the question one wishes to ask about communication and considers how various philosophical thoughts can best inform one's project.

This project began with the recognition of an intellectual web of ideas about philosophy of communication emerging from the University of Marburg in Marburg, Germany.⁶⁶ Directly or indirectly, each of the philosophers whose work is addressed was involved with views that emerged there. For example, at various points Martin Heidegger, Hans-Georg Gadamer, and Jürgen Habermas each taught at the University of Marburg. Heidegger's major work *Being and Time* was published while he was on the faculty there. Gadamer (born in Marburg) completed his second doctorate under Heidegger's direction and later returned to teach at the University of Marburg. Habermas's *Habilitationsschrift* (post-doctoral thesis), which was presented at the University of Marburg, formed the basis of his work *The Structural Transformation of the Public Sphere*. Emmanuel Levinas first met Heidegger at the University of Freiburg (Heidegger's alma mater), where Levinas pursued studies in phenomenology under Edmund Husserl. At different times, both José Ortega y Gassett and Hannah Arendt attended the University of Marburg as students. In all likelihood, Mikhail Bakhtin became familiar with the ideas of the Marburg school through the work of Matvei Kagan, a member of his intellectual circle.⁶⁷ Born in Germany, Jean Gebser was undoubtedly aware of the influence of the Marburg school. Maurice Merleau-Ponty and Michel Foucault both studied at the École Normale Supérieure in Paris. Merleau-Ponty, greatly influenced by Husserl, rejected Husserl's theory of the knowledge of other persons and generalized Heidegger's insights to include the analysis of perception.⁶⁸ Merleau-Ponty's work then made way for his poststructuralist successor, Foucault.⁶⁹ The philosophers' ideas often intend/extend toward and/or diverge from each other as each develops his/her philosophy of communication. Each essay provides an understanding of the work of the philosopher of communication and provides openings for how his/her work creatively informs issues of human communication.

"Searching for Perfection: Martin Heidegger (with Some Help from Kenneth Burke) on Language, Truth, and the Practice of Rhetoric," is authored by Michael J. Hyde. Rhetorical theorists and critics have turned to Heideggerian philosophy to illuminate the ontological nature of the orator's art and to provide direction in assessing how this art is actually practiced in our everyday lifes. This essay offers a critical assessment of Heidegger's hermeneutic phenomenology of language, especially as it dates back to his (yet unpublished and untranslated) lecture course on Aristotle's *Rhetoric*. In light of this assessment, Hyde offers a discussion of Heidegger's lifelong struggle to answer the question of Being (*die Seinsfrage*).

"Callicles' Parlor: Revisiting the *Gorgias* after Dwelling with Gadamer," is authored by Lenore Langsdorf. The venerable dispute between rhetoric and philosophy can take a new direction when engaged in from the perspective of Hans-Georg Gadamer's hermeneutic phenomenology. Within the broad rereading of the philosophical-rhetorical tradition that Gadamer's work inspires, Langsdorf focuses on the separation of learning and knowledge from action and belief that occurs in Callicles' parlor when Socrates arrives. Her thesis is that Plato devises, through their dialogue, a separation of transcendent and transcendental truth that is denied by evidence supplied by rhetorical action. Using the evidence to reject that separation holds implications for the contemporary debate concerning the materiality of rhetoric.

"Hannah Arendt: Dialectical Communicative Labor," is authored by Ronald C. Arnett. This essay situates Hannah Arendt's contribution to social/philosophical praxis within the metaphor of communicative labor. Her philosophy united communication and labor as a necessary carrier of ideas into action. She pointed to a philosophy of communication labor, not to describe, but to engage the labor of social/philosophical praxis and change. Arnett examines Arendt through a communication lens with the coined term "communicative labor" guiding the interpretive task. Communicative labor situates communication as the carrier of philosophically shaped action into the "private" and "public" domains of human life. Communicative labor suggests a view of communication incongruous with what Arendt called the "social."

"The Engagements of Communication: Jürgen Habermas on Discourse, Critical Reason, and Controversy," is authored by G. Thomas Goodnight. This essay explicates the approach of social theory in the study of human communication. The post-cold war works of Habermas are read as he develops a theory of communicative action and mobilizes this point of view to engage in debates with philosophers, historians, and advocates of the public realm. Goodnight addresses how Habermas mobilizes this communicative point of view to engage and critique positions in philosophical and political debates, including discussions over systems reasoning, genetics, terrorism, and the Holocaust. The essay concludes with a discussion of the prospects of social theory for learning from evolving communication controversy.

"Ethical Selfhood: Emmanuel Levinas's Contribution to a Philosophy of Communication" is authored by Bettina Bergo. This essay investigates Levinas's response to the question "How does communication arise?" Bergo articulates the significance of individual passions which reveal a layer of experience that contributes to communication. Three inflections of Levinas's work are outlined: the affective roots of his philosophy of communication, the realm of exteriority and communication, and his understanding of ethical sensibility and the possibility of communication through the flesh, as inspired by Merleau-Ponty.

"Maurice Merleau-Ponty: Communicative Practice," is authored by Algis Mickunas. This essay explores Merleau-Ponty's understanding of the primacy of "I can" in bodily communication. Mickunas shows that "higher" levels of communication are metaphoric extensions of the already understood body and intercorporeal constitution of concrete and immediate communication providing both for individuation and communalization. The explication of the "I can" is grounded on the primary, perceptual, corporeal engagement with the world and others comprising an overlapping field of phenomena that, as perceived, are also involved in perceptual communication. This is to say that the intercorporeal communication is also worldly communication. As we engage with the perceived phenomena, the phenomena are equally engaged in communicating our axes of activity. In this sense, we can be communicative agents only because we are engaged agents in the world. The essay delimits the way that language and bodily activities, the "I can," mutually overlap, vary, and extend one another. This also requires an analysis of the "in between domain," wherein the communicative overlapping in bodily communication is constituted prior to action-reaction and form and matter: communication is in constant self-generation.

"Communicology: The French Tradition in Human Science," is authored by Richard L. Lanigan. Together, Roman Jakobson, Maurice Merleau-Ponty, and Michel Foucault create a comprehensive theory of a semiotic phenomenology of human discourse and practice. Merleau-Ponty's focus on perception and Foucault's complementary focus on expression constitute the building blocks of a human science grounded on the quadratic of discourse : parole :: language : langue. In addition, Pierre Bordieu extends this theory to practice, completing the application of embodied discourse as a human science in research method and product.

"Jean Gebser's Cosmology: Poetic Openings and Dialogic Possibilities," is authored by Pat Arneson. Jean Gebser's work considered the basic forms of perception present in culture. This essay overviews Gebser's cosmological theory and further discusses potentialities in his work for enhancing communication scholarship by addressing the historical context that propelled Gebser's writing and identifying the significance of his ideas for a postmodern age. Arneson outlines Gebser's dimensions of consciousness, which include the archaic, vital-magic, psychic-mythic, mental-rational, and integral structures. Each "structure" or "dimension" holds distinct nuances that contribute differently to configure cultures in varying ways. Poetic expression provides an opening through which the comprehensive integral dimension can be revealed. The work of Martin Buber, a philosopher of dialogue, exhibits how dimensions of consciousness are available in the "between" of dialogue. His use of Hasidic tales, or "poetic narratives," in dialogue aware or call the listener to Gebser's integral dimension of consciousness.

"There Is Nothing Outside Circumstance: Near, Against, With(in) Ortega y Gasset" is authored by Ramsey Eric Ramsey (with an accompanying "Ghostly Hand" compiled and arranged by Ramsey Eric Ramsey and J. N. Sturgess). Ortega gives us not only much to ponder concerning *what* we may say and think about communication, but, with equal importance, *how* we might go about articulating what we might come to say. His meditations on depth and surface and the clarity each demands, as well as his thoughts on circumstance, are both in form and content exemplified in his *Meditations on Quixote*. Trying to embody what he calls the brief gesture that leads to the pedagogy of suggestion, Ramsey shares some of the many insights that Ortega's philosophy of communication has to offer.

"Mikhail Bakhtin: The Philosophy of Dialogism" is authored by Leslie A.

Baxter. This essay overviews those aspects of Bakhtin's dialogism theory that hold particular relevance to communication scholars. Dialogism decenters the monadic self; instead, Bakhtin advocates viewing "self" as an ongoing process of emergence in the interanimation of voices—perspectives, values, horizons of seeing. Baxter considers the centrality of Bakhtin's work on "utterance," understood not as the act of an autonomous speaker but as a site where multiple voices interpenetrate. Voices are rarely on equal footing; rather, it is possible to identify centripetal voices (voices that are privileged or centered) and centrifugal voices (those marginalized or muted voices that represent "Other"). "What voices interanimate in communication?" is a central question to ask of communication from a dialogic perspective. Baxter summarizes the primary kinds of voices that can be present (and absent) in talk and examines the implications of a dialogic perspective for the study of communication.

Together these essays provide insight into various philosophies of communication. Each philosopher conceives communication differently and holds potential for generating further insight into the process of human communication.

Inclusion of Bibliographies

A comprehensive bibliography of the first editions of books, seminars, and lectures of each philosopher, along with English translations, is included after each essay. This provides readers with a useful research tool and also source citations for reading first editions of works in the philosopher's first language. Gadamer urged, "We must learn more languages. That is the main point. English will naturally become the worldwide language of commerce, but there will be mother tongues everywhere. And that is what we must fight for. Every language has a new point of view, and one will become more tolerant when one permits the way that other speaks. I believe that by learning more foreign languages, one will be educated in the end to a greater self-critique."[70] The bibliographies are provided to encourage readers to extend themselves into other writings to increase their depth of understanding about the philosopher's work. Together, the biography, essay, and bibliography for each philosopher of communication are designed to provide entrée for readers to explore the expanse of issues included in philosophy of communication.

Ongoing Conversation

The conversation about philosophy of communication provides a rich opening for understanding the multiplicities at work in the process of human communication. This introduction offered an overview of postmodernity; encouraged understanding of a shifting education that calls for altering the contemporary fragmentation of theoria, poiesis, and praxis; addressed "defining" philosophy of communication; and encouraged attuning oneself to a philosophical spirit which enables insight for social action that alters the way we understand and approach self, others, and society. This invitation to "think with" philosophers of communication and augment one's understanding of lived experience enables one to, in turn, pose further questions about the experience of being-in-the-world that is our communicative life.

> "This is what my hermeneutics always had in view: there is no last, definitive word. That is given to no one. If the other misunderstands me, then I must speak differently until he understands me. We are all always only underway."—Hans-Georg Gadamer[71]

Notes

1. Dennis K. Mumby, "Modernism, Postmodernism, and Communication Studies: A Rereading of an Ongoing Debate," *Communication Theory* 7 (1997): 1.
2. Stuart Sim, "Postmodernism and Philosophy," in *The Routledge Companion to Postmodernism*, ed. Stuart Sim (New York: Routledge, 2001), 3.
3. Jean-François Lyotard, *The Postmodern Condition: A Report on Knowledge,* trans. Geoff Bennington and Brian Massumi (1979; Minneapolis: University of Minnesota Press, 1984): 34–37.
4. Sim, *The Routledge Companion to Postmodernism*, vii.
5. Norman K. Denzin, *Images of Postmodern Society: Social Theory and Contemporary Cinema* (Newbury Park, CA: Sage, 1991), 151.
6. Sim, *The Routledge Companion to Postmodernism*, vii.
7. A plethora of books are currently available on the market suggesting techniques for simplifying one's life. For example, Jerry D. Jones, *201 Great Questions to Help Simplify Your Life* (Colorado Springs, CO: NavPress, 1999); Patrick Fanning and Heather Garnos Mitchener, *The 50 Best Ways to Simplify Your Life: Proven Techniques for Achieving Lasting Balance* (Oakland, CA: New Harbinger Publications, 2001); Tiki Kustenmacher, *How to Simplify Your Life: Seven Practical Steps to Letting Go of Your Burdens and Living a Happier Life* (Frankfurt am Main: Campus, 2004).
8. Seyla Benhabib, *Situating the Self: Gender, Community, and Postmodernism in Contemporary Ethics* (New York: Routledge, 1992), 2.
9. Calvin Schrag, "Foreword" in Ramsey Eric Ramsey, *The Long Path to Nearness: A Contribution to a Corporeal Philosophy of Communication and the Groundwork for an Ethics of Relief* (Amherst, NY: Humanity Books, 1998), xi.
10. Gary Brent Madison, *The Politics of Postmodernity: Essays in Applied Hermeneutics* (Dordrecht: Kluwer Academic Publishers, 2001), 71.
11. Lenore Langsdorf, "The Homecoming of Rhetoric," in *The Philosophy of Communication:* Volume II, ed. Konstantine Boudouris and Takis Poulakos (Alimos, Greece: International Center for Greek Philosophy and Culture, 2002), 109. "A variety of translations of the word Techne (singular form of technai) can be found in contemporary Greek-English dictionaries, including 'art,' 'artistry,' 'craft,' 'liberal arts,' and 'applied skill.' . . . [T]echne is a term hard to translate, but perhaps best rendered as 'art' if one remembers that it meant primarily the useful arts and handicrafts and only latterly, if at all, the fine arts"; Hunter Groninger, "What Do

We Mean by 'The Art of Medicine'?" *The Pharos,* Autumn 2004, 28, http://www.al-phaomegaalpha.org/Pharos/New/Articles/ Autumn2004Groninger.pdf (accessed October 23, 2005).

12. Langsdorf, "The Homecoming of Rhetoric," 110. See also Richard A. Lanham, *The Electronic Word: Democracy, Technology, and the Arts* (Chicago: University of Chicago Press, 1995).

13. Langsdorf, "The Homecoming of Rhetoric," 117 n. 30.

14. Ibid., 110.

15. Ibid.

16. Ibid., 111.

17. Ibid.

18. Ramsey Eric Ramsey and David James Miller, "From the Loving Struggle to the Struggle to Love: A Conversation with Calvin O. Schrag," *Experiences Between Philosophy and Communication: Engaging the Philosophical Contributions of Calvin O. Schrag,* ed. Ramsey Eric Ramsey and David James Miller (Albany: State University of New York Press, 2003), 21. See also Lenore Langsdorf, "In Defense of Poiesis: The Performance of Self in Communicative Praxis," *Calvin O. Schrag and the Task of Philosophy after Postmodernity,* ed. Martin Beck Matuštík and William L. McBride (Evanston, IL: Northwestern University Press, 2002).

19. Lenore Langsdorf, "Philosophy of Language and Philosophy of Communication: Poiesis and Praxis in Classical Pragmatism," *Recovering Pragmatism's Voice: The Classical Tradition, Rorty, and the Philosophy of Communication* (Albany: State University of New York Press, 1995), 198.

20. Langsdorf, "In Defense of Poiesis," 288–289.

21. Ibid., 289.

22. Ibid.

23. Ramsey and Miller, "From the Loving Struggle to the Struggle to Love," 21.

24. Ibid.

25. Calvin O. Schrag, *Communicative Praxis and the Space of Subjectivity* (West Lafayette, IN: Purdue University Press, 2003), 22.

26. Langsdorf, "In Defense of Poiesis," 281.

27. John Stewart, *Language as Articulate Contact: Toward a Post-Semiotic Philosophy of Communication* (Albany: State University of New York Press, 1995), 229.

28. Stewart, *Language as Articulate Contact,* 232.

29. Calvin O. Schrag, "Rhetoric Resituated at the End of Philosophy," *Quarterly Journal of Speech* 71 (1985): 172.

30. Ramsey and Miller, "From the Loving Struggle to the Struggle to Love," 21.

31. Langsdorf, "In Defense of Poiesis," 281.

32. Ibid., 290.

33. Ibid.

34. Ibid., 282.

35. Ibid., 207–208.

36. Langsdorf, "In Defense of Poiesis," 282.

37. Ramsey and Miller, "From the Loving Struggle to the Struggle to Love," 14.

38. Calvin O. Schrag and David James Miller, "Communication Studies and Philosophy: Convergence without Coincidence," in *The Critical Turn: Rhetoric and Phi-*

losophy in Postmodern Discourse, ed. Ian Angus and Lenore Langsdorf (Carbondale: Southern Illinois University Press, 1993), 126.

39. Ramsey Eric Ramsey, *The Long Path to Nearness: A Contribution to a Corporeal Philosophy of Communication and the Groundwork for an Ethics of Relief* (Amherst, NY: Humanity Books, 1998), 6–8.

40. Ramsey, *The Long Path to Nearness,* 2.

41. Ibid., 41.

42. Ibid., 95.

43. Ramsey and Miller, "From the Loving Struggle to the Struggle to Love," 16.

44. Langsdorf, "Philosophy of Language and Philosophy of Communication," 197.

45. My use of the term "philosophical spirit" is not meant to allude to Hegel's sense of the phenomenology of spirit. My intention is not, as he notes, to guide "The journey of spirit through the various shapes of consciousness constitutes . . . a veritable *itinerarium mentis* in Deum: the phenomenology of spirit is a religious quest, a pilgrimage"; Peter C. Hodgson, *G. W. F. Hegel: Theologian of the Spirit* (Minneapolis, MN: Fortress Press, 1997), 92. Nor do I intend this disposition, as Hegel suggested, to be "a forepiece that can be dropped and discarded once the student, through deep immersion in its contents, has advanced through confusions and misunderstanding to the properly philosophical point of view"; J. N. Findley, "Foreword," *Hegel's Phenomenology of Spirit,* trans. A. V. Miller (New York: Oxford University Press, 1967), v.

46. Schrag, *Communicative Praxis,* 170.

47. Lenore Langsdorf, "Words of Others and Sightings/Citings/Sitings of Self," The Critical Turn: Rhetoric and Philosophy in Postmodern Discourse, ed. Ian Angus and Lenore Langsdorf (Carbondale: Southern Illinois University Press, 1993), 22.

48. Ramsey, *The Long Path to Nearness,* 96.

49. Scott McLemee, "Questioning the Past: A New Biography Fuels Debate over the Relationship between Hans-Georg Gadamer's Philosophy and the Nazi Era," *Chronicle of Higher Education,* July 18, 2003, A15.

50. Langsdorf, "Philosophy of Language and Philosophy of Communication," 205.

51. Edgar Sheffield Brightman, *An Introduction to Philosophy* (New York: Henry Holt and Co., 1925), 21.

52. Konstantine Boudouris and Takis Poulakos, "Introduction," in *The Philosophy of Communication,* vol. 2, ed. Konstantine Boudouris and Takis Poulakos (Alimos, Greece: International Center for Greek Philosophy and Culture, 2002), 11.

53. Ramsey, *The Long Path to Nearness,* 16.

54. See, for example, Richard E. Palmer, *Hermeneutics* (Evanston, IL: Northwestern University Press, 1969); Kurt Mueller Vollmer, ed., *The Hermeneutics Reader: Texts of the German Tradition from the Enlightenment to the Present* (New York: Continuum, 1988); Hans-Georg Gadamer, *Philosophical Hermeneutics,* trans. and ed. David E. Linge (Berkeley: University of California Press, 1977); Hans-Georg Gadamer, *Truth and Method,* trans. Joel Weinsheimer (New York: Continuum, 1999).

55. John C. Kelly, *A Philosophy of Communication* (London: Centre for the Study of Communication and Culture, 1981).

56. Ibid., 7.

57. Ramsey and Miller, "From the Loving Struggle to the Struggle to Love," 11.
58. McLemee, "Questioning the Past," A14. See also Jean Grondin, *Hans-Georg Gadamer: A Biography* (New Haven, CT: Yale University Press, 2003); Richard Wolin, "Nazism and the Complicities of Hans-Georg Gadamer: Untruth and Method," *New Republic,* May 15, 2000, 36–45; Richard E. Palmer, "A Response to Richard Wolin on Gadamer and the Nazis," *International Journal of Philosophical Studies* 10 (2002): 467–482.
59. McLemee, "Questioning the Past," A16.
60. Ibid.
61. Vernon E. Cronen, "Communication Theory for the Twenty-First Century: Cleaning Up the Wreckage of the Psychology Project," *Communication: Views From the Helm for the 21st Century,* ed. Judith Trent (Boston, MA: Allyn & Bacon), 19.
62. Stewart, *Language as Articulate Contact,* 234.
63. Madison, *The Politics of Postmodernity,* 102.
64. Ramsey and Miller, "From the Loving Struggle to the Struggle to Love," 6.
65. Stewart, *Language as Articulate Contact,* 231–232.
66. The University of Marburg (Philipps-Universität in Marburg an der Lahn) was founded in 1527 during the Reformation. The University of Marburg is the oldest Protestant university in existence. The university system initially had four faculties (Theology, Law, Medicine, and Philosophy) and includes many small faculties which are often represented by just one professor. See "History of Philipps-Universität Marburg," http://www.uni-marburg.de/zv/geninf/historie_e.html (accessed October 28, 2003).
67. Craig Brandist, "The Bakhtin Circle," in *The Internet Encyclopedia of Philosophy,* ed. James Fieser and Bradley Dowden (Martin, TN: University of Tennessee, 2003), http://www.utm.edu/research/eiep/b/bakhtin.htm (accessed October 28, 2003).
68. Encyclopedia of Marxism, "Merleau-Ponty, Maurice," http://www.marxists.org/glossary/people/m/e.htm (accessed October 28, 2003).
69. Gary Brent Madison, "Merleau-Ponty, Maurice," *The Cambridge Dictionary of Philosophy,* ed. Robert Audi (Cambridge, UK: Cambridge University Press, 1999), 558–560.
70. Ansgar Kemmann, "Heidegger as Rhetor: Hans-Georg Gadamer Interviewed," *Heidegger and Rhetoric,* trans. Lawrence Kennedy Schmidt, ed. Daniel M. Gross and Ansgar Kemmann (Albany: State University of New York Press, 2005), 62.
71. Ibid.

Martin Heidegger (1889–1976)

Biographical Sketch

Martin Heidegger was born on September 26, 1889 in Messkirch, in southwestern Germany to sexton and master cooper Friedrich Heidegger and Johanna née Kempf. He grew up in a modest Catholic family that was active in the local church. Heidegger went to high school in Constance on scholarship and lived in a Catholic boarding house, beginning to prepare for the priesthoood. In high school he was introduced to the work of Franz Brentano, a forebear of the phenomenological movement, which evoked his interest in philosophy.

Different sources report inconsistent information about the life of Martin Heidegger. Information for this biographical sketch was drawn from Alfred Denker, "Heidegger's Chronology"—http://evans-experientialism.freewebspace.com/heideggerschronology.htm (accessed October 9, 2003); Charles B. Guignon, "Heidegger, Martin," *The Cambridge Dictionary of Philosophy*, 2nd ed., ed. Robert Audi (Cambridge: Cambridge University Press, 1999); Michael Inwood, *Heidegger: A Short Introduction* (New York: Oxford University Press); Thomas Sheehan, "Heidegger, Martin (1889–1976)," *Routledge Encyclopedia of Philosophy*, vol. 4, ed. Craig Edward (New York: Routledge, 1998); Stuart Sim, "Heidegger, Martin," *The Routledge Companion to Postmodernism* (New York: Routledge, 2001). Photograph of Martin Heidegger by Digne Meller-Marcowicz.

Heidegger studied theology and philosophy at the University of Freiburg, but by the summer of 1911 had abandoned his plans to become a Jesuit priest. In 1911, he switched his course of study to mathematics and the natural sciences. While at Freiburg he began to study the writings of Edmund Husserl and Wilhelm Dilthey. By 1913 Heidegger earned his doctorate in philosophy with a dissertation entitled "Die Lehre vom Urteil im Psychologismus" (The Doctrine of Judgment in Psychologism).

Heidegger taught at the University of Freiburg as a lecturer from 1915 to 1923. In 1917, Heidegger married a Protestant woman, Elfriede Petri. Heidegger's academic career was interrupted when he was drafted into military service in 1918. Found unsuited for active duty, he was relegated to postal and meteorological duties. Heidegger's first son, Jörg, was born in 1919, and his second son, Hermann, was born in 1920.

When Heidegger returned to Freiburg in 1919, he announced his break with Catholic philosophy. Heidegger was appointed to the junior position in philosophy at the University of Marburg (1923–1928). In 1925, Heidegger began a year-long affair with his then student Hannah Arendt. The relationship ended when Heidegger emerged as a Nazi sympathizer: Arendt was Jewish.

In 1928, Heidegger was appointed as Edmund Husserl's successor to the chair of philosophy at the University of Freiburg (1928–1945). On April 21, 1933, Heidegger was elected rector (president) of the University of Freiburg. On May 3, 1933, Heidegger joined the Nazi Party. He delivered several lectures in support of the National Socialist revolution and Hitler and his policies.

This position and his support of the Nazi Party and Adolf Hitler himself would come to divide Heidegger from friends (such as Husserl) and colleagues in the academy. After the war, Heidegger was suspended from teaching because of his Nazi activities in the 1930s. In 1950, however, he was allowed to resume teaching, and thereafter he occasionally lectured at the University of Freiburg and elsewhere.

Martin Heidegger died at his home in Zähringen, Freiburg, on May 26, 1976, and was buried in his home town of Messkirch.

Searching for Perfection
Martin Heidegger (with Some Help from Kenneth Burke) on Language, Truth, and the Practice of Rhetoric

Michael J. Hyde

The phenomenological investigations of Martin Heidegger unfold in a life-long endeavor to answer a specific question as completely (perfectly) as possible: What is the meaning, the truth, of Being? The truth of Being is necessarily present in the particular existence of any entity. With the existence of *human* being in mind, Heidegger's answer to the question makes much of the relationship between Being and language:

> Language is not a mere tool, one of many which man possesses; on the contrary, it is only language that affords the very possibility of standing in the openness of the existent [the presencing of Being]. Only where there is language, is there world, i.e., the perpetually altering circuit of decision and production, of action and responsibility, but also of commotion and arbitrariness, of decay and confusion.[1]

The human world is only possible through our use of language, which "presences" Being.

Heidegger's appreciation of language is ontologically oriented. What he observed to be "the essence of language" does not originate in the everyday sociopolitical and rhetorical workings of discourse. Rather these workings presuppose the existence of a more primordial discourse that opens us to the disclosure of what the world presents for comprehension and what, in turn, can be re-presented by us in a meaningful (i.e., symbolic) manner. The essence of language is primarily associated with our *being open* to the disclosing of what *is*. This association raises the issue of "truth." Phenomenologically speaking, truth happens, first and foremost, as an act of disclosure, a "showing-forth" (*epi-deixis*) or epideictic display of something that presents itself to us. The assertion and validity of any "truth claim" presupposes the occurrence of such an act.

Heidegger's first detailed and most famous assessment of the matter is found in his *Being and Time* (1927); although in his earlier lecture course on Aristotle's *Rhetoric* (1924)—which the rhetorical scholar Nancy Struever credits as providing "arguably . . . the best 20th century reading" of Aristotle's text—one finds Heidegger breaking ground for his continuing investigations of the relationship between Being and language.[2] Heidegger not only agrees with Aristotle, especially with the first two books of the *Rhetoric*, he also credits him with providing an interpretation of the everyday, communal workings of discourse that is unsurpassed in its insightful treatment of the topic. Aristotle helps make it possible for Heidegger to begin understanding in a rigorous way the relationship between Being and language.

I expand on these introductory comments throughout this essay. Some of what I have to say about the relationship between Being and language should be familiar to those who know the literature in communication and rhetorical studies that draws direction from Heidegger's early and later philosophy. The novelty of my project comes with the topic that I employ to help organize my discussion and that, to the best of my knowledge, is not identified in this literature as a major theme: the metaphysical pursuit of perfection. I know of no place in Heidegger's writings where he explicitly deals with this topic in any detail. Yet, as one who gives much thought to the relationship between Being and language and the issue of truth that is necessarily associated with the relationship, Heidegger's writings overflow with indirect references to the metaphysical pursuit of perfection. His entire philosophy, as well noted, is a response to a call to come to complete terms with the truth of Being. The rhetorical dimension that this task entails is suggested by Heidegger when he notes: "Even the essential word, if it is to be understood and so become a possession *in common*, must make itself ordinary."[3]

The most famous discussion of perfection found in the communication and rhetorical literature is provided by Kenneth Burke when, clarifying how it is that human beings are "rotten with perfection," he examines the "perfectionist" nature of language. I include some of Burke's insights regarding this matter in this essay. In doing so, I hope to offer readers a way of understanding Heidegger's philosophical project that may be especially helpful to those who would feel more comfortable following my lead while in Burke's company. Bringing Heidegger and Burke into conversation with each other about the topic of perfection will enable to me to clarify limitations and problems in their respective treatments of the topic and its relationship to language, truth, and the practice of rhetoric. In the rare remarks that Burke offers on Heidegger's philosophy, there is a hint that this union might prove helpful in trying to understand humankind's metaphysical propensities. I am motivated by this hint, even though Burke's remarks offer, at best, a minimal understanding of Heidegger's interest in the question of Being and the metaphysical impulse that grants the question significance.[4]

Animalia Metaphysica

Human beings are metaphysical creatures: beings fated to struggle with the ever present challenge of "getting things right," "making thinks better, "improving" themselves, being as "complete" as they can be as they grow, mature and become wise with the years. A well-known saying "of progress" is associated with this struggle and challenge: "Practice makes perfect." Indeed, we are beings capable of performing activities that, although at times quite demanding, are nevertheless satisfying because they are perceived as advancing our "goodness" and thereby testify to our "hope in the future" where humankind's potential for perfectibility can continue to be actualized. Especially when coupled with past successes, the metaphysical strength of this hope registers itself as a longing or "nostalgia" to feel secure and at home with ourselves and others—in short, to have it, as they say, "all together." A state of perfection is a state of completeness.

Such all togetherness is what the formal philosophical doctrine of metaphysics is all about: it seeks a unifying perspective of the totality of what *is*—Being. Human beings are born philosophers, whether or not they are ever awarded an advanced degree in the discipline. Everyday existence calls us to this vocation, especially when things go wrong. The philosopher Karl Jaspers emphasizes this point when he notes that the

> philosophical life springs from the darkness in which the individual finds himself, from his sense of forlornness when he stares without love into the void, from his self-forgetfulness when he feels that he is being consumed by the busy-ness of the world, when he suddenly wakes up in terror and asks himself: What am I, what am I failing to do, what should I do?[5]

If only for a moment, we are likely to lose our bearings in life when, for whatever reason, we find ourselves in situations that disrupt our current "comfort zones" such that we must address these questions "for our own goodness," as well as for the goodness of others. The disruption exposes an incompleteness to our being and thus triggers a metaphysical impulse. We are creatures whose nostalgia (from the Greek *nostos:* to return home) for security and completeness makes us susceptible to the ailment of becoming homesick for familiar and welcoming surroundings.

This ailment infects our well-being and the peace of mind that can accompany it; and this, to be sure, is not a perfect way to be. Indeed, have you ever met a person who enjoyed being in a constant state of homesickness? Wanderlust can certainly have its rewards, but having a "dwelling place" (*ethos*) where some reprieve is offered from the grind of everyday life and that we can call home defines a need that seems to be written into our genes. Moses and his people wandered in the desert for forty years, but not without the hope that they would eventually reach the "promised land." In Judaism, the word for dwelling-place (*makom*), be it "promised" or not, is also a word that refers to God's presence. Even God needs a place (e.g., the planet earth) to be heard and responded to ("Where art thou?" "Here I am!"), a home away from home (heaven), if you will. Judaic tradition stresses that we are capable of responding to God because we are gifted with a "heart"—the ability to be awed by and to wonder and care about others. "I will give them a heart to know Me, that I am the Lord (Jeremiah 24:7). "The Lord appeared to Abram and said unto him, I *am* the Almighty God; walk before me, and be thou perfect [Hebrew: *tamin* or 'wholehearted']" (Genesis 17:1–2). The heart allows for a genuine acknowledgment of, and a "knowing-together" (Gk. *sunei-desis*; Lat. *con-scientia*) with, God. In the New Testament, the word "heart" becomes the moral operation of "conscience" (1 Corinthians 8 and 10).[6]

Western religion is filled with moralistic rhetoric that addresses the guiding question of metaphysics: Why is there something (Being) rather than nothing (non-being)? Heidegger answers the question without resorting to what cosmologists term "God-in-the-gaps" thinking. As he puts it:

> Only from the truth of Being can the essence of the holy be thought. Only from the essence of the holy is the essence of divinity to be thought. Only in light of the essence of divinity can it be thought or said what the word "God" is to signify. . . . How can man at the present state of world history ask at all seriously and rigorously whether the god nears or withdraws, when he has above all neglected to think into the dimension in which alone that question can be asked?[7]

The "dimension" referred to here is the event of existence (Being) as it discloses itself in and to human being.

For Heidegger, the truth of Being is most apparent in the existence of that being whose consciousness of the world is most advanced in its related capacities of reflection (critical thinking) and articulation (symbolic expression). Heidegger initially puts it this way: Human being "is an entity which does not just occur among other entities. Rather it is ontically distinguished by the fact that, in its very Being, that Being is an *issue* for it."[8] In other words, what Heidegger designates as the "special distinctiveness" of human being that differentiates it from other entities is that this entity is concerned with its existence, its Being, its way of becoming what it is. This concern for Being is constantly demonstrated in one's everyday involvement with things and with others. Reflecting on the meaningfulness of what is being demonstrated, one can, and often does (especially in times of crisis), raise the question of what it means to be. The question makes explicit a human being's concern for Being. Only human being is consciously concerned enough to do this. And because it is also capable of understanding to various degrees what it is doing out of concern for its Being, human being can provide an answer to the question. Heidegger thus tells us that "man should be understood, within the question of Being, as *the* site which Being requires in order to disclose itself. Man is the site of openness, the there," the place within all of existence where Being finds a "clearing," where it can be observed with care and then shared in language that is remarkable for its disclosive (truth-telling) capacity.[9]

Much is made possible by our being a "dwelling-place" for Being. This ontological character of our existence, as Heidegger constantly reminds us, originates with the spatial and temporal structure of human being that—although typically measured by human beings with such inventions as clocks, calendars, maps, and computers—is *not* itself a human creation. The way in which what was (the past) and what is (the present) are constantly open to the objective uncertainty of what is not yet (the future) defines an event that is always already at work before we decide to notice and to calculate its presence. Human being, in other words, has something about its Being that is *more* and thus *other* than its own making—

something whose objective uncertainty is the basis of "mystery." What will happen tomorrow? Who can say for sure? What is the source of this "otherness" of Being that discloses itself in our lives but is not of our own making?

The most common and "obvious" answer to this last question is, of course, "God." Heidegger neither denies nor affirms the "correctness" of this answer. He is more interested in being true to the empirical demands of phenomenological inquiry and thus does not deviate from the task of advancing a description of the ontological workings of this otherness. How exactly does this phenomenon work itself out in our lives? In both his early and later philosophy, Heidegger addresses this question by examining how human beings embody some aspect of otherness in the way we exist as a "being-toward death." We *are* finite creatures. Life carries with it its own negation. As soon as we are born (or conceived), we are old enough to die. The otherness ("nothingness") of death names "a presence of absence" that is at "play" in the midst of Being, that can make its nullifying move into our everyday lives at any moment, and that is well-known for inciting the "dread" of anxiety. Individuals who suffer from "communication apprehension" (the "stage fright" of speaking in public before an audience), for example, are well acquainted with this emotion. What will people think of them as they express themselves to others? Some of these reticent-prone souls are even known to say that they "felt like they were dying" while in the situation.[10]

For Heidegger, however, this example points to something of "greater" ontological significance. When trying to come to *complete* terms with the experience—terms that grapple with how it is that Being can be so disturbing, disruptive, and overpowering—we eventually find ourselves at a loss for words. Being (its presence *and* absence) is! That's life! Short of the word "God," the play going on here "gives" only itself to go on. As Heidegger puts it, the revealing or "presencing" of Being is at the same time a concealing, for the play of Being is also that which "holds itself back and withdraws" whenever we attempt to grasp *the* reason for its happening, for its Being the way it is. "The play is without 'why,'" writes Heidegger. "It plays since it plays. It simply remains a play: the most elevated and the most profound."[11] Hence, following Heidegger, it may be said that the play of Being—which gives itself to us by way of the presencing of all that lies before us—is itself a "mystery," for it is never without an element of "absence."

Heidegger describes this absence as the void of "nothingness," the "Nothing" out of which the coming to presence of all that is appears. The ancient metaphysical question—"Why is there something rather than nothing?"—has it wrong. The Nothing of Being is real; it exists as the "annihilating" nature of Being itself, the way in which Being holds itself back and slips away from our grasp, refusing to be known completely, perfectly.[12] Using one of Burke's favorite terms to describe the resistance of material reality to be disclosed by acts of interpretation, one might say that the truth of Being, or what Burke refers to as "the eternally unsolvable Enigma," is exceptionally "recalcitrant." Burke puts matters this way:

We in cities rightly grow shrewd at appraising man-made institutions—but beyond these tiny concentration points of rhetoric and traffic, there lies the eternally unsolvable Enigma, the preposterous fact that both existence and nothingness are equally unthinkable. Our speculations may run the whole qualitative gamut, from play, through reverence, even to an occasional shiver of cold metaphysical dread—for always the Eternal Enigma is there, right on the edges of our metropolitan bickerings, stretching outward to interstellar infinity and inward to the depths of the mind. And in this staggering disproportion between man and no-man, there is no place for purely human boasts of grandeur, or for forgetting that men build their cultures by huddling together, nervously loquacious, at the edge of an abyss.[13]

Human beings, *animalia metaphysica,* pursue perfection as exhibited through the presencing and concealing play of Being revealed in language.

Language, Truth, and Rhetoric

Burke is far more interested in the resistance of reality to be disclosed in an act of interpretation than he is in the truth of Being. As a literary, rhetorical, and social critic, he is drawn to the material world of symbolic action and the way such action functions to make the world meaningful, for better or for worse. Regarding the nature of the abyss, Burke remains content to describe it as "the eternally unsolvable Enigma." Notice that he refers to this phenomenon by using the negative: "nothingness," "no-man." For Burke, however, these terms are not meant to describe some material "thing" (nothingness) that actually exists. There "are no negatives in nature," claims Burke. This "ingenious addition to the universe is solely a product of human symbol systems. . . . To look for negatives in nature would be as absurd as though you were to go out hunting for the square root of minus-one." Burke thus speaks only of "the sheer symbolicity of the negative." The "quickest way to demonstrate" this "fact," argues Burke, "is to look at any object, say, a table, and to remind yourself that, though it is exactly what it is, you could go on for the rest of your life saying all the things that it is not." Burke condenses the argument to the second clause of his "definition of man": this symbol-using creature is the "inventor of the negative."[14]

I will have more to say about the validity of this claim when I return to a discussion of Heidegger. Before doing that, however, it will be helpful to see how Burke further emphasizes the truth of this claim in his related discussion of what he terms the "perfectionist" nature of language.

Burke's understanding of "perfection" is rooted in Aristotle's "metaphysical" notion of "entelechy," which emphasizes how any entity—be it a stone, a tree, a bird, or a human being—comes about and develops in such a way that it aims at the perfection or completeness natural to its kind: the essence of what it *is.* Wanting to avoid additional metaphysical and ontological issues that accompany a full blown appreciation of this idea, Burke opts to confine his use of this "principle of perfection" to the material and thus empirical realm of symbolic action where it shows something of itself in the perfectionist impulse of language to "define" situations. He writes:

> The mere desire to name something by its 'proper' name, or to speak a language in its distinctive ways is intrinsically 'perfectionist.' What is more 'perfectionist' in essence than the impulse, when one is in dire need for something to so state this need that one in effect 'defines' the situation? And even a poet who works out cunning ways of distorting language does so with perfectionist principles in mind, though his ideas of improvement involve recondite stylistic twists that may not disclose their true nature as judged by less perverse tests.[15]

The impulse of language to define situations reveals a metaphysics of perfection.

Burke investigates the rhetoric of religious discourse in order to demonstrate just how far the perfectionist impulse of language can go in aiding human beings to satisfy their metaphysical desire to gain a complete understanding of the truth writ large—the Word—and whatever its opposite may be termed. Burke puts it this way: ". . . without regard for the ontological truth or falsity of the case, there are sheerly technical reasons, intrinsic to the nature of language, for belief in God and the Devil. . . . Heaven and Hell together provide the ultimate, or perfect, grounding for sanctions."[16]

Burke also emphasizes that, in being moved by the perfectionist impulse at work in a given doctrine, human beings too often take for granted the necessary shortcomings of the process. Although the definitions made possible by this impulse are meant to constitute vocabularies intended to be "reflections" of reality, they also at the same time are "selections" of reality. And any selection of reality must function as a "deflection" of reality, whereby the origin of manipulation begins to take form.[17] This selection/deflection function of language-use introduces "negation" into the process as it makes clear what the truth of the matter in question supposedly *is not*. The perfectionist impulse of language must always be attended to by the critic, argues Burke, in order to safeguard against those possibilities of interpretation that are marginalized and eliminated in the process but that still may possess degrees of truthfulness in what they have to say. Failing this critical task, we invite a potential and serious problem to manifest itself in our lives: that a given doctrine will condition its adherents to become close-minded to alternative possibilities of thought and action such that these people become "rotten with perfection." Burke maintains that this capacity is "revealed most perfectly in our tendency to conceive of a 'perfect enemy'. . . . The Nazi version of the Jew, as developed in Hitler's *Mein Kampf,* is the most thoroughgoing instance of such ironic 'perfection' in recent times."[18]

Ever since I began writing about Heidegger and Burke, I wished that the first of these influential thinkers would have read the works of the second and then offered an honest assessment of the similarities and differences that exist in their respective understandings of the essence of language and related matters. I also wished that Burke's brief references to Heidegger gave a stronger indication that he had carefully read and appreciated Heidegger's program of phenomenological research. Heidegger certainly would take exception to Burke's claim that human beings are the inventors of the negative. I think, however, that nothing less than embarrassment should be felt by Heidegger when considering the problem of being "rotten with perfection." Such embarrassment would be fueled by the similarities between the two thinkers regarding the "authentic" practice of rhetoric. A fuller discussion of these points is offered below in considering their shared interest in the metaphysical pursuit of perfection.

Recall that Heidegger identifies an "otherness" of Being that is not a human creation yet discloses something of itself in the experience of anxiety. We are not the inventors of that primordial spatial/temporal structure of existence that opens us to what is not yet. This openness grants human existence the status of being that place where Being finds a clearing, where it can be observed for whatever truth it reveals at the moment, and where it can then be represented symbolically. Burke shows no appreciation of Heidegger's discussion of the matter. I suspect he might grant that Heidegger is possibly on to something here. But Burke would not grant that this something—this otherness of Being that displays itself in the presence and absence of what is—is, in fact, a "nothingness" out of which the coming to presence of all that is appears. Heidegger's idea of "the Nothing" is, for Burke, a "something": "Insofar as an *idea* of 'Nothing' involves an *image,* it must be an image of 'something,' since there can be no other kinds of image."[19]

Indeed, Heidegger offers us an "image" of something that he terms "the Nothing." The image evolves out of a phenomenological inquiry concerning the truth of Being that far exceeds the scope of Burke's philosophy. Heidegger thus presents a detailed description of a primordial event, a process, as it happens everyday in our lives but that tends to be taken for granted until our everyday lives are disrupted by some "shocking" occurrence. The description captures the way the event presents itself while at the same time "holding itself back and withdrawing" from complete understanding. An example of Western religion's version of this specific happening is offered in the story of how Moses is only allowed to see God's back (never God's face) as God passes (withdraws) before him on Mount Horeb (Exodus 33, 18:23). Heidegger is not speaking of God; rather, he is speaking of an event that takes place before we can even begin to think about God. Everything that exists presupposes the presence of Being and the otherness that always accompanies it. If God created all of this, so be it. Burke substitutes labels ("The Eternal Enigma," "the abyss") for a careful phenomenological analysis of the process in question. Heidegger takes us even further beyond Burke as he continues his analysis of the matter.

Human existence provides an opening, a clearing, a dwelling place for Being to present itself to witnesses who can think about what truths it discloses, represent these truths symbolically, and, whenever necessary, contest their meaning and significance in an attempt to perfect human understanding. Heidegger describes the process as the ongoing "conversation" of humankind that informs the various ways that traditions, customs, rules, and norms of culture help to define the everyday public practices ("publicness") of social life. Although these practices and the rhetoric that informs them can and oftentimes do provide a breeding ground for the evils of conformism, they nevertheless also provide the necessary background for coming to terms with who we are first and foremost as social beings and for determining whether or not our extant ways of seeing, interpreting, and becoming involved with things and with others might be changed "for the better." Heidegger's positive take on the workings of this entire process is suggested when he noted in his 1924 lecture course on Aristotle's *Rhetoric* how the understanding constituting the received opinion (*doxa*) of a given public "reveals authentic being-with-one-another in the world" ("Die Doxa ist die eigentliche Entdecktheit des Miteinanderseins in der Welt").[20]

Heidegger's use of the word "authenticity" (*Eigentlichkeit*) is associated with the ability of human beings to assume the ethical responsibility of affirming their freedom through resolute choice. Aristotle's *Rhetoric* is Heidegger's guide for understanding and appreciating how this task is worked out rhetorically in the communal setting and how such rhetorical action can be employed to move people toward the just, the good, and, of course, the truth. The art of rhetoric has a necessary role to play when we attempt to communicate to others our individual thoughts on these matters. Rhetoric is a means for opening others to ideas, judgments, and proposed courses of action that, when appropriated and enacted, purportedly can enrich a community's understanding of what *is* and what *ought* to be. Rhetoric, in other words, exhibits a "disclosing" (truth-telling) capacity that serves the perfectionist (entelechial) impulse that informs and motivates human thought and action. Remember, "Even the essential word, if it is to be understood and so become a possession *in common*, must make itself ordinary."[21]

Heidegger, however, finds in this capacity something more than what Aristotle and Burke have to say about the topic. Any attempt to disclose the truth symbolically presupposes the workings of a more primordial process of truth-telling. The source of this process is not of our making. Rather, as discussed above, it is the spatial-temporal structure of existence that *opens* us to the contingency of the future and thereby, within this openness, *gives us a place to be* toward all that stands before us. We are creatures who are always caught up in the play of Being, always on the way toward understanding what can or will be in our lives but is *not yet*, and thus always confronted with the task of trying to make sense of and to do something with our lives. Human being is structured ontologically as an evocation and a provocation, or what Heidegger describes as the most original instance of "the call of conscience": As it discloses itself to us, existence calls for the responsiveness of concerned thought and action, for that which enables us, even in the most distressful situations, to take charge of our lives as we assume the responsibility of affirming our freedom through resolute choice and thereby become personally involved in the creation of a meaningful existence. This is how systems of morality come into being in the first place. The perfectionist driven language of morality is the language of responsiveness and responsibility that is called for by the ontological workings of Being.

At the heart of these workings lies an "otherness" that is as real as real can be and that lends itself to being described as a void, an abyss, a region of nothingness that simultaneously presents itself to, and withdraws from, human understanding. As he develops his phenomenological account of this process in his later philosophy, Heidegger makes much of how the actual disclosing of this process and "the call" that emanates from it define the "being of language" (*Logos*) in its most primordial state: the original presenting and "saying" of all that lies before us. Here, at this ontological level of existence, language is not understood first and foremost as a capacity for communication but rather as the original and silent manifestation, the "showing" (*Aufzeigen*) of *what is*.[22] This original act of disclosure comes before any symbolic act that attempts to disclose whatever truth is at issue at the time. The call of conscience (of our Being and its otherness) that calls for concerned thought and action "dispenses with any kind of utterance," writes Heidegger. "It does not put itself into words at all; . . . *Conscience discourses solely and constantly in the mode of keeping silent.*"[23]

Heidegger speaks to us of a discourse that is more original than anything he or anyone else has to say about it:

> The essential being of language is Saying as Showing. Its showing character is not based on signs of any kind; rather, all signs arise from a showing within whose realm and for whose purposes they can be signs. . . . Even when Showing is accomplished by our human saying, even then this showing, this pointer, is preceded by an indication that it will let itself be shown.[24]

Elsewhere Heidegger provides a description of what he is doing when articulating such observations: "To speak means to say, which means to show and to let [something] be seen. It means to communicate and, correspondingly, to listen, to submit oneself to a claim addressed to oneself and to comply and respond to it."[25] Conscience calls and Heidegger, listening attentively, phenomenologically, responds with a discourse meant to communicate to us the ontological workings of this call, its way of saying and showing itself to that particular being who has the linguistic ability to put into words what is perceived to be.

Heidegger turns to the workings of the "great" poet or artist in order to further philosophize about and illustrate the dynamics of this call (to perfection). In their capacity to open themselves to Being, these talented souls display extraordinary ability in using their materials to disclose something of the truth of a more original disclosure, or what Heidegger, in being true to his artistic preference, describes as the original "bringing-forth" (*poiesis*) of the truth of what *is* to our attention.[26] Another Greek term that is appropriate to use here is *epi-deixis*: a "showing-forth" of truth. This term, of course, heads us in the direction of rhetoric rather than poetry. Regarding the genre of rhetoric (epideictic) most steeped in this primordial discursive event of the saying (showing) of Being, Quintilian has said: "Indeed I am not sure that this is not the most important department of rhetoric in actual practice."[27] A phenomenology of the truth of Being and its call of conscience lends ontological support to this claim. The "saying" or disclosing of our temporal existence defines the most primordial form of epideictic speech and "public address." The call of conscience calls us to witness the disclosing of truth and then to disclose it to others in a meaningful way. It calls for concerned thought and decisive action. In short, it calls for what itself is: a rhetorical performance in the spreading of the word.

Aristotle does not speak of epideictic discourse in the *Rhetoric* in such an ontologically robust way; instead, he associates it more with speech that is designed to "praise" and to "blame" individuals. With Heidegger's reading of this work, then, he was not alerted enough to show how, in the discourse of everyday existence, there lies an "essential" clue for understanding the essence of language and the truth of Being. Taken to certain metaphysical ("heavenly") limits, this discovery about rhetoric suggests that God is not only the "greatest poet" but also the "greatest rhetorician." In the original showing and saying of existence, God offers what Kierkegaard terms "the essential sermon [of] one's own existence. A person preaches with this every hour of the day and with power quite different from that of the most eloquent speaker in his most eloquent moment."[28] The "saying" of human being is informed by a rhetorical impulse that speaks to the importance of remaining open to the disclosing of "otherness" (e.g., other things, other people) in the search for truth and perfection.

One can only wonder what, if anything, would have changed in Heidegger's work if he had taken notice of just how far rhetoric can be traced back into the heart of human being. Perhaps, for example, he would have demonstrated a more heart-felt response to the showing-forth of death that came with the Nazi regime in the 1930s and 1940s and that he eventually acknowledged in 1949 when he noted simply: "Agriculture is today a motorized food industry, in essence the same as the manufacture of corpses in gas chambers and extermination camps, the same as the blockade and starvation of countries, the same as the manufacture of atomic bombs."[29] The moral and rhetorical inappropriateness of this claim is obvious and embarrassing. For the particular showing-forth of death in question here calls for witnesses who can speak the truth of the horror that faces them by using words in such a way that the resulting rhetoric becomes itself a showing-forth of what is. With this specific epideictic event, witnesses might realize how dreadful the consequences can be when people do not know how to take to heart the presence and cries of others who would have us "never forget" what was done to them.

In the Old Testament one reads: "I will give them a heart to know Me, that I am the Lord" (Jeremiah 24:7). The gift here is that of "conscience": the capacity to remain open to and be awed and instructed by the happenings and mysteries of life.[30] Where was Heidegger's conscience as he spoke about the truth of Being and poetry at a time when a most competently created work of epideictic rhetoric was desperately needed in order to instruct the thinking and actions of others who lived on during and after the Holocaust? Burke's essay, "The Rhetoric of Hitler's Battle," which details what can happen to discourse when it is shaped by one who is utterly "rotten with perfection," provides an excellent example of what remains unsaid in Heidegger's writings.

In his *Truth and Method*, Hans-Georg Gadamer (arguably Heidegger's most famous student) writes: "What man needs is not just the persistent posing of ultimate questions, but the sense of what is feasible, what is possible, what is correct, here and now. The philosopher, of all people, must, I think, be aware of the tension between what he claims to achieve and the reality in which he finds himself."[31] For me, this statement is another way of warning the philosopher or any other person about the disease of becoming rotten with perfection. When his life-long philosophical project is seen in the historical light of a specific social and political context, Heidegger shows signs of having been infected by the disease and the blindness that goes with it.

The tragic irony here is that Heidegger's reading of Aristotle's *Rhetoric*—a reading that informs his notion of "authentic community" developed in *Being and Time*—speaks strongly against the dangers of this disease.[32] In working out an answer to the question of Being and its relationship to language, truth, and the practice of rhetoric, Heidegger saw the light, but for too short of a time. In that moment, however, something showed itself about Being that is rhetorical. Communication and rhetorical scholars have appropriated Heidegger's work in order to extend the ontological reach of their research. Doing this with someone like Burke whispering in our ears supplies an antidote against a certain ailment that can turn deadly in the course of "perfecting" our endeavors.

Notes

1.   Martin Heidegger, "Hölderlin and the Essence of Poetry," trans. Douglas Scott, in *Existence and Being* (South Bend, IN: Gateway Editions, 1949), 276.
2.   Martin Heidegger, "Grundbegriffe der Aristotelischen Philosophie," unpublished transcript of Heidegger's 1924 summer semester lecture course at Marburg, in the Marcuse Archive, Stadtsbibliotek, Frankfurt; Nancy S. Struever, "*Alltäglichkeit*, Timefulness, in the Heideggerian Program," in Daniel M. Gross and Ansgar Kemmann (eds.), *Heidegger and Rhetoric* (Albany: State University of New York Press, 2005).
3.   Heidegger, "Hölderlin and the Essence of Poetry," 275 (my italics).
4.   See Kenneth Burke, *The Rhetoric of Religion: Studies in Logology* (Berkeley: Univer-

sity of California Press, 1970), 20–21; and his *Language as Symbolic Action: Essays on Life, Literature, and Method* (Berkeley: University of California Press, 1966), 454. The most extensive comparison of Heidegger and Burke that I am aware of is Samuel B. Southwell, *Kenneth Burke and Martin Heidegger: With a Note against Deconstructionism* (Gainesville: University of Florida Press, 1987). The topic of "perfection" is not a central theme in his discussion.

5. Karl Jaspers, *Way to Wisdom*, trans. Ralph Manheim (New Haven, CT: Yale University Press, 1954), 121.

6. For expanded discussions of the relationship between "dwelling place" and the "heart," especially as this relationship in considered in ancient Greek and Judaic thought, as well as in phenomenological inquiry, see Michael J. Hyde, "Introduction: Rhetorically, We Dwell," in Michael J. Hyde (ed.), *The Ethos of Rhetoric* (Columbia: University of South Carolina Press, 2004), xiii–viii; Michael J. Hyde, *The Life-Giving Gift of Acknowledgment: A Philosophical and Rhetorical Inquiry* (West Lafayette, IN: Purdue University Press, 2006), chapter 4 ("Dwelling Places").

7. Martin Heidegger, "Letter on Humanism," in *Basic Writings*, ed. David Farrell Krell (New York: Harper & Row, 1977), 230. For a critique of "God-in-the-gaps" thinking by a Nobel Prize–winning physicist, see Steven Weinberg, *Dreams of a Final Theory: The Scientist's Search for the Ultimate Laws of Nature* (New York: Vintage Books, 1994), 241–261.

8. Martin Heidegger, *Being and Time*, trans. John Macquarrie and Edward Robinson (New York: Harper & Row, 1962), 32.

9. Martin Heidegger, *An Introduction to Metaphysics*, trans. Ralph Mannheim (New Haven, CT: Yale University Press, 1959), 205.

10. For a comprehensive discussion of this communication problem, see Gerald M. Phillips, *Communication Incompetencies: A Theory of Training Oral Performance Behavior* (Carbondale: Southern Illinois University Press, 1991).

11. Martin Heidegger, *The Principle of Reason*, trans. Reginald Lilly (Bloomington: Indiana University Press, 1991), 113.

12. See Martin Heidegger, "What Is Metaphysics?" in *Existence and Being*, 325–361.

13. Kenneth Burke, *Permanence and Change: An Anatomy of Purpose* (New York: Bobbs-Merrill, 1965), 272.

14. Kenneth Burke, *Language as Symbolic Action: Essays on Life, Literature, and Method* (Berkeley: University of California Press, 1966), 9.

15. Burke, *Language as Symbolic Action*, 26.

16. Ibid., 20. Also see Kenneth Burke, *Rhetoric of Religion: Studies in Logology* (Berkeley: University of California Press, 1970), 18–23, 273–316.

17. Burke, *Language as Symbolic Action*, 44–62.

18. Ibid., 18.

19. Burke, *The Rhetoric of Religion*, 19.

20. Heidegger, "Grundbegriffe der Aristotelischen Philosophie," 19.6.24.

21. Heidegger, "Hölderlin and the Essence of Poetry," 275.

22. Heidegger, *Being and Time*, 49–58, 314, 310–325; also see, for example, Martin Heidegger, *On the Way to Language*, trans. Peter D. Hertz (New York: Harper & Row, 1971), 57–136. In this and other later works, Heidegger speaks of the "call of Being" rather than the "call of conscience."

23. Heidegger, *Being and Time*, 318.

24. Heidegger, *On the Way to Language*, 123.

25. Martin Heidegger, *Zollikon Seminars: Protocols-Conversations-Letters*, trans. Franz Mayr and Richard Askay, ed. Medard Boss (Evanston: Northwestern University Press, 2001), 215.

26. See, for example, Martin Heidegger, *The Question Concerning Technology and Other Essays*, trans. William Lovitt (New York: Harper & Row, 1977), 10–11; Martin Heidegger, *Poetry, Language, Thought*, trans. Albert Hofstadter (New York: Harper & Row, 1971), 62–74.

27. Quintilian, *Institutio oratoria*, trans. H. E. Butler (Cambridge: Harvard University Press, 1985), 2.1.10.

28. Søren Kierkegaard, *Provocations: Spiritual Writings of Kierkegaard*, ed. Charles E. Moore (Farmington, PA: The Plough Publishing House, 1999), 263.

29. Quoted in Richard Wolin, *The Politics of Being: The Political Thought of Martin Heidegger* (New York: Columbia University Press, 1990), 168.

30. For an extended discussion of this point, see Michael J. Hyde, *The Call of Conscience: Heidegger and Levinas, Rhetoric and the Euthanasia Debate* (Columbia: University of South Carolina Press, 2001), 1–17.

31. Hans-Georg Gadamer, *Truth and Method*, 2nd rev. ed., trans. Joel Weinsheimer and Donald G. Marshall (New York: Crossroad, 1989), xxxviii.

32. For an expanded treatment of this point, see my *The Call of Conscience*, 57–64.

Bibliography of Works

Books by Martin Heidegger

1910s

Die Lehre vom Urteil im Psychologismus. Leipzig: J. A. Barth, 1914.

Die Kategorien und Bedeutungslehre des Duns Scotus. Tübingen: Mohr, 1916.

1920s

Sein und Zeit. Halle: Niemeyer, 1927.

Kant und das Problem der Metaphysik. Bonn: F. Cohen, 1929.

Vom Wesen des Grundes. Halle: Niemeyer, 1929.

Was ist Metaphysik? Bonn: F. Cohen, 1929.

1930s

Die Selbstbehauptung der deutschen Universität: Rede, gehalten bei der feierlichen Über-nahme des Rektorats der Universität Freiburg i. Br. am 27.5.1933. Breslau: Korn, 1934.

1940s

Hölderlins Hymne "Wie wenn am Feiertage . . ." Halle a. d. S.: M. Niemeyer, 1941.

Vom Wesen der Wahrheit: Zu Platons Höhlengleichnis und Theätet. Frankfurt am Main: V. Klostermann, 1943.

Erläuterungen zu Hölderlins Dichtung. Frankfurt am Main: V. Klostermann, 1944.

Platons Lehre von der Wahrheit. Bern: Francke, 1947.

Über den Humanismus. Frankfurt am Main: V. Klostermann, 1949.

1950s

Anteile. Frankfurt am Main: V. Klostermann, 1950.

Holzwege. Frankfurt am Main: V. Klostermann, 1950.

Einführung in die Metaphysik. Tübingen: M. Niemeyer, 1953.

Der Feldweg. Frankfurt am Main: V. Klostermann, 1953.

Aus der Erfahrung des Denkens. Pfullingen: G. Neske, 1954.

Vorträge und Aufsätze. Pfullingen: G. Neske, 1954.

Was heißt Denken? Tübingen: M. Niemeyer, 1954.

Was ist das—die Philosophie? Pfullingen: Neske, 1956.

Zur Seinsfrage. Frankfurt am Main: V. Klostermann, 1956.

Identität und Differenz. Pfullingen: G. Neske, 1957.

Der Satz vom Grund. 2nd ed. Pfullingen: Neske, 1958.

Hegel, der Hausfreund. 2nd ed. Pfullingen: G. Neske, 1958.

Unterwegs zur Sprache. Pfullingen: Neske, 1959.

1960s

Gelassenheit. 2nd ed. Pfullingen: Neske, 1960.

Nietzsche. Pfullingen: Neske, 1961.

Die Frage nach dem Ding: Zu Kants Lehre von den transzendentalen Grundsätzen. Tübingen: M. Niemeyer, 1962.

Die Technik und die Kehre. Pfullingen: Neske, 1962.

Über Abraham a Santa Clara. Meßkirch: Stadtverwaltung, 1964.

Der europäische Nihilismus. Pfullingen: Neske. 1967.

Der Ursprung des Kunstwerkes. Stuttgart: Reclam, 1967.

Wegmarken. Frankfurt am Main: V. Klostermann, 1967.

Zur Sache des Denkens. Tübingen: Niemeyer, 1969.

1970s

Phänomenologie und Theologie. Frankfurt am Main: V. Klostermann, 1970.

Schellings Abhandlung über das Wesen der menschlichen Freiheit (1809). Tübingen: M. Niemeyer, 1971.

Frühe Schriften. Frankfurt am Main: V. Klostermann, 1972.

Frau Dr. Hildegard Feick: Der langjährigen getreuen Mitarbeiterin zum Gedächtnis. Frankfurt am Main: Klostermann, 1974.

Gesamtausgabe. Frankfurt am Main: Klostermann, 1976.

Seinsfrage. 4th ed. Frankfurt am Main: Klostermann, 1977.

1980s

Aristoteles, Metaphysik IX, 1–3: Von Wesen und Wirklichkeit der Kraft. Frankfurt am Main: V. Klostermann, 1981.

Aus der Erfahrung des Denkens: 1910–1976. Ed. Hermann Heidegger. Frankfurt am Main: Klostermann, 1983.

Denkerfahrungen, 1910–1976. Ed. Hermann Heidegger. Frankfurt am Main: Klostermann, 1983.

Frage nach der Bestimmung der Sache des Denkens. St. Gallen: Erker-Verlag, 1984.

Phänomenologische Interpretationen zu Aristoteles: Einführung in die phänomenologische Forschung. Frankfurt am Main: Klostermann, 1985.

Briefwechsel, 1953–1974: Martin Heidegger, Erhart Kästner. Ed. Heinrich W. Petzet. Frankfurt am Main: Insel, 1986.

Zollikoner Seminare: Protokolle, Gespräche, Briefe. Ed. Medard Boss. Frankfurt am Main: V. Klostermann, 1987.

Aufenthalte. Frankfurt am Main: V. Klostermann, 1989.

Beiträge zur Philosophie: Vom Ereignis. Ed. Friedrich-Wilhelm von Herrmann. Frankfurt am Main: V. Klostermann, 1989.

Briefwechsel, 1918–1969: Martin Heidegger, Elisabeth Blochmann. Ed. Joachim W. Storck. Marbach am Neckar: Deutsche Schillergesellschaft, 1989.

1990s

Briefwechsel 1920–1963/Martin Heidegger, Karl Jaspers. Ed. Walter Biemel and Hans Saner. Frankfurt am Main: V. Klostermann, 1990.

Nietzsches Metaphysik: Einleitung in die Philosophie: Denken und Dichten. Ed. Petra Jaeger. Frankfurt am Main: V. Klostermann, 1990.

Phänomenologie der Anschauung und des Ausdrucks: Theorie der philosophischen Begriffsbildung. Frankfurt am Main: Klostermann, 1993.

Hegel [Abhandlungen 1938/39, 1941 und 1942]. Ed. Ingrid Schüßler. Frankfurt am Main: V. Klostermann, 1993.

Bremer und Freiburger Vorträge. Ed. Petra Jaeger. Frankfurt am Main: Klostermann, 1994.

Feldweg-Gespräche (1944/45). Ed. Ingrid Schüßler. Frankfurt am Main: V. Klostermann, 1995.

Phänomenologie des religiösen Lebens. Frankfurt am Main: V. Klostermann, 1995.

Einleitung in die Philosophie. Frankfurt am Main: V. Klostermann, 1996.

Besinnung. Ed. Friedrich-Wilhelm von Herrmann. Frankfurt am Main: V. Klostermann, 1997.

Deutscher Idealismus (Fichte, Schelling, Hegel) und die philosophische Problemlage der Gegenwart. Frankfurt am Main: V. Klostermann, 1997.

Satz vom Grund. Frankfurt am Main: V. Klostermann, 1997.

Briefe 1925 bis 1975 und andere Zeugnisse: Hannah Arendt, Martin Heidegger. Ed. Ursula Lutz. Frankfurt am Main: V. Klostermann, 1998.

Die Geschichte des Seins: 1. Die Geschichte des Seins (1938/40), 2. Koinon, aus der Geschichte des Seyns (1939/40). Ed. Peter Trawny. Frankfurt am Main: V. Klostermann, 1998.

Geschichte des Seins. Frankfurt am Main: V. Klostermann, 1998.

Logik als die Frage nach dem Wesen der Sprache. Frankfurt am Main: V. Klostermann, 1998.

Metaphysik und Nihilismus. Ed. Hans-Joachim Friedrich. Frankfurt am Main: V. Klostermann, 1999.

2000s

Briefwechsel 1959–1976: Martin Heidegger, Imma von Bodmershof. Ed. Bruno Pieger. Stuttgart: Klett-Cotta, 2000.

Reden und andere Zeugnisse eines Lebensweges: 1910–1976. Ed. Hermann Heidegger. Frankfurt am Main: V. Klostermann, 2000.

Zu Hölderlin: Griechenlandreisen. Ed. Curt Ochwadt. Frankfurt am Main: V. Klostermann, 2000.

Briefe an Max Müller and andere Dokumente. Ed. Holger Zaborowski and Anton Bösl. Freiburg: Alber, 2003.

——, and Bernhard Welte. *Briefe und Begegnungen*. Ed. Alfred Denker and Holger Zaborowski. Stuttgart: Klett-Cotta, 2003.

Zu Ernst Jünger. Ed. Peter Trawny. Frankfurt am Main: V. Klostermann, 2004.

(Coedited with Ludwig von Ficker). *Briefwechsel 1952–1967*. Ed. with commentary by Matthias Flatscher. Stuttgart: Klett-Cotta, 2004.

Mein liebes Seelchen! Briefe von Martin Heidegger an seine Frau Elfride, 1915–1970. Ed. Gertrud Heidegger. Munich: DVA, 2005.

Seminars and Lectures by Martin Heidegger

1910s

Zur Bestimmung der Philosophie: Mit einer Nachschrift der Vorlesung "Über das Wesen der Universität und des akademischen Studiums" [frühe Freiburger Vorlesung Kriegsnotsemester 1919 und Sommersemester 1919]. Ed. Bernd Heimbüchel. Frankfurt am Main: V. Klostermann, 1987.

Grundprobleme der Phänomenologie (1919/20) [frühe Freiburger Vorlesung, Wintersemester 1919/20]. Ed. Hans-Helmuth Gander. Frankfurt am Main: V. Klostermann, 1993.

1920s

Phänomenologie der Anschauung und des Ausdrucks: Theorie der philosophischen Begriffsbildung [frühe Freiburger Vorlesung Sommersemester 1920]. Ed. Claudius Strube. Frankfurt am Main: V. Klostermann, 1993.

Phänomenologische Interpretationen zu Aristoteles: Einführung in die phänomenologische Forschung [frühe Freiburger Vorlesung Wintersemester 1921/22]. Ed. Walter Bröcker and Käte Bröcker-Oltmanns. Frankfurt am Main: V. Klostermann, 1985.

Ontologie: Hermeneutik der Faktizität [frühe Freiburger Vorlesung Sommersemester 1923]. Ed. Käte Bröcker-Oltmanns. Frankfurt am Main: V. Klostermann, 1988.

Einführung in die phänomenologische Forschung [Marburger Vorlesung Wintersemester 1923/24]. Ed. Friedrich-Wilhelm von Herrmann. Frankfurt am Main: V. Klostermann, 1994.

Der Begriff der Zeit: 1. Der Begriff der Zeit (1924), 2. Der Begriff der Zeit [Vortrag 1924]. Ed. Friedrich-Wilhelm v. Herrmann. Frankfurt am Main: V. Klostermann, 2004.

Grundbegriffe der aristotelischen Philosophie [Marburger Vorlesung Sommersemester 1924]. Ed. Mark Michalski. Frankfurt am Main: V. Klostermann, 2002.

Platon: Sophistes [Marburger Vorlesung Wintersemester 1924/25]. Ed Ingeborg Schüßler. Frankfurt am Main: V. Klostermann, 1992.

Prolegomena zur Geschichte des Zeitbegriffs [Marburger Vorlesung Sommersemester 1925]. Ed. Petra Jaeger. Frankfurt am Main: V. Klostermann, 1979.

Logik: Die Frage nach der Wahrheit [Marburger Vorlesung Wintersemester 1925/26]. Ed. Walter Biemel. Frankfurt am Main: V. Klostermann, 1976.

Die Grundbegriffe der antiken Philosophie [Marburger Vorlesung Sommersemester 1926]. Ed. Franz-Karl Blust. Frankfurt am Main: V. Klostermann, 1993.

Grundprobleme der Phänomenologie [Marburger Vorlesung Sommersemester 1927]. Frankfurt am Main: V. Klostermann, 1975.

Phänomenologische Interpretation von Kants Kritik der reinen Vernunft [Marburger Vorlesung Wintersemester 1927/28]. Frankfurt am Main: V. Klostermann, 1977.

Metaphysische Anfangsgründe der Logik im Ausgang von Leibniz [Marburger Vorlesung Sommersemester 1928]. Frankfurt am Main: V. Klostermann, 1978.

Einleitung in die Philosophie [Freiburger Vorlesung Wintersemester 1928/29]. Ed. Otto Samme and Ina Saame-Speidel. Frankfurt am Main: V. Klostermann, 1996.

Der deutsche Idealismus (Fichte, Schelling, Hegel) und die philosophische Problemlage der Gegenwart [Freiburger Vorlesung Sommersemester 1929; mit einem Anhang einer Nachschrift der zweiten Vorlesung Sommersemester 1929 "Einführung in das akademische Studium"]. Ed. Claudius Strube. Frankfurt am Main: V. Klostermann, 1997.

Die Grundbegriffe der Metaphysik: Welt, Endlichkeit, Einsamkeit [Freiburger Vorlesung Wintersemester 1929/30]. Ed. Friedrich-Wilhelm von Herrmann. Frankfurt am Main: V. Klostermann, 1983.

1930s

Vom Wesen der menschlichen Freiheit: Einleitung in die Philosophie [Freiburger Vorlesung Sommersemester 1930]. Ed. Hartmut Tietjen. Frankfurt am Main: V. Klostermann, 1982.

Hegels Phänomenologie des Geistes [Freiburger Vorlesung Wintersemester 1930/31]. Ed. Ingtraud Görland. Frankfurt am Main: V. Klostermann, 1980.

Vom Wesen der Wahrheit: Zu Platons Höhlengleichnis und Theätet [Freiburger Vorlesung Wintersemester 1931/32]. Ed. Hermann Mörchen. Frankfurt am Main: V. Klostermann, 1988.

Sein und Wahrheit [Freiburger Vorlesungen Sommersemester 1933 und Wintersemester 1933/34]. Ed. Hartmut Tietjen. Frankfurt am Main: V. Klostermann, 2001.

Logik als die Frage nach dem Wesen der Sprache [Freiburger Vorlesung Sommersemester 1934]. Ed. Günter Seubold. Frankfurt am Main: V. Klostermann, 1998.

Hölderlins Hymne: "Germanien" und "Der Rhein" [Freiburger Vorlesung Wintersemester 1934/35]. Ed. Susanne Ziegler. Frankfurt am Main: V. Klostermann, 1980.

Einführung in die Metaphysik [Freiburger Vorlesung Sommersemester 1935]. Ed. Petra Jaeger. Frankfurt am Main: V. Klostermann, 1983.

Die Frage nach dem Ding: Zu Kants Lehre von den transzendentalen Grundsätzen [Freiburger Vorlesung Wintersemester 1935/36, wurde unter dem Titel "Grundfragen der Metaphysik" gehalten]. Ed. Petra Jaeger. Frankfurt am Main: V. Klostermann, 1984.

Schelling: Vom Wesen der menschlichen Freiheit (1809) [Freiburger Vorlesung Sommersemester 1936]. Ed. Ingrid Schüßler. Frankfurt am Main: V. Klostermann, 1988.

Nietzsche: Der Wille zur Macht als Kunst [Freiburger Vorlesung Wintersemester 1936/37]. Ed. Bernd Heimbüchel. Frankfurt am Main: V. Klostermann, 1985.

Nietzsches metaphysische Grundstellung im abendländischen Denken: Die ewige Wiederkehr des Gleichen [Freiburger Vorlesung Sommersemester 1937]. Ed. Marion Heinz. Frankfurt am Main: V. Klostermann, 1986.

Nietzsche: Seminare 1937 und 1944: 1. Nietzsches metaphysische Grundstellung (Sein und Schein); 2. Skizzen zu Grundbegriffe des Denkens [Übungen Sommersemester 1937 und Sommersemester 1944; Aufzeichnungen und Protokolle]. Ed. Peter von Ruckteschell. Frankfurt am Main: V. Klostermann, 2004.

Grundfragen der Philosophie: Ausgewählte "Probleme" der "Logik" [Freiburger Vorlesung WS 1937/38]. Ed. Friedrich-Wilhelm von Herrmann. Frankfurt am Main: V. Klostermann, 1984.

Zur Auslegung von Nietzsches II. Unzeitgemässen Betrachtung: "Vom Nutzen und Nachteil der Historie für das Leben" [Freiburger Seminar Wintersemester 1938/1939]. Ed. Hans-Joachim Friedrich. Frankfurt am Main: V. Klostermann, 2003.

Nietzsches Lehre vom Willen zur Macht als Erkenntnis [Freiburger Vorlesung Sommersemester 1939]. Ed. Eberhard Hanser. Frankfurt am Main: V. Klostermann, 1989.

Vom Wesen der Sprache: die Metaphysik der Sprache und die Wesung des Wortes; zu Herders Abhandlung "Über den Ursprung der Sprache" [Oberseminar Sommersemester 1939; Aufzeichnungen und Protokolle]. Ed. Ingrid Schüßler. Frankfurt am Main: V. Klostermann, 1999.

1940s

Nietzsche: Der europäische Nihilismus [Freiburger Vorlesung II. Trimester 1940]. Ed. Petra Jaeger. Frankfurt am Main: V. Klostermann, 1986.

Grundbegriffe [Freiburger Vorlesung Sommersemester 1941]. Ed. Petra Jaeger. Frankfurt am Main: V. Klostermann, 1981.

Die Metaphysik des deutschen Idealismus: Zur erneuten Auslegung von Schelling: Philosophische Untersuchungen über das Wesen der menschlichen Freiheit und die damit zusammenhängenden Gegenstände (1809) [Freiburger Vorlesung 1. Trisemester 1941, Freiburger Seminar Sommersemester 1941]. Ed. Günter Seubold. Frankfurt am Main: V. Klostermann, 1991.

Hölderlins Hymne: "Andenken" [Freiburger Vorlesung Wintersemester 1941/42]. Hrsg. Curd Ochwadt. Frankfurt am Main: V. Klostermann, 1982.

Hölderlins Hymne "Der Ister" [Freiburger Vorlesung Sommersemester 1942]. Ed. Walter Biemel. Frankfurt am Main: V. Klostermann, 1984.

Heraklit [Freiburger Vorlesung, Sommersemester 1943 und Sommersemester 1944]. Frankfurt am Main: V. Klostermann, 1979.

Parmenides [Freiburger Vorlesung Wintersemester 1943/44]. Ed. Manfred S. Frings. Frankfurt am Main: V. Klostermann, 1982.

1950s

Colloquio sulla dialettica e ultima lezione non tenuta del semester estivo 1952 [Muggenheim: 1952.09.15]. Padua: CEDAM, 1999.

1960s

Heraklit [Seminar Wintersemester 1966/67]. Ed. Eugen Fink. Frankfurt am Main: V. Klostermann, 1970.

Vier Seminare: Le Thor 1966, 1968, 1969, Zähringen 1973. Übers. d. franz. Seminarprotokolle von Curd Ochwadt. Frankfurt am Main: V. Klostermann, 1977.

Seminare. Ed. Curd Ochwadt. Frankfurt am Main: V. Klostermann, 1986.

English Translations of Books by Martin Heidegger

1940s

Existence and Being. Translation by Douglas Scott, F. G. C. Hull, and Alan Crick. South Bend, IN: Regnery/Gateway, 1979 (first published in 1949 by H. Regnery Co.).

1950s

Question of Being. Trans. William Kluback and Jean T. Wilde. New York: Twayne Publishers, 1958.

An Introduction to Metaphysics. Trans. Ralph Manheim. New Haven: Yale University Press, 1959.

1960s

Essays in Metaphysics: Identity and Difference. Trans. Kurt F. Leidecker. New York: Philosophical Library, 1960.

Being and Time. Trans. John Macquarrie and Edward Robinson. New York: Harper, 1962.

Kant and the Problem of Metaphysics. Trans. James S. Churchill. Bloomington: Indiana University Press, 1962.

German Existentialism. Trans. Dagobert D. Runes. New York: Wisdom Library, 1965.

What Is a Thing? Trans. W. B. Barton, Jr., and Vera Deutsch. Chicago: H. Regnery Co., 1968.

What Is Called Thinking? New York: Harper & Row, 1968.

Discourse on Thinking. Trans. John M. Anderson and E. Hans Freund. New York, Harper & Row, 1969.

Essence of Reasons. Trans. Terrence Malick. Evanston, IL: Northwestern University Press, 1969.

Identity and Difference. Trans. Joan Stambaugh. New York: Harper & Row, 1969.

1970s

Hegel's Concept of Experience. New York: Harper & Row, 1970.

On the Way to Language. Trans. Peter D. Hertz. New York: Harper & Row, 1971.

Poetry, Language, Thought. Trans. Albert Hofstadter. New York: Harper & Row, 1971.

On Time and Being. Trans. Joan Stambaugh. New York: Harper & Row, 1972.

The End of Philosophy. Trans. Joan Stambaugh. New York: Harper & Row, 1973.

Early Greek Thinking. Trans. David Farrell Krell and Frank A. Capuzzi. New York: Harper & Row, 1975.

Piety of Thinking: Essays. Trans., notes and commentary by James G. Hart and John C. Maraldo. Bloomington: Indiana University Press, 1976.

Basic Writings: From Being and Time (1927) to The Task of Thinking (1964). Ed. David Farrell Krell. New York: Harper & Row, 1977.

Question Concerning Technology and Other Essays. Trans. William Lovitt. New York: Harper & Row, 1977.

Heraclitus Seminar, 1966/67: Martin Heidegger and Eugen Fink. Trans. Charles H. Seibert. University, AL: University of Alabama Press, 1979.

Nietzsche. Trans. David Farrell Krell. San Francisco: Harper & Row, 1979.

1980s

Basic Problems of Phenomenology. Trans. Albert Hofstadter. Bloomington: Indiana University Press, 1982.

Metaphysical Foundations of Logic. Trans. Michael Heim. Bloomington: Indiana University Press, 1984.

History of the Concept of Time: Prolegomena. Trans. Theodore Kisiel. Bloomington: Indiana University Press, 1985.

Schelling's Treatise on the Essence of Human Freedom. Trans. Joan Stambaugh. Athens: Ohio University Press, 1985.

Hegel's Phenomenology of Spirit. Trans. Parvis Emad and Kenneth Maly. Bloomington: Indiana University Press, 1988.

1990s

Principle of Reason. Trans. Reginald Lilly. Bloomington: Indiana University Press, 1991.

Concept of Time. Trans. William McNeill. Cambridge, MA: B. Blackwell, 1992.

Parmenides. Trans. André Schuwer and Richard Rojcewicz. Bloomington: Indiana University Press, 1992.

Basic Concepts. Trans. Gary E. Aylesworth. Bloomington: Indiana University Press, 1993.

Basic Questions of Philosophy: Selected "Problems" of "Logic." Trans. Richard Rojcewicz and André Schuwer. Bloomington: Indiana University Press, 1994.

Aristotle's Metaphysics [theta] 1–3: On the Essence and Actuality of Force. Trans. Walter Brogan and Peter Warnek. Bloomington: Indiana University Press, 1995.

Fundamental Concepts of Metaphysics: World, Finitude, Solitude. Trans. William McNeill and Nicholas Walker. Bloomington: Indiana University Press, 1995.

Hölderlin's Hymn "The Ister." Trans. William McNeill and Julia Davis. Bloomington: Indiana University Press, 1996.

Phenomenological Interpretation of Kant's Critique of Pure Reason. Trans. Parvis Emad and Kenneth Maly. Bloomington: Indiana University Press, 1997.

Plato's Sophist. Trans. Richard Rojcewicz and André Schuwer. Bloomington: Indiana University Press, 1997.

Pathmarks. Edited by William McNeill. Cambridge, UK: Cambridge University Press, 1998.

Contributions to Philosophy (from Enowning). Trans. Parvis Emad and Kenneth Maly. Bloomington: Indiana University Press, 1999.

Ontology: The Hermeneutics of Facticity. Trans. John van Buren. Bloomington: Indiana University Press, 1999.

2000s

Elucidations of Hölderlin's Poetry. Trans. Keith Hoeller. Amherst, NY: Humanity Books, 2000.

Towards the Definition of Philosophy: With a Transcript of the Lecture Course "On the Nature of the University and Academic Study." Trans. Ted Sadler. New Brunswick, NJ: Athlone Press, 2000.

Phenomenological Interpretations of Aristotle: Initiation into Phenomenological Research. Trans. Richard Rojcewicz. Bloomington: Indiana University Press, 2001.

Zollikon Seminars: Protocols, Conversations, Letters. Ed. Medard Boss. Trans. Franz Mayr and Richard Askay. Evanston, IL: Northwestern University Press, 2001.

Essence of Human Freedom: An Introduction to Philosophy. Trans. Ted Sadler. New York: Continuum, 2002.

Essence of Truth: On Plato's Parable of the Cave Allegory and Theaetetus. Trans. Ted Sadler. New York: Continuum, 2002.

Off the Beaten Track. Ed. and trans. Julian Young and Kenneth Haynes. Cambridge, UK: Cambridge University Press, 2002.

Supplements: From the Earliest Essays to Being and Time and Beyond. Ed. John van Buren. Albany: State University of New York Press, 2002.

Four Seminars. Trans. Andrew Mitchell and François Raffoul. Bloomington: Indiana University Press, 2003.

Heidegger-Jaspers Correspondence, 1920–1963. Ed. Walter Biemel and Hans Saner. Trans. Gary E. Aylesworth. Amherst, NY: Humanity Books, 2003.

Phenomenology of Religious Life. Trans. Matthias Fritsch and Jennifer Anna Gosetti-Ferencei. Bloomington: Indiana University Press, 2004.

Hans-Georg Gadamer (1900–2002)

Biographical Sketch

Hans-Georg Gadamer was born on February 11, 1900, in Marburg, Germany. He grew up in Breslau, where his father was a professor of pharmacy. His mother died when he was four years old, and his father remarried a short time later. Gadamer's older brother suffered from epilepsy and was institutionalized when Gadamer was a teenager.

Religion played only a small role in Gadamer's life as he was growing up.

Different sources report inconsistent information about the life of Hans-Georg Gadamer. Information for this biographical sketch was drawn from Robert L. Bernasconi, "Gadamer, Hans-Georg," *The Cambridge Dictionary of Philosophy*, 2nd ed., ed. Robert Audi (Cambridge, UK: Cambridge University Press, 1999); Robert J. Dostal, *Cambridge Companion to Gadamer* (Cambridge, UK: Cambridge University Press, 2002); "Hans-Georg Gadamer," *Stanford Encyclopedia of Philosophy*—http://plato.stanford.edu/entries/gadamer (accessed August 17, 2005); "Hans-Georg Gadamer Bio"—http://www.svcc.cc.il.us/academics/classes/gadamer/gadbio.htm (accessed October 9, 2003). "Hans-Georg Gadamer Dies; Noted German Philosopher," *Washington Post*, 16 March 2002, p. B5—http://www.washingtonpost.com/ac2/wp-dyn?pagename=article&contentId=A35910-2002Mar15&notFound=true (accessed August 20, 2005); Richard Palmer, "Wolin's Misguided Attacks on Gadamer and Hermeneutics"—www.vahidnab.com/palmer.htm (accessed August 17, 2005). Photograph by Richard Palmer.

Socially and culturally much faith was placed in science and technology. His father was a strict disciplinarian—authoritarian and, at times, antidemocratic. Gadamer found that although his father was highly educated, the latter had little respect for the humanities. While his father tried to instill a strong scientific influence, Gadamer was more interested in Shakespeare, Greek philosophy, and German thinkers/writers.

Gadamer began university studies at the University of Breslau (now the University of Wroclaw in Poland) in 1918, transferring to the University of Marburg in 1919. He earned his first doctorate in 1922, at the age of twenty-two under Paul Natorp with his work "Das Wesen der Lust nach den platonischen Dialogen" (The Essense of Pleasure in the Platonic Dialogues). In 1923, he married Frida Kratz; they had one daughter. Gadamer began serving as Heidegger's assistant in 1923, and in 1928 he completed his second doctorate, entitled "Platos dialektische Ethik" (Plato's Dialectical Ethics) under the guidance of Paul Friedländer and Martin Heidegger.

Gadamer taught philosophy at the University of Marburg, spent a short time at the University of Kiel (1934–1935), and then returned to Marburg, where he was honored as "extraordinary professor" in 1937. In 1939, he began teaching at the University of Leipzig, where he served as rector from 1946 to 1947. During World War II Gadamer was contemptuous toward Hitler; living in a police state, he concentrated attention on his work. In 1947, Gadamer accepted a call to the University of Frankfurt, and in 1949 he succeeded Karl Jaspers as chair at the University of Heidelberg. After his earlier divorce, in 1950 he married Käte Lekebusch.

Upon retirement from the University of Heidelberg in 1968, Gadamer lectured throughout the United States, Canada, and in other countries. Hans-Georg Gadamer died on March 13, 2002, in Heidelberg, Germany.

Callicles' Parlor
Revisiting the Gorgias *after Dwelling with Gadamer*

Lenore Langsdorf

> "What man needs is not just the persistent posing of
> ultimate questions, but the sense of what is feasible,
> what is possible, what is correct, here and now. The
> philosopher, of all people, must, I think, be aware of
> the tension between what he claims to achieve and
> the reality in which he finds himself."
>
> —Hans-Georg Gadamer[1]

The venerable dispute between rhetoric and philosophy can take a new direction when engaged from the perspective of Hans-Georg Gadamer's hermeneutic phenomenology. Within the broad rereading of the philosophical-rhetorical tradition that Gadamer's work inspires, I focus, in this chapter, on the separation of learning and knowledge from action and belief that occurs in Callicles' parlor when Socrates arrives. Plato promotes, through their dialogue, a hierarchical division between knowledge and belief that denies the value of the kind of knowing that informs rhetoric, in order to valorize the kind of knowing that informs philosophy. Neglect and even dismissal of the distinctive character and value of rhetorical knowing enables Plato to treat the difference between them as a division, rather than as a productive tension. The kind of knowing that Plato dismisses, I propose, is hermeneutic in character and applied through rhetorical action. I do not advocate a correlative dismissal of the propositional knowing that Plato (and thus, the Platonic Socrates) values. Rather, in keeping with hermeneutic principles, I advocate a productive relationship between both kinds.

In what follows, I summarize the initial conversation on the nature of rhetoric that begins between Socrates' companion, Chaerephon, and Gorgias's companion, Polus, and then is carried for some time primarily by Gorgias and Socrates (449b–461b) before it is taken up by Polus and Socrates (461b–481b).[2] My focus is on the conceptions of knowing that are brought to the exchange between Gorgias and Socrates. What emerges from that exchange is a characterization of rhetoric as aligned with "flattery" and the body, rather than instruction and the soul (463b; 464b), which is a "knack" rather than an "art," which cannot be taught, and which relies upon an inferior form of cognition—belief—rather than upon "sure knowledge" (454e). In the next section of the paper, I explicate Gadamer's conception of hermeneutic as providing an alternative conception of knowing that is used by rhetoric. In the concluding section, I consider how rhetoric functions within the art of conversation and propose that including both senses of knowing would enable us to acknowledge the differences between philosophy and rhetoric as a productive tension, rather than a division.

Gorgias and Socrates on Knowing

> "The question is whether there can be any such thing as philosophical knowledge of the moral being of man. If man always encounters the good in the form of the particular practical situation in which he finds himself . . . the person acting must view the concrete situation in light of what is asked of him in general. But—negatively put—this means that knowledge that cannot be applied to the concrete situation remains meaningless and even risks obscuring what the situation calls for."
>
> —Hans-Georg Gadamer[3]

Socrates accomplishes a separation between knowledge and belief early on in the dialogue. We are told that Gorgias is already tired after what Callicles, the host, characterizes as "a most elegant feast," which was followed by "a fine and varied display" of Gorgias's ability to respond to any and all questions. Socrates, in contrast, has dallied in the marketplace and so arrives in Callicles' parlor too late for the feast as well as the discourse. The latter is framed from the very first words of the dialogue as a "fight or a fray" (447a), the kind of performance in which the will and desire of both partners is prominently displayed. Gorgias wants new challenges by way of "whatever questions anyone in the house might like to ask" and complains that "nobody has asked [him] anything new for many years now" (447c; 448a). Socrates, correlatively, declares what he wants from Gorgias: "I want to find out . . . what is the function of his art, and what it is that he professes and teaches" (447c).

The conversation that follows exemplifies the classic form of Socratic dialectic: it seeks a definition of what something is (in this case, what art it is that Gorgias practices) and then applies the method of division to the genus that is articulated in that definition. In other words, the variety of aspects and components that comprise an activity are unified under one heading; the dialectician then delineates the parts of that unity by identifying essential characteristics, the presence or absence of which serve to divide the genus into its species. Socrates immediately uses analogy to focus the definition on the object—the product of the activity of art. The product of weaving, he says, is clothes, and the product of music is tunes; "tell me," he continues, "with what particular thing rhetoric is concerned" (449d). Gorgias declares that the product of rhetoric is "speech" (449e). In response to Socrates' question of whether rhetoric is "concerned with all kinds of speech," Gorgias offers a differentiation based on how much "action" or "work" is involved. Gorgias aligns rhetoric with a "class of arts" ("numeration, calculation, geometry, draught-playing") that relies upon cognitive application of rules (450d), and then differentiates within that genus: rhetoric does so in relation to the "greatest of human affairs," the "power" to "persuade" in "public gatherings" and especially in the courts and legislature, when "what is just and unjust" is at issue (451d; 452e; 454b).

To summarize: through use of Socrates' chosen procedure, dialectic's method of definition and division, Socrates and Gorgias have agreed, first, that the product (object) of rhetoric is persuasive speech. They went on to agree on the separation of persuasion that is effective within speech from persuasion that transcends speech to have its effect in action. Socrates abruptly shifts to "consider[ing] another point": the nature of learning and believing (454c). They already agreed that teaching involves persuasion (453d). Now they agree that there are "two forms of persuasion—one providing belief without knowledge, and the other sure knowledge" (454e). Gorgias then agrees with Socrates' proposal that the rhetorician's product—persuasion as used in public gatherings, when deliberation leads to actions and policies that govern action—is "persuasion for belief, not for instruction in the matter of rights and wrong" (455a). Thus, we have the separation of learning and knowledge from action and belief, and the association of rhetoric with the latter.

Agreement on that division leads Socrates to proclaim that he remains unclear in regard to just what advice the rhetorician is able to give those who are skilled in, for instance, construction or military affairs. Gorgias responds with an example: his brother is a doctor, and Gorgias has gone with him and other doctors on visits to noncompliant patients. "When the doctor failed to persuade him [the patient] I succeeded, by no other art than that of rhetoric," Gorgias claims, and goes on to add that "there is no subject on which the rhetorician could not speak more persuasively than a member of any other profession" (456b–c). When Socrates questions him more closely, however, Gorgias acknowledges that this power is only effective with "the ignorant"—since "to those who know, he [the rhetorician] will not be more convincing than the doctor" (459a). The method of division has now so reduced rhetoric's nature that Socrates declares it not an art at all, but a mere "habitude or knack" of engaging in "flattery" (463a–b), a counterfeit of politics, as cookery is a counterfeit of medicine. Its power is one that moves the ignorant to act without knowledge.

In the course of my own experience of teaching the Platonic dialogues, I have found that students often complain that Socrates' interlocutors are poor defenders of their own claims. Probably all readers, teachers and students alike, have wanted to intervene on behalf of dialogue partners who, all too often, seem to be reduced to the status of "yes men." In more than one class, I have proposed that we exercise our imaginations in the service of such interventions by finding the moment in the dialogue when the interlocutor's divergent position has not yet been dismissed, and introducing alternative lines of thinking that might save the day. I would like to engage in that exercise now, by intervening with a third option at the point at which Socrates concludes that "rhetoric is a producer of persuasion"—a definition which Gorgias declares is "satisfactory" (453a). This agreement opens a line of thinking that results in their agreeing to divide the field of persuasion into two kinds: "one providing belief without knowledge and the other sure knowledge" (454e). My intervention introduces a third kind of learning and knowing that problematizes both the clear division between "belief" and "knowledge" that Socrates brings to the conversation, and the restriction of rhetoric to persuasion that Gorgias brings. The source for this intervention is the hermeneutic tradition, and particularly that tradition as developed by Hans-Georg Gadamer.

Hermeneutic Knowing

"From the hermeneutical situation originates the primordial function of rhetoric . . . to 'make known' meaning both to oneself and to others . . . through the interpretive understanding of reality."
—Michael J. Hyde and Craig R. Smith[4]

The division between arts and mere habitudes that emerges in the *Gorgias* presumes the physician's reliance upon knowledge, which is always understood by Plato as "sure," i.e., certain and stable, in contrast to the rhetorician's reliance upon "belief without knowledge" (454e). The latter, Socrates argues, can only move physicians' patients (as well as members of juries and legislatures) to action on the basis of their ignorance. What is neglected in this dichotomy is the possibility of a further differentiation within "knowledge" between the "sure" and the "situated." Sure knowledge is of things as they represent immutable and transcendent Ideas, and is applicable in all times and places. Situated knowledge is relevant to fluid circumstances and uses diverse "interpretive understanding[s] of reality" to guide action without certainty, although with degrees of plausibility ranging from the possible to the probable. Plato's epistemology and ontology valorize the stable and certain and presumes "sure knowledge" as the whole of what is to count as the goal of inquiry. Gadamer's hermeneutics, however, develops a different conception of the goal of inquiry. His model is more Aristotelian than Platonic; in particular, it takes Aristotle's phronesis (moral knowledge) rather than Plato's episteme (theoretical knowledge) as its model. Since hermeneutics involves a particular conception of learning, I will need to say a bit about that learning process before turning to sketching the kind of knowing that is its result.

Aristotle reminds us that "all teaching starts from what is already known" (*Nic. Ethics* 1139b.26).[5] In contrast to Plato's valorization of innate knowledge, Aristotle valorizes knowledge acquired by induction from experience: "science and art come to men through experience," which gives us "knowledge of individuals" (*Meta.* 981a4, 15). Experience, in turn, is "produced" from memory

(*Meta.* 980b.5). Ultimately, memory relies upon perception: "So from perception there comes memory . . . and from memory (when it occurs often in connection with the same thing), experience" (*Post. Anal.* 100a4–5).

Following Martin Heidegger, hermeneutics understands the knowledge that results from this process (perception, memory, and experience as the source of science and art) as one of interpretation. "In interpreting," Heidegger argues, "we do not, so to speak, throw a 'signification' over some naked thing which is present-at-hand."[6] Rather, interpretive activity uses a "fore-structure" with three aspects: fore-having, fore-sight, and fore-conception.[7] *Fore-having* is the gift of culture, which provides us with patterned ways of acting and thinking that become part of memory and practice so early and pervasively in our lives that we take them for granted; which is to say, we use them without knowing that we do so. For instance, even before we are old enough to engage in conversation, we may perceive others looking directly at some conversation partners and looking downward while talking with others. *Fore-sight* utilizes that cultural gift to inform the ways in which we respond to particular situations. In other words, fore-sight informs the viewpoints from which we develop knowledge. Using that same example, we may come to see the latter (downward-looking) conduct as appropriate when conversing with superiors—which means that we have learned to interpret the object of an averted gaze as a superior. *Fore-conception* provides implicit ways of conceiving correlated to our actions. For instance, we bring a structure of "superiors," "equals," and "inferiors" to our interactions with other human beings that we do not bring to our interactions with furniture. Heidegger concludes that "something becomes intelligible as something" as "it gets its structure from a fore-having, a fore-sight, and a fore-conception."[8]

It is important to note that the precision and even singularity of definition that can be achieved in regard to our explicit conceptual structures does not extend to the fore-sight that informs our attitudes, or the fore-having from which those attitudes develop, or the fore-conceptions that inform our perceptions. In our example, although my explicit definition of "superior" may well be in accord with other speakers of English, my viewpoint (fore-sight) in regard to "superiors" may be one of admiration, respect, mistrust, fear, or scorn—or a fluid shifting among and even blending of those possibilities, depending upon the particularities of the situation. In any case, I would be remiss to assume that others' ways of thinking and acting share my viewpoint (fore-sight) or retain traces of the same patterns of conduct (fore-having) that directed the fore-conceptions that inform my understanding of situations.

We can now bring this theory of forestructure back to Aristotle's acknowledgment that "all teaching starts from what is already known" (*Nic. Ethics* 1139b.26) and to Socratic dialectic as the mode of teaching exemplified in the Platonic dialogues. What is always "already known" is the forestructure—which we do not learn as "sure knowledge" taught by a teacher, but as situated and thus contingent knowledge transmitted in communal practices, which are informed by beliefs sedimented from a community's history and constitutive of its culture. Forestructural knowledge as a whole—encompassing fore-having and fore-sight, as well as fore-conception—is not amenable to propositional form, and thus, to the categorical precision that is the goal of dialectical definition and division.

Gadamer emphasizes that this contingent cultural knowledge, which is basic to hermeneutic knowledge is so different from the propositional knowledge that Socrates seeks through dialectical method that we are unable to identify any method for possessing it. Indeed, there is a sense in which we do not and even cannot possess it; rather, it is more fitting to recognize that it possesses us, by analogy with Gadamer's remark about history: "history does not belong to us, but we belong to it."[9] This lack of possession gives us a vital clue: the propositional knowledge prized by Socrates—from the evidence of his pressing Gorgias to identify rhetoric's object, correlative to the relationship of weaving to clothes and music to tunes—presumes that there are propositional claims to be made about objects that are known, by subjects who know them. The cultural knowledge prized by hermeneutic, however, is that which constitutes both subjects and objects as the beings they are. Thus, it would be more accurate to say that we are this knowledge, than that we have this knowledge.

What the rhetorician must know (more accurately, what the rhetorician must share) is knowledge of how the patient thinks and feels about illness and health and about the limits and justification of doctors' authority as well as the limits and justification of patients' independent judgment. This would include a variety of culturally supported, but individually attuned, evaluations of the situation. We might go on to say that the knowledge that Gorgias uses to persuade the recalcitrant patient who does not share the physician's knowledge—and thus, by Socrates' standard, is "ignorant"—is knowledge of that patient as a subject, as constituted in and through (and thus, in a sense, possessed by) a particular forestructure that encourages resistance to or reliance upon the doctor's knowledge. Perhaps what is most basic in the rhetorician's knowledge is acknowledgment of that constitutive function of forestructural knowledge. As Walter Fisher summarizes these priorities: "If a story denies a person's self-conception, it does not matter what it says about the world."[10]

The interests of clarity as well as the desire to move beyond the contest of wills and hierarchical conceptual structure that we witness in the *Gorgias* might be better served by acknowledging that the differences between these kinds of knowledge are too vast to subsume within one concept, or even within one discipline.[11] We could confine the term "knowledge" (and its accompanying forestructure) to the kind of inquiry that seeks information about subjects and objects. Correlatively, we could speak of understanding human subjects and the subject matter of interest to them (us) as the kind of inquiry that's relevant to rhetoric.[12] Given the history of division and hierarchy that marks the relationship of philosophy and rhetoric, however, I prefer to use the term "knowledge," modified by "propositional" or "hermeneutic," for I would argue that hermeneutic knowing of the forestructure, brought by participants to a conversation, is what rhetoric employs along with the propositional knowing contributed by (e.g.) the doctor. Both medicine and rhetoric, then, are arts that rely upon knowledge—although the knowing that's crucial to each is of importantly different kinds.

The Art of Conversation

> "We say that we 'conduct' a conversation, but the more genuine a conversation is, the less its conduct lies within the will of either partner."
>
> —Hans-Georg Gadamer[13]

Our intervention in the *Gorgias* in order to develop an alternative to Socrates' conclusions needs a second element of Gadamer's hermeneutic. We have intervened in the original dialogue with a line of thinking that establishes rhetoric as an art that relies upon a specific kind of knowledge complementary to that of, for example, the physician, the general, or the architect (455c). Now we need to thematize Gadamer's understanding of art as play, his explication of meaning and truth as emergent from that play, and his proposal that both the participants in that play and the "cultural scene"[14] that is that play are constituted in the very art of playing. In other words, we need to understand the being of speech—which Gorgias has identified as rhetoric's product (449e)—as a particular work of art.

Gadamer's hermeneutic is a phenomenological one, which is to say that he adopts Edmund Husserl's starting point in experience, understood as the interaction between noesis (a directedness toward some aspect of the world, including the actor (agent) who is always already part of that world), and noema (some aspect of the actor's lifeworld, i.e., of the actual cultural scene toward which the actor is directed). In other words, Gadamer follows Husserl in denying that experience arises from the subject-object structure of traditional epistemology.[15] Rather, he explicates experience as interactive play: both the players and the work of art (the "subjects" and "objects" of traditional analysis) emerge in and through the interaction itself. Those who participate in the play that comprises any work of art come to it with a forestructure that constitutes them; but in participating, their very "mode of being" is reconstituted by partaking in that experience.[16] Correlatively, the very being of the work of art (be that a conversation or a painting) is reconstituted as the forestructure sedimented in it engages with those who experience it. In other words, Gadamer explicates the work of art as perpetually unfinished, continually becoming itself with every presentation that calls participants to it. Its "actual being cannot be detached from its presentation"[17] lest the persistently deferred completion of its being become a demise—a closure that brings it to an end.[18] This is not to say, however, that the work of art is dependent upon its participants for its being. Rather, it displays an "autonomy"[19] by virtue of the forestructure that constitutes it at any moment of its engagement with participants, who are changed in and through that engagement.[20] In brief, in genuine conversation (in contrast to the "fray" enacted by opposed wills and desires in the *Gorgias*), the participants constitute the conversation even as the conversation constitutes them.

We can now explicate the kind of knowledge with which rhetoric is concerned, in conjunction with and contrast to that with which philosophy is concerned. The philosopher's work, as amply illustrated in Socratic dialectic, is the clarification and appreciation of ideas. These serve as the not-so-"raw" material of conversation. The philosopher's material, in other words—comparable to the musical notes of the composer and the knowledge of medicines and their effects used by the physician—is conceptual. For Platonic philosophy, those concepts are eternal and immutable, universally applicable, in principle, and available to those who take up the philosophical life in contrast to the life of the composer, the physician, or the rhetorician.

For rhetoric, however, concepts are historical and mutable. The rhetorician's work, correlatively, is the application—and so, actualization—of those concepts as meanings that are always already situated in particular cultural scenes. The "raw" material rhetoricians use to produce speech that persuades (as Socrates and Gorgias would say) is hermeneutic knowledge of their audience's historically and culturally formed forestructures—the sedimented extant interpretations of the philosopher's ideas that are embedded in our initial understanding of any situation and that the rhetorician judges are relevant to that situation. Rhetoricians, in other words, make known—communicate—interpretations of reality that shape the beliefs, emotions, feelings, and values of their audiences. Their interpretations, adapted to the exigencies of a situation, are given with the intention of moving audience members to direct their actions, beliefs, feelings, and values in one way rather than another, toward one goal rather than another.

In the course of conducting themselves in one way rather than another, the members of an audience are themselves changed along with their forestructures and their situations. The productive tension between our philosophical and rhetorical endeavors is suggested by Gadamer's remark on the partiality and wholeness implicit in speech:

> Every word causes the whole of the language to which it belongs to resonate and the whole worldview that underlies it to appear. Thus every word, as the event of a moment, carries with it the unsaid, to which it is related by responding and summoning. The occasionality of human speech is not a causal imperfection of its expressive power; it is, rather, the logical expression of the living virtuality of speech that brings a totality of meaning into play, without being able to express it totally.[21]

For the rhetorician as well as the philosopher, then, there is value in applying knowledge (whether of the ideas or of the forestructure) to human life. In conversation value is added to the philosopher's material as transcendent ideas become actualized in discourse (words, gestures, and images) that moves participants to actions of diverse kinds—ranging from continued conversation that persistently reconstitutes the work of art that is the conversation, to conduct that's informed by the beliefs, emotions, feelings, or values that are shaped (crafted) in that conversation, to transformation of the participants themselves. For philosophy, that value is extrinsic to the ideas themselves: insofar as the ideas are immutable, actualization adds nothing to them, as such.[22] However, intrinsic value is added to the rhetorician's material as the forestructures he or she brings to a conversation are reconstituted by their use in this particular cultural scene. The ideas and practices embedded or sedimented in forestructures are transcendental, rather than transcendent—which is to say that they are conditions for the possibility of making sense of a situation. Thus their value is intrinsic: the knowledge at issue is fluid, contingent, and persistently open to contextual expansion and elaboration. Knowledge is not "sure" and closed to influence by action in the actual world, or limited to being a difference within a system of ideas. Nor is it open to arbitrary change by way of "anything goes" redefinition, for changes in the hermeneutic knowing that's useful in rhetorical praxis emerge from interpretations of actual practices that constitute lived experience.[23]

Gorgias's and Socrates' example of doctor-patient conversation illustrates the complementarity of both these endeavors within the art of conversation. We can return to the story, now understood through the "seen, but unobserved relationship" between rhetoric and hermeneutic.[24] Gorgias accompanies his physician brother on a visit to a patient who (let us grant Socrates' point) is ignorant of the ideas that inform the doctor's advice and "is unwilling either to take the medicine or submit to the surgeon's knife" (456b). The patient is brought into compliance by Gorgias's use of his rhetorical skill in a "rightful" way (457a)—which I take to be one that is informed by Gorgias' trust in and reliance upon his brother's propositional knowledge, as well as his own hermeneutic and rhetorical skills. Gorgias uses hermeneutic skills as he listens to the patient's story as to why he or she is unwilling to undergo the treatment prescribed by the physician. If Gorgias is to succeed in altering the patient's convictions, he needs to use his rhetorical skills to craft an alternate story that takes account of the patient's story but offers a plausible alternative interpretation of the situation that could move the patient from resistance to compliance. I would emphasize that "could": there is no certainty in rhetoric, for the hermeneutical knowing on which rhetoric depends is never complete.

Thus the goal of Gorgias's listening must be twofold. First, and following Aristotle's recognition that "all teaching starts from what is already known" (*Nic. Ethics* 1139b.26), Gorgias needs to start from the assumption that the patient has "good reasons" for resisting the physician's advice. To understand those reasons, the physician must come to share the forestructural knowledge that the patient—although "ignorant" of the physician's propositional knowledge—always already knows and is using to interpret this particular situation. "Good reasons express practical wisdom," Walter Fisher reminds us; "they are . . . an encompassment of what is relative and objective in situations [and] function to resolve exigencies by locating and activating values."[25]

The "whole power of rhetoric" (455d), then, is the ability to bring together the audience's particular historical and cultural forestructure with the expert's abstract information about particular ideas—be those of medicine, engineering, or statecraft—so that propositional knowledge may be taken up into the experience that constitutes both knowing subjects and their subject matter. Bringing these together is no simple, once-for-all accomplishment. It requires taking account of the philosophical tradition of valuing episteme for itself, of valuing knowing gained through the analysis of propositions, and wisdom found in the contemplation of ideas. The rhetorical tradition, in contrast, values episteme insofar as it informs phronesis and contributes to the learning process that shapes the community's (including, the rhetorician's own) forestructure.

John Shotter speaks of these differences as seeking knowledge "by looking" in contrast to "by being in touch": "Our ways of knowing seem to be at least two-sided," he proposes.[26] The Platonic Socrates stands on one side, defending the kind of knowing that Gilbert Ryle summarizes as "knowing that" and—as second in importance, and modeled on "knowing that"—"knowing how."[27] "Knowing that" is articulated in propositional knowledge. Gorgias stands on the other side, personifying a kind of knowing that Shotter, with reference to Ryle's dichotomy, calls "knowing from within" or "knowing whether": a "practical-moral" kind of knowing that "one has only from within a social situation, a group, or an institution, and which thus takes into account (and is accountable to) the others in the social situation in which it is known."[28] This is, he concludes, a "special kind of knowledge, *sui generis*, which is prior to both ["knowing that," *episteme*, and "knowing how," *techne*] and, in being linked to people's social and personal identities, determines the available forms of these other two kinds of knowledge."[29] "Knowing from within" is articulated in the stories we tell about the origins and aims of the "good reasons" that inform the choices of our lives—stories to which rhetoricians must listen carefully if we would propose alternatives to those choices.

In this essay, we revisited the opposition of wills and positions that characterizes the *Gorgias*, after dwelling with Gadamer's understanding of the complementarity of the universal and the particular, the infinite and the finite, the transcendence of episteme and the immanence of phronesis, the possibilities of philosophy and the realities of rhetoric. Discerning the complementarity of these ways of knowing may enable us to accomplish the genuine conversation that eluded Gorgias and Socrates.

Notes

1. Hans-Georg Gadamer, *Truth and Method*, 2nd rev. ed. (New York: Continuum, 2002), xxxviii.

2. Plato, *Lysis. Symposium. Gorgias*, trans. W. R. M. Lamb (London: W. Heinemann [The Loeb Classical Library], 1925). All references to the *Gorgias* are from this translation.

3. *Truth and Method*, 313.

4. Michael H. Hyde and Craig R. Smith, "Hermeneutics and Rhetoric: A Seen but Unobserved Relationship," *Quarterly Journal of Speech* 65 (1979): 347–348.

5. Aristotle, *The Complete Works of Aristotle: The Revised Oxford Translation*, ed. Jonathan Barnes (Princeton: Princeton University Press, 1984). All quotations from Aristotle are from this edition.

6. Martin Heidegger, *Being and Time*, trans. John Macquarrie and Edward Robinson (New York: Harper & Row, 1962), 190.

7. *Being and Time*, 191.

8. *Being and Time*, 193.

9. *Truth and Method*, 276.

10. Walter R. Fisher, *Human Communication as Narration: Toward a Philosophy of Reason, Value, and Action* (Columbia: University of South Carolina Press, 1987), 75.

11. Gadamer suggests that the power of Sophistic oratory was so strong that Plato needed to "discipline it" by teaching it "its proper limits" (*Philosophical Hermeneutics* [Berkeley: University of California Press, 1976], 22). The exigency of this need for discipline may have been Plato's desire to institute a new discipline that was insecurely rooted in the fore-structure of his audience. There are two lines of thinking about the historical situation of that desire that seem to me relevant to understanding why this desire led to a denigration of rhetoric. The first is Eric Havelock's argument that Platonic knowledge depended upon the comparatively new technology of alphabetic literacy, rather than the cultural tradition of orality, in which Sophistic oratory was rooted:

    > One is entitled to ask however, given the immemorial grip of the oral method of preserving group tradition, how a self-consciousness could ever have been created. If the educational system which transmitted the Hellenic mores had indeed relied on the perpetual stimulation of the young in a kind of hypnotic trance, to use Plato's language, how did the Greeks ever wake up? The fundamental answer must lie in the changing technology of communication . . . which enabled a reader to dispense with most of that emotional identification . . . [and] could release psychic energy, for a review and rearrangement . . . of what could be seen as an object and not just heard and felt." (*Preface to Plato* [Cambridge, MA: Harvard University Press, 1963], 208)

    In terms of fore-structure, then, Plato was contending with sedimented ways of seeing (fore-sight) and patterns of conduct (fore-having) that constituted "emotional identification," and that clashed with the conceptual structures advocated by the Platonic Socrates. (Athens's condemnation of Socrates might be seen, in this light, as another confirmation of the value of evolutionary change that begins in practices rather than revolutionary change that is imposed upon a lifeworld.)

That line of thinking is compatible with the argument that Plato coined the very term "philosophy" to differentiate his teaching from that of the Sophists. Economic motives (competition for students), all too familiar to our contemporary academic institutions, lurk behind that differentiation. See, for the latter, Thomas Cole, *The Origins of Rhetoric in Ancient Greece* (Baltimore: The Johns Hopkins University Press, 1991); and Edward Schiappa, "*Rhetorike*: What's in a Name? Toward a Revised History of Early Greek Rhetorical Theory," *Quarterly Journal of Speech* 78 (1992): 1–15). Correlatively, we could consider the advantages of sharing the field, i.e., acknowledging the mutually productive tension between objectivistic and knowledge and situational understanding, in contrast to the hierarchy of "sure knowledge" and "belief without knowledge," which is our inheritance from the *Gorgias*.

12. Hermeneutic theory teaches us that such a change in conceptual structures is more likely to be accepted if there are appropriate viewpoints (fore-sight) and patterns of conduct (fore-having) that support it. I would argue that there are, although limited space precludes making that argument here.

13. *Truth and Method*, 383.

14. I borrow the phrase "cultural scene" from Donal Carbaugh, *Situating Selves: The Communication of Social Identities in American Scenes* (Albany: SUNY Press, 1996), 16. Carbaugh develops this phrase from the work of Dell Hymes and Clifford Geertz. The cultural scene is the focus of "the analyst's investigation of the larger system of communication, the 'culturescape,' of which any one particular situated practice is a part. Whether participants say it is relevant or not, one would want to know the history of the community, the communicative practices, and social identities. This 'cultural knowledge' then becomes a general resource with which to describe and interpret, to account for, the communication in any one particular scene." Thus understood, the term reminds us (as "situation" does not) of historicity, and has a greater sense of fluidity than "context," which tends to connote a stable frame.

15. This is not to say that Gadamer follows Husserl in the latter's understanding of speech. When Husserl analyzes "communicative speech" or "living discourse" in the first of the *Logical Investigations*, he makes an "essential distinction" between two concepts, "indications" and "expressions" (*Logical Investigations*, trans. J. N. Findlay (New York: Humanities Press, 1970), 269). In speech, Husserl holds, expressions function as indications "of the 'thoughts' of the speaker, i.e., of his sense-giving inner [*psychischen*; psychic] experiences," which are informed by ideal meanings (177). Husserl's primary focus on ideal meanings, rather than the actual situations (such as conversations) in which those meanings are communicated, contrasts with Gadamer's focus on actual communicative activity.

16. *Truth and Method*, 101–106.

17. *Truth and Method*, 122.

18. *Truth and Method*, 105.

19. *Truth and Method*, 111.

20. *Truth and Method*, 102, 110–111.

21. *Truth and Method*, 458.
22. Husserl retains this philosophical conception in his analysis of "expression" and "indication" in the first of the *Logical Investigations* (see note 15).
23. More precisely, I find that this knowing emerges from the moment of poiesis within praxis. See my "In Defense of Poiesis: The Performance of Self in Communicative Praxis," in *Calvin O. Schrag and the Task of Phenomenology after Postmodernity*, ed. William McBride and Martin Beck Matustik (Evanston, IL: Northwestern University Press, 2002), 281–296.
24. The phrase is from Hyde and Smith (see note 4).
25. *Human Communication as Narration*, 94. Fisher indicates his agreement with much in Gadamer's work, although he disagrees with Gadamer's division of labor between hermeneutic and rhetoric (95).
26. John Shotter, *Cultural Politics of Everyday Life* (Toronto: University of Toronto Press, 1993), 19–20, 23.
27. *Cultural Politics*, 7. Shotter cites Gilbert Ryle, *The Concept of Mind* (London: Methuen, 1949).
28. *Cultural Politics*, 7.
29. *Cultural Politics*, 7.

Bibliography of Works

Books by Hans-Georg Gadamer

1920s

Das Wesen der Lust nach den platonischen Dialogen. Marburg, Phil. Diss., 17 Aug. 1922.

1930s

Platos dialektische Ethik: Phänomenologische Interpretationen zum "Philebos." Leipzig: Meiner, 1931.

Plato und die Dichter. Wissenschaft und Gegenwart, no. 5. Frankfurt am Main: V. Klostermann, 1934.

1940s

Regards sur l'histoire. Cahiers de l'institut allemande, 2. Paris: Fernand Sorlot, 1941.

Volk und Geschichte im Denken Herders: Nach einem am 29. Mai 1941 in Paris. geh. Vortrag. Frankfurt am Main: Kostermann, 1942.

Bach und Weimar. Weimar: Böhlaus Nachf., 1946.

——, ed. *Philosophische Texte.* Frankfurt am Main: V. Klostermann, 1946.

Beiträge zur geistigen Überlieferung. Godesberg: Helmut Küpper, 1947.

Goethe und die Philosophie. Leipzig: Volk und Buch, 1947.

Über die Ursprünglichkeit der Wissenschaft. Leipzig: J. A. Barth, 1947.

——, ed. and trans. *Aristoteles, Metaphysik VII.* Frankfurt am Main: V. Klostermann, 1948.

Über die Ursprünglichkeit der Philosophie. Berlin: Chronos, 1948.

Vom geistigen Lauf des Menschen: Studien zu unvollendeten Dichtungen Goethes. Godesberg: H. Küpper, 1949.

1960s

Wahrheit und Methode: Grundzüge einer philosophischen Hermeneutik. Tübingen: Mohr, 1960.

Gadamer, Hans-Georg, and Martin Heidegger. *Der Ursprung des Kunstwerkes.* Stuttgart: P. Reclam, 1960.

Dialektik und Sophistik im siebenten platonischen Brief. Heidelberg: C. Winter, 1964.

———, ed. *Heidelberger Hegel-Tage 1962.* Bonn: Bouvier, 1964.

———, ed. *Hegel-Tage, Royaumont 1964.* Bonn: Bouvier, 1966.

———, ed. *Beiträge zur Deutung der Phänomenologie des Geistes, Hegel-Studien.* Bonn: Bouvier, 1966.

Das Problem der Sprache. Munich: W. Fink, 1967.

Kleine Schriften. 4 vols. Tübingen: J. C. B. Mohr, 1967–1979.

Platos Dialektische Ethik und andere Studien zur platonischen Philosophie. Hamburg: F. Meiner, 1968.

Um die Begriffswelt der Vorsokratiker. Darmstadt: Wissenschaftliche Buchgesellschaft, 1968.

Werner Scholz. Recklinghausen: A. Bongers, 1968.

———, ed. *Hegel-Tage, Urbino 1965*. Bonn: Bouvier, 1969.

Beaufret, Jean, and Hans-Georg Gadamer. *Die Frage Martin Heideggers: Beiträge zu einem Kolloquium mit Heidegger aus Anlaß seines 80. Geburtstages*. Heidelberg: C. Winter, 1969.

Il Problema della coscienza storica. Naples: Guida, 1969.

Gadamer, Hans-Georg, and Wolfgang Schadewalt. *Idee und Zahl: Studien zur platonischen Philosophie*. Heidelberg: C. Winter, 1968.

1970s

Die Begriffsgeschichte und die Sprache der Philosophie. Oplanden: Westdeutscher Verlag, 1971.

Hegels Dialektik: Fünf hermeneutische Studien. Tübingen: Mohr, 1971.

Gadamer, Hans-Georg, Max Müller, and Emil Staiger. *Hegel, Hölderlin, Heidegger*. Karlsruhe: Badenia, 1971.

Wer bin ich und wer bist du? Ein Kommentar zu Paul Celans Gedichtfolge "Atemkristall." Frankfurt am Main: Suhrkamp, 1973.

Vernunft im Zeitalter der Wissenschaft: Aufsätze. Frankfurt: Suhrkamp, 1976.

Gadamer, Hans-Georg, and Gottfried Boehm. *Seminar—Philosophische Hermeneutik*. Suhrkamp Taschenbuch, Wissenschaft, 144. Frankfurt am Main: Suhrkamp, 1976.

Gadamer, Hans-Georg, and Joachim Jungius-Gesellschaft der Wissenschaften. *Rhetorik und Hermeneutik: Als öffentl. Vortrag gehalten am 22.6.1976 in Hamburg*. Veröffentlichung der Joachim Jungius-Gesellschaft der Wissenschaften. Göttingen: Vandenhoeck und Ruprecht, 1976.

Die Aktualität des Schönen: Kunst als Spiel, Symbol u. Fest. Stuttgart: Reclam, 1977.

Philosophische Lehrjahre: e. Rückschau. Frankfurt am Main: V. Klostermann, 1977.

Poetica: Ausgewählte Essays. Frankfurt am Main: Insel, 1977.

Gadamer, Hans-Georg, Werner Marx, and Carl Friedrich von Weizsäcker. *Heidegger: Freiburger Universitätsvorträge zu seinem Gedenken*. Ed. Werner Marx. Freiburg i. Br.: Alber, 1977.

Die Idee des Guten zwischen Plato und Aristoteles. Sitzungsberichte der Heidelberger Akademie der Wissenschaften, Philosophisch-historische Klasse, 1978, 3. Heidelberg: C. Winter, 1978.

———, ed. and trans. *Plato, Texte zur Ideenlehre*. Frankfurt am Main: V. Klostermann, 1978.

Gadamer, Hans-Georg, and Paul Ricoeur. *Le Temps et les philosophies: Au carrefour des cultures: Etudes préparées pour l'UNESCO, bibliothèque scientifique*. Paris: Payot/ Unesco, 1978.

1980s

Hegels Dialektik: Sechs hermeneutische Studien. Tübingen: J.C.B. Mohr, 1980.

Was ist Literatur? Munich: Alber, 1981.

Gadamer, Hans-Georg, and Heinrich Fries. *Mythos und Wissenschaft*. Freiburg: Herder, 1981.

Heideggers Wege: Studien zum Spätwerk. Tübingen: Mohr, 1983.

Lob der Theorie: Reden und Aufsätze. Frankfurt am Main: Suhrkamp, 1983.

Gadamer, Hans-Georg, Roman Jakobson, and Elmar Holenstein. *Das Erbe Hegels II*. Suhrkamp Taschenbuch Wissenschaft, 440. Frankfurt am Main: Suhrkamp, 1984.

Die Vielfalt Europas: Erbe und Zukunft. Stuttgart: Robert-Bosch-Stiftung, 1985.

Griechische Philosophie I. Gesammelte Werke, vol. 5. Tübingen: Mohr, 1985.

Griechische Philosophie II. Gesammelte Werke, vol. 6. Tübingen: Mohr, 1985.

Hermeneutik: Wahrheit und Methode, 1: Grundzüge einer philosophischen Hermeneutik. Gesammelte Werke, vol. 1. Tübingen: Mohr, 1986.

Neuere Philosophie I. Gesammelte Werke, vol. 3. Tübingen: Mohr, 1987.

Neuere Philosophie II. Gesammelte Werke, vol. 4. Tübingen: Mohr, 1987.

Das Erbe Europas: Beiträge. Frankfurt am Main: Suhrkamp, 1989.

1990s

Gedicht und Gespräch: Essays. Frankfurt am Main: Insel, 1990.

Gadamer, Hans-Georg, Bernhard Welte, and Fernand Couturier. *Herméneutique: Traduire, Interpreter, Agir.* Saint-Laurent: Éditions Fides, 1990.

Griechische Philosophie: Plato im Dialog. Gesammelte Werke, vol. 7. Tübingen: Mohr, 1991.

Ergänzungen, Register. Gesammelte Werke, vol. 2. Tübingen: Mohr, 1993.

Hermeneutik, Ästhetik, praktische Philosophie: Hans-Georg Gadamer im Gespräch. Ed. Carsten Dutt. Heidelberg: C. Winter, 1993.

Kunst als Aussage. Gesammelte Werke, vol. 8. Tübingen: Mohr, 1993.

Über die Verborgenheit der Gesundheit: Aufsätze und Vorträge. 2nd ed. Frankfurt am Main: Suhrkamp, 1993.

Hermeneutik im Vollzug. Gesammelte Werke, vol. 9. Tübingen: Mohr, 1993.

Hermeneutik im Rückblick. Gesammelte Werke, vol. 10. Tübingen: Mohr, 1995.

Die Moderne und die Grenze der Vergegenständlichung. Munich: Bernd Kluser, 1996.

Der Anfang der Philosophie. Stuttgart: Reclam, 1997.

Gadamer, Hans-Georg, and Kuno Fischer. *System der Logik und Metaphysik oder Wissenschaftslehre.* Heidelberg: Manutius, 1998.

2000s

Erziehung ist sich Erziehen. Heidelberg: Kurpfälzischer Verlag, 2000.

Hermeneutische Entwürfe: Vorträge und Aufsätze. Tübingen: Mohr Siebeck, 2000.

Gadamer, Hans-Georg, Theodor W. Adorno, and Max Horkheimer. *Nietzsche l'antipode: Le drame de Zarathoustra.* Paris: Allia, 2000.

Gadamer, Hans-Georg, and Reinhart Koselleck. *Zeitschichten: Studien zur Historik.* Frankfurt am Main: Suhrkamp, 2000.

Gadamer, Hans-Georg, and Riccardo Dottori. *Die Lektion des Jahrhunderts: Ein Interview von Riccardo Dottori.* Ed. Silke Günnewig. Münster: Lit, 2001.

Derrida, Jacques, and Hans-Georg Gadamer. *Der ununterbrochene Dialog.* Ed. Martin Gessmann. Frankfurt am Main: Suhrkamp, 2004.

Seminars and Lectures by Hans-Georg Gadamer

1950s

Gedächtnisrede auf Oskar Schürer. Darmstadt: Neue Darmstädter Verl. Anst., 1952.

1970s

Idee und Wirklichkeit in Platos Timaios. 10. November 1973. Heidelberg: C. Winter, 1974.

Die Idee des Guten zwischen Plato und Aristoteles. 10.1.1976. Heidelberg: C. Winter, 1978.

Gadamer, Hans-Georg, and Gottfried Boehm. *Seminar: Die Hermeneutik und die Wissenschaften.* Frankfurt am Main: Suhrkamp, 1978.

1980s

Die Universität Heidelberg und die Geburt der modernen Wissenschaft. Rede, gehalten am 12. Oktober 1986 bei d. Eröffnung d. Festwoche zum Jubiläum "600 Jahre Univ. Heidelberg." Berlin: Springer, 1987.

Hermeneutik und Historik. Sitzungsberichte der Heidelberger Akademie der Wissenschaften, Philosophisch-historische Klasse, 1987, 1. Heidelberg: C. Winter, 1987.

Platon als Porträtist: Vortrag gehalten aus Anlaß d. Erwerbung d. Platon-Bildnisses für d. Glyptothet am 29. Febr. 1988. Munich: Verein d. Freunde u. Förderer d. Glypthothek u. d. Antikensammlungen München, circa 1988.

Gadamer, Hans-Georg, and Günther Pflug. *Kultur und Medien: Vorträge, gehalten im Auditorium Maximum am 1. Februar 1988 und am 14. April 1988 im Philosophenturm d. Universität Hamburg.* Hamburg: Hamburg Universität, 1989.

1990s

"Zukunft ist Herkunft." Hans-Georg Gadamer and Emil Schumacher. Mit e. Gespräch u. Beitr v. Hans-Georg Gadamer. Jena: Friedrich Schiller Universität, 1997.

English Translations of Books by Hans-Georg Gadamer

1970s

Gadamer, Hans-Georg, ed. *Truth and Historicity.* The Hague: Martinus Nijhoff, 1972.

Truth and Method. Trans. Garrett Barden and John Cumming. London: Sheed & Ward, 1975.

Hegel's Dialectic: Five Hermeneutical Studies. Trans. P. Christopher Smith. New Haven: Yale University Press, 1976.

Philosophical Hermeneutics. Trans. David E. Linge. Berkeley: University of California Press, 1976.

1980s

Dialogue and Dialectic: Eight Hermeneutical Studies on Plato. Trans. P. Christopher Smith. New Haven, CT: Yale University Press, 1980.

Reason in the Age of Science. Trans. Frederick G. Lawrence. Cambridge, MA: MIT Press, 1981.

Philosophical Apprenticeships. Trans. Robert R. Sullivan. Cambridge, MA: MIT Press, 1985.

The Idea of the Good in Platonic-Aristotelian Philosophy. Trans. P. Christopher Smith. New Haven, CT: Yale University Press, 1986.

The Relevance of the Beautiful and Other Essays. Ed. Robert Bernasconi. Trans. Nicholas Walker. New York: Cambridge University Press, 1986.

Gadamer, Hans-Georg, Werner Marx, Steven W. Davis, and Carl Friedrich Weizsäcker. *Heidegger Memorial Lectures.* Pittsburgh, PA: Duquesne University Press, 1982.

Gadamer, Hans-Georg, John M. Connolly, Thomas Keutner, E. K. Specht, and Wolfgang Stegmüller. *Hermeneutics versus Science? Three German Views: Essays: Revisions,* vol. 8. Notre Dame, IN: University of Notre Dame Press, 1988.

1990s

Plato's Dialectical Ethics: Phenomenological Interpretations Relating to the Philebus. Trans. Robert M. Wallace. New Haven, CT: Yale University Press, 1991.

Gadamer, Hans-Georg, and Hugh J. Silverman. *Gadamer and Hermeneutics: Science, Culture, Literature: Plato, Heidegger, Barthes, Ricoeur, Habermas, Derrida.* Continental Philosophy, 4. New York: Routledge, 1991.

Hans-Georg Gadamer on Education, Poetry and History: Applied Hermeneutics. Ed. Dieter Misgeld and Graeme Nicholson. Trans. Lawrence Schmidt and Monica Reuss. Albany: State University of New York Press, 1992.

Heidegger's Ways. Trans. John W. Stanley. Albany: State University of New York Press, 1994.

Literature and Philosophy in Dialogue: Essays in German Literary Theory. Trans. Robert H. Paslick. Ed. Dennis J. Schmidt. Albany: State University of New York Press, 1994.

The Enigma of Health: The Art of Healing in a Scientific Age. Trans. Jason Gaiger and Nicholas Walker. Stanford, CA: Stanford University Press, 1996.

Gadamer on Celan: "Who Am I and Who Are You?" and Other Essays. Trans. and ed. Richard Heinemann and Bruce Krajewski. Albany: State University of New York Press, 1997.

Gadamer, Hans-Georg, and Edwin Hahn Lewis. *The Philosophy of Hans-Georg Gadamer.* The Library of Living Philosophers, vol. 24. La Salle, IL: Open Court, 1997.

The Beginning of Philosophy. Trans. Rod Coltman. New York: Continuum, 1998.

Praise of Theory: Speeches and Essays. Trans. Chris Dawson. New Haven, CT: Yale University Press, 1998.

Hermeneutics, Religion, and Ethics. Trans. Joel Weinsheimer. New Haven, CT: Yale University Press, 1999.

2000s

Gadamer, Hans-Georg, and Lawrence K. Schmidt, eds. *Language and Linguisticality in Gadamer's Hermeneutics.* Lanham, MD: Lexington Books, 2000.

The Beginning of Knowledge. Trans. Rod Coltman. New York: Continuum, 2001.

Gadamer in Conversation: Reflections and Commentary. Trans. and ed. Richard E. Palmer. New York: Continuum, 2001.

A Century of Philosophy: Hans-Georg Gadamer in Conversation with Riccardo Dottori. Trans. Rod Coltman and Sigrid Koepke. New York: Continuum, 2003.

Hannah Arendt (1906–1975)

Biographical Sketch

Hannah Arendt was born on October 14, 1906, in Hanover, Germany, to Paul and Martha Cohn Arendt. Her parents were both well-educated and leftist in their political convictions. In 1910, her family moved to Königsberg. Arendt attended synagogue and religious instruction in Judaism. Her father died of paresis (syphilitic insanity) when she was seven years old, leaving her mother as a single parent to raise Arendt in the house of her affluent grandfather. Her mother

Different sources report inconsistent information about the life of Hannah Arendt. Information for this biographical sketch was drawn from "Hannah Arendt," The European Graduate School—http://www.egs.edu/resources/arendt.html (accessed August 18, 2005); Peter Baehr, *Portable Hannah Arendt* (New York: Penguin Books, 2000); Edward Craig, ed., *Routledge Encyclopedia of Philosophy* (New York: Routledge, 1998); Richard E. Glathman, "Arendt, Hannah," *The Cambridge Dictionary of Philosophy*, 2nd ed., ed. Robert Audi (Cambridge, UK: Cambridge University Press, 1999); Luise F. Pusch, "Women of Hanover: Hannah Arendt," trans. Joey Horsley—www.fembio.org/women-from/hannover/hannah-arendt.shtml (accessed October 9, 2003); Dana Villa, ed., *Cambridge Companion to Hannah Arendt* (Cambridge, UK: Cambridge University Press). Photograph courtesy of Jerome Kohn of the Hannah Arendt Literary Trust.

married Martin Beerwald in 1920, bringing two older stepsisters, Eva and Clara Beerwald, into their home.

Arendt was an avid reader. As a child, she encountered racism and was ostracized by students and teachers while in grade school. Both she and her mother fought back aggressively as World War I came and went. In 1924, she graduated from high school in Königsberg.

In 1925, Arendt attended the University of Marburg, where she studied theology with Rudolph Bultmann. Martin Heidegger was lecturing at Marburg in 1927, and they had a year-long affair, which ended when Arendt, who was Jewish, learned of Heidegger's involvement with the National Socialist Party. She continued her studies at the University of Freiburg, where she studied under phenomenologist Edmund Husserl. Then, at the University of Heidelberg, Arendt studied philosophy under existential philosopher-psychologist Karl Jaspers, completing her dissertation, entitled "Der Liebesbegriff bei Augustin. Versuch einer philosophischen Interpretation" (The Concept of Love in Augustine: An Attempt of a Philosophical Interpretation) in 1928.

In 1929 Arendt married Günther Stern and moved to Berlin. They offered their home as a place of refuge for Jews in transit fleeing Nazi persecution. While her first dissertation was published in 1929, she was prevented from habilitating (writing a second dissertation, which would have earned her permission to teach in German universities) in 1933 because she was a Jew. She fled Germany to France, where Stern had already moved. They divorced in 1939. She brought her mother to Paris from Königsberg in 1939. Through her involvement with Judaism, Arendt became acquainted with Heinrich Blücher, a member of the German Communist Party, who stimulated her interest in Marxism and political theory. They married in 1940.

At the onset of World War II, soon after her marriage, Arendt was interned in southern France at the infamous internment camp Gurs. Arendt managed to escape from Gurs, reunited with Blücher and in 1941 fled to New York via Lisbon, Portugal, with her husband and mother.

In 1941, Arendt settled in the United States. She found work as a journalist and eventually became the lead editor of a large publishing house. In 1951, her work *The Origins of Totalitarianism* was published, the same year she became a citizen of the United States. The book made Arendt an intellectual celebrity. Before long, she was widely recognized as a political philosopher. She held professorships or guest professorships at several universities, including Princeton, Harvard, and Berkeley.

Hannah Arendt died on December 5, 1975, in New York.

Hannah Arendt
Dialectical Communicative Labor

Ronald C. Arnett

> Eyes so used to darkness as ours will hardly be able to
> tell whether their light was the light of a candle or that
> of a blazing sun.[1]

This essay underscores the significance of "dialectical communicative labor" for the study of the philosophy of communication by examining Hannah Arendt's ongoing legacy and continuing contribution to a philosophy of communication. This work outlines major concepts from her work and their communicative implications and extends her ideas into philosophy of communication using the metaphor "dialectical communicative labor" as a heuristic conceptual key for understanding a postmodern world attentive to differentiation and the danger of unreflective consensus.

The term "dialectical communicative labor," coined by the author, is contrasted with a second metaphor, "alienated communicative work." This extension of Arendt's ideas privileges content over process in communication, differentiating labor in "public" and "private" communicative domains with "alienated communicative work" in the "social" sphere. As Seyla Benhabib suggests with the title of her work *Situating the Self,* how and where the self finds itself situated makes a difference.[2] How one does communication (labor or work) and where one engages the communication (private, public, or social) situates communicative life, moving either within the sphere of "dialectical communicative labor" or the sphere of "alienated communicative work."

Arendt's project sheds light upon the modern error, a failed effort to replace dialectical questioning, naturally generated by public and private differentiation, with unreflective confidence in the inevitability of progress. Arendt brings a candle to the table of thoughtfulness, permitting light to illuminate our way to questioning both the old and the new; neither is inherently correct. The distance needed for questioning lives naturally in public and private difference, which affords the questioner two sets of eyes from which to ask the question: "Is a given decision the best action in a particular historical moment?" Arendt herself takes on modernity, not with a gun or the call to power, but with a candle that offers light—reclaiming differentiated sight, fueled by public and private difference.

Introduction

This essay engages the social criticism of Hannah Arendt from a communication perspective, guided by an interpretive metaphor of "dialectical communicative labor." Arendt neither wrote specifically on communication nor used the term "dialectical communicative labor." The metaphor of dialectical communicative labor is a term used by this author to summarize Arendt's mission from a communication perspective, while honoring the horizon of her critical social project. Entrance into Arendt's work begins with a basic assumption—she outlined the reason for the collapse of confidence in modernity. Her work foreshadowed postmodern rejection of modernity, a conception of life resting upon the bad-faith foundation of optimism and progress.

Arendt unveiled a fundamental fault line in the modern world, detailing her conception of the reason for viewing modernity as a failed "social" experiment. The notion of the social as the amalgamation of public and private life is the resultant conclusion of a false sense of hope. Arendt deconstructed the foundation of modernity and then offered a constructivist critique, a pragmatic argument for the necessity of rebuilding and reconstituting a vibrant public and private life. She sought to redeem, out of the wreckage of the modern experiment, the natural dialectical communicative act of questioning.

Arendt's work is a major political and philosophical force that provides a counterargument and profound alternative to modernity. Her suggestion is itself a critique of progress in that she returned to the past to reclaim the fallen space of differentiated public and private life. Arendt's call for the rebuilding of public and private life invites us to paradigmatically reconsider the study of communication, deprivileging the taken-for-granted modern metaphor of progress, whether in accepting the "new" over the traditional or in the contemporary pursuit of the personally novel as a form of self-development.

Arendt understood modernity as a social experiment run amok. Her counter argument against the ideological assurance of modernity calls us to re-invigorate, nourish, and differentiate public and private communicative contexts. Arendt's scholarship detailed the social consequences of the collapse of differentiated public and private life and more pointedly named the reason for the failed modern social experiment, questioning false confidence in the inevitability of human progress.

The collapse of public and private life, into a modern amalgamation of undifferentiated space and unrecognized space, was fueled from the unbounded optimism in the inevitability of progress. Such optimism was unable to embrace the ongoing inescapability of rhetorical interruptions in the stream of progress. Optimism and progress live on a gradual and upwardly sloping field of increasing expectations—unprepared for major setbacks, false paths, and ill-conceived new ventures. The differentiation of public and private space provides a natural form of questioning, prompted by a dialectical tension between public and private life. The grand call to optimism and to progress loses textured questioning when public and private difference "morph" into a single uniform view of life.

From a communication perspective, the heart of Arendt's constructivist critique/project does not rest primarily in deconstruction of the "social," but within her rationale for reclaiming differentiated public and private life space. Working within the spirit of Arendt's project, this essay affirms the pragmatic necessity of differentiating public and private life as a natural dialectical encouragement of communicative complexity and interpretive texture. This essay coins a term of communicative action, "dialectical communicative labor," as the hermeneutic entrance into Arendt's project that sheds light on everyday questioning by dialectically texturing communicative understanding.

Situating Hannah Arendt's Legacy

Arendt's insights emerged from the intellectual heritage of the Greeks and her understanding of the emerging work of Edmund Husserl, Martin Heidegger, and Karl Jaspers. Additionally, she contended repeatedly with the work of Karl Marx. Most importantly, Arendt was engaged in the issues of her time—she lived in a human condition that invited totalitarian life in overt forms of aggression and more subtle forms of social life. Her work mirrors our day as she contended with her own. She witnessed totalitarian domination in both overt and subtle fashion, lending to her critique of both—offering a reason for the postmodern emphasis on differentiation.

Her engagement with a historical moment of domination pointed to the coming "banality" of modernity[3]—an extreme commonness of narrative confusion, virtue contention, and fragmented lives signaled by the tragic events of Nazism. She sensed the power of the "social" as a place that exacerbated a "shirking mentality," an inability to look at the world through another's eyes. She understood the collapse of the modern project without the increasing totalitarian and subtle perpetuation of the social sphere, in which conformity became increasingly hostile to differentiation.

Arendt's project was propelled by an intense concern for conformity within the social sphere that shaped the lives of those who knowingly and those who unknowingly were limited by conformity and consensus. Arendt lived in a ruptured moment in the modern project, signaling the oncoming inevitability of postmodern concern for differentiation. As a Jewish woman scholar in the era of Adolf Hitler, she witnessed the modern collapse of the social in world-scale form of the Third Reich. While conformity in this form was obviously destructive, Arendt had the wisdom to see the destructive life of the social in much less obvious and politically powerful places. The destructive call for consensus demanded by the social domain, which for Arendt defined "modernity," made the call for postmodern narrative confusion, virtue contention, and fragmented lives a call for liberation. Postmodernity was a response to the destructive power of the social domain, not a loss of agreement. Postmodernity opened the door to questioning and reengagement of public and private life.

Hitler's Third Reich was a public call to conformity, framing power within the social domain, a place inhospitable to differentiation and difference. The "final solution" employed by Nazi Germany was a cruel reminder of the limits of consensus, a social space shaped by forced conformity, inclusion/exclusion based upon unalterable factors such as religion, race, and physical characteristics. Arendt's engagement with that social sphere provided a stark view of the danger and the evil of forced consensus, whether politically motivated or tied to a desire to join particular social groups. Arendt did not call for unrecognized fragmentation. She would not necessarily agree with the extreme postmodern responses to modernity, but she would understand them and understand how those responses were potentially inevitable. She might, as this essay suggests, begin to question both postmodernity and modernity and begin the search for a third alternative, which her work suggests.

Seyla Benhabib is a contemporary scholar of the philosophy of communication who extends the work of Arendt and Jürgen Habermas, linking questions of procedure, public space, and communicative justice. Benhabib's engagement with Arendt offers significant contemporary insight into the philosophy of communication, as the final pages of the afterword to *The Communicative Ethics Controversy* reveals, by stressing the importance of Arendt's use of Kant's "enlarged mentality."[4] An enlarged mentality situates judgment within both particular and universal principles. An enlarged mentality presupposes one's ability to reverse perspectives, to see from another's position, permitting one to creatively implement a given universal as one gathers more and more particular understandings. Seeking to understand another's position enriches one's own insights, leading to an "enlarged mentality" that permits one to reflect upon positions different than one's own. One works within a universal of respect for the Other that necessitates understanding another's position through the reversal of perspectives, which then enlarges one's own mentality—one's ability to see, judge, and implement with attentiveness to differences and particulars.

An "enlarged mentality" forges the ongoing construction and sophistication of narrative and interpretive skills, which includes the importance of an "enlarged mentality" for judgment. Such a capacity to see another's perspective moves one from—in fact liberates one from—provincial thinking and judgment situated solely within "subjective private conditions."[5] An enlarged mentality for judgment requires reflective communicative content attentive to one's own position and that of others. Reflective communication, attentive to the perspective of particular others, moves communicative life beyond one's own presuppositions and into "dialectical communicative labor."

Benhabib's book on Arendt begins with an introductory question, "Why Hannah Arendt?"[6] Benhabib answers her own initial question, pointing to the power of Arendt's ideas for understanding the marginalization and the necessity of differentiating public and private space in order to lessen the power of conformity that constitutes the social sphere. Benhabib stresses the importance of Arendt's work in a postmodern time of increasing emphasis on "insiders" and "outsiders." Arendt "borrowed the terms *pariah* and *parvenu* from the French journalist Bernard Lazare: while the pariah is the one who is cast aside, marginalized, and treated with contempt by society because of his or her otherness, the parvenu denies her otherness so as to become accepted by the dominant society."[7] Without public and private space in place, a dialectic of accountability is lost as the social collapses these contrasting spaces of human life.

Benhabib acknowledges the controversy around Arendt's scholarship on the question of totalitarianism, while preserving a key message from Arendt, "the fragility of human rights."[8] Benhabib understands the power of the term "parvenu" for recognizing the social sphere as a place that captures one's attention and energy. One works to enter a space that is forever off-limits unless one conforms to the extent of losing all uniqueness. Hans-Georg Gadamer suggests that we invite new information through the bias, prejudice, and uniqueness we bring to a given text or historical moment.[9] The power and constraint of the social sphere is that it denies uniqueness, calling for a parvenu, an adopter of social conventions void of uniqueness. The sphere of the social goes undisturbed, unchanged by the presence of a newcomer—one must simply fit in. The social sphere demands consensus, eradicating any uniqueness of the Other.

To diminish the power of the social and the demands to function as a parvenu—and to thus protect human rights—Arendt repeatedly announced the importance of differentiating public and private space. The latter part of the twentieth century witnessed a collapse of public and private spheres, against which Benhabib currently contends and against which Hannah Ardent warned. Arendt saw the inevitable movement of modern life toward increasing power and significance of a social domain. The power of the story of "progress" rests within the scope of "social progress," not expansive participation in public and private life. Businesses using the term "family" to describe life in the organization, churches using the term "friend" for those unknown or little engaged, and schools using the term "self-esteem" as a key to education collectively point to the rise of the social, a domain of consensus in which disagreement with conventions about family, friends, and esteem are considered out of place—out of place within the power of the social sphere.

In the concluding pages of Benhabib's book on Arendt, the ongoing significance of Arendt's project of reclaiming difference in public and private space and the danger of the social finds expression in stark contemporary terms:

> After two decades of criticizing the private/public split, and the way in which this dichotomy has served to camouflage domestic violence, child molestations, and marital rape in the private reality, contemporary feministic theory is entering a new phase of thinking about these issues. The binarity of the public and the private spheres must be reconstructed, and not merely rejected. From abortion rights to debates about pornography, from the struggles of gay and lesbian couples to become foster parents and to be recognized as "domestic partners," a renewed affirmation of the value of the private [and public spheres] is afoot.[10]

By failing to differentiate public and private space, we invite a social sphere of conformity that works well in a small town of little diversity, but fails miserably in urban centers of difference. The global community is more akin to an urban life of difference where people of contrary positions work together than it is to life within a provincial small town.

Arendt understood the power and necessity of differentiation—the key to a postmodern world. She understood the social sphere as a failed experiment, signaling the decline of modern assumptions of progress and integration. She witnessed firsthand the attempt of new ideas (progress) to annihilate a people and saw integration resulting in the acceptance of some people without the approval of others. The social approves too quickly of whatever conforms. If one believes in "progress," then what is "new" receives more attention and, too often, unreflective social agreement that the new is more important than the old. Just as tradition cannot become an unchallenged assumption, neither can the new. The social is a place of conformity and consensus for both unreflective tradition and unreflective engagement of the new. The social sphere is a place of conformity and, simultaneously, exclusion. Unreflective enactment of tradition and change invites exclusion of those outside the arena of agreement.

In Benhabib's *Situating the Self: Gender, Community, and Postmodernism in Contemporary Ethics*, she devotes a chapter to Arendt that once again examines the themes of enlarged mentality and public and private[11]; both spheres point to the importance of Arendt's work for understanding the pragmatic necessity of differentiation in a postmodern world of recognized narrative/virtue contention. Benhabib underscores Arendt's use of the term "thoughtlessness,"[12] Arendt's response to Adolf Eichmann. Arendt contended that the inability to think invites depravity. Her comments make even more sense in a postmodern world of difference. We must think and understand our lives together. The provinciality of "emotivism" cannot be condoned.[13] Moral decision-making by emotivism or personal preference misses engagement with one's situated existence and with the Other, lacking an enlarged mentality beyond one's own skin and unreflectively situated life.

Modernity's Race

Modernity sought to lessen one's perceived depth of the lived world and to exploit each extension of the new and the novel. Modernity flattens and levels with calls for implementation, forgoing dialectical questioning of a given phenomenon. Such a perspective works to "biggy size" whatever works without asking "What should be done?" Metaphors that emphasize bigger as better are indeed apt for sustaining the illusion of the metanarrative of progress—metaphors of bigger, faster, ever efficient, and "more" guide the dark side of unrestrained growth. Jacques Ellul's critique of the West was that we do what "can" be done, too often failing to ask what "should" be done.[14] Dialectical questioning inherently suggests

a minimal gesture toward discerning the notion of "should" in a given historical situation, rather than falling prey to the demand to implement what is new.
Modernity lives within the metaphor of unfettered progress, hostile to the call of
tradition. Postmodernity opens the ground for tradition once again within the
frame of multiplicity. Deconstruction attacks the universal of progress and the
notion of universality, not the reality of multiple traditions. Public and private
differentiation naturally points to a multiplicity of traditions. Modernity sought
to kill tradition, only to discover with its demise that postmodernity had given
birth to a conversation among traditions—without the underpinning of unfettered optimism in progress or the individual disembedded from the clutches of
limits that live within traditions. Arendt takes us back to traditions, rejecting
the assumption that progress rests with the individual self.

Modernity assumes the commonplace of "progress"; one hears the echo of
the chant of progress throughout history from the Enlightenment through the
Reformation to the Industrial Revolution. Optimistic faith in progress is the common link among philosophical, theological, and business advancements. Each
major historical movement challenged tradition with an agreed-upon alternative
foundation—progress. Modernity challenged tradition as the fulcrum point for
decision making. Confidence in the reality of progress became the artificial turf
upon which the modern self stands and seeks to advance. The movement from
tradition to modernity's confidence in progress made the ground under one's
feet—tradition—irrelevant. Without the ground of tradition the self was disembedded, left to fend alone, standing above history. Tradition became irrelevant
and the self became the focus of attention, unleashing unfettered confidence in
the new. No longer was the task one of reinterpreting a tradition to meet the demands of the historical moment. The task shifted to the self as social construc-
tor of a "brave new world." Progress as the keystone of modernity moved the self
into the limelight, acting as if one could function without ground under one's
feet—attempting to ignore the recalcitrance of being as situated in the ground
upon which we stand. The postmodern emphasis on ethnic, racial, gender, and
socioeconomic ground revisits the recalcitrance of being, taking seriously the
ground—the grounds—upon which we stand.

For those absorbed by modernity, the place of fear and terror rests within
tradition, which functions as quicksand—terrain alien to progress and mobility. Modernity challenges tradition, and postmodernity recharges the necessity
of tradition with an "s"—tradition becomes traditions or "petite narratives."[15]
Even popular fare underscores this reading. At first glance, *Fiddler on the Roof*
offers a critique of tradition; yet it is placed against the backdrop of the Marxist revolution in Russia. The message is not simply about the limits of tradition,
but about the limits of progress as well. Such a critique of progress rested at the
core of the parting of Albert Camus and Jean-Paul Sartre. Camus's rejection was
not of Marxism, but of the intemperate hope in progress that the revolutionary
language carried. Modernity has been the site of conflict of ideologies with a

common first principle—the march toward progress. The fight of progressive ideologies, from capitalism to Marxism and from self-situated humanism to self-situated religion (*deus ex machina*), shapes the face of modernity. Life made ever better, ever better—such is the refrain of the modern hymn of progress.

Modernity adopted progress as a universal good, a god-word, the taken-for-granted ground of contemporary life. Arendt centers her contention against the "social," the collapsed space that offers only a blurred remnant of public and private life in its unleashing of the notion of progress and unrestrained growth:

> . . . it was as though the growth element inherent in all organic life had completely overcome and overgrown the processes of decay by which organic life is checked and balanced in nature's household. The social realm, where the life process has established its own public domain, has let loose an unnatural growth, not merely against society but against a constantly growing social realm, that the private and intimate, on the one hand, and the political (in the narrower sense of the word), on the other, have proved incapable of defending themselves.[16]

The "social" is the keeper of progress, providing implicit and explicit ground from which a communicator meets the world; the notion of metanarrative lives within the assumption that progress is the universal given. Such confidence in the ground of progress made discussion of tradition irrelevant in modernity. What then makes for the good life is not tradition, but the onward and upward trajectory toward what is not yet. Progress provides the ground for an unwarranted sense of self-confidence. The self no longer feels compelled to learn about a given tradition, whether one's own or that of another, but assumes that a commitment to progress, which both explicitly and implicitly unleashes the self as a heroic contributor to the future, is a sufficient answer to questions of existence. The self becomes the super-agent of the metanarrative of progress. From Arendt's perspective and from a postmodern reading, the self stands on the artificial turf of progress, unaware of the loss of narrative soil that situates the person, forgoing artificial clarity for the mud of everyday life. This unexamined confidence in the ground of progress places "bad faith" under the feet of the modern agent, which ironically results in a rapid run toward conformity.[17]

The artificial ground that supports confidence in progress fuels an uncomplicated understanding of the self—ignoring public space and diminishing the complexity and texture of differing engagements in private life. Modernity assumed a final resting place for the "good life," replaced by the counterfeit ground of progress. The "good life" then lives within the self with the self unreflectively walking with assurance and confidence on the soil of bad faith—progress. Such unreflective confidence announces itself in the metaphors of modernity—self-development, self-actualization, and self-presentation. These modern metaphors act as natural extensions of modernity's blighted "social" project.

By attacking the notion of the social, Arendt's work points to the pragmatic necessity of communicative ground that is dialectically nourished in public and private life. Upon this dialectical ground, the self finds temporal guidance; communicative action as ground rejects the artificial turf of the "social," which obscures the complexity of dialectical co-informing through the communicative interplay of public and private life. Arendt's work seems to suggest a key question for the study of human communication in an era of narrative and virtue contention: "How does one find temporal communicative ground for guiding a life?" This essay hinges an answer on the metaphor of "dialectical communicative action." Modernity lessens difference, flattening and leveling, opening the door for an inauthentic "herd mentality" constituted by the commonality of commitment to the self.

Modernity's race rests on a collapsed track of public and private life. The collapse is obscured by the synthetic surface of progress. Upon this assumption of progress stand many selves, moving in different directions with a common origin of progress, hence the social becomes the collapsed space of individualism, which cloaks a deep-seated conformity based upon "universal" agreement that progress guides human life. The social provides the ironical base for individualism.

The "Social" as Ironical Ground for Individualism

The "bad faith" ground of the "social" displays itself most vividly in times of narrative and virtue contention. The social assumes adherence to societal practices that foster movement toward progress and do not question the privileged status of progress via social climbing. Arendt witnessed narrative contention as a Jewish woman in Nazi Germany. From the standpoint of the outsider, Arendt differentiated between "pariah" and "parvenu" as social actor types engaged in social climbing. For Arendt the pariah remains on the outside, never invited into a place, actively ignored. The parvenu, on the other hand, works energetically to find a door that opens access to social mobility.

> As a Jew Rahel had always stood outside, had been a pariah, and discovered at last, most unwillingly and unhappily, that entrance into society was possible only at the price of lying, of a far more generalized lie than simply hypocrisy. She discovered that it was for the parvenu . . . to sacrifice every natural impulse, to conceal all truth, to misuse all love, not only to suppress all passion, but worse still, to convert it into a means for social climbing.[18]

The parvenu takes on the practices of the "social" world with the hope of profiting from its "magic" center, which houses progress and masks the hidden requirement of conformity. Yet, for the parvenu to enter competition inherent in social climbing, one must give oneself to standards that render one's contribution without uniqueness. Parvenus must give themselves to a subtle form of social imperialism. Engaging work without the support of a tradition, a community of

people, and with the inevitability of disconfirmation of one's contribution defines alienated communicative work, witnessed in the life and on the face of the
parvenus, the one never able to join a predefined social sphere.

The "social" is a place of conformity, which permits only limited accepted
social practices. The necessity of postmodernity emerged as an alternative to the
social. This author views Arendt's notion of the "social" as the dark side of the
Enlightenment. The conformity of the social rests within the assumptions of the
universal and of progress. Postmodernity opened up differences among various
traditions, recognizing differing narrative grounds. The reality of multiple petite narratives offers exit from the prison of conformist practices that germinate
within the social—providing a third option to pariah (the outsider) and parvenu
(the conforming social climber). Postmodernity destroys the hegemony of the
social, expanding life choices. In postmodernity, individuals become persons in
communities that form around a common center; petite narratives offer identity
and the possibility of uniqueness. In contrast to the social, which lessens differences, postmodern recognition of multiple petite narratives opens up spaces for
those deemed "unfit" for a defined social space.

Benhabib reminds us of the importance of Alexis de Tocqueville's insights
to Arendt's work.[19] Arendt understood that Tocqueville's warning to early Americans about the importance of "habits of the heart" makes no sense in an era of
narrative change.[20] Instead, it was Bonhoeffer's response to the Nazi's habits of
the heart that clearly announced a change of habits of the heart in a "world come
of age."[21] Such habits arise from the interaction of our public and private lives.
Situating habits of the heart in the communicative interplay of public and private
life counters the unreflective suspension of habits in a "social" space, a space of
conformity that embraces the illusion of self-autonomy.

The social space of modernity gathers nourishment from the assumption
of unimpeded growth and progress. To reject the growth assumption of modernity opens the door to the question of communicative ground without the false
bravado of an imperial self, but with an awareness and expectation that progress
diminishes accomplishments in our march from war to war and from employment
in one company to another. Interpreting otherwise than confidence in the notion
of progress and the growth potential of the self rests with a term that suggests the
practical heart of Arendt's work in action—'dialectical communicative labor.'

Arendt's scholarship points to the inevitability of the "postmodern" task
of reclamation, reclaiming spaces of difference. The metaphor of 'dialectical
communicative labor' provides a hermeneutic entrance into Arendt's critique
of modernity, congruent in tone and responsive to the meaning horizon of her
re-constitutive critical project. Modernity with the dual focus upon progress
and the self constitutes itself as a moral cul de sac. Modernity bears out the social consequence of misplaced confidence in the ideal of constant and inevitable
growth. In modernity, progress functions as a metanarrative with the notion of
the self as an action-receptacle for development and change.

The unity of a metanarrative of progress and uniform commitment to self-development enriches the "social," a space of conformity, and simultaneously augments Tocqueville's warning about individualism without narrative restraint. The leveled space of the "social" spawns life under the "bad faith" of individualism as difference, while the social actually lives within an imperialist agreement of conformity hostile to competing traditions, receptive to the expectation of progress alone. It is not the self, but rather the story-laden richness of tradition, that informs and situates selves and makes difference possible. When public space morphs into communities of affinity[22] and the rigors of structured play called leisure collapse into undemanding moments of recreation,[23] public and private life collapse into the void of the "social." The "social" becomes the arena for gladiators of self-development. Such is the reason the founder of conflict theory, Georg Simmel, considers "jealousy" the most pernicious and damaging infection within a community.[24] The fusion of public and private life unifies a space that positions the self on a common ground; one no longer looks for difference in the stories that shape another, but confidently attends to oneself, unresponsive to the narrative ground that shapes the relationship between self and Other.

The "social" functions as a universal paradigm unresponsive to difference[25]—it is this taken-for-granted commitment to progress, a form of paradigmatic assurance, that marshals the self into an implementer of progress. The confidence with which people engage the social ignores Thomas Kuhn's notion of competing paradigms.[26] The headlong pursuit into what Arendt called the "social" was only possible in a historical moment when the enlightenment project of agency compressed public and private life into a paradigmatic runway for self-confidence. Nourished by public and private spheres, this collapse resulted in inattentiveness to Otherness and hyper-reflection upon the self. Within the "social" sphere, an individual seeks approval and acceptance; if successful in gaining "membership" within a given social sphere, the person forfeits the ability to unite communication and labor. If, however, one cannot find one's way into a given "social" arena, yet unceasingly engages the effort of social acceptance, an individual courts a contorted view of dialectical communicative labor, which this essay terms "alienated communicative work." Alienated communicative work is the communicative result of the parvenu seeking entrance into a world that exploits his or her toil without confirming the doer of the work. Alienated communicative work permits one to work without entrance into a "sacred" space, the "social." It is this "social" space that uses, tempts, and then excludes that harbors a banality of evil that Arendt sought to deconstruct; she displayed the poverty of acceptance in the social.

Knowledge nourished by the natural dialectic of public and private life is irrelevant when people hold unbridled confidence in the universal, exercise the inevitable march toward truth, and pay unlimited attention to the self. The unleashed self ignores the story-laden nature of life, as Arendt states.

> Although everybody started his life by inserting himself into the human world through action and speech, nobody is the author or producer of his own life story. In other words, the stories, the results of action and speech, reveal an agent, but this agent is not an author or producer. Somebody began it and is its subject in the twofold sense of the word, namely, its actor and sufferer, nobody is its author.[27]

The self was unleashed by the collapsed boundaries of public and private life, leaving in its place the social, a place where false optimism propels self-confidence, ever certain of the ground for progress and achievement.

From Optimistic Confidence to Realistic Hope

Unrealistic optimism in progress is central to Christopher Lasch's critique of progress in *The True and Only Heaven*.[28] He outlined the importance of realistic hope, textured by success and failure and ever nourished by hard work—with the recognition that hard work does not always prevail. Lasch rejected a story of ever expanding progress based upon a misplaced confidence in growth. The self assumes that all is possible under the spell of such a story, unable to fathom the possibility of disappointment. Cynicism finds a home in unmet expectations and demands for optimism.[29] Cynicism is the home of those angered by the unfulfilled story of progress.

Arendt did not accept a story of modern confidence, a story of progress that emboldened the self to fashion itself as creator standing above traditions, dependent upon the tradition of progress alone. Situated within and responsive to the failed Nazi project of unifying the modern world, Arendt interpreted otherwise, questioning not the Nazi project alone, but what in the modern experiment made the Nazi project possible. Instead of calling for the uniformity of the social, Arendt called for difference; her work foreshadowed the postmodern necessity of appreciating differentiation. Her critique of modernity, in short, is the desire to unify society by having faith in a common assumption of progress—people foregoing the effort and challenge to learn from and engage difference in public and private life. The collapse of public and private life into the realm of the "social" fits the modern hope of obliterating tradition(s) and person(s) into interchangeable units. The metaphor of machine guides the confidence of modernity, including confidence in the modern self, who grows with machine-like precision. Such a view of communicative life rests within the assumption that people have paradigmatically "arrived," permitting traditions to be ignored as irrelevant and placing primary attention upon the self.

Arendt critiqued modernity as a place that masquerades as an arena of difference, inviting "dark times," where only conformity permits one to survive. Modernity does not honor tradition(s); its altar is the self. The irony of modernity is that from the colonization of traditional life one invites what a colleague called "interpersonal colonization" within the realm of the "social."[30] Modernity kills traditions that nurture persons, offering instead the social, a place of inter-personal colonization where one conforms not to tradition, but to the whim of a collective. The social is the place of agreed-upon colonization where one seeks approval to join, not a tradition, but a "herd."

One's communicative life within traditions, whether social, ethnic, or religious, informs the self in a postmodern age. The self is constructed by the traditions that guide us. To ignore traditions is to cease to learn about another, asking instead for the other to conform to me—such is the place of Arendt's "social" within the realm of conformity. The work of Walter Fisher on "narrative rationality" points in this direction.[31] Without a story-laden tradition there is no rationality. Rationality is a modern construct assuming universal agreement on basic presuppositions that situate and provide background for interpretation. If one disagrees with such premises—i.e., progress and the ability of the "self" to stand above the historical moment and claim objective insight—rationality becomes divertive of the story and stories that shape a given communicator.

Arendt reminds us of "dark times," moments when the social collapses public and private life, when "the unhidden and unprotected by the privacy of the self appears in public."[32] Such a view of "dark times" does not underscore moments of tragedy, but rather finds kinship with the insights of Martin Buber when he discussed the demonic of "psychologism,"[33] trying to attribute motives to another's behavior, and of Dietrich Bonhoeffer, who suggested that one must permit and expect another to wear a mask.[34] One does not have the right to know all the intricacies of another's life. Dark times blur public and private, forgoing dialectical insight that can call one arena into question by the other.

Hannah Arendt's interpretive insights engage the reader with a story about a communicative place of danger—the realm of the "social." For a postmodern age, the "social" is the modern arena of consensus and "common" taste that made the renewed call for differentiation inevitable. Contrasting the conformity of the "social" arena, Arendt invited the reader into action and responsibility, repeatedly framing an argument about the menace that resides within pretense and conformity of the "social" realm. Dialectical communicative labor reclaims the importance of differentiating one idea or action from another, which makes differentiation of public and private communicative domains possible. Dialectical communicative labor moves beyond or through passive accommodation to and with the social arena into the realm of difference.

Dialectical Communicative Labor

"Dialectical communicative labor" functions as a form of conceptual shorthand for the unity of philosophical, reflective, and differentiated understanding of ideas and practices that undergird and shape communicative interaction in the public and private domains of communicative life. In short, dialectical communicative labor does not work with melting pot efforts to confuse "this with that," for whatever reason the effort at combination gathers social legitimacy.

"Dialectical communicative labor" is a metaphor that suggests the necessity of differentiation, making possible public and private communicative life contentious with demands for conformity in the social sphere. The realm of the "social" sacrifices this critical questioning mode for an unreflective sense of belonging. The social arena defines modernity as a failed experiment; new ideas emerge via differentiation, not feigned agreement or superficial consensus.

Framing Arendt's philosophy as a union of communication and human labor seeks to construct communicative insight through dialectical differentiation. Dialectical communicative labor suggests that communication is a process of laboring with ideas/content in a reflectively differentiated manner that moves ideas into action within the "public" and "private" spheres of human interaction. Arendt's writing illustrates a philosophy of "dialectical communicative labor" that forgoes a description of the "given," a description of consensus about the "social," and engages dialectical communicative labor in the act of social/philosophical *praxis*, which allows for differentiation and change. Dialectical communicative labor suggests an understanding of communication incongruous with what Arendt called the "social." Dialectical communicative labor necessitates reflective philosophical and practical content of ideas, requiring differentiation of one idea and action from another to avoid the pitfall of the "social," which calls for feigned consensus. Differentiation is the propelling metaphor for dialectical communicative labor, which makes private and public domains of human life distinguishable from the social. Labor is a necessity; reframing communicative engagement as labor takes the power from a "social" enclave that seeks to use the work of the parvenu while discarding the doer of the work. The notion of dialectical communicative labor rests on the assumption of difference. Without differentiating public and private life and deconstructing the social, communicative insight lives forever with the routine of implementation. Arendt points to the necessity of engaging difference in the natural act of labor, central to the human condition.

Arendt's differentiation of labor and work offers textured insight for understanding one of the major "communicative limits" of modernity—support of and conformity to the social. Her work points to a postmodern reclaiming of the necessity of public and private space, enhanced by communicative differentiation. Arendt's scholarship, understood from the vantage point of philosophy of communication, reminds us of a form of communication situated within the labor of communicative practices, contrary to conventions that herd us into unreflectively embraced compliance and, at times, an actively sought after compliance with the social sphere in order to gain access into the communicative life within a particular aspect of that domain.

Communicative life without dialectical questioning moves us into Arendt's social or what George Ritzer called *The McDonaldization of Society*—a world of extreme commonness. Francis Fukuyama referred to this era as the end of history.[35] Each metaphor offers insight into the realm of the social, a place that loses differentiation and difference.

In differentiating public and private communicative space, the term "dialectical communicative labor" offers an alternative to an emphasis on discourse or communicative process, not supplanting such terms, but offering a metaphor that unites communication and labor, carrying conceptual content into action, enriching public and private space. The "social" is shaped by conformity, not intellectual and relational labor that shapes the uniqueness of public and private space with communicative content. The social is shaped by agreement on the importance of the space, not the content. Simply put, if one watches an ad on television and is unable to remember the importance of the product and in some cases the product itself, what finds marketability is the social. The public importance of the product and the private use of the product fall as secondary to conformity to a given social space.

The danger of conformity in the social propelled Arendt's work in one book after another. From her dissertation on Saint Augustine, published as *Love and Saint Augustine,* where she cited the importance of "absolute distance"[36] outlined in *The Human Condition,* where she framed her most powerful critique of the social, Arendt called for distance to reflect. The social obliterates the distance that is essential for differentiation and insight rather than conformity.

Dialectical communicative labor presupposes that the purpose of communication is to carry informational and relational *content* into public and private life, minimizing the power of the social domain. Contrasted with dialectical communicative labor is "alienated communicative work," which stresses conformity to and with the social and unites communication with "work," not "labor." Arendt offers conceptual insight, differentiating labor and work, offering implications for distinguishing "dialectical communicative labor" that shapes "public" and "private" space from communicative work, which conforms to demands of the "social."

Communicative Relevance

Arendt points to a communicatively enlarged mentality that has moral implications for the study of communication in a postmodern age. Her work reclaims traditions, identifying the "social" self, which can stand above history as a figment of imagination. She reclaims the differentiated space of public and private life, offering dialectical communicative insight. Arendt points to identity of the self as embedded within "a web of relationships and enacted stories."[37] The relationships shift in public and private life, and the stories are enacted differently. Arendt takes us back to a realm of the "hero," not as an individual standing above life, but someone standing up to one's ankles and sometimes one's knees in the mud of everyday life.

The character of the hero, understood by Homer and cited by Arendt, is simply a free man involved in the Trojan enterprise. One finds one's courage in the ability to speak and act in the story-laden contexts. One does not stand above, but in the midst of, the everyday confusion of life. The hero lives everyday life with blurred vision, blurred by being in the world, not above the world. The hero does not live on abstract principles or objective insight, but on the fragile will to acknowledge the storied nature of life and one's obligation to contribute to such a story. For Arendt, "courage is not necessarily or even primarily related to a willingness to suffer the consequences; courage even boldness are already present in leaving one's private hiding place and showing who one is, in disclosing and exposing one's self."[38] The labor of the hero is threefold: to acknowledge the story-laden nature of life, to contribute to the story, and to walk from the confines of private life into the heat of public debate.

The communicative labor of Arendt's hero is to forgo the false confidence of the social and walk into the story-laden nature of life. The differentiated spaces of public and private life offer dialectical insight, each shedding some light upon the other. Arendt would contend with the modern effort to dispense with the hero. The hero walks within stories. The hero extends stories. Only the willingness to walk from private to public accountability makes the hero possible. The hero is not special for Arendt—the title is bestowed upon all those unwilling to fall prey to the seduction of the social and its siren song of progress.

It is not progress of an isolated self seeking to join a social enclave that guides human significance; meaningful guidance comes from stories, traditions, and petite narratives with real people struggling within them. For Arendt, courage rests in the web of everyday life—a web of stories that naturally illuminate differently the context of lives through the dialectical labor of differentiating public and private space. Arendt offered a counter to the banality of evil nourished by the "social." She pointed to engagement with the world that was otherwise than convention, framing a different commonness. Arendt reminded us of a liberation nourished by the banality of labor, a human commonness that sustains without the social. She gave and gives the parvenu hope—reminding us that creative labor, meaningful engagement, and thoughtful ideas happen outside the social, often in the outskirts, the provinces—places unresponsive to the social climbing of the parvenu cloaked by a delusion of individualism and locked within the paradigmatic conventions of a given "social" space.

Notes

1. Hannah Arendt, *Men in Dark Times* (New York: Harcourt, Brace & World, 1968), ix–x.
2. Seyla Benhabib, *Situating the Self: Gender, Community, and Postmodernism in Contemporary Ethics* (New York: Routledge, 1992).
3. Hannah Arendt, *The Human Condition* (Chicago: Univ. of Chicago Press, 1998), 252.

4. Seyla Benhabib, *The Communicative Ethics Controversy* (Cambridge, MA.: MIT Press, 1990), 361.
5. Ibid., 300.
6. Seyla Benhabib, *The Reluctant Modernism of Hannah Arendt* (Lanham, MD: Rowan & Littlefield, 2003), xxxvii.
7. Ibid., xxvi.
8. Ibid., xxxiii.
9. Hans-Georg Gadamer, *Truth and Method* (New York: Continuum, 1994), 239.
10. Benhabib, *Reluctant Modernism*, 214.
11. Benhabib, *Situating the Self,* 121–144.
12. Ibid., 122.
13. Alasdair MacIntyre, *After Virtue* (Notre Dame: Univ. of Notre Dame Press, 1981), 11–14, 16–33.
14. Jacques Ellul, *In Season, Out of Season* (New York: Harper & Row, 1981), 172–200.
15. J.-F. Lyotard, *Theory and History of Literature,* vol. 10: *The Postmodern Condition: A Report on Knowledge,* trans. G. Bennington and B. Massumi (1979; reprint, Minneapolis: Univ. of Minnesota Press, 1993), 60.
16. Arendt, *Human Condition*, 47.
17. Jean-Paul Sartre, *Being and Nothingness: An Essay on Phenomenological Ontology,* trans. Hazel E. Barnes (New York: Washington Square Press, 1953), 86–116.
18. Hannah Arendt, *Rahel Varnhagen: The Life of a Jewess* (Baltimore: Johns Hopkins Univ. Press, 1997), 244.
19. Benhabib, *Reluctant Modernism*, 68.
20. Alexis de Tocqueville, *Democracy in America* (Chicago: Univ. of Chicago Press, 1996), 287.
21. Dietrich Bonhoeffer, *Letters and Papers from Prison,* ed. Eberhard Bethge (New York: Simon & Schuster, 1971).
22. Maurice Friedman, *The Confirmation of Otherness in Family, Community, and Society* (New York: The Pilgrim Press, 1983).
23. Gadamer, *Truth and Method*, 116–17, 134.
24. Georg Simmel, *Conflict and the Web of Group-Affiliations* (New York: The Free Press, 1955), 50–55.
25. Arendt, *Human Condition*, 38–49.
26. Thomas Kuhn, *The Structure of Scientific Revolutions* (Chicago: Univ. of Chicago Press, 1962), 43–51.
27. Arendt, *Human Condition*, 184.
28. Christopher Lasch, *The True and Only Heaven: Progress and Its Critics* (New York: W.W. Norton, 1991).
29. Ronald C. Arnett and Pat Arneson, *Dialogic Civility in a Cynical Age* (Albany: State Univ. of New York Press, 1999), 13.
30. Janie Harden Fritz, Conversation with author, Pittsburgh, PA, October 23, 2002.
31. Walter Fisher, "Narrative as a Human Condition Paradigm: The Case of Public Moral Argument," *Communication Monographs* 51 (1984): 1–22.
32. Arendt, *Men in Dark Times,* ix.
33. Martin Buber, *Between Man and Men* (1947; reprint, New York: Macmillan, 1965).

34. Dietrich Bonhoeffer, *Life Together* (New York: Harper & Row, 1954).

35. George Ritzer, *The McDonaldization of Society: New Century Edition* (Thousand Oaks, CA: Pine Forge Press, 2000); Francis Fukuyama, *The End of History and the Last Man* (New York: Free Press, 1992), 56, 58, 64–67, 136–39, 144, 207, 288, 289, 310–11, 320.

36. Hannah Arendt, *Love and Saint Augustine* (Chicago: Univ. of Chicago Press, 1996), 98.

37. Arendt, *Human Condition*, 181.

38. Ibid., 186.

Bibliography of Works

Books by Hannah Arendt

1920s

Der Liebesbegriff bei Augustin: Versuch einer philosophischen Interpretation. Berlin: J. Springer, 1929.

1940s

Sechs Essays. Heidelberg: L. Schneider, 1948.

1950s

Elemente und Ursprünge totaler Herrschaft. Frankfurt am Main: Europäische Verlagsanstalt, 1955.

Fragwürdige Traditionsbestände im politischen Denken der Gegenwart. Frankfurt am Main: Europäische Verl. Anst., 1957.

Die Krise in der Erziehung. Bremen: Angelsachsen-Verlag, 1958.

Die ungarische Revolution und der totalitäre Imperialismus. Munich: R. Piper, 1958.

Rahel Varnhagen, Lebensgeschichte einer deutschen Jüdin aus der Romantik. Munich: R. Piper, 1959.

1960s

Vita Activa: Oder, Vom tätigen Leben. Stuttgart: W. Kohlhammer, 1960.

Von der Menschlichkeit in finsteren Zeiten: Rede über Lessing. Munich: R. Piper, 1960.

Dempf, Alois, Hannah Arendt, and F. Engel-Janosi, eds. *Politische Ordnung und menschliche Existenz: Festgabe für Eric Voegelin zum 60 Geburtstag*. Munich: Beck, 1962.

Eichmann in Jerusalem: Ein Bericht von der Banalität des Bösen. Munich: R. Piper, 1964.

Gespräch mit Hannah Arendt. Munich: R. Piper, 1965.

Über die Revolution. Munich: R. Piper, 1965.

1970s

Macht und Gewalt. Munich: R. Piper, 1971.

Walter Benjamin, Bertolt Brecht: Zwei Essays. Munich: R. Piper, 1971.

Wahrheit und Lüge in der Politik: Zwei Essays. Munich: R. Piper, 1972.

Erinnerungen an Karl Jaspers. Munich: R. Piper, 1974.

Gespräche mit Hannah Arendt. Ed. Adelbert Reif. Munich: Piper, 1976.

Die verborgene Tradition: Acht Essays. Frankfurt am Main: Suhrkamp, 1976.

Vom Leben des Geistes. Vol. 1: *Das Denken*. Munich: R. Piper, 1979.

Vom Leben des Geistes. Vol. 2: *Das Wollen*. Munich: R. Piper, 1979.

1980s

Das Urteilen. Texte zu Kants politischer Philosophie. Ed. and with an essay by Ronald Beiner. Aus dem Amerikanischen von Ursula Ludz. Munich: R. Piper, 1985.

Arendt, Hannah, and Karl Jaspers. *Briefwechsel Arendt/Jaspers, 1926–1969*. Ed. Lotte Köhle and Hans Saner. Munich Piper, 1985.

Zur Zeit. Politische Essays. Ed. Marie Luise Knott. Aus dem Amerikanischen von Eike Geisel. Berlin: Rotbuch-Verlag, 1986.

Die Krise des Zionismus: Essays und Kommentare 2. Ed. Eike Geisel and Klaus Bittermann. Berlin: Tiamat, 1989.

Menschen in finsteren Zeiten. Ed. Ursula Ludz. Munich: R. Piper, 1989.

Nach Auschwitz: Essays und Kommentare 1. Ed. Eike Geisel and Klaus Bittermann. Berlin: Tiamat, 1989.

1990s

Was ist Existenz-Philosophie? Berlin: Hain, 1990.

Israel, Palästina und der Antisemitismus: Aufsätze. Ed. Eike Geisel and Klaus Bittermann. Berlin: Wasenbach, 1991.

Besuch in Deutschland. Aus dem Amerikanischen von Eike Geisel. Foreword by Henrik M. Broder; sketch by Ingeborg Nordmann. Berlin: Rotbuch, 1993.

Was ist Politik?: Fragmente aus dem Nachlaß (1956–1959). Ed. Ursula Ludz. Foreword by Kurt Sontheimer. Munich: R. Piper, 1993.

Zwischen Vergangenheit und Zukunft: Übungen im politischen Denken I. Munich: R. Piper, 1994.

". . . in keinem Besitz verwurzelt": Die Korrespondenz/Hannah Arendt, Kurt Blumenfeld. Ed. Ingeborg Nordmann. Hamburg: Rotbuch-Verlag, 1995.

Ich will verstehen: Selbstauskünfte zu Leben und Werk. Ed. Ursula Ludz. Munich: R. Piper, 1996.

Arendt, Hannah, and Martin Heidegger. *Briefe 1925 bis 1975: Und andere Zeugnisse.* Frankfurt am Main: V. Klostermann, 1998.

Über den Totalitarismus: Texte Hannah Arendts aus den Jahren 1951 und 1953. Commentary by Ingeborg Nordmann. Dresden: Hannah-Arendt-Inst. für Totalitarismusforschung.

Von Wahrheit und Politik. Munich: R. Piper, 1999.

Arendt, Hannah, and Hermann Broch. *Briefwechsel: 1946 bis 1951.* Ed. Paul Michael Lützeler. Frankfurt am Main: Jüdischer Verlag, 1996.

Arendt, Hannah, and Mary McCarthy. *Im Vertrauen.* Ed. Carol Brightman. Trans. Ursula Ludz and Hans Moll. Munich, Piper, 1995.

2000s

In der Gegenwart: Übungen im politischen Denken II. Ed. Ursula Ludz. Munich: R. Piper, 2000.

Denktagebuch: 1950 bis 1973, vol. 1. Ed. Ursula Ludz and Ingeborg Nordmann. Munich: R. Piper, 2002.

Denktagebuch: 1950 bis 1973, vol 2. Ed. Ursula Ludz and Ingeborg Nordmann. Munich: R. Piper, 2002.

Denken ohne Geländer: Texte und Briefe. Ed. Heidi Bohnet and Klaus Stadler. Munich: Piper, 2005.

Arendt, Hannah, and Uwe Johnson. *Der Briefwechsel; 1967–1975: Hannah Arendt-Uwe Johnson.* Ed. Eberhard Fahlke and Thomas Wild. Frankfurt am Main: Suhrkamp, 2004.

Seminars and Lectures by Hannah Arendt

1940s

Vor dem Antisemitismus ist man nur noch auf dem Monde sicher: Beiträge für die deutsch-jüdische Emigrantenzeitung "Aufbau" 1941–1945. Ed. Marie Luise Knott. Munich: R. Piper, 2000.

1950s

Rede am 28. September 1959 bei der Entgegennahme des Lessing-Preises der Freien und Hansestadt Hamburg. Hamburg: Europäische Verlagsanstalt, 1999.
Lectures on Kant's Political Philosophy. Ed. Ronald Beiner. Chicago: University of Chicago Press, 1982.

1960s

Von der Menschlichkeit in finsteren Zeiten: Gedanken zu Lessing. Rede anlässl. d. Verleihung d. Lessingpreises 1959 d. Freien u. Hansestadt Hamburg. Hamburg: Hauswedell, 1960.

English Translations of Books by Hannah Arendt

1950s

Origins of Totalitarianism. New York: Harcourt Brace, 1951.
The Human Condition. Chicago: University of Chicago Press, 1958.
Rahel Varnhagen: The Life of a Jewess. Trans. Richard and Clara Winston. London: Published for the Institute by the East and West Library, 1958.

1960s

Between Past and Future: Six Exercises in Political Thought. New York: Viking Press, 1961.
Eichmann in Jerusalem: A Report on the Banality of Evil. New York: Viking Press, 1963.
On Revolution. London: Faber & Faber, 1963.
Between Past and Future: Eight Exercises in Political Thought. New York: Viking Press, 1968.
Men in Dark Times. New York: Harcourt, Brace, & World, 1968.

1970s

On Violence. New York: Harcourt, Brace, & World, 1970.
Walter Benjamin, Bertolt Brecht: Zwei Essays. Munich: R. Piper, 1971.
Crises of the Republic: Lying in Politics, Civil Disobedience on Violence, Thoughts on Politics and Revolution. New York: Harcourt Brace Jovanovich, 1972.
Jew as Pariah: Jewish Identity and Politics in the Modern Age. New York: Grove Press, 1978.
Life of the Mind: Thinking. New York: Harcourt Brace Jovanovich, 1978.
Life of the Mind: Willing. New York: Harcourt Brace Jovanovich, 1978.

1990s

Essays in Understanding: 1930–1954. Ed. Jerome Kohn. New York: Harcourt, Brace, & Co., 1994.

Between Friends: The Correspondence of Hannah Arendt and Mary McCarthy, 1949–1975. Ed. Carol Brightman. New York: Harcourt Brace, 1995.

Hannah Arendt/Heinrich Blücher: Briefe 1936–1968. Ed. Lotte Köhler. Munich: R. Piper, 1996.

Love and Saint Augustine. Ed. Joanna Vecchiarelli Scott and Judith Chelius Stark. Chicago: University of Chicago Press, 1996.

2000s

Portable Hannah Arendt. Ed. Peter Baehr. New York: Penguin Books, 2000.

Within Four Walls: The Correspondence between Hannah Arendt and Heinrich Blücher, 1936–1968. Ed. Lotte Kohler. Trans. Peter Constantine. New York: Harcourt, 2000.

Responsibility and Judgment. Ed. Jerome Kohn. New York: Schocken Books, 2003.

Letters, 1925–1975. Ed. Ursula Ludz. Trans. Andrew Shields. Orlando: Harcourt, 2004.

Jürgen Habermas (1929–)

Biographical Sketch

Jürgen Habermas was born June 18, 1929, in Düsseldorf, Germany, to Ernst and Grete Habermas. He grew up in the town of Gummersbach, where his father was head of the Bureau of Industry and Trade, and his grandfather was a minister and director of the local seminary.

Different sources report inconsistent information about the life of Jürgen Habermas. Information for this biographical sketch was drawn from Simon Blackburn, "Habermas, Jürgen," *The Oxford Dictionary of Philosophy* (Oxford, UK: Oxford University Press, 1996), Oxford Reference Online—http://www.oxfordreference.com/views/ ENTRY.html?subview+Main&entry+t98.001063 (accessed October 9, 2003); Sonja K. Foss, Karen A. Foss, and Robert Trapp, *Contemporary Perspectives on Rhetoric*, 2nd ed. (Prospect Heights, IL: Waveland Press, 2002); "Jürgen Habermas," The European Graduate School—http://www.egs.edu/resources/ habermas.html (accessed August 17, 2005); Nina Maasan Greenberg and Michael Martin, "Habermas, Jürgen," *Dictionary of Literary Biographies: Twentieth Century European Cultural Theorists*, ed. Paul Handsom (Detroit, MI: Gale Group, 2001); Douglas Kellner, "Habermas, Jürgen (1929–)"—http://www.gseis.ucla.edu/faculty/kellner/essays/Habermas.pdf (accessed August 18, 2005); Stuart Sim, ed., "Habermas, Jürgen," *The Routledge Companion to Postmodernism* (New York: Routledge, 2001); Mitchell Stephens, "The Theologian of Talk," *The Los Angeles Times Magazine*, October 23, 1994, 26—http://www.nyu.edu/classes/stephens/ Habermas%20page.htm (accessed August 20, 2005). Photograph © Reuters/CORBIS.

During this time, the Nazi regime had a heavy influence upon Habermas's thought and future work. Habermas was a member of the Hitler Youth (as most non-Jews were) and was sent to defend the Western Front during the final months of World War II. In 1945, at age fifteen, he began to determine his own political views. Following the Nüremberg trials, Habermas realized the criminality of the Nazi regime, which had shaped his world view, and recognized his need to be reeducated. He graduated from high school in 1949.

His negative perspective on Nazi Germany was fueled by problems relating to society and communal ethics. He attended the universities of Göttingen and Bonn, where he studied philosophy, history, psychology, German literature, and economics. He earned his doctorate from the University of Bonn with a dissertation on the work of Friedrich von Schelling in 1954 entitled "Das Absolute und die Geschichte. Von der Zwiespältigkeit in Schellings Denken" (The Absolute and History: On the Ambivalent Character in Schelling's Thinking). The following year he married Ute Wesselhoft; they have three children.

From 1956 to 1959, Habermas worked as an assistant to Theodor W. Adorno. In 1961, he accepted a professorship at the University of Heidelberg. In 1964, Habermas was made professor of philosophy and sociology at the University of Frankfurt. Habermas left Frankfurt for the University of Starnberg in 1971 to become codirector of the Max Planck Institute for Research into Conditions of Living in a Scientific and Technological World. After a series of disputes with students and colleagues, he resigned in 1982 and returned to the University of Frankfurt, where he served as professor of philosophy and historical studies until his retirement in 2002. Habermas continues to be an active scholar, associated with the University of Frankfurt as an emeritus professor.

The Engagements of Communication
Jürgen Habermas on Discourse, Critical Reason, and Controversy

G. Thomas Goodnight

A philosophy of communication—as communication itself is ordinarily believed to be—should be clear, straightforward, supple, in a word, transparent to all who would engage others. After all, communication is as familiar as breathing and as firmly felt as walking. Humans routinely express needs, articulate interests, disclose feelings, make inquiries, take guesses, and assert truths. In short, we produce and participate through sign and symbol in any of the innumerable actions that can be made with words and reasons, gestures and deeds. Communication is an ability, individually evolved from a natural human capacity, learned while young, developed over time, available to all—or so the world routinely suggests to us. A critical philosophy of communication comes to terms, in various ways, with why humans generally, and each generation particularly, sustain such confidence in the everydayness of communication. Such a philosophy also endeavors to explore, explain, and repair rips and snags in the fabrics of social exchange and cultural understandings that result when communication fails to do its work, individually and collectively. Sometimes communication problems appear minor, and repairs are easily made; at other times whole populations are marginalized, and the range of communication narrows during times when people are socially ostracized, enslaved, or at war. The theoretical challenge of a philosophy of communication is at one and the same time to engage the multiform practices of communication in the dazzling complexity of cultural, social, institutional and individual developments and disruptions, while maintaining true to the intuitive feel of everyday use. The practical challenge of a philosophy of communication is to critically appreciate and learn from cultural, social, and institutional communicative accomplishments, both by advancing a reconstructive interpretation of grounded communicative norms and by performing a critique of systematically distorted communication—the traditions of practice that perpetuate injustice for society and auger more harm than good for a community.

Jürgen Habermas is a preeminent philosopher. Since the mid-1960s, he has developed a sophisticated, elaborate, and wide-ranging philosophy of communication that has challenged, puzzled, frustrated, provoked, engaged, and inspired his publics, for his "theory of communicative action" is among the most ambitious philosophical projects ever undertaken. Habermas argues for nothing less than the philosophical reshaping of modernity, in the interest of sustaining the project of the Enlightenment itself. Such a project of recovery would appear to run against the tides of the twentieth century, which began amidst the hypocrisies of colonialism, the abuses of the industrial revolution, and the sundering of the equation between technological and moral progress in the killing fields of the First World War. Even as science subsequently evolved a far-ranging, complicated communications revolution in publishing, telephony, media, and other instruments of exchange, the charnel houses of the Second World War brought into permanent question the proud claims of philosophy to reason, emancipation, and culture. Like his teacher, Theodor Adorno, Habermas is not blind to the failures of the Enlightenment; his philosophy is squarely rooted in the experiences of the twentieth century.[1] Yet, seeking to overcome the "dark night" of reason, he has developed a philosophy of reconstruction and recuperation, a program that puts the idea of communication at the center of human endeavor.

The idea of communication is not new, of course. Over the past half-century, it has become embedded in the cultural lore of modernity. The model that Claude Shannon and Warren Weaver envisioned for communication is a standard modern form. Sender and receivers exchange signals to encode and decode messages that travel through a channel of some sort, only to be returned in the form of feedback to the original source.[2] The whole process takes place within a seamless loop reduplicated by the behavior of chemicals, machines, animals, or persons. They all partake in the exchange of information. Context is said to make a difference, of course, depending upon whether there are two humans engaged in interpersonal exchange, in group interaction, or large audiences in mass-mediated messages. The model is universal, analytically parsed, neutrally described, static, complete, and efficient. Further, problems in communication can be ascertained by identifying defects, deficiencies, and distortions in encoding, transmission, decoding, or feedback—just as the power of communication can be measured by appraising strength of signal, fidelity of transmission, robustness of feedback, pliability of channel, and fit to audience characteristics. The idea of communication as a neutral medium of social exchange and a network of contacts is woven into the very fabric of the technological, commercial, professional, and scientific superstructures of modern society. This is not all there is to communication, however.

In response to modern versions of a scientifically and technologically informed traditional society, a number of authors have taken up the issue of reason, ethics, communication, and language. On the one hand, their projects of deconstruction together with the forays of postmodernity have checked Western hubris by enacting strategies of antagonism, skepticism, and minimalism, reaching back to Nietzsche to question the overweening claims of science to reason, and to question institutional power.[3] On the other hand, a number of philosophical projects have arisen to recover, repair, or reconstruct the broken links between reason and communication, including the work of John Rawls, Charles Taylor, Karl-Otto Apel, and Albrecht Wellmer.[4] Habermas's project maintains an antagonism with the former group, as he engages negative dialectics, deconstructionist critique, and strategies of genealogy by posing challenges to Jacques Derrida, Michel Foucault, and others to avoid "performative contradictions" and to make the affirmative space the ground that aligns their own projects with the aims of emancipation and justice.[5] Additionally, Habermas appropriates, transforms, and differentiates his own project of universal pragmatics from its competitors by defending a universalist philosophy, a revised Kantianism, attendant to the interactional quality of discourse, its cognitive dimensions, and its procedural adherence to universal norms. The project is dialectically constructed, a singular philosophy of communication with argumentation at its core, unfolding through argumentative engagements with supporters and opponents alike.

Early work published in English initiated Habermas's neo-Marxist critique of scientific reason, particularly focusing on the notion of legitimation crisis. Legitimation is important for a democratic society because capitalism produces inequalities of wealth; thus the contemporary social welfare state must negotiate constantly between the needs of society and the demands of capital to retain profits.[6] Legitimation crises occur when the justifications are no longer satisfactory, and widespread disaffection results. Communicative distortions are both a symptom and cause of the crisis, which can be uncovered and analyzed through critique of systematically distorted political communication. Habermas's magisterial two-volume *Theory of Communicative Action,* published in the early 1980s, establishes his basic ideas of discourse and critique while taking issue with the "colonization of the lifeworld" affected by "expert cultures" acting on behalf of reigning institutions.[7] The English-language publication of his dissertation in 1989, *The Structural Transformation of the Public Sphere* (first published in 1962), extended our understanding of his ideas. In that work, Habermas raised the issue that democracy itself was in decline because the very constitutional rights that were prized for the performance of citizenship and an informed vote were being eroded by the "spectacle" of mass-mediated performances (e.g., political party conventions, horse race coverage).[8] The declinist thesis set off a lively debate on the public sphere. Subsequently, Habermas published *Between Facts and Norms,* a work that develops critical theory in relation to the emergence of new social movements and new publics brought about by the end of the Cold War.[9] In this work, the communicative relationships between and among fringe movements, civil society, and state institutions are explored, as publics emerge from the periphery with new ideas and new definitions of needs, and engage in dialogue with civil society institutions, which in turn translate protest to influence. Additionally, Habermas examines the unique argumentative functions of the judiciary, legislative, and executive branches of government in translating the "communicative power" of public discourse into "bureaucratic power," extended through the judiciary under a legitimate rule of orders. *Between Facts and Norms* is a book that powerfully influenced the fruitful discussion that has subsequently taken place on the issues of "deliberative democracy," a wide-ranging debate on the prerequisites of communication and argument for a vital public sphere.

During the 1990s, Habermas continued to develop his ideas of a universal pragmatics, evolving a theory of "discourse ethics," which elaborates his initial theory of "communication action" but keeps true to its core assumptions.[10] Habermas maintains that the challenge of establishing a communicative ethics is not solely, or even primarily, a matter for discussion among philosophers. So in the past fifteen years he has entered a number of public debates, questioning positions and claims from his own communicative standpoint. He has intervened into public debates concerning history and the Holocaust, religion, terrorism, human rights, globalism, European unification, and genetics.[11] In each case, Habermas examines both sides of the question, giving a hearing to competing arguments, while reconstructing the normative dimensions of the issues along the lines of pursuing emancipation, nondistorted communication, and justice. Uniquely, Habermas conjoins theory and practice in his philosophy of communication along a very broad front.

The difficulty and the promise of engaging Habermas cannot be described just by the complexity and breadth of the project. Rather, his philosophy makes an argument most fundamentally about how one should change one's thinking about communication in order to begin to learn—that is he argues that thinkers should reflectively appraise the constitutive assumptions about how communication itself is and should be practiced, in order to assess what our practices are, in the interests of understanding what they might yet become. In such work, Shannon-Weaver-inspired models are to be considered, for they have influenced and continue to figure in the practices of our time. Yet, as Habermas shows, such technical understanding exists within a greater horizon of struggle over the constitution of human communication. As part of that struggle, Brant Burleson and Susan Kline write, "Critical theories ultimately aim to aid the members of a society to become more liberated, responsible, and enlightened agents by exposing and overcoming the forms of individual, social, and political domination that unduly constrain autonomy of thought and freedom of action."[12]

In this paper I will examine Jürgen Habermas's critical theory of communication as a struggle to articulate a universal pragmatics that promises liberation, reclamation of reason, and a reconstructive path to Enlightenment. The intent of the essay is to provide a hermeneutic of sufficient strength to understand the spirit of Habermas's project, even though in this limited space it cannot trace out the richness of technical detail.[13] The essay consists of three parts: tracing out core assumptions of communication, a review of the range of argumentation, and a discussion of Habermas's criticism of contemporary controversies.

"A Theory of Communicative Action"

The basic idea of communication is really quite simple, Habermas never tires of reminding us. "When saying something in the context of everyday life, the speaker refers not only to something in the objective world (as the sum total of what is or could be the case) but also to something in the social world (as the sum total of legitimately ordered interpersonal relations) and to something in the speaker's own world (as the sum total of experience that can be manifested and to which he has privileged access)."[14] Speech is spoken as an utterance within an extended community of native language users. Every speaker is situated, and all utterances initially entwine all three worlds; yet, each utterance intended to be understood—to be communicated—connects a speech act to a situation in such a way as to invite understanding uniquely grounded in one of our three worlds. "Speech acts serve not only to represent (or presuppose) states and events in which case the speaker makes reference to something in the objective world," Habermas says. "They also serve to produce (or renew) interpersonal relationships in which case the speaker makes reference to something in the social world of legitimately ordered interactions. And they serve to express lived experience, that is, they serve the process of self-representation in which case the speaker makes reference to something in the subjective world to which he [or she] has privileged access." In sum, "agreement in the communicative practice of everyday life rests simultaneously on intersubjectively shared propositional knowledge, on normative accord, and on mutual trust."[15]

The "three world" theory is borrowed from Karl Popper, who noted that especially to remain reasonable, a speaker must regard a claim as fallible that is valid only insofar as it has yet to be disconfirmed by evidence.[16] This presupposition imparts to communication a cognitive dimension, namely that what is said is open to criticism, and from critical discussions learning is possible. Habermas's difference with Popper is that he himself understands the relationships among the three worlds to be relatively autonomous; that is, there is no single template, method, or procedure that yields rational knowledge, but rather—around a common core—each world has its own standards of appraising communication through argument. Representations can be in error, norms can be falsely attributed as shared, and expressions can be inappropriate. Communicative rationality thus admits to a range of validity standards broad enough to encompass the activities of the everyday world.[17]

Everyday communication is a bedrock feature of the lifeworld. Habermas believes that individuals routinely participate in the varied modes of communication without much reflection. "Is this the case?" "Will it work?" "Is our conduct right?" "Should we do it?" "Is the expression authentic?" "Is he or she being truthful?" These are common questions, asked and answered appropriately because, in the interest of understanding, communication adapts its forms to accommodate a *range* of different assertions and replies. Or as Habermas says: "In the attitude toward reaching understanding, the speaker raises with *every* intelligible utterance that the claim in question is true (or that the existential presuppositions of the propositional content hold true), that the speech act is right in terms of a given normative context (or that the normative context it satisfies is itself legitimate), and the speaker's manifest intentions are meant in the way they are expressed."[18] In communicating, we mutually select, cooperatively enact, and reciprocally adjust these forms of rationally supportable claim-making as appropriate to a situation.

The situated enactment of a particular kind of speech act (locutionary, il-locutionary, or perlocutionary) "thematizes" claims to objective truth, norma-tive rightness, or authentic expression. Conversely, raising a claim obligates its utterer to provide support—if requested—to show *why* he or she asserts that the proposition is true, that the invocation of a regulative standard is right, or that the expression of private experience is truthful. In practice, validity standards—the worthiness of a claim to be recognized—vary because the requirements of proof for claims to know about the objective world, to regulate what is just or fitting for our social world, and to truthfulness for personal expressions are not the same. Yet, communication sustains reasonability—defined by willingness to offer and receive criticism—as its common core. Everyone seems to intuitively grasp how to express identities, plan activities, and coordinate action because we trust that communication essentially aims at understanding, consensus, intelligibility, and legitimate collaborations. Thus, "in smoothly functioning everyday communi-cation these four validity claims are naively accepted by participants. That is, the possibility of routine communication is dependent on the implicit reciprocal im-putation by social actors that the other is intelligible, truthful, sincere, and behav-ing according to appropriate social norms."[19]

"As soon as the hearer accepts the guarantee offered by the speaker, obli-gations are assumed that have consequences for interaction, obligations that are contained in the meaning of what was said."[20] Yet, what happens when the smooth flow of communication is interrupted, when an interlocutor finds the reason for making a claim insufficient for going forward with plans, activities, or a relation-ship? Of course, everyday life is "fueled by disappointing experiences and sur-prising contingencies." Nevertheless, individuals are rarely at a loss in the face of such turbulence. "The constant upset of disappointments and contradiction, contingency and critique in everyday life crashes against a sprawling, deeply set, and unshakable rock of background assumptions, loyalties, and skills."[21] In con-sidering the inventional possibilities of the lifeworld to restore cooperation in a situation, a speaker has multiple choices, not all of which reinforce the bonds of communication with a listener. A speaker could rely upon the "loyalties" of tradi-tion, custom, or role to demand adherence. Alternatively, he or she could skillfully resort to force, inducement, or trickery to gain compliance. Yet, to restore the com-mon understanding necessary for reasoned agreement requires working through the bases for concern and objection—which neither resorting to the invocation of authority nor to the execution of strategy can do. Rather, communicative partners must engage in an exchange of reason-giving and criticism—argumentation— which Habermas defines as "that type of speech in which participants thematize contested validity claims and attempt to vindicate or criticize them through ar-guments." An argument "contains reasons or grounds that are connected in a systematic way with the validity claim of a problematic expression."[22]

Argumentation is a special relationship based on the reflexive assumptions that "Rule-guided conduct is fallible and therefore requires two simultaneous, exchangeable roles: one for A, who follows a rule and thereby seeks to avoid mistakes, and one for B, who can critically judge the correctness of the rule-guided conduct of A."[23] Just as the giving of reasons falls into one of three worlds, so does criticism. As Habermas claims, "every speech act as a whole can always be criticized as invalid from three perspectives: as untrue in the view of a statement made (or of the existential presuppositions of the propositional content), as untruthful in view of the expressed intention of the speaker, and as not right in view of the existing normative context (or the legitimacy of the presupposed norms themselves)."[24] Yet, criticism retains a common core based around its particular claim to be a "problem-solving procedure that generates convictions."[25] An argument is not serious, Habermas claims, "if certain individuals are not allowed to participate, issues or contributions are suppressed, agreement or disagreement is manipulated by insinuations or by threat of sanctions, [or] the like."[26] There is only one ultimate regulative criterion for argumentation. If "participants genuinely want to convince one another they must make the pragmatic assumption that they allow their 'yes' and 'no' responses to be influenced solely by the force of the better argument."[27]

There is no term more central to Habermas's project than "the force of the better argument," yet there is no concept left more open-ended. It is clear that he believes this regulative ideal to be commonly invoked, rarely enacted fully, and yet universally presupposed in philosophical disputes as well as everyday practice. "Argumentation serves to focus on and test validity claims that are initially raised implicitly in communication action and naively carried along with it," he writes. Testing requires a special communicative relationship where "argumentation is characterized by the hypothetical attitude of those who take part in it. From this perspective, things and events become states of affairs that may or may not exist. Similarly, this perspective transforms existing norms, norms that are empirically recognized or socially accepted, into norms that may or may not be valid, that is, worthy of recognition."[28] In this "ideal speech situation," actors take the role of a participant in discussion, suspend strategic action, regard the provision of support or justification as serious offers, and are reciprocally guided toward reaching understanding. Thus, the taken-for-granted world is put into question, action justifications questioned, disagreements made explicit, counterfactual and counterintuitive alternatives discussed—with no pressure acknowledged other than to get it right. The "force" behind the communication comes from transforming competitive advocacy behind the "yes" and "no" positions of the arguers into a cooperative search for the truth. The idea of seeking a "better" argument acknowledges the inherent fallibility and open-endedness of the process, while rooting communicative rationality in practice. Thus it becomes the duty of interlocutors, not the definitional prerogative of philosophers, to pursue truth, justice, the common good, and trust in the activities of communication. Only if these conditions are met can mistakes be admitted, problems isolated, assumptions corrected, and learning accrued.

Argumentation yields justified claims that its proponents can defend "with reasons against the objections of possible opponents; in the end . . . [any interlocutor] should be able to gain the rationally motivated agreement of the interpretation community as a whole."[29] A truth claim must be transparent, open to debate, self-regulating, and consensus-forming, or else it cannot be defended. Understanding cannot be reached if speech acts are insincere, closed to argument, self-excepting, and exclude competent and interested audiences. Truth is grounded in communicative reason by its adherence to "ideal assertability, that is, as the vindication of criticizable validity claims under the communication conditions of an audience of competent interpreters that extends ideally across social space and historical time."[30] Put bluntly: "What is valid must be able to prove its worth against any future objections that might actually be raised."[31] Thus, in argumentation, interlocutors raise to the level of discussion both the content of the assertion—that is, whether a speech act is true, right, or truthful—as well as whether its justification is advanced in ways that do not inappropriately limit, if not completely undercut, the accessibility of support upon which its acceptance depends. This "double structure" of communication permits argumentation to result in an appreciation of speakers for reasoning "with one another," which, in turn, enables a commonly tested knowledge of "experiences" or "states of affairs about which they want to reach an understanding."[32]

Argument as Product, Procedure, and Process

There is perhaps no philosopher since Aristotle who has found such a central role for argumentation as Habermas. Just as Aristotle divided the domains of cognition into scientific, dialectical, and rhetorical reasoning, so Habermas appropriates the contemporary views of argumentation as product, procedure, or process.[33] Drawing upon Aristotle, Habermas asserts that science tests reasons logically "from the product perspective" with "the intention of grounding or redeeming a validity claim with arguments" and interest in the locutionary force.[34] Dialectical argument aims at "gaining general assent from the procedural perspective, by the intention of ending a dispute about hypothetical validity claims with a rationally motivated agreement," testing the reasons standing behind the interpersonal relations invited by illocutionary speech acts. Regarding rhetorical reasoning, "[t]he fundamental intuition connected with argumentation can best be characterized from the process perspective by the intention of convincing a universal audience," he says, borrowing Chaïm Perelman's notion of persuasion (perlocutionary speech acts) aimed at a universal audience.[35] Testing states of affairs in the objective world, the appropriateness of norms for interlocutors caught up in complex moral and ethical problems, as well as issues of trust, trigger different validity conditions for sustaining communication.[36]

A key distinction among conditions of validity exists between the requirements to provide "grounds" and "reasons." The grounds of *theoretical and practi-*

cal argument are offered proofs made public and ideally subject to symmetrical testing, presentation, and review opportunities among interlocutors. In *critique,* reasons are offered proofs made only partially public between inherently asymmetrical relationships to understand the truthfulness of a rendered claim. Consider the distinctions among the requirements of argumentation as theoretical discourse, practical discourse, and critique.

"Discourse" is Habermas's term for argumentation that pertains either to theoretical or practical concerns. Theoretical discourse is that which guides inquiry into the natural world. The power of theoretical discourse is in accurately representing a "state-of-affairs," which, with appropriate tests, enables manipulating the natural world. Theoretical discourse is dependent upon logical standards of validity, rigorously constructed out of the deep "intersubjective understanding" of the sciences. The constantive speech acts of theoretical discourse state, assert, describe, or reference an objective world and "give rise to obligations only insofar as the speaker and the hearer agree to base their actions on situational definitions that do not contradict the propositions they accept as true at any given point."[37] This form of information produces technical knowledge, and the deeply held intersubjective understandings of science generate the theoretical discourses that underwrite the communication practices of expert communities. Theoretical discourse underpins instrumental or purposive rationality, where the basic question to be answered is what comprises the most effective means to a given end. Science has risen to its current significant level of prestige because its formulations permit learning through successful manipulation of the natural world, standardization of procedures for testing and assessing evidence, and institutional values of openness to criticism. However, what works well for science does not translate to the communicative conditions of practical discourse.

If theoretical discourse derives meaning from its arguments over "what is the case," practical discourse gives rise to discussions over "what ought to be." What action is justifiable in the situation in which we are caught up? Characteristic speech acts of practical discourse are regulatives, statements that command, forbid, allow, warn, or in some way communicate what is appropriate or expected of considered conduct given the circumstances at hand. Whereas theoretical discourse proceeds ordinarily along positivistic lines, practical discourse is dialectically constructed. The grounds upon which practical discourse is constructed lead progressively toward emancipatory ends. The more time interlocutors devote to reflective inquiry and discussion about "what is the right thing for us to do," the greater the likelihood that understandings about "what ought to be done" will be predicated on genuine insights supportable by universal, transcendent norms.

In basic interactions, cooperation is based on self-interest. One's self-interest is defined by an authority who initiates an asymmetrical relationship which is based on the inducements of punishment and rewards, combined with appeals to loyalty. These interactions are held together by threat of sanction and promise of compensation, thereby limiting communication to giving commands and offering expressions of obedience. In interactions where reasons among interlocutors are shared, cooperation is rooted in role behavior that is internalized from observation and participation in the social world. Conformity to roles is expected and reinforced by socialization processes that merge individual identity with the behavioral patterns of a primary group. The group system of norms is internalized and self-promoted as a duty which restrains inclination.

In modern, postconventional interaction, ideal role taking is performed in discourses that integrate the speaker, not with a narrow sense of role conformity, but with broader, world perspectives. The rules for testing whether new norms ought to be applied from new insights are principles of argumentation. Interlocutors argue for what is right, notwithstanding traditional notions of self-interest, group sanction, or personal habit. Thus, validity is tested through counterfactual argumentation concerning both what is right to do and what are the right procedures for justifying norms. In any given situation, two questions drive critical argumentation: "Is this right for us?" *against* "Is this right for everyone, caught in similar circumstances?" "Responsibility becomes a special case of accountability, the latter here meaning the orientation of action toward an agreement that is rationally motivated and conceived as universal: to act morally is to act on the basis of insight."[38] Thus, interpersonal reason is dialectically constructed to move through reason-giving on a limited basis toward the greater autonomy of "ideal role taking" in gaining moral insight into doing what is expected for its own sake.[39]

Critique is a form of argument that is different from discourse insofar as it engages truthfulness. Aristotle's rhetoric constituted a productive art. The discourse of public deliberation deploys norms, discovered through dialectic, situated as rhetoric to regulate excesses and deficiencies of the public sphere. Habermas's argumentative counterpart of practical deliberation concerning individual and communal values achieves this function, but nests argumentation related to persuasion as a critical, rather than a primarily productive, process of individual and communal argumentation.

In contrast with Aristotelians, Habermas holds that deliberation does not necessarily yield the common good if the presuppositions of a community—its traditions—leave a gap between aspired common identities and real enactments, between what is attributed as a satisfactory resolution of needs for all and the actual, emergent needs, which can only be communicated through the struggle of social movement and debate in the public sphere. Thus, deliberative argument is divided into two different functions. Discourse produces reasons whose end is justice and is regulated by procedural guarantees of fairness and counterfactual reconstruction; critique prompts the sort of deliberation that doubly exposes hypocrisies, inconsistencies, and outworn traditions while opening a space for articulating common values, ends, and goals for a community. The critical deliberative, public argument of communities must at the same time honor the traditions of custom, which are fused with the identity of the community while reflecting carefully on which of those customs should remain in light of both changed circumstances and closing the gap between a community's professed self-identity and its historical record of achievement.[40] The invitation to criticism is one that Habermas himself takes up in turning his theories of communicative action toward the nettles of the present, the controversies that put at stake the practices of communication in the lifeworld and the public sphere.

The Critical Theory of Communication and Controversy

The triumph of modernity in the twentieth century came at a great price, for as Habermas notes, the "phenomena of violence and barbarism mark the distinctive signature of the age."[41] While tempting to do otherwise, critical intervention into contemporary controversies should set aside philosophies of pessimism and approach the great issues of the age with a balanced critique and reconstruction of issues, he believes. Thus, the aim of a critical philosophy of communication is to reshape, broaden, and rebuild confidence in ideals—Western ideals themselves long-tarnished, invoked too often in promiscuous, self-serving fashion in order to rationalize the violent, exploitative, and repressive actions of colonial governments and nationalist causes. The present revolutions of globalization with the attendant explosion of new populations and new communications technology, however, offer a compelling opportunity for undertaking the projects of Enlightenment anew because changes in our common lifeworlds are accelerating.

"The mode of village life, which has been formative for all cultures, from the Neolithic period until well into the nineteenth century, survives only in imitation form in developed countries," Habermas writes. The global upsurge of the megapolises "where growth is only two or three decades old, face[s] us with a mode of experience that we are at a loss to comprehend," he concludes.[42] The "mental consequences" of accelerating changes in the lifeworld are "very hard to assess," he admits, but argues that, even while new communicative infrastructures are rapidly emerging, globalization is creating "only a new infrastructure, and not a new orientation or a new form of consciousness."[43] Thus, Habermas's program of critical intervention into the controversies of the age is conducted with the aim of examining both sides of the argument and developing a program of adjustment, renewal, or even radical renovation, rather than performing either a totalizing critique or uncritical celebration of rapidly changing conditions. Three areas constitute his most significant interventions: globalization, human rights, and the lifeworld.

At the level of the nation-state, Habermas observes the "rise of ethnocentric reactions against anything foreign," a situation calling for a "politics of recognition" within and across national frontiers.[44] While acknowledging that the nation is becoming ever less able to control its own sovereignty, he nonetheless notes that state constitutions have become crucial in a struggle to retain those hard-won guarantees of citizen rights and freedoms. He therefore advocates a balanced appraisal that avoids the "uncritical welcome of the globalization process" or its "uncritical demonization." The central challenge is "how to make the most effective and innovative functions of self-regulating markets, while simultaneously avoiding unequal patterns of distribution . . . ," a problem confronting the formation of the European Union, with its ancient states and institutions driving globalization.[45]

The problem of recognition is reduplicated in the issue of human rights, a Janus-faced set of norms that are in one sense advocated universally, but in another only protected on the ground in the more limited constitution of a citizenry. Habermas conducts a critique of the uses of human rights as false promises, coverings for exploitation, and empty rationalizations for market power. Yet, on the other hand, he concludes: "In Asia, Africa, and South America, they also constitute the only language in which the opponents and victims of murderous regimes and civil wars can raise their voices against violence, repression, and persecution, against injuries to their human dignity."[46] A critical reconstruction of human rights as a shared realization of humanity is both possible and desirable, and would act as a necessary brake on exploitation. Further, attention to emergent public spheres with new sensitivities toward human needs offers progressive hope in the confrontation with oppression.

Habermas also constructs a critical intervention in a defense of the lifeworld, which he believes is depleted by the openness of communicative practices to modernist institutions regulated by cultures of expertise. Habermas starts by noting the fragmentation among institutional specialists who deploy technical reason, not only in the interests of efficiency, but also as implicit justifications to maintain institutional power and money. The result may well be the "colonization of the lifeworld" for those defined as "clients" of institutional services. Yet, in the main the relation between ordinary communicative practices—with their meanings attached to personal choices and individual life projects—and the legal, bureaucratic idioms of modern institutions constitutes a continuing dialectic. It is not so much that knowledge is in short supply from respective arenas of expertise, but the problem persists of "how to overcome the isolation of science, morals, and art and their respective expert cultures."[47] The particular issue that draws Habermas's attention in this respect is genetic engineering, whose advances cannot be evaluated by resorting to the language of science and medicine alone, but requires an ethic of care that takes into account the communicative norms of the lifeworld of an individual in which concerns intervene.[48] Given the pervasive influence of modern institutions, their rapid change, and the need to test old norms and evolve new ones, the critical work of communicative action should continue for some time to come. The critical philosophy of communication puts a brake on market-bureaucratic-scientific collaborations by drawing into discussion questions of human value and the ends of justice and the good life. In this respect, Habermas's own work is self-consciously to transform the "telos of reaching understanding" developed in religious traditions to the secular, argumentative realm of making informed, meaningful, collaborative life choices.[49]

Globalization, human rights, and modernity define major dimensions of contemporary controversy which invite intervention—description, assessment, prediction, and advocacy. Habermas's theory of communicative action creates the grounds for asking how issues in these complex debates can be read from the perspective of those having a say in collocation with interested others. Conversely, the theory itself is a product of times when norms are changing, technology evolving, publics emerging, states contesting for power, and institutions developing. A philosophy of communication adequate to such a world of social, cultural, and individual turbulence and change is not static—it evolves around a set of core notions, finds allied thinking, challenges opposing views, and finally proceeds onto the stage of practice. Jürgen Habermas has opened such a route, toward a critical, self-reflective theory of communication, for all those who would follow.

Notes

1. Theodore Adorno, *Negative Dialectics* (New York: Seabury Press, 1973). See also Fred R. Dallmayr and Thomas A McCarthy, *Understanding and Social Inquiry* (Notre Dame: University of Notre Dame Press, 1977); Raymond Geuss, *The Idea of a Critical Theory: Habermas and the Frankfurt School* (New York: Cambridge University Press, 1981); David Held, Introduction to *Critical Theory: Horkheimer to Habermas* (Berkeley: University of California Press, 1980).

2. Claude E. Shannon and Warren Weaver, *The Mathematical Theory of Communication* (Urbana: University of Illinois Press, 1949/1964).

3. For Habermas's response to postmodernity and deconstruction, see Jürgen Habermas, *The Philosophical Discourses of Modernity: Twelve Lectures,* trans. Frederick Lawrence (Cambridge: MIT Press, 1987).

4. Karl-Otto Apel, *Towards a Transformation of Philosophy* (London: Routledge and Kegan Paul, 1980); Karl-Otto Apel, *Understanding and Explanation: A Transcendental Pragmatic Perspective* (Cambridge: MIT Press, 1984); Seyla Benhabib and Fred R. Dallmayr, *The Communicative Ethics Controversy* (Cambridge: MIT Press, 1990); John Rawls, *A Theory of Justice* (Cambridge: Belknap Press, 1971); Charles Taylor, Garbis Kortian, Jürgen Habermas, and Alan Montefiore, *Metacritique* (Cambridge: Cambridge University Press, 2004); Albrecht Wellmer, *Critical Theory of Society,* trans. John Cumming (New York: Herder and Herder, 1971); Albrecht Wellmer, *The Persistence of Modernity: Essays on Aesthetics, Ethics, and Postmodernity,* trans. David Midgley (Cambridge: MIT Press).

5. Habermas, *Philosophical Discourses of Modernity.*

6. Jürgen Habermas, *Communication and the Evolution of Society,* trans. Thomas McCarthy (Boston: Beacon Press, 1979); Jürgen Habermas, *Knowledge and Human Interests,* trans. Jeremy Shapiro (Boston: Beacon Press, 1972); Jürgen Habermas, *Legitimation Crisis,* trans. Thomas McCarthy (Boston: Beacon Press, 1975); Jürgen Habermas, *Observations on the "Spiritual Situation of the Age,"* trans. Andrew Buchwalter (Cambridge: MIT Press, 1984).

7. Jürgen Habermas, *The Theory of Communicative Action,* vol. 1: *Reason and the*

Rationalization of Society, trans. Thomas McCarthy (Boston: Beacon Press, 1985). Jürgen Habermas, *The Theory of Communicative Action,* vol. 2: *Lifeworld and System, A Critique of Functionalist Reason,* trans. Thomas McCarthy (Boston: Beacon Press, 1989). These views developed out of an earlier turn to communication. See Jürgen Habermas, *On the Logic of the Social Sciences,* trans. Shierry Weber Nicholson and John Stark (Cambridge: MIT Press, 1988); Jürgen Habermas, *Theory and Practice,* trans. John Viertel (Boston: Beacon Press, 1973). Jürgen Habermas, *Toward a Rational Society: Student Protest, Science, and Politics,* trans. Jeremy J. Shapiro (Boston: Beacon Press, 1971).

8. Jürgen Habermas, *The Structural Transformation of the Public Sphere: An Inquiry into a Category of Bourgeois Society,* trans. Thomas Berger (Cambridge: MIT Press, 1989). See also James Bohman, *Public Deliberation, Pluralism, Complexity, and Democracy* (Cambridge: MIT Press, 1996); Craig Calhoun, ed., *Habermas and the Public Sphere* (Cambridge: MIT Press, 1992).

9. Jürgen Habermas, *Between Facts and Norms: Contributions to a Discourse Theory of Law and Democracy,* trans. William Rehg (Cambridge: MIT Press, 1996).

10. Jürgen Habermas, *Justification and Application: Remarks on Discourse Ethics,* trans. Ciaran Cronin (Cambridge: MIT Press, 2004); Jürgen Habermas, *Moral Consciousness and Communicative Action,* trans. Christian Lenhardy and Shierry Weber Nicholson (Cambridge: MIT Press, 1990); Jürgen Habermas and Maeve Cooke, *On the Pragmatics of Communication* (Cambridge: MIT Press, 1998); Jürgen Habermas, *Postmetaphysical Thinking,* trans. William Mark Hohengarten (Cambridge: MIT Press, 1992); Jürgen Habermas, *On the Pragmatics of Social Interaction: Preliminary Studies in the Theory of Communicative Action,* trans. Barbara Fultner (Cambridge: MIT Press, 2000).

11. Giovanna Borradori, Jürgen Habermas, and Jacques Derrida, *Philosophy in a Time of Terror: Dialogues with Jürgen Habermas and Jacques Derrida* (Chicago: University of Chicago Press, 2003); Jürgen Habermas and Peter Dews, *Autonomy and Solidarity: Interviews with Jürgen Habermas,* 2nd. rev. ed. (New York: Verso, 1992); Jürgen Habermas, Ciaran Cronin, and Pablo DeGreiff, *The Inclusion of the Other: Studies in Political Theory* (Cambridge: MIT Press, 1998); Jürgen Habermas and Peter Dews, *The Liberating Power of Symbols: Philosophical Essays* (Cambridge: MIT Press, 2001); Jürgen Habermas, *The Future of Human Nature* (Cambridge, UK: Polity, 2003); Jürgen Habermas and Max Pensky, *The Postnational Constellation: Political Essays* (Cambridge: MIT Press, 2002); Jürgen Habermas, *Time of Transitions* (Oxford: Blackwell, 2004); Jürgen Habermas and Frederick G. Lawrence, *Philosophical Political Profiles* (Lincoln: University of Nebraska Press, 1994); Shierry Weber Nicholsen and Jürgen Habermas, *The New Conservatism: Cultural Criticism and the Historians' Debate* (Cambridge: MIT Press, 1989).

12. Brant R. Burleson and Susan L. Kline, "Habermas' Theory of Communication: A Critical Explication," *Quarterly Journal of Speech* 65 (1979): 413.

13. Richard Berstein, *Habermas and Modernity* (Cambridge: MIT Press, 1985); Jane Braaten, *Habermas's Critical Theory of Society* (Albany, NY: State University of New York Press, 1991); Erik Oddvar Eriksen and Jarle Weigard, *Understanding Habermas* (London: Continuum, 2004); Thomas McCarthy, *The Critical Theory of Jürgen Habermas* (Cambridge: MIT Press, 1978); Michael Pusey, *Jürgen Haber-*

mas (London: Tavistock Publications, 1987); Rick Roderick, *Habermas and the Foundations of Critical Theory* (New York: St. Martin's, 1986).

14. Habermas, *Moral Consciousness and Communication Action*, 25.
15. Ibid., 136.
16. Karl Popper, *The Logic of Scientific Discovery* (New York: Basic Books, 1959).
17. Popper, *The Logic of Scientific Discovery.*
18. *Moral Consciousness and Communication Action*, 136–137.
19. Burleson and Kline, "Habermas' Theory of Communication," 417.
20. Habermas, *Moral Consciousness and Communicative Action*, 59.
21. Habermas, *Between Facts and Norms*, 22.
22. Habermas, *Theory of Communicative Action*, 1:18.
23. Habermas, *Postmetaphysical Thinking*, 69.
24. Ibid., 76–77.
25. Habermas, *Justification and Application*, 158.
26. Ibid., 56.
27. Ibid., 31.
28. Habermas, *Moral Consciousness and Communicative Action*, 158–159.
29. Habermas, *Between Facts and Norms*, 14.
30. Ibid., 15.
31. Ibid., 35.
32. McCarthy, *The Critical Theory of Jürgen Habermas*, 282.
33. The core of Habermas's theory of argumentation may be found in the first section of the *Theory of Communicative Action*. He borrows heavily from argumentation studies, especially Stephen Toulmin. Unfortunately, Habermas has rarely revisited argumentation studies since the initial work, although he continues to deploy the basic precepts of his theory.
34. Habermas, *Theory of Communicative Action*, 1:26.
35. Ibid., 26. See Chaim Perelman and L. Olbrechts-Tyteca, *The New Rhetoric: A Treatise on Argumentation*, trans. John Wilkinson and Purcell Weaver (Notre Dame: University of Notre Dame Press, 1969), 30–35.
36. For a study of discourse and ethics see William Rehg, *Insight and Solidarity: A Study in the Discourse Ethics of Jürgen Habermas* (Berkeley, CA: University of California Press, 1994).
37. Habermas, *Moral Consciousness and Communicative Action*, 59.
38. Habermas, *Moral Consciousness*, 162.
39. The universalization principle: "For a norm to be valid, the consequences and side effects that its general observance can be expected to have for the satisfaction of the particular interests of each person affected must be such that all affected can accept them freely" (Habermas, *Moral Consciousness and Communicative Action*, 120).
40. Just as Aristotle finds that self-deliberation and public deliberation are counterparts, so Habermas argues that critique can work to eradicate individual and communal self-deception. Thus, therapeutic critique is equated to art criticism in their capacity to discover the grounds of "genuine" value by testing what is professed to be the case against actual behavior or experience. Since all claims to the "life projects" of an individual or community are contingent, inevitably varied in

a pluralistic culture, critique is always an unfinished project, even though certain "goods" can be established and constitutionally protected. Crucially these goods are the rights which secure or guarantee freedoms necessary to practice open communication.

41. Habermas and Pensky, *The Postcolonial Constellation,* 45.
42. Ibid., 41, 43.
43. Habermas, *Religion and Rationality: Essays on Reason, God, and Modernity,* ed. Eduardo Mendieta (Cambridge, MA: MIT Press, 2002), 149.
44. Ibid., 74, 81.
45. Habermas, *Postnational Constellation,* 49.
46. Ibid., 153.
47. Habermas, *Moral Consciousness and Communicative Action,* 19.
48. Habermas, *The Future of Human Nature.*
49. Habermas, *Religion and Rationality,* 148.

Bibliography of Works

Books by Jürgen Habermas

Das Absolute und die Geschichte: Von der Zwiespältigkeit in Schellings Denken. Inaugural-Dissertation Philosophie. Bonn, 1954.

1960s

With Ludwig von Friedeburg, Christoph Oehler, and Friedrich Weltz. *Student und Politik: Eine soziologische Untersuchung zum politischen Bewusstsein frankfurter Studenten.* Neuwied: H. Luchterhand, 1961.
Strukturwandel der Öffentlichkeit: Untersuchungen zu einer Kategorie der bürgerlichen Gesellschaft. Neuwied: H. Luchterhand, 1962.
Theorie und Praxis: Sozialphilosophische Studien. Neuwied am Rhein: Luchterhand, 1963.
Erkenntnis und Interesse. Frankfurt am Main: Suhrkamp, 1968.
Technik und Wissenschaft als "Ideologie." Frankfurt am Main: Suhrkamp, 1968.
Protestbewegung und Hochschulreform. Frankfurt am Main: Suhrkamp, 1969.

1970s

Zur Logik der Sozialwissenschaften. Frankfurt am Main: Suhrkamp, 1970.
Über Sprachtheorie: Einführende Bemerkungen zu einer Theorie d. kommunikativen Kompetenz. Vienna: Verein Gruppe Hundsblume, 1970.
Philosophisch-politische Profile. Frankfurt am Main: Suhrkamp, 1971.
With Niklas Luhmann. *Theorie der Gesellschaft oder Sozialtechnologie: Was leistet d. Systemforschung?* Frankfurt am Main: Suhrkamp, 1971.
Arbeit, Freizeit, Konsum: Frühe Aufsätze. The Hague: Van Eversdijck, 1973.
Erkenntnis und Interesse: Mit e. neuen Nachw. Frankfurt am Main: Suhrkamp, 1973.
Kultur und Kritik: Verstreute Aufsätze. Frankfurt am Main: Suhrkamp, 1973.
Legitimationsprobleme im Spätkapitalismus. Frankfurt am Main: Suhrkamp, 1973.
Zur Rekonstruktion des historischen Materialismus. Frankfurt am Main: Suhrkamp, 1976.
Politik, Kunst, Religion: Essays über zeitgenössische Philosophen. Stuttgart: Reclam, 1978.

1980s

Kleine politische Schriften (I–IV). Frankfurt am Main: Suhrkamp, 1981.
Theorie des kommunikativen Handelns. Frankfurt am Main: Suhrkamp, 1981.
Zur Logik der Sozialwissenschaften. Frankfurt am Main: Suhrkamp, 1982.
Coedited with Ludwig von Friedeburg. *Adorno-Konferenz 1983.* Frankfurt am Main: Suhrkamp, 1983.
Moralbewußtsein und kommunikatives Handeln. Frankfurt am Main: Suhrkamp, 1983.
Coedited with Wolfgang Edelstein. *Soziale Interaktion und soziales Verstehen.* Frankfurt am Main: Suhrkamp, 1984.

Vorstudien und Ergänzungen zur Theorie des kommunikativen Handelns. Frankfurt am Main: Suhrkamp, 1984.

Die neue Unübersichtlichkeit: Kleine politische Schriften (V). Frankfurt am Main: Suhrkamp, 1985.

Der philosophische Diskurs der Moderne: Zwölf Vorlesungen. Frankfurt am Main: Suhrkamp, 1985.

Eine Art Schadensabwicklung: Kleine politische Schriften (VI). Frankfurt am Main: Suhrkamp, 1987.

L'Espace public: Archéologie de la publicité comme dimension constitutive de la société bourgeoise. Trans. Marc B. de Launay. Paris: Payot, 1988.

Nachmetaphysisches Denken: Philosophische Aufsätze. Frankfurt am Main: Suhrkamp, 1988.

Die nachholende Revolution: Kleine politische Schriften (VII). Frankfurt am Main: Suhrkamp, 1989.

1990s

Die Moderne, ein unvollendetes Projekt: Philosophisch-politische Aufsätze, 1977–1990. Leipzig: Reclam, 1990.

Erläuterungen zur Diskursethik. Frankfurt am Main: Suhrkamp, 1991.

Texte und Kontexte. Frankfurt am Main: Suhrkamp, 1991.

Faktizität und Geltung: Beiträge zur Diskurstheorie des Rechts und des demokratischen Rechtsstaats. Frankfurt am Main: Suhrkamp, 1992.

Die Normalität einer Berliner Republik. Frankfurt am Main: Suhrkamp, 1995.

Die Einbeziehung des Anderen: Studien zur politischen Theorie. Frankfurt am Main: Suhrkamp, 1996.

Vom sinnlichen Eindruck zum symbolischen Ausdruck: Philosophische Essays. Frankfurt am Main: Suhrkamp, 1997.

Die postnationale Konstellation: Politische Essays. Frankfurt am Main: Suhrkamp, 1998.

Wahrheit und Rechtfertigung: Philosophische Aufsätze. Frankfurt am Main: Suhrkamp, 1999.

2000s

Kommunikatives Handeln und detranszendentalisierte Vernunft. Stuttgart: P. Reclam, 2001.

Zeit der Übergänge: Kleine politische Schriften (IX). Frankfurt am Main: Suhrkamp, 2001.

Die Zukunft der menschlichen Natur: Auf dem Weg zu einer liberalen Eugenik? Frankfurt am Main: Suhrkamp, 2001.

English Translations of Books by Jürgen Habermas

1970s

Toward a Rational Society: Student Protest, Science, and Politics. Trans. Jeremy J. Shapiro. Boston: Beacon Press, 1970.

Knowledge and Human Interests. Trans. Jeremy J. Shapiro. Boston: Beacon Press, 1971.

Theory and Practice. Trans. John Viertel. Boston: Beacon Press, 1973.

Legitimation Crisis. Trans. Thomas McCarthy. Boston: Beacon Press, 1975.

Communication and the Evolution of Society. Trans. Thomas McCarthy. Boston: Beacon Press, 1979.

1980s

Philosophical-Political Profiles. Trans. Frederick G. Lawrence. Cambridge, MA: MIT Press, 1983.

Theory of Communicative Action. Trans. Thomas McCarthy. Boston: Beacon Press, 1984.

Autonomy and Solidarity: Interviews. Ed. Peter Dews. London: Verso, 1986.

Philosophical Discourse of Modernity: Twelve Lectures. Trans. Frederick Lawrence. Cambridge, MA: MIT Press, 1987.

On the Logic of the Social Sciences. Trans. Shierry Weber Nicholsen and Jerry A. Stark. Cambridge, MA: MIT Press, 1988.

New Conservatism: Cultural Criticism and the Historians' Debate. Trans. and ed. Shierry Weber Nicholsen. Cambridge, MA: MIT Press, 1989.

Structural Transformation of the Public Sphere: An Inquiry into a Category of Bourgeois Society. Trans. Thomas Burger with the assistance of Frederick Lawrence. Cambridge, MA: MIT Press, 1989.

1990s

Moral Consciousness and Communicative Action. Trans. Christian Lenhardt and Shierry Weber Nicholsen. Cambridge, MA: MIT Press, 1990.

Postmetaphysical Thinking: Philosophical Essays. Trans. William Mark Hohengarten. Cambridge, MA: MIT Press, 1992.

Justification and Application: Remarks on Discourse Ethics. Trans. Ciaran Cronin. Cambridge, MA: MIT Press, 1993.

Past as Future: Vergangenheit als Zukunft. Trans. and ed. Max Pensky. Lincoln: University of Nebraska Press, 1994.

Between Facts and Norms: Contributions to a Discourse Theory of Law and Democracy. Trans. William Rehg. Cambridge, MA: MIT Press, 1996.

Debating the State of Philosophy: Habermas, Rorty, and Kolakowski. Ed. Józef Niznik and John T. Sanders. Westport, CT: Praeger, 1996.

A Berlin Republic: Writings on Germany. Trans. Steven Rendall. Lincoln: University of Nebraska Press, 1997.

Inclusion of the Other: Studies in Political Theory. Ed. Ciaran Cronin and Pablo De Greif. Cambridge, MA: MIT Press, 1998.

On the Pragmatics of Communication. Ed. Maeve Cooke. Cambridge, MA: MIT Press, 1998.

2000s

The Liberating Power of Symbols: Philosophical Essays. Trans. Peter Dews. Cambridge, MA: MIT Press, 2001.

On the Pragmatics of Social Interaction: Preliminary Studies in the Theory of Communicative Action. Trans. Barbara Fultner. Cambridge, MA: MIT Press, 2001.

Postnational Constellation: Political Essays. Trans. and ed. Max Pensky. Cambridge, MA: MIT Press, 2001.

Religion and Rationality: Essays on Reason, God, and Modernity. Ed. Eduardo Mendieta. Cambridge, MA: MIT Press, 2002.

The Future of Human Nature. Cambridge, UK: Polity, 2003.

Truth and Justification. Trans. and ed. Barbara Fultner. Cambridge, MA: MIT Press, 2003.

Emmanuel Levinas (1905–1995)

Biographical Sketch

Emmanuel Levinas was born in Kaunas, Lithuania, on December 30, 1905 (Gregorian calendar). His father owned a bookstore. Levinas was educated as an orthodox Jew and a Russian citizen, speaking both Yiddish and Russian. He studied the Talmud and read the Bible in Hebrew. He also read Pushkin, Dostoevsky, Tolstoy, and Gogol. The family moved to Ukraine when World War I broke out but returned to Lithuania after the Russian Revolution, where Levinas graduated from the Jewish Russian-language lyceum.

Different sources report inconsistent information about the life of Emmanuel Levinas. Information for this biographical sketch was drawn from Robert Audi, ed., *Cambridge Dictionary of Philosophy*, 2nd ed. (Cambridge, UK: Cambridge University Press, 1999); Edward Craig, ed., *Routledge Encyclopedia of Philosophy* (New York: Routledge, 1998); Jacques Derrida, *Adieu to Emmanuel Levinas* (Stanford, CA: Stanford University Press, 1997); "Emmanuel Levinas," The European Graduate School—http://www.ega.edu/rsources/levinas.html (accessed August 18, 2005); Peter Steinfels, "Emmanuel Levinas, 90, French Ethical Philosopher: A Thinker Who Placed Ethics in the Foreground of His System," *The New York Times*, December 27, 1995—http://home.pacbell.net/atterton/levinas/Obituary.htm (accessed 8-17-05). Photograph courtesy of Mme. Simone Hansel, daughter of Emmanuel Levinas.

Levinas entered Strasbourg University in France (1924–1929), where he studied Latin, classics, psychology, sociology, and philosophy. In 1928, he moved to the University of Freiburg, where he studied under Edmund Husserl and Martin Heidegger. In 1930, he published his dissertation, entitled "Théorie de l'intuition dans la phénoménologie de Husserl" (The Theory of Intuition in Husserl's Phenomenology). Levinas later translated Husserl's *Cartesian Meditations* into French and in 1932 wrote an essay on Heidegger entitled "Martin Heidegger et l'ontologie" (Martin Heidegger and Ontology"). Levinas subsequently regretted his enthusiasm for Heidegger's work due to the latter's accommodation to Nazism.

In 1930, Levinas became a naturalized French citizen. In 1932, he married his wife, Raissa, a musician originally from Vienna. Together they had a daughter, Simone Hansel, and a son, Michael.

After Levinas earned his doctorate from Strasbourg University, he taught at the École Normale Israélite Orientale in Paris. Levinas entered the French Army in 1939 and served as a Russian and German interpreter. He was a prisoner of war for four years in a German labor camp. By the end of the war, most of Levinas's family was killed by the Nazis; his wife and daughter escaped death by hiding in a French monastery. His experience with the war and the Holocaust influenced his political and ethical thought and he began to articulate his own philosophy.

After the war Levinas returned to the École Normale Israélite Orientale in Paris and became director of the school until 1961, when he took a position at the University of Poitiers. In 1967, he accepted a position at the Nanterre branch of the University of Paris and in 1973 he accepted a position at the Sorbonne.

Emmanuel Levinas retired in 1979 and devoted himself to writing books. He died of heart failure in Paris, France, on December 25, 1995.

Ethical Selfhood
Emmanuel Levinas's Contribution to a Philosophy of Communication

Bettina Bergo

> "If an an-archeology is possible."
> —Levinas, *Otherwise than Being,* p. 7

Introductory Remarks

The figure of Emmanuel Levinas is ambiguous, yet significant, within a philosophy of communication.[1] The encounter with the other person that he describes—under phenomenological brackets so that we observe without judging the "event" of our consciousness—has been called, provocatively, a "failure of communication." Reconstructed from within the face-to-face experience, a self feels itself answerable, spontaneously, to another. Yet that self, that "me," is not answerable in the sense of being called to identify itself, converse, or even listen to the other. The initial experience is one of being drawn out of oneself, unable to elude the face of the other, and thus "responsible" to it. The response can take a host of forms, from violence to an attempt at flight. However, the response that Levinas argues is primordial could be phrased as "here I am" (*me voici*), or "after you, sir." This is failed communication only in the sense that it is not concerned primarily with setting out the groundwork for a philosophy of dialogue or communication.

The primordial response concerns a unique quality of human intersubjectivity, one that Levinas's teacher, and founder of contemporary phenomenology, Edmund Husserl, appeared to have overlooked: the other human being, when she faces me, *affects me* before I constitute her as a woman of some age, race, class or region. In Husserl's most familiar works, consciousness *constructs* the other as *alter ego*, another being like the self in appearance and actions. Levinas's work has explored the impact of another on a self at the level of passivity or *paskhein*; that level at which one undergoes or suffers a force, whether it is internal or external. The exploration of passivity—of events that hold together in their unity without intervention on the part of a subject—was already begun by Husserl in his studies of our internal consciousness of time. But it was his students, Levinas, Max Scheler, Martin Heidegger and others, who turned Husserlian phenomenology toward passivity and intersubjectivity, passivity and the experience of values, and passivity and moods, respectively.

Such a phenomenology seeks, beneath conscious imagining or its reconstruction of dialogical situations, a level of sense experience that otherwise goes unremarked. We can call it, with Levinas, sensuous vulnerability. For him, sensuous vulnerability is a property of our being creatures with skins, with flesh. If it is possible to reach beneath conscious imagining to this level, the price of such descriptions is invariably skeptical, bringing about questions of the kind: Is that really what happens when "I" am face to face with another person? These questions prove ineradicable, because the gap in time between the actual event of the encounter and its being re-experienced for the sake of philosophical insight is never wholly bridgeable. Nevertheless that gap itself is constitutive of *any* reflective approach to experience in its immediacy, and phenomenology provides some correctives to keep it from naturalist abstractions, such as the division between subjective experience and objective experience. In this, phenomenology's work is not so dissimilar from psychoanalysis, which itself attempts to approach consciousness as multilayered and constituted of sedimented, modified memories. Given the difficulties intrinsic to such a task, Levinas elected to focus on and unfold the complexities within the face-to-face "moment." Despite the many apparent similarities with Martin Buber, Levinas is a philosopher of responsibility before he is a philosopher of dialogue or communication.

Yet communication, if understood as more than the exchange of signals or information, comes into existence for reasons often clearly more complex than the desire for communication (which would situate it wholly on the side of the one who desired to initiate communication). If we inquire into the conditions that make communication possible, we gain from Levinas's analyses of affect, of being in flesh and blood, and of "sincerity." All of these are ingredients in that moment of failed communication he describes. Communication is none other than the unchosen and unwilled event by which a self's enclosure in self is momentarily broken and its self-directed movement is temporarily halted. Never a philosophy of the will or one of the decision, Levinas's philosophy of communication is a prolonged reflection on what an "I" receives, of its selfhood, from an other human being—election, if you will, but election as a call to answer for itself, not to converse.

Reflection on the impact of the human gaze is not unknown to us in philosophy or psychology. We only have to think of Jean-Paul Sartre's invisible gaze, which leaves a subject feeling reified and in danger. Psychoanalysts such as Melanie Klein have studied the gaze of the mother in the consolidation of subjectivity.[2] Jacques Lacan's discussions of the gaze include a struggle of mastery and constitution perhaps not unlike Georg Wilhelm Friedrich Hegel's: think of his ironic presentation in *Seminar XI* of the man who boasted that, at least the shiny tin can floating on the water could not *see* him (which implies that the sense that objects might have a gaze is essential to the phantasmatic). Yet, despite his own study of psychology in France, Levinas's work steadfastly refuses any rapprochement with psychology or psychoanalysis. The work, he insists *à la* Husserl, is descriptive; it unfolds a dimension of human experience that *is*, that *happens,* yet that is different from what philosophy calls "being" if being is characterized by mortality, change, and struggle.

This chapter considers Levinas's philosophy of communication. First, Levinas's response to the question "How does communication arise?" is suggested. Second, the significance of individual passions which reveal a layer of experience that contribute to communication is considered. Third, three inflections of Levinas's work are outlined: the affective roots of his philosophy of communication, the realm of exteriority and communication, and his understanding of ethical sensibility and the possibility of communication through the flesh, as inspired by Merleau-Ponty.

A Phenomenology of "Pre-synthetic Experience" and Its Vicissitudes

If Levinas as a philosopher acknowledges responsibility as the necessary condition for the possibility of any communication, then we have already seen the curious twist that his descriptions entail. To answer the question, "How do we communicate?"—that is, beyond engaging in the exchange of information or enacting some drive—we must faithfully describe the affective dimension of a face-to-face situation. We must describe its impact on my *fleshly* sense of integrity, my emotions, and the self-containment of my mental activity in solitude. This description leads us to the following observation. For Levinas, failed communication calls forth responsibility, in which the other approaches me as if she were at a level higher than I (though neither she nor I *willed* such a thing), which gives rise to communication as sincere listening and attending to the other. Therein lies the twist we noted. Yet another one awaits us.

The other twist looks more like a paradox. In describing events that take place in a brief time, and in trying to reach their meaning without distorting that meaning in our representation of the event (i.e., from the third-party, or removed, stance that we conquer by representing an event to ourselves in which we were at one time directly implicated), we must reconstruct both the event and its meaning. We must set these into concepts (though Levinas strives to describe a metaphoric level of experience that is prior to language and conceptuality, because it makes language possible as speaking to another person). Yet, in doing this, we have to recross the temporal gap, or lag between experience and its representation; in doing so, and against our best intentions, we betray the force of the event as well as its meaning. This is why it is difficult to return to an affective experience in its immediacy. Indeed, it may be unbearable to relive, or it may be dumbfounding or appear implausible on reflection. Psychology has shown us that we cover over certain affects or ensconce them. Above all, philosophers and psychologists recognize that the "order" to which sensibility (as vulnerability and immediacy) and affects belong is different in significant ways from the discursive order of rationality and calculation. Thus, as Levinas writes, when it comes to affective meaning, "consciousness by itself would be incapable" of it (OBBE

152). Moreover, he cautions us that, in the interpretation of this meaning, "there is a possibility both of ideology [as a religious or political hypostatization] and of sacred delirium, [and] delirium must be *reduced* by philosophy, [it must] be reduced to *signification*" (OBBE 152). For Levinas, the function of philosophy is to embrace the paradox of affectivity as communication and as ethical investiture. This means his philosophy must reduce and "betray" the excess of communication by giving it a conceptual and phenomenological form. Now, if Levinas's phenomenology is still a phenomenology, then it is so as a *description* of affectivity in the midst of communication, rather than an analysis of intentionality or a description of perceptual essences. That said, though his philosophy explores the conditions for the possibility of signification, it is not a semiotics if by this we mean that the sign presented to the other should be analyzed in terms of its structure or referent. Rather, Levinas's inquiry concerns what makes the sign possible in the first place, and what precedes everyday intentionality. Levinas is looking for the groundwork of all human communication, for that moment prior to dialogue when an "I" responds to another and accounts for itself.

To that end, Levinas practices a nontraditional phenomenological reduction. Husserl never reduced human emotion to its condition of possibility, conceived of as our skin, and its inside-outside structure. Husserl's reduced consciousness almost always showed a mental movement aiming at an intentional object, which it grasped. Levinas's strategy is to uncover the ethical meaning of human emotion—generally in the form of a traumatized affect. It might seem strange that traumatized affect opens the possibility of communication. However, "traumatized affect" (OBBE, 138,146) means, here, that the face-to-face situation breaks through my usual self-containment as ego (whether phenomenological *or* psychological). As against Husserl, Levinas's ego is *not* the source of all its intentions and meaning. The other comes on the scene, is experienced emotionally before perceptually. He is "felt" through the skin rather than being constituted as an object. I do not communicate with objects because I do not feel summoned to account for myself before a chair or even before an animal. Of course, not all affectivity has an ethical component. Only certain affects—or, better, *passions* (i.e., intense recurring emotions that we "suffer")—that we find in the wake of what Levinas calls "trauma" are liable to have this ethical character. This ethical character suggests that there is in Levinas a possible opening, through affect, that goes beyond what psychoanalysis called the "pleasure principle."[3] Indeed, the opening goes even beyond the characteristic "reality principle,"[4] toward what Levinas might call an "ethical principle." That is, under certain circumstances, an "I" can unwittingly be "for-the-other" (OBBE, 170). It is here that Levinas situates the possibility of communication.

This strange vulnerability or passion that Levinas calls for-the-other, at the core of communication, is not a state of being or existence. The idea that something is *not* of being is part of his ongoing struggle with Martin Heidegger. Levinas's two philosophical adversaries are Hegel and Heidegger. For Levinas, being is not the answer to the question, "Why is there something instead of nothing?" Against Heidegger, Levinas returns to an older conception of being which we recognize as Hobbesian or Malthusian. Being is mechanistic: it entails struggle, *gravitas*, and sometimes pleasure. This conception was probably influenced by the times in which Levinas lived, though today being is no less violent than it was in his lifetime and, by his own logic, it could not be so. For Levinas being is literally transcended in the encounter with the other person. Nevertheless, this is not a philosophy of utopia; neither is it a rhetoric of peace—Levinas is deeply critical of rhetorics. Given the vulnerability that is characteristic of fleshly existence, the trauma or suffering of the encounter with the other can give rise to a violent response, especially so far as the ego thus forced open remains governed by a pleasure principle. That is, I can choose not to see you, not to respond to you; I can thrust you away. Despite this, my violent rejection remains a reaction, even a protection from what Levinas conceives to be the strange "desire" that has come up in the face-to-face relation. This desire is unique to intersubjectivity, which, under certain circumstances, effectively suspends the pleasure principle. Obviously, such a thesis deserves questioning, especially in light of psychoanalysis's notion of the Ego Ideal and the way it can hold sway over the ego. In other words, the other who calls to me is neither my leader nor the projection of who I would like to be. But what gives him the peculiar power he exerts on me? If one could answer that question, then that would mean we could reach beneath body and flesh and explain why our sensibility is an open structure.

What is surprising is that Levinas's investigation into the possibility of human communication insists it remains faithful to his teacher, Husserl's, phenomenology. He criticizes rhetoric in philosophy, rejects conceptions of style such as we find in Nietzsche, and attacks psychoanalysis as a method throughout his career. Thus, the great value of Levinas lies in his descriptions of precognitive affective events, which involve such a loss of ego before another human that we can only conclude that what we call human communication is grounded on a preconscious, intersubjective connection, which is what allows us to speak of human fraternity. That means that we have, here, a phenomenology reaching toward depths comparable to those sought by psychoanalysis, even as it dismisses the discoveries and structures of psychoanalysis. That ambition leads Levinas into an impasse that has been beautifully sketched by Julia Kristeva in her essay on Proust's *Remembrance of Things Past*.[5] Let us take a look at that impasse.

On the Aporia of Affectivity

Philosophies of communication may inquire into the nature of dialogical relationships, the conditions under which information is exchanged, or the constitutive dynamics between communication and communities. Philosophers of communication have rarely examined *individual* passions as capable of revealing a layer of experience that lies generally hidden because this layer is resistant to both discourse and analysis. This concern with passions as surreptitious modes of knowing that are prediscursive, arguably begins with Søren Kierkegaard. For him, anxiety was the passion that revealed our freedom for what it is *simpliciter:* a hesitation between possibilities, cognized or not. Subsequent existential philosophies, like Heidegger's, approached certain passions as signs, pointing toward what escapes us conceptually. To be sure, the list of thinkers of affectivity becomes longer when we consider those who sought philosophical insights in literary texts.

One such philosopher is Julia Kristeva, who began her career in structuralist semiotics. In her study of Marcel Proust's work *Time and Sense,* she argues that understanding human affectivity involves a paradox comparable to Levinas's impasse. Against cognitive psychology she argues that sensations and emotions are *not* inferior forms of judgment, and that they belong to an order different from rationality.[6] Yet they must be set into discursive forms to be communicated to others, not to mention being recognized fully by ourselves. The paradox arises thus: in subjecting passions and emotions to linguistic structures, we express them as (quasi-)judgments and thereby betray what is unique to them, making them *look* like reasoning in search of itself. Clearly, there is no choice in the matter. Kristeva calls this "an aporia of sensation." She traces the first philosophical illustration of it to Plato's cave dwellers, who watch a screen at the back of their cavern. The screen would be the intermediate reality between a pure, or solar, rationality, which blinds us, and complete darkness. The shadows on the screen are "symbols of sensory experience," she says. Yet, by the same token, these are *bona fide* "intelligible realities," once translated into ideas. While they may thus become judgments, they do not share the same form as the rational objects found outside the cave (TS 234).

If Kristeva is right, then what she calls the reality of "sensation-emotion" does and does *not* enter the form of a rational judgment but nevertheless *requires* translation if it is to become an object for thought. For this reason, it ceases to matter whether emotion is or is not deficient judgment, because representation never does reach the metaphoric shadows on Plato's screen. People must interpret and shape these emotions into conceptual statements in order to pull the selves caught in the throes of emotion out of the cave that is their affective self-absorption. Failing this, we have no effective communication.

But is this not the contribution that psychoanalysis makes to a philosophy of communication? More than in any other discipline, psychoanalysts developed the concepts with which to "translate" a multilayered affectivity. And they insisted that mental life cannot be reduced to mere consciousness (any more than conscious contents can be reduced to the *form* of consciousness itself, as phenomenology shows). Levinas also ventures a subtle translation of affectivity. In so doing, both he and psychoanalysis run up against Kristeva's aporia of sensation. That is to say, we *feel* our imperatives and our affective impediments even before we *know* them. Indeed, we require this *truth* of emotion in order to judge our situations (though what we attain in judging may prove wrong or simply renew the ambiguous process of translation). This accounts for what Freud called "analysis terminable and interminable."[7] Attempting to bring into language what is always decentered in its regard means seeking modes of communication of a realm of existence that is deeply human yet elusive. For Kristeva, the importance of Proust lies in the way he constructs his communication. And therein lies also the contribution of psychoanalysis to a philosophy of communication.

Indeed, psychoanalysis's much criticized topologies (of primary and secondary processes, and then of the ego, id, and superego) may begin with a philosophically *traditional* conception of subjectivity as agency. But that conception is quickly outstripped at two levels: psychoanalysis's structure of communication, which is dialogical and hermeneutical, and its discovery of two types of desire— one at the level of the primary process of bodily drives, the other at work in the secondary process, which is symbolic consciousness. In 1961, Levinas was also working with the double structure of desire, one conscious and object-rooted, the other preconscious and inaugurating communication.

Levinas's later work adds a new fold to Kristeva's logic of the translation of affect. This fold, enactment, is crucial to a philosophy of communication. Rather than describing the contents of his everyday consciousness, Levinas communicates, he says, and then he *unsays* the trauma of the ethical encounter—and this in a voice that moves between the first and third persons. Levinas's enactment contains a limited self-legitimation comparable to the *meaning* of memory in psychoanalysis: "I tell you, *here and now,* that I suffer this; in so doing, I have already betrayed the meaning of the event I am remembering, but it is imperative that I tell you." Analogously, memory claims: "This happened to me; even the obscurity you perceive here is part of the event." The extension of the search for intelligibility into sensation and passion is the core of the analytic and the Levinasian gambit.

This maneuver brings into communication something recalcitrant to the logics of causality, identity, and noncontradiction. The gambit is inevitable insofar as affect contains its own practical imperatives. But such an extension makes sensation and passion adjuvants to the philosophy of communication. And even when sensation strains the pleasure and reality principles (as it does in Levinas and in certain cases of transference in Sigmund Freud, where Freud finds a "death drive"[8] at work), communicated affect carries with it the illocutionary questions: "What is this?" and "Why me?"—or even, "What *me* is this?" For this reason, Michel Henry observed that psychoanalysis shares with phenomenology

> the implicit yet crucial intuition . . . that the psyche's essence *does not reside in the world's visible becoming or in what is set forth as an object.* As a radical refusal of [Heidegger's] ecstatic [structure of consciousness] and its claim to define the psyche's essence, the unconscious assures man of a hold on his most intimate being.[9]

The significance of psychoanalysis is thus close to the insights of Levinas's mature thought. We desire, to the point of requiring, such an approach to our intimate being in the process of communication—even if it loses its reality as we bring it under reflective scrutiny.

The Evolution of Levinas's Phenomenology

We can observe Levinas's idiosyncratic "phenomenological" reduction to the meaning that is sensibility and affect, unfolded fully in *Otherwise than Being* (1974). I will proceed in presenting this by following the history of his formulations of the reduction backward, starting from 1974. Let us keep in mind, throughout, the ultimate task Levinas assigns himself: "In renouncing [Husserlian] intentionality as a guiding thread toward the *eidos* of the psyche . . . our analysis will follow sensibility in its *pre-natural signification* to the maternal, where, in proximity, signification signifies before it gets bent into *perseverance in being* in the midst of a Nature" (OBBE 68, first emphasis added).

Levinas thus gives up his phenomenological focus on intentionality in favor of an interpretative phenomenology of sensibility as vulnerability, and a curious containment to which he attributes the figure of maternity—a figure not unfamiliar to Jewish mysticism. He argues that sensibility falls outside "natural" behaviors and attributes, which clearly include his conception of willing. Prior to willing or desiring, and determined through its emotional effects, is a *self* carrying what is not itself—a nearly schizophrenic situation—however rapidly this comes to pass. This would be ethical sensibility, which is anti-ecstatic and which stops one from being simply "for oneself" or "out ahead of oneself toward one's ownmost possibilities," as in Heidegger. We might call it a desire against the grain, which repeats and increases over time, rather like a neurosis, though it requires another human being in her facticity, if it is to come to pass at all. Despite Levinas's rejection of psychoanalysis, how can we fail to be reminded here of the origin of Freud's superego—similarly an "other-in-the-same," and similarly heterogenic (born of an other). Striking too is the violence with which Levinas's other and Freud's superego sound their call within the self. Further study might show that, in the 1974 work, Levinas reproduces (unconsciously?) a speculative three-part logic that recalls Freud's second *topos*. What brought Levinas to such a logic? To understand this, we must look at the phenomenological reduction and the way Levinas's use of it evolved.

Levinas's phenomenological career seems to go through three basic inflections. The first is concerned with the affective roots of a philosophy of communication. It focuses on interiority in the 1940s. The second inflection turns to exteriority and communication in the 1950s and '60s. It rethinks Heidegger's *Dasein*, itself open to the world, giving priority to enjoyment, teaching, and communication over the use of worldly things. The third inflection approaches ethical sensibility as immanence, and the possibility of communication through the flesh (*la Chair*), a notion whose inspiration he owes to Merleau-Ponty.[10]

Affective Roots of Levinas's Philosophy of Communication

The first inflection in Levinas's work distills influences from Edmund Husserl, Martin Heidegger, and Henri Bergson, and Levinas's early teachers of psychology at Strasbourg, Maurice Pradines and Maurice Blondel.[11] When Levinas first published his dissertation on Husserl, *Theory of Intuition in Husserl's Phenomenology*,[12] he praised Husserl's work for its "attempt at delineating what is called sensibility and understanding" (TIPH 79). Husserl's specific technique of the phenomenological-transcendental *reduction* makes this attempt "interesting." This is because his phenomenological reduction allowed Husserl to start with "the intrinsic meaning of sensible or categorial [tied to Kant's categories, or structures of understanding] life itself" (TIPH 79). This meaning is always available to description because, no matter how many perspectives one might have on an event of sensibility and perception, sense objects come to us directly as wholes, "all at once" (TIPH 79). The lesson of our sensuous and affective consciousness is that, through it, successive sensations and their elements continuously re-fuse, synthetically, in a kind of understanding that is not firstly propositional. Husserl's thought thus afforded Levinas access to sensuous experience as the condition for the possibility of communication without imposing subsequent intellectual constructions such as "objective" perceptions versus merely "imagined" ones.

Husserl's phenomenological reduction provided access to the *primacy of the lived experience* on the proviso of maintaining a division in psychic life between our functioning constituting consciousness *in the world* and the world-free, phenomenological spectator that is revealed ultimately by his transcendental reduction. Thus a duality arises, as structurally unavoidable, in a single consciousness, from the moment it seeks to approach lived experience. The duality poses the question: Which is first, consciousness as intentionality or consciousness always already situated in a world? Levinas grasped the difficulty of this situation early.[13] Already in 1930, he argued that the absoluteness of Husserl's phenomenological spectator (and the solipsism of a pure "I" that results from it) *cannot give us* the actual, full life of consciousness:

> We have interpreted the constitutional problems as ontological and we have seen their essential task: to throw light on the meaning of existence. This . . . clarifies the philosophical role . . . of the phenomenology of consciousness, [and it] may be the aspect in which we have been more explicit than Husserl himself. . . . [Anyhow] only Heidegger dares to face this problem [of the primacy of the lived] deliberately. (TIPH 154)

Levinas's work considers the primacy of lived experience, which situates communication, without presupposing a psychic division between one's conscious functioning in the lived world and the phenomenal world itself.

By the 1940s, Levinas not only faced the problem himself, but had worked out an alternative phenomenology of consciousness to that of Husserl or Heidegger.

Levinas's descriptions unfolded a consciousness whose time structure was not firstly ecstatic, or aimed toward the future, but rooted in the weight of the present (as was Bergson's *duration*)[14] and taking up a stance toward things (*Stellungnahme*) (as Husserl's consciousness had done). More important, and like Husserl *and* Freud, for whom the pure "I" or "ego" functions as a nonconscious unifying principle, Levinas took a decisive turn toward an interiority that did *not* firstly presuppose a world, much less Heidegger's being-in-the-world.

As Levinas writes in his 1947 *Existence and Existents,*

> It is, therefore, a regrettable confusion in contemporary philosophy [notably, Heidegger's philosophy] to have placed events—which it had the incontestable merit of discovering under the purely negative term of the "unconscious"—[that are unconscious] inside of a world, and to have denounced as hypocrisy, as *fall* . . . before the essential, a behavior in the world whose secularity and contentment translate simply the very destiny of that world. (EE 64, my translation)

Instead of placing psychic events within the frame of *Dasein*'s openness to the world—thereby holding fast to the inside-outside binarity that results, and focusing on the question of being—the young Levinas turned back to Husserl and his "famous epochè" (EE 64) or reduction, to dispute Heidegger's "ontological finality" (EE 64). Just as Husserl had argued in his 1900 *Logical Investigations,* Levinas insisted that when it is described in its fullness—as affect, passions, mood, and reflection—consciousness is our primary world. His focus on the scene of immanence (though as a scene, it is not posited first as "inside" *or* "outside") allows the spectrum of modes of consciousness to be their own courts of appeal in matters of ethics and intersubjectivity generally.[15]

To show the depth of this immanence, Levinas resorts to modes of consciousness that shade off—increasingly far from Husserl's conscious intentionality—into intermediaries between full consciousness and unconsciousness. These include fatigue, lassitude, insomnia, and sleep, but also nausea and the urge to get out of oneself and one's present time. His descriptions of "insomnia," elaborated between 1940 and 1947, utterly rewrite Heidegger's description of anxiety. Levinas's purpose was to make anxiety a pre- or semiconscious state that did *not* reveal the uncanniness of *Dasein* and his dialectic of the nothing-that-nihilates (the function of anxiety), but merely the fragility of the insomniac self. Writes Levinas,

> The distinction between the attention [or intentionality] that is directed upon objects—whether external or internal—and the wakefulness that is absorbed in the rustling of inevitable being goes farther still. The I [*moi*] is carried off by the fatality of being. There is no longer any outside or any inside.[16]

Here, then, is Levinas's critique of Heidegger's being-in-the-world, and of the latter's understanding of anxiety.

Levinas has set Husserl's phenomenological reduction to revealing the modes of being of a self whose character is, like Sartre's, transcendental: *this* self simply *is* its pain, its anxiety, or its sleepiness. At this level, it is never a detached spectator of these modes. Levinas continues, "This wakefulness is absolutely empty of objects. Which does not come down to saying that it is the experience *of nothingness*" (EE 110). Again, we find the critique of Heidegger's reduction—that is, of his anxiety as he presented it in works from 1927 and 1929—where it was an experience of precisely *nothing*, of active "nihilating" isolating *Dasein* before itself and before the question of being.

"Rather," writes Levinas, "[anxiety] is as anonymous as the night itself. Attention supposes the freedom of the I who directs it; the wakefulness of insomnia that holds our eyes open *has no subject*" (EE 110). With the stroke of a pen, Levinas begins his lifelong investigation of the pre-egological states of consciousness, *which have neither an intentional subject nor offer themselves for re-collection by some ego-agency*. This is *his* pre-conscious. In a broad sense, it is motivated by the same search that drove Freud, namely, for a truth of the subject that extended past its own deliberate acts of subjective intentionality. "Shall we say," he writes, "that kinaesthesia [the awareness of movement inside and out] is more than a knowledge, that, in internal sensibility . . . I am my pain, my respiration, my organs, . . . that I do not only *have* a body, but *am* a body?" (EE 123).

Levinas's early project was to unfold an embodied ego, using Heidegger's deformalized "reductions," tied to human practices and to daily existence. He proceeded all the way to unconsciousness. This may be why he criticized Freudian psychology as too shaped by a traditional view of consciousness, and neglectful of the "ontological meaning" of the unconscious. In reality, the psychoanalytic "reduction," facilitated by analytical listening and bringing to light dynamic regions of immanence, seems more abstract and speculative. But then, Freud also distilled his egology from a large number of observed subjects—something Levinas could not do.[17] He writes,

> . . . the unconscious that consciousness shelters [*couve*] is not, in turn, an intention that could prolong, by integrating it into a vaster system of finalities, the very sincerity of the intentions we direct upon the world, as though a dark world, identical in every way to the world of light, survived [*se survivait*] under the veil of the night. [No,] the background-thoughts [*arrière-pensées*] of unconsciousness are not thoughts promised to the same rank as thinking, and merely awaiting their promotion. The manner in which consciousness refers to the unconscious is not an intention in its turn. (EE 117)

The assimilation of the unconscious and its "events" to conscious life or intentionality was Freud's (and Husserl's) error for Levinas, but *not* the notion of the unconscious itself.

Exteriority and Communication: The Open Subject and Its Being-in and Transcendence of the World

The second phase of Levinas's career, in the 1950s and 1960s, directs the phenomenological to the openness of the subject to its world. This was a theme not so dissimilar from Heidegger's being-in-the-world. In Levinas, however, it focused on the enjoyment and love of life, in preference to care and utility.[18] *Totality and Infinity* (1961) presents his fully developed philosophy of *jouissance*, from eating and experiencing the wind and the sun, through communication, sexuality, and parenthood. It is not a philosophy of desire, since desire in the philosophical discourse typical of 1961 was largely the Kojèvian desire *for the desire* of the other, which led to struggle rather than communication. Alexandre Kojève's desire, like Jacques Lacan's following him, was a tragic one predicated on a will to absolute negativity, and manifesting itself in the temporary "master" position. Many criticized this reading of Hegel, which confounds his *lord-and-bondsman* with Nietzsche's *master-slave* positions and set the master-slave dialectic as definitive of desire and operative at the heart of the *Phenomenology*.[19] Aware of these criticisms and opposed to Hegelian dialectics, Levinas adopted Jean Wahl's reading of the *Phenomenology* and highlighted the ground of consciousness as a sensuous-based love of life,[20] which, again, ultimately makes human communication possible.

In Levinas's middle career, this ground of consciousness is one of plenty. The enjoyment of consciousness affords us the possibility of generosity and speaking to another. However, the experienced time that structures "love of life" is broken by the temporal interruption and the spatial inflection implicit in Levinas's conception of the face-to-face encounter. Now, the so-called spatial inflection is primordial: if, by its activity, a subject opens realms of objects by using or consuming them, it is the human other that *opens* the subject in turn. Thus, it is the human other, and *not the preexisting world*, that makes the subject a *Da*, or a "there," a site. Levinas borrows the notion of "trans-ascendence" from Jean Wahl (TI 35, 41). Levinas speaks of the "curvature of intersubjective space" (TI 291), where the other opens and refocuses the subject by virtue of his face. The subject has lost control of the circle of space around him (in Freud: the subject has lost his defenses). He is halted by a gaze whose nature is different from his own.

Thus in 1961, conversation will arise from the "relation with a reality infinitely distant from my own reality, yet without this distance destroying the relation and without this relation destroying this distance" (TI 41). Conversation, as speaking to one another face-to-face, is not firstly symmetrical or competitive; it is "metaphysical desire" (TI 42), "where power, by essence murderous of the other, becomes, faced with the other and 'against all good sense', the impossibility of murder, the consideration of the other, or justice" (TI 47). This exceptional space, and occasional but repeated moments of an inversion of power, "form the fabric of being itself," (TI 81) writes Levinas in *Totality and Infinity*. Being is thus

woven out of disparate elements that are other than *phusis* or natural development, and political history, and other than Heidegger's being as the dynamic
quod or "how" of beings. In Levinas, being is tensed between pluralism and the
polar opposites of immanent enjoyment and ethical transcendence, or desire for
life's goods and metaphysical desire.[21] The reduction reaches this being through
the singularization that the enjoyment of life's goods permits the subject and, at
a deeper level, by the isolation of the same by the other person.

These two reductions are deeply Heideggerian in inspiration: just as Heidegger's broken tool *reveals* the unfamiliarity of the world without its network of
practical references, Levinas's enjoyment of the sunlight *reveals* the unfamiliarity
of the nature when it turns, by its intrinsic excess, from warmth to burning fire.
Or again, anxiety, by isolating *Dasein*, reveals its structure as a being-with-others and shows it, now, to itself alone (Heidegger).[22] So too, in Levinas, the approach of the other individuates the subject by directing its unspoken command
and gaze toward that subject: this is Levinas's disclosive reduction, which shows,
paradoxically, the subjective structure of being-with-others as well—only with
the added dimension of being-able-to-be-*for*-the-others, which opens to communication with them.

Levinas's Phenomenological Reduction and Communication

The deeper question of existence is, for Levinas, the human other. His phenomenological reduction—transformed from Husserl's model in much the way that
Heidegger had done, by integrating the reduction into lived existence—*reveals*
the world of enjoyment as ambiguous and the other person as constitutive of
the subject's own "where" and "how," in an ethical sense. But though the other
is a partner in human dialogue, the Other (as "force" of her face), which brings
about what Nietzsche called the trans-valuation of my being-in-the-world, is a
disclosure or revelation that also hides its facticity. The face of the Other is like
a force of passive resistance. Levinas says that we do not have the time to *see* the
face in its objectivity. That is, we have not seen it before it has (already) com-
manded us ("do not harm me").

Being or existence is thus problematical in *Totality and Infinity,* because
conversation, dialogue, here combines the practical experience of addressing another with Levinas's famous "trans-ascendence" (TI 35) upward, toward answering and assisting the other person spontaneously. Although she is my partner in
dialogue, the other person, as expression and force of resistance, is also the Other,
capital "O." And Levinas repeats this at a moment where he becomes conscious
of the other's invisible presence *as his reader,* in a strange here-and-now moment.
"These relations [between self and other], which I claim form the fabric of being
itself, first come together in my discourse *presently addressed* to my interlocutors:
inevitably across my idea of the Infinite the other faces me—hostile, friend, my
master, my student. . . . The face to face remains an ultimate situation" (TI 81).

Words that Freud might himself have written. The irreducibility of the face-to-face relation is lodged in language given, where it is not signs that are exchanged but where the self, the I, itself becomes a signifier whose meaning is open, is sincerity as awaiting and as aware of the other. This becomes what Levinas also calls "justice"—the suddenly becoming aware that my speaking is "presently addressed to my interlocutors" (TI, 81). It is interesting that we find in Lacan a moment comparable to this, in the analytic situation.

Examining the incipience of those moments that Sigmund Freud called *Übertragungsphänomene*, or transference phenomena, Jacques Lacan notes in 1954 (seven years before Levinas published *Totality and Infinity*):

> We have asked the question of what memory, remembering, techniques of remembering mean; asked what free association means in as much as it permits us to accede to a formulation of the subject's history. But what does the subject become . . . is it always the same subject? Here we are before a phenomenon where we grasp a knot in the progress [of analysis] . . . a resistance. We see produced, at a certain point in this resistance, what Freud called the transference, that is, here, the actualization of the person of the analyst. . . . [The] subject [at that moment] experiences it like the brusque perception of something that is not easy to define, *presence*.[23]

To this idea of presence of the other, Lacan adds,

> This is a sentiment that we don't have all the time. . . . You sense, certainly, that it is a sentiment which, I would say, we tend ceaselessly to erase from life. This wouldn't be easy to live if, at every instant, we had the sentiment of this presence, with all the mystery that it contains. This is a mystery that we hold aside, but of which, to tell the truth [*pour tout dire*], we are made. (SI, 53)

What Lacan grasped in his analytic practice—and what Levinas rethought in 1961 under such heavy phenomenological brackets that it looked like a brute accident—was the intersection of the everyday dimension of conversation and its profound ethical, but also *strange*, "foundation."

The "foundation" gets "revealed" in the uncanny presence that the other evinces occasionally, and at the sentient and affective level, when the everyday circuit of talk breaks down. But the circuit depends upon the constitution that is always already invisible, or becoming invisible. This is where Levinas's metaphysical desire is situated, and, as Lacan notes, gets forgotten. We normally speak to others as to forms or to *statuts civils;* the experience that Levinas himself calls "this moral experience, so commonplace" (TI 53) is the moment where we strike up against "the impossibility of *forgetting* the intersubjective experience that leads to the social experience and endows it with meaning" (TI 53). This is Levinas, not Lacan. But what separates Lacan and Levinas here is not the moment they describe, but the fundamental *meaning* of it: the transference is a moment where the self cannot bring its own expression to effectivity; it cannot bring the word into the circle of communication, because the circle has dissolved before the strangeness of the other. Writes Lacan, "The I is constituted in relation to the other. It is correlative with the other. The level at which the other is lived situates precisely the level at which, literally, the I exists for the subject" (SI, 61). Levinas would hardly deny this. He would invite Lacan to conceive the interruptive moment as an experience of a call, a demand—one that is structural to intersubjective life, and possible even in the analyst's office.

Levinas's second phase unfolds at this de facto and practical level. *Totality and Infinity* (1961) is an "essay on exteriority," by which he means "*metaphysical* exteriority." Levinas's understanding of exteriority embraces metaphysics precisely as desire, and fights a war on two fronts: against Kojève's Hegel and his desire and against Heidegger's being as extra-ethical; and against his understanding of mortality. The goal is to keep exteriority from lapsing into ecstatic temporality, those times typical of a *Dasein* continually out-ahead-of-itself or isolated, and alone before its *own* uncanniness.

Ethical Sensibility as Immanence: Communication through the Flesh

The third phase in the development of Levinas's phenomenology as it contributes to an understanding of communication is the most radical. This phase consists of the work done above all in the chapter entitled "Substitution" in *Otherwise than Being or beyond Essence*, published in 1974. This third phase resembles the work on states of consciousness in the 1940s. However, there is a difference. The final phenomenology places at its center the notion of flesh. This concept Levinas no doubt borrows from Maurice Merleau-Ponty. If Merleau-Ponty's interest in the flesh, *la Chair*, lay in the interconnection of the sensible body and the sentient body (feeling itself inside and the world outside, simultaneously), Levinas will explore this flesh first in 1961 in light of enjoyment,[24] then in 1974 in light of suffering. He never pursues the relationship of body flesh to world flesh, as Merleau-Ponty did. Instead, Levinas examines the interpenetration of self and other *in the self*, seeming to spiritualize Merleau-Ponty's subtle phenomenological materialism.

Merleau-Ponty pushed Husserl's philosophical wavering about phenomenological origins between an egological subject that constitutes intentional objects and a pre-egological self of "impressional" intentionality.[25] Levinas follows Merleau-Ponty's expanded, "operative intentionality" (*fungierende Intentionalität*) into the investigation of objectless intentionalities having the curious form of carnal self-affection.[26] Unlike Merleau-Ponty, however, Levinas's self-affection will come to pass through an affective self, *but also* through the other *in* that self, inexplicable in its spatiality but redolent of psychoanalytic discussions of the split subject. This alterity-in-immanence represents a greater departure from Husserl than did Merleau-Ponty's *flesh*, because Levinas insisted both on the absolute alterity of the other, and that this other be *in* but *not of* the same—

while Merleau-Ponty construed our affective life as the intertwining of sentience-and-externally-sensed.

Explicitly rejecting the objective and constructivist side of Husserl's thought, Levinas writes in 1974,

> The notion of access to being, representation, and thematization of a said presuppose sensibility, and thus proximity, vulnerability and signifyingness. Between the signification proper to the sensible and that of thematization and the thematized as thematized, the *abyss is much greater than the parallelism constantly affirmed by Husserl* between all the "qualities" or "theses" of intentionality would allow one to suppose. (OBBE 68)

Levinas's wager is that "signification" as the inconceivable structure of the flesh could serve as the "dephased" or decentered ground of what he calls the "psyche" in the late work. Although he calls it "signifyingness par excellence" (OBBE 69), the psyche intended here is a Greek, a peripatetic and Stoic psyche that is a living unity of feeling and thinking. But "signifyingness par excellence" clearly means that Levinas will now set the root of his earlier concept of conversation into a vulnerability that always already *means* something. This something is simply "exposure to the other" and "the possibility of giving" (OBBE 69). As such, it is exceptional to what Levinas calls the "nature" of mechanistic causalities (OBBE 68). However, as the source of speaking, this exposure is not wholly unlike the middle-career Lacan and his unconscious, structured like a language.

Now, Levinas's concept of "signifyingness," *signifiance*, points to a specific sensitivity to another human, which is also a tie of some kind with her, and which lies both at the root of "ethical" communication with her, *and* at that of erotic enjoyment. Levinas sometimes calls this a "reverse *conatus*" (OBBE 70), similar to Freud's counter-erotic drive toward release and relaxation, which he deemed the *Todestrieb* (death drive) in 1920. But what is a "reverse *conatus*?" It is hard to say, because Levinas rules out all but the most spiritual of answers, leaving us with a mystery: "It is neither a structure, nor an inwardness of a content in a container, nor a causality, nor even a dynamism, which still extends in a time that could be collected into a history" (OBBE 70).[27] This is, he argues, an "ambivalence" (OBBE 162), "a dilemma or an alternative if one sticks to the phenomena" (OBBE 154). Above all, it is a challenge posed to philosophy—and, it is worth adding, to psychoanalysis. This is a challenge to psychoanalysis because, more than any other discipline, psychoanalysis embraces what appear to be the dilemmas of conscious life when "one sticks to the phenomena." Moreover, it does so through an attention to the truth of passions and pathology. But we find this—also and in an ethicized form—in Levinas's "extraordinary . . . reversal of the same into the other," which is, at the level of sensibility, a "patience of passivity . . . always at the limit, exceeded by a demented suffering, 'for nothing', a suffering of pure misery" (OBBE 153).

This is Levinas's exploration, at a formal level, of the possibility of the intersubjective circuit of empathy and communication, discussed by Merleau-Ponty and others. Levinas's investigation is close to Lacan, again, when Levinas denies that his concept of "substitution" is psychology. Levinas asserts, "substitution is not the psychological event of compassion or intropathy in general, but makes possible the paradoxical psychological possibilities of putting oneself in the place of another" (OBBE 146). This ground, outside space and time, Levinas calls "the outdated notion of the soul" (OBBE 103) or "the hypostasis" (OBBE 106)—his term for an unconscious.[28] Let us listen to the qualification, which comes afterward in the form of a question:

> How in consciousness can there be an undergoing or a passion whose active source does not, in any way, occur in consciousness? . . . It is not objective or spatial, recuperable in immanence and thus falling under the orders of . . . consciousness; it is obsessional, non-thematizable and . . . anarchic. (OBBE 102)

This answers the *how* of Levinas's assertion: "Subjectivity is structured as the other in the same . . . in a way different from that of consciousness" (OBBE 25).

In elaborating something like the logic of Moses Maimonides's negative theology—applied to the mystery of subjectivity—Levinas employs figures both dramatic and varied to the point of promiscuity. He will borrow concepts and figures from psychoanalysis, Christian dogmatics, Lurianic kabbalah, and literature. The figures from psychoanalysis are especially powerful for him: trauma, psychosis, obsession, recurrence, and repetition. Formally, the "constitution" (better: the *election*) of the self by another poses no difficulties to psychoanalysis, nor to Merleau-Ponty's genetic phenomenology. Indeed, the incipience of this selfhood in trauma and suffering reminds us of the causes of neurosis that prove to be a structuring factor in all subjectivity when Freud adapts Otto Rank's notion of birth-trauma (physiological self-intoxication). Moreover, a divided subject is a significant contribution of psychoanalysis, variously worked out by Freud and Lacan. Thus, Levinas's work provides an an-archaeology, "If an an-archeology is possible" (OBBE 7), which situates communicators in their lived-world.

In Closing

In considering Levinas's philosophy of communication, his response to the question "How does communication arise?" was suggested. The significance of individual passions which reveal a layer of experience that contributes to communication was considered. Finally, three inflections of Levinas's work were outlined: the affective roots of his philosophy of communication, the realm of exteriority and communication, and his understanding of ethical sensibility and the possibility of communication through the flesh, as inspired by Merleau-Ponty.

I have noted the necessity, for Levinas, of tying sensibility and affectivity to signification, or the capacity to signify and to speak to another. Despite his protests about formal structures, this claim suggests a minimalist one at the least. But then, to argue that the unconscious is structured like a language is comparably minimalist, because it points to an operative but invisible grammar of combinations of signifiers and images.

Levinas's concerns tying sensibility and affectivity to signification are ethical. And they become religious in an extraordinary way. The nearness of the other human being gives rise to a desire . . . to open, to "say," as he puts it. What one says does not matter, except that in the wake of this excess one sometimes says the extraordinary word "God." Levinas's claim that the origin of the signifier "God" lies precisely in the human, ethical situation becomes marked in the period of *Otherwise than Being*. Given his repugnance for ontologizing the other, capital "O," we find the other-in-the-same ultimately indescribable (or interminably describable). Levinas's exploration of the rise of and incipience of "impossible signifiers" like "God" (OBBE, 152, 156, 158, 162) is rooted in his concern to unearth the conditions under which human communication comes to be.

Notes

1. In the main, I will cite Levinas's two major works, *Totality and Infinity: An Essay on Exteriority* (Pittsburgh, PA: Duquesne University Press, 1969) and *Otherwise than Being: Or Beyond Essence* (Pittsburgh, PA: Duquesne University Press, 1998). These are the most recent editions of the works, which appeared in French, respectively, in 1961 and 1974. Hereafter cited in the text as TI and as OBBE.

2. Melanie Klein, *Love, Guilt and Reparation: And Other Works 1921–1945* (New York: Free Press, 2002); M. Klein, *Envy and Gratitude: 1946–1962* (New York: Free Press, 2002).

3. Cf. Sigmund Freud, "Beyond the Pleasure Principle" (1920), in *The Freud Reader*, ed. Peter Gay (New York: W.W. Norton & Co., 1989), 594–626.

4. Cf. Freud, "Beyond the Pleasure Principle," 603.

5. Julia Kristeva, *Time and Sense: Proust and the Experience of Literature*, trans. Ross Guberman (New York: Columbia University Press, 1996). Cited in the text as TS.

6. The argument for inferior forms of judgments becomes circular the moment we posit that "judgment" is exclusively and definitionally discursive and rational. How would one ascertain this without formulating an affect in propositional form, and thereby emitting a judgment?

7. Sigmund Freud, "Analysis Terminable and Interminable" (1937), in *The Standard Edition of the Complete Psychological Works of Sigmund Freud*, vol. 23, trans. and ed. James Strachey (London: Hogarth Press, 1968).

8. Cf. Freud, "Beyond the Pleasure Principle," 617–618.

9. Michel Henry, *Genealogy of Psychoanalysis*, trans. D. Brick (Stanford, CA: Stanford University Press, 1993), 285–86. Cited in the text as GP with page numbers.

10. Before his sudden death Maurice Merleau-Ponty was slated to be a member of the jury presiding over Levinas's Sorbonne defense of his *doctorat d'état*, which resulted in the publication *Totality and Infinity* (1961). Merleau's influence on Levinas was not, then, as significant as Jean Wahl's, to whom Levinas dedicated his 1961 work. But it cannot be doubted that Levinas was familiar with Merleau-Ponty's 1948 *Phenomenology of Perception*, and perhaps with his 1954–1955 Collège de France lectures on passivity in sleep, dreams, and psychoses—work that radicalized Husserl's discussions of passivity as memory and temporal syntheses.

11. Their influences are discussed by Anne-Marie Lescourret in her intellectual biography, *Emmanuel Levinas* (Paris: Flammarion, 1974).

12. Levinas, *Theory of Intuition in Husserl's Phenomenology*, trans. André Orianne (Evanston, IL: Northwestern University Press, 1973). Hereafter abbreviated and cited in the text as TIHP. The theme of intuition (as opposed to intentionality) probably came from Maurice Pradines's extensive research into sensibility as "metaphysics' ancient problem of intuition" in his *Philosophie de la sensation*, vol. 2: "La Sensibilité élémentaire" (Elementary Sensibility) (Paris: Les Belles Lettres, 1928). It may be Pradines who first introduced Levinas to Husserl's phenomenology in the 1920s (see TIHP, 91). In any case, the question of "intuition" had to be distilled from Husserl's work, since the latter's concerns focused on the nature and types of "intentionality" and "eidetic intuitions" (intuitions of constructed essences of things) and since intuition was basically a concept drawn from psychology.

13. This situation sums up a part of the debate between Husserl and his erstwhile student Martin Heidegger, who situates human existence in a world, in being or existence, from the first.

14. Henri Bergson, *Duration and Simultaneity* (1921) (New York: Bobbs-Merrill Press, 1965).

15. Abstractions like these (objective, subjective, consciousness itself)—are held out of play by Husserl. In his Sorbonne lectures, *The Cartesian Meditations* (1931), he insisted that phenomenology, as the science of pure consciousness, should itself *found* psychology and other sciences, as acts of constituting consciousness at ever higher levels of complexity. He points out, "The eidetic (concerning essences of things) theory of lived processes must take the lived processes with the whole content with which they present themselves in eidetic intuition, *whether it be on psychological experience or on psychological fiction*." See Edmund Husserl, "The Relations between Psychology and Phenomenology" in *Cartesian Meditations*, a work Levinas first translated from the German notes for French readers.

16. Levinas, *De l'existence à l'existant* (Paris: Vrin, 1978), 110, my translation. Generally cited in the text as EE.

17. Freud also misunderstood what Levinas called "*volupté*" or erotic *jouissance* within the larger scheme of existence and history. In Levinas's "Time and the Other," first presented as lectures between 1946 and 1947, he presented *his* phenomenology of desire and enjoyment as a function of ordering the present.

18. Not surprisingly, Levinas's friend and mentor Jean Wahl had given a seminar on Heidegger's 1928–1929 *Einleitung in der Philosophie* and his 1929 *Was ist Metaphysik?* The seminar bore Wahl's interpretive mark and language. Some of

this language—for example, the *voici* with which Wahl translated Heidegger's *da*, or "there," will later be integrated by Levinas into his own philosophy as our *first response* to the Other: "Me voici." Of Heidegger's *Dasein*, Wahl observes, "Being among things, elementary and non-mediated, non-truncated . . . lets us approach the human being immediately in things. And, precisely because it is a natural opening upon things, the idea of reflection need not come in. We are here at a more fundamental level. What we mean, simply, is that the human being *carries with him a circle of opening*. . . . The *Da-* of *Dasein* signifies this circle (*Umkreis*) of opening, in which the being is . . . by nature, and in which it is revealed." See Jean Wahl, *Introduction à la pensée de Heidegger: Cours donnés en Sorbonne, janvier à juin 1946* (Paris: L.G.F., 1998), 70.

19. Thereby reading the whole as the "anthropo-genesis of the structure of human desires rather than a series of moments with parallels in the *Logic*. See Otto Pöggeler's essay "Phénoménologie et logique," in Jean-Luc Marion and G. Planty-Bonjour, eds., *Phénoménologie et métaphysique* (Paris: PUF, 1984), 29. Pöggeler argues, as Levinas's teacher Jean Wahl also did, that Hegel was more influenced by the romantic movement of his time, and by works such as Jacobi's novel *Woldemar,* in which human recognition was more significant than the struggle of two solipsistic counterparts. Pöggeler argues that the *Phenomenology* is simply a working out, in moments, of Hegel's logic; Wahl argues that the *Phenomenology* is the last expression of the young Hegel, profoundly conscious of the scissions between the philosophy and political life of his time. Wahl sets the figure of the unhappy consciousness forth as the more fundamental figure of history; this interpretation of Hegel, I believe, influenced Levinas. But Levinas remained opposed to the triumphalism of Kojève. I suspect that, like Pöggeler, Levinas would have found ill-conceived the flattening of history implicit in Kojève's reading of the later moments of the *Phenomenology*—where God appears amidst "those who know him as absolute knowledge"—as a reference to Napoleon.

The crucial point is this: the desire that Hegel's philosophy expresses, as read by Kojève and by Lacan and others, is not a desire that interested Levinas. Kojève's desire was a distillation of the master-valet dialectic *in history*, and as the primary structuring force in the unfolding of consciousness. As Pöggeler put it, "Hegel experienced early on that it is only in history and by history that man becomes himself." From early on, Lessing's *Nathan* centered his perspective on the historical promise of reconciliation of religious and political differences. Pöggeler adds, "Lessing presupposes that man could raise himself . . . above all through the experience of suffering over the positive and above what is only historical, to purified reason" (Pöggeler, "Phénoménologie," 23).

20. Sensuous love of life is a theme Levinas has drawn from Pradines, see the latter's *Philosophie de la sensation*, vol. 2, 85ff.

21. He writes, "It should have served as a foundation for a pluralist philosophy in which the plurality of being would not disappear . . ." (see *TI*, 80). The pluralist conception of being will soon give way to a "nature" that is will, *conatus*, and increase.

22. As Rudolf Bernet writes, "The world to which the works of the preoccupied *Dasein* relate, is sooner a common world than a shared world; it is a world prior to sharing and prior to the parceling out [mise en commun] and of no one, the world of

anonymous *Dasein* . . . [The] absence of the others has the particularity of rendering the *Dasein* attentive to the fact that its existence always takes the form of being-with." See Rudolf Bernet, *La Vie du sujet: Recherches sur l'interprétation de Husserl dans la phénoménologie* (Paris: Presses Universitaires de France, 1994), 29, my translation.

23. See note 18. Hereafter Lacan's *Seminaire I* is abbreviated in the text as SI.

24. See Merleau-Ponty, "The Intertwining—The Chiasmus," in *The Visible and the Invisible,* trans. A. Lingis, ed. C. Lefort (Evanston, IL: Northwestern University Press, 1968), 130–155, first published in French in 1964, although related notes and lectures were available prior to then. In that crucial section, Merleau-Ponty uses the concept of "element" to define the flesh. This is a notion that we find used in Levinas's *Totality and Infinity* with one difference: the Elemental for Levinas is exteriority; it does not really engage our body as profoundly as it does in Merleau-Ponty. The latter is intent upon dissolving barriers and boundaries between self and world. He writes, "Where are we to put the limit between the body and the world, since the world is flesh?" and he adds, "The world seen is not 'in' my body, and my body is not 'in' the visible world ultimately: as flesh applied to a flesh, the world neither surrounds it nor is surrounded by it. . . . There is reciprocal insertion and intertwining of one in the other. Or rather, . . . there are two circles, or two vortexes, or two spheres, concentric when I live naïvely, and as soon as I question myself, the one slightly decentered with respect to the other"; cf. "The Intertwining—The Chiasmus," 138.

 Merleau-Ponty adds that both world and "I" are "flesh" and that "flesh" is "not matter, is not mind, is not substance" but "'element' in the sense it was used to speak of water, air, earth. . . ." (139). Levinas will define this chiasmatic relationship in relation to the self and the other, rather than the seer and the seen, body and world.

25. And with this, Husserl's ambivalence between constituting a phenomenology of objectifying intentionalities and tentative ventures into non-objectifying intentionalities (in which neither world nor things need be "objects" ready to hand, *vorhanden*).

26. For an extensive discussion of the French reception of Husserl, and the French options taken in light of his oscillation between strict objectifying intentionality and preintentional "states," see Bernet, *La Vie du sujet,* 297–327.

27. Levinas admits as much, repeatedly. Note, "Spirituality is sense, and sense is not a simple penury of being. Spirituality is no longer to be understood on the basis of knowing. In the splendid indifference of radiant being, there is an overwhelming of this being into sense, into proximity, which does not turn into knowing. It signifies as a difference" (*OBBE,* 97). This theme has been extended by Jean-Luc Marion to his icono-graphy.

 But the term-question that is "spirituality" arises repeatedly here. As Levinas writes, "In this spirituality, infinity comes to pass, more ancient than the time of remembering, a diachrony without memory and thus out of season" (*OBBE,* 64).

28. The term goes all the way back to 1940–1945, when it was used in *Existence and Existents.*

Bibliography of Works

Books by Emmanuel Levinas

1930s

La Théorie de l'intuition dans la phénoménologie de Husserl. Paris: F. Alcan, 1930.

1940s

De L'existence à l'existant. Paris: Fontaine, 1947.
En Découvrant l'existence avec Husserl et Heidegger. Paris: J. Vrin, 1949.

1960s

Totalité et infini: Essai sur l'extériorité. The Hague: M. Nijhoff, 1961.
Difficile liberté: Essais sur le judaïsme. Paris: A. Michel, 1963.
Quatre lectures talmudiques. Paris: Éditions de Minuit, 1968.

1970s

Humanisme de l'autre homme. Montpellier: Fata Morgana, 1972.
Autrement qu'être, ou, au-delà de l'essence. The Hague: M. Nijhoff, 1974.
Sur Maurice Blanchot. Montpellier: Fata Morgana, 1975.
Noms propres: Agnon, Buber, Celan, Delhomme, Derrida, Jabès, Kierkegaard, Lacrois, Laporte, Picard, Proust, Van Breda, Wahl. Paris: Beauchesne, 1976.
Sacré au saint: Cinq nouvelles lectures talmudiques. Paris: Éditions de Minuit, 1977.

1980s

Dieu qui vient à l'idée. Paris: J. Vrin, 1982.
Ethique et infini: Dialogues avec Philippe Nemo. Paris: Fayard, 1982.
L'au-delà du Verset: Lectures et discours talmudiques. Paris: Editions du Minuit, 1982.
Die Spur des Anderen; Unters. zur Phänomenologie u. Sozialphilosophie. Trans., ed., and introduction by Wolfgang Nikolaus Krewani. Munich: Alber, 1983.
Temps et l'autre. Paris: Presses Universitaires de France, 1983.
Transcendance et intelligibilité: Suivi d'un entretien. Geneva: Labor et Fides, 1984.
Hors sujet. Frontfroide-le-Haut: Fata Morgana, 1987.
A l'heure des nations. Paris: Editions de Minuit, 1988.

1990s

L'oblitération: Entretien avec Françoise Armengaud à propos de l'œuvre de Sosno. Paris: Editions de la Différence, 1990.
Außer sich: Meditationen über Religion und Philosophie. Ed. Frank Miething. Munich: Hanser, 1991.
Entre Nous: Essais sur le penser-à-l'autre. Paris: Bernard Grasset, 1991.
La Mort et le temps. Paris: Libr. Générale Française, 1992.
Dieu: La Mort et le temps. Paris: B. Grasset, 1993.
Liberté et commandement. Saint-Clément-la-Rivière: Fata Morgana, 1994.
Nouvelles lectures talmudiques. Paris: Minuit, 1996.
Quelques réflexions sur la philosophie de l'hitlérisme. Paris: Payot & Rivages, 1997.

2000s

Positivité et transcendance: *Suivi de Levinas et la phénoménologie*. Paris: Presses Universitaires de France, 2000.

Visage de l'autre. Paris: Seuil, 2001.

Paul Celan, de l'être à l'autre. Saint-Clément-la-Rivière: Fata Morgana, 2002.

Seminars and Lectures by Emmanuel Levinas

La Différence comme Non-indifférence: Éthique et altérité chez Emmanuel Levinas; le séminaire du Collège International de Philosophie. Ed. Arno Münster. Paris: Éd. Kimé, 1995.

English Translations of Books by Emmanuel Levinas

1960s

Totality and Infinity: An Essay on Exteriority. Trans. Alphonso Lingis. Pittsburgh, PA: Duquesne University Press, 1969.

1970s

Theory of Intuition in Husserl's Phenomenology. Trans. André Orianne. Evanston, IL: Northwestern University Press, 1973.

Existence and Existents. Trans. Alphonso Lingis. The Hague: Nijhoff, 1978.

1980s

Otherwise Than Being or Beyond Essence. Trans. Alphonso Lingis. Dordrecht, Netherlands: Martinus Nijhoff, 1981.

Ethics and Infinity. Pittsburgh, PA: Duquesne University Press, 1985.

Collected Philosophical Papers. Trans. Alphonso Lingis. Dordrecht, Netherlands: Martinus Nijhoff, 1987.

Time and the Other and Additional Essays. Trans. Richard A. Cohen. Pittsburgh, PA: Duquesne University Press, 1987.

1990s

Difficult Freedom: Essays on Judaism. Trans. Seán Hand. Baltimore, MD: Johns Hopkins University Press, 1990.

Nine Talmudic Readings. Trans. Annette Aronowicz. Bloomington: Indiana University Press, 1990.

Outside the Subject. Trans. Michael B. Smith. London: Athlone, 1993.

Beyond the Verse: Talmudic Readings and Lectures. Trans. Gary D. Mole. Bloomington: Indiana University Press, 1994.

In the Time of the Nations. Trans. Michael B. Smith. Bloomington: Indiana University Press, 1994.

Emmanuel Levinas: Basic Philosophical Writings. Edited by Adriaan T. Peperzak, Simon Critchley, and Robert Bernasconi. Bloomington: Indiana University Press, 1996.

Proper Names. Trans. Michael B. Smith. Stanford, CA: Stanford University Press, 1996.

Discovering Existence with Husserl. Translated and edited by Richard A. Cohen and Michael B. Smith. Evanston, IL: Northwestern University Press, 1998.

Entre Nous: On Thinking-of-the-Other. Trans. Michael B. Smith and Barbara Harshav. New York: Columbia University Press, 1998.

Alterity and Transcendence. Trans. Michael B. Smith. New York: Columbia University Press, 1999.

New Talmudic Readings. Trans. Richard A. Cohen. Pittsburgh, PA: Duquesne University Press, 1999.

Of God Who Comes to Mind. Trans. Bettina Bergo. Stanford, CA: Stanford University Press, 1998.

2000s

God, Death, and Time. Trans. Bettina Bergo. Stanford, CA: Stanford University Press, 2000.

Is It Righteous to Be? Interviews with Emmanuel Levinas. Ed. Jill Robbins. Stanford, CA: Stanford University Press, 2001.

Humanism of the Other. Trans. Nidra Poller. Chicago: University of Illinois Press, 2003.

On Escape: De l'évasion. Trans. Bettina Bergo. Stanford, CA: Stanford University Press, 2003.

Unforeseen History. Trans. Nidra Poller. Urbana: University of Illinois Press, 2004.

Maurice Merleau-Ponty (1908–1961)

Biographical Sketch

Maurice Merleau-Ponty was born March 14, 1908, in Rochefort-sur-Mer, France. His father was killed in World War I, and he and his sister were raised by their mother in Paris. His childhood was happy, and he retained a close connection with his mother. He attended the Lycées Janson-de-Sailly and Louis-le-Grand, entering the École Normale Supérieure in 1926 and graduating in 1930. He began teaching philosophy at high schools in Beauvais, Chartres, and Paris. In 1935, Merleau-Ponty became a junior member of the faculty at the École Normale Supérieure.

Different sources report inconsistent information about the life of Maurice Merleau-Ponty. Information for this biographical sketch was drawn from Taylor Carman and Mark Hansen, eds., *Cambridge Companion to Merleau-Ponty* (Cambridge, UK: Cambridge University Press, 2005); Edward Craig, ed., *Routledge Encyclopedia of Philosophy,* vol. 6 (New York: Routledge, 1998); G. B. Madison, "Merleau-Ponty, Maurice," *The Cambridge Dictionary of Philosophy*, 2nd ed., ed. Robert Audi (Cambridge, UK: Cambridge University Press, 1999); "Maurice Merleau-Ponty," The European Graduate School—http://www.egs.edu/resources/ponty.html (accessed August 17, 2005); "Maurice Merleau-Ponty Main Biography"—www.bookrags.com/ biography/maurice-merleau-ponty (accessed August 17, 2005); Stephen Priest, *Merleau-Ponty* (New York: Routledge, 1998). Photograph courtesy of Mme. Suzanne Merleau-Ponty.

After the Nazi invasion of Poland, Merleau-Ponty entered the French Army. He served as a lieutenant in the infantry and was imprisoned and tortured by the Germans. With the collapse of France he returned to teaching. He completed his *docteur des lettres* based on two dissertations, *La Structure du comportement* (*The Structure of Behavior,* completed in 1938 and published in 1942) and *Phénoménologie de la perception* (*Phenomenology of Perception,* 1945).

Merleau-Ponty became politically active after his service in the military and his experience as a prisoner of war. Merleau-Ponty joined forces with friends Jean-Paul Sartre and Albert Camus in the Socialisme et Liberté resistance group. During this time, Merleau-Ponty disassociated from Catholicism and became an atheist.

In 1945 when the liberation came, Merleau-Ponty joined the faculty as professor of philosophy at the University of Lyons. From 1945 to 1952 he served as unofficial co-editor (with Jean-Paul Sartre) of the journal *Les Temps modernes.* He became disillusioned with the Korean War and Sartrian politics and resigned from the editorial board.

In 1949, Merleau-Ponty accepted the chair of child psychology and pedagogy at the Sorbonne, working with Jean Piaget. In 1952 he took the chair of philosophy at the Collège de France, formerly occupied by Henri Bergson. Merleau-Ponty was the youngest philosopher ever to hold this position, and he retained it until his death.

Maurice Merleau-Ponty died of a heart attack on May 3, 1961. At the time, he was working on a manuscript investigating the relation between what he saw as two distinct phases in his philosophy (*The Visible and the Invisible*). Reconciled with the Catholic Church prior to his death, he was buried with the solemn rites of the church. He is survived by his wife, Suzanne Berthe Jolibois Merleau-Ponty, a physician and psychiatrist, and their daughter, Marianne.

Maurice Merleau-Ponty
Communicative Practice

Algis Mickunas

Introduction

Among the numerous conceptions focused on communicative practice there seems to be no consensus. A Hegelian understanding of labor, as the absolute working of itself through history, requires mediation through ideal concepts. The initial views of Marx, proposing concrete sensuous activity, became absorbed in a system of iron-clad laws of materialistic dialectics. The ideologically practical Americans designed pragmatism and lost it to scientific reductionisms and technical innovations for the solution of concrete challenges. More recently the critical school, prompted by the PRAXIS group, was designed to fill the gap left by previous philosophies between thought and language, language and act. The PRAXIS group consisted of Yugoslavian philosophers who challenged both east and west on the principle that a judgment about a society does not depend on what is written on its flags but what real social, political, and economic relationships obtain among the members of a society. The critical school became more concerned with critiques of other "practical" philosophies and got entangled in moralities, principles, and rules of action, while neglecting communicative activities themselves. The latter are always presumed but constantly left out of account by shifting one's attention toward explanatory causes, statistical curves, phonetic variations, cultural structures, and even social or economic interests. The scientization of communication completely avoids communicative practice and tends toward genetic, physiological, biological, chemical, and even psychological compilations of "empirical" data as the given reality of communication. As a matter of course, major communication departments could buy "database" materials so that the faculty could write papers without having to understand anything about communicative activities. No doubt, communicative practice is extolled as the subject matter of explanation, but it vanishes under the weight of numbers, graphs, and reductionistic explanations. In this sense the practical domain, which was the catalyst for the transformation of philosophy away from homogeneous and all-encompassing conceptual systems, became reduced, and yet elevated to another homogeneous system devoid of the practical.

Another prevalent demand, perhaps less obvious than the loss of communicative praxis, is generating and testing "applied" theory in "real life." This suggests that practical communication is in itself lacking and needs a theory, and that theory is more significant than actual communication. Such claims are possible if one accepts uncritically a tradition that theories, and above all scientific theories, are instrumental in mastering the environment in order to reshape it in terms of human "needs." Communicative applications cannot be taken as an innocent testing of a theory in practical life, since the very theory will transform such a life. By design, theories are metaphysical constructs that have become normative concerning the ways that activities are to be prescribed. This leads to the unquestioned acceptance of metaphysical theories and the presumption of their concreteness. In such an approach, practical communication becomes an embodiment of metaphysical constructs, otherwise it is not communication. Hence the very view of communicative practice is formed along metaphysical, conceptual systems, lending the theoretical constructs an inordinate preeminence against the concrete. One major example of this is the so-called empirical studies, where the metaphysical preeminence of mathematics rules the practical. Practical communication does not consist of numerical formulations and their presumed precision, but is replete with ambiguities, tensions, decisions that have unexplored results, implications, possibilities, and metaphoric variations and extensions.

This state of affairs precludes a discovery of communicative activity that would reflect some pure metaphysical construct, such as mathematical mean, to be applied to all communication as a universal standard. Indeed, such constructs may be intertwined with historical prejudgments, tacit valuations, and explanatory assumptions that need to be explicated at the level of actual engagements in communication—whether the communication is daily activity or scientific practice. Both assume a fundamental communicative awareness that transgresses, pervades, and cannot be subsumed under partial explanations or even a sum of them, such as different disciplines offering their versions of communicative activity. The assumption of such a communicative "level" is not present in some unconscious process—sometimes designated as "cultural unconscious"—or some unrecognized biological drives, but is lived *without* a distance, *without* a position either as subjective or objective.

Before the exposition of this domain of immediacy in the works of Merleau-Ponty, a number of main trends must be avoided that at times tend to suggest that Merleau-Ponty's thesis is identical with one of such trends. This is not to suggest that Merleau-Ponty excludes such trends a priori; rather, his investigations in the domain of communicative practice explicate such trends at a deeper level.

The work of Merleau-Ponty is different from and primordial to such readings of human communication. This discussion will first consider how Merleau-Ponty's work is distinct from the primacy of historical tradition as informing communication. After unraveling quandaries within common assumptions about communication, a discussion of Merleau-Ponty's work addressing the situated and expressive body is offered.

Against the Primacy of Historical Tradition

There is a convergence of opinion that human activities are embedded in an intersubjective and historical horizon of sense, comprising the life world. This convergence is characteristic of hermeneutical and linguistic schools with a pre-vailing claim that communicative practice is founded in historical situatedness of human life, and framed in a particular form of language, interpretation and understanding. In a historical view, it is impossible to extricate experienced phenomena from their historical context and linguistic interpretation to make a universal claim to the primacy of direct awareness of the world. The claims to direct awareness, so goes their argument, forget the fact that phenomena are accessible on a vast buoyancy of a tradition and interpretation which inevitably envelop the individual's experience in an intersubjective, social, and historical context of understanding into which the individual's awareness dissolves. Such a context and language contain common usages, means, norms, rules, customs, prejudgments and a life world. The individual's awareness is a direct example or a representative of such a context. The individual lives, feels, senses, acts and thinks in a sphere of commonality that lends her a world and understanding. Perceptual experience is completely inadequate to account for the much broader linguistic world of a historical tradition. The historical tradition is inexhaustible and is regarded to be as objective as any empirical account of events; it could be called "objective spirit" or "historically effective consciousness." In that view, every coming to awareness and every activity is traditionally and institutionally delimited and specified. This situation supposedly comprises a more encompass-ing and more concrete phenomenological awareness. Individual activity con-sists of a situational application of general modes of prescribed rules, such that the individual is comprehensible as a project within a common understanding. In principle, the historical and linguistic sense interconnections of a common practical activities, given as a form of life and a life world, precede individual engagements in practical communication, and historicality enables the concrete activity as a specification of this encompassing ground. Thus the subject is already intersubjective because of the primacy of historical and linguistic understanding. The individual is situation-bound and transcended by historical horizons that lend the individual a power of transcendence over her own situation.

The sense interconnections must somehow be already in place and under-stood—mainly through educational formation of individuals—if the practical sense of communication is to be grasped and enacted. With the natural language analysts, one could even say that the condition for understanding consists of a convergence of conventions, and meaning can be derived only from such linguis-tic conventions. The issue here is with the "only" and "derived." If one presumes that any activity is understandable only as a derivation from conventions and rules, then one would have to account for interpretations and ambiguities that offer variations of the "same" rule. The variations would have to be attributed to the incompetence of the subject or to one's incorrect use of language, or to another level of language, such as the interpretive dimension. This would mean that we have a dual language, one of correct rules and forms of life, and a second that is always a deviation from such rules and forms. One would have to face the issue of their connection; the rules and forms have a strict and precise life, while their instantiation is couched in a language that is varied, loose, and ambiguous and can never reach the "high" standards of pure grammar. In brief, everyday communication seems to proceed in its own life of ambiguous communication. Neither the presumption—historical, linguistic, social—nor the proposed situated individuation can account for the generality and its specification without assuming that all rules are understood universally as situated. As such, nothing is resolved and the issue of communication is merely postponed.

A somewhat different quandary remains. The historically and linguistically given judgments and forms, present in their intersubjective generality, are understood only situationally, wherein linguistic forms "individuate" and specify such generalities. The use of linguistic forms presupposes a prior understanding of what comprises an individual situation, stemming from another source than the historical and linguistic generalities, since, as already mentioned, one cannot derive a contingent situation from the presumed generality of rules, grammars, and life forms. Recognizing a situation within a frame of rules, grammars, and life forms does not allow for uniqueness. The selectivity of rules and how they are applied in a unique situation must have a more fundamental source in awareness that makes a pregiven language coextensive as a variant that modulates the situation. At the outset the notion of an a priori history and language must be avoided in order not to fall in the problematic of the access of such history and language. If the access is individual and situated, then it would be impossible to claim that one knows the rules, grammar, and form of life as they are in themselves without introducing an encompassing transcendental awareness that is neither historical nor linguistic but purely eidetic subjectivity. The assumed primacy of history and language must exclude the transcendental domain in principle, and thus such theories are left to their own devices to account for the possibility of accessing history and language. In turn, if history and language are an accumulation of situated contingent individual events, then no necessary generalities of rules, grammar, and life forms can be devised. Historical intersubjectivity can be maintained if it is taken at another level of awareness, one that is more concrete than the historically prescribed contingent individuals with their idiosyncratic and psychological functions. Merleau-Ponty demonstrates how a situated actor is intersubjective at a prelinguistic and subhistorical domain of awareness that contains both perceptual generality and singularity, and singular generality, which comprise communicative practice.

Moreover, the claim to rules and forms of life becomes equally problematic with respect to their being "conventions." Allowing for the moment the priority of historical and linguistic domains as the basis for intersubjectivity and the possibility of mutual and general understanding, still we would have to offer an answer to the question concerning the assumption of universality that would result from conventions. In what sense do history and language, in their own right, contain universality when it is a process of specific individual and not repeatable events, and indeed contingent and situated events? After all, there are no continuous councils that sit and form conventions for others to follow. Unless we grant, as we shall see subsequently with Merleau-Ponty, the primacy of the "I can" that accesses and is intertwined with the phenomena prior to history and language as givers of meaning, we shall be running in theoretical circles. The trick of historical and linguistic theses is to take the accessibility of phenomena; reduce it to a historically particular, situated, and incommunicable individual and her awareness; and then charge that such an individual cannot yield universally accessible awareness and communication without being supported by an a priori history and language. Yet by their own theses, historical and linguistic positions are equally particular, situated, and must silently import the primacy of perceptual and situated awareness in order then to discover the generality of the rules governing awareness by a self generating history and language. No doubt, there is historically and linguistically transmitted awareness that may have general characteristics, but the conditions for such transmitted awareness are not solely historical or linguistic. They presuppose perceptual awareness that has its own generality in order to make sense of its ability to locate and transmit the historical and linguistic treasures.

Finally, one must avoid the rage of "culturalism," which is basically a postmodern syndrome where everything is culture and is bound by culturally devised modes of discursive practices. The latter phrase, "discursive practices," is used to designate all sorts of events, from daily gossip about one's relatives through scientific logic, to the very power of language to shape every facet of our lives and the rhetorical confrontations between ideologies, interests, and prejudices. At base, each culture is a formation of a unique discursive practice and cannot be imposed upon another discursive practice without violation and unwarranted imperialism. Each culture has its own rules that allow its members to communicate without obstructions and ambiguities. Outsiders could not comprehend such a communication because their cultural discursive practice is different and the meaning of signs is not the same. At the outset, such understanding precludes cross-cultural communication for the following reasons. First, each person is restricted by the discursive practice of her culture and thus must interpret the discourses of other cultures in terms of her own discursive practice. Second, such an interpretation has no communicative understanding of the others. What the others say is precisely what we say of them. Third, even if we immerse ourselves in and learn the discursive practice of another culture, we could not tell members of our culture what another culture communicates without translating such communication into our own discursive practice and hence interpreting the other in our own cultural discourse. Unintended as this may be, it would still be cultural imperialism. Fourth, the others could not understand us, since they too would have to interpret what we wish to express in their own discursive practice and be equally, although unintentionally, imperialistic. Fifth, the notion that each culture has a unique discursive practice belongs to a particular culture's discursive practice and hence cannot be a universal claim without becoming imperialistic. If there is no awareness that transgresses cultural boundaries, then cross-cultural communication makes no sense unless one were to presume some metaphysical sense of universal human nature. But this presumption is excluded by the thesis that each culture's discursive practice determines one's perception of the world, including one's metaphysical pronouncements. For solutions to these quandaries we must turn to the work of Merleau-Ponty and his groundbreaking contributions to the understanding of communicative practice.

The Situated Body

The unfolding of communicative practice with Merleau-Ponty will require analyses of various levels of structural and active corporeity and the constitution of the phenomenal field wherein such structures and activities intertwine. These analyses are required to disclose active generalities prior to brute facts and generalized structures. Such active generalities will lay the ground for understanding the meaning of situation, intersubjectivity, and individuality as inseparable correlates and the institutions of practical, communicative technologies. This does not imply that the different levels function separately, but only that the mode of presentation requires their separate analyses. No doubt, numerous thinkers have extolled the theoretical need to consider the primacy of corporeity and even of instrumental interconnections of implements as functions in a system of significations in all thinking, but Merleau-Ponty demonstrates such interconnections to be all-pervasive phenomena of corporeal interaction with the world of phenomena, and intercorporeal communication about such phenomena. One should note that traditional communication theories, premised as they are on language, grammar, codes, senders and receivers, messages and interpreters, are concerned with meaning. And meaning is usually ascribed to the function of the subject. For Merleau-Ponty the phenomena of our active engagements are inescapably meaningful, requiring no subject to project meaning on an indifferent world. Hence, in his work, communicative practice includes meanings that comprise the experienced world. Here subject and object, subject and subject, become redundant, even if interesting residua of traditional metaphysics.

Merleau-Ponty takes to task the above-suggested theories of communicative practice on the basis of the primacy of engaged bodily perception, which is always oriented toward, and intertwined with, the phenomenal field. The phenomenal field consists of various levels, first of which is its diacritical or differentiated character. Every aspect of the experienced field, such as a specific color, signifies other colors in the field and thus has a meaning in a mutually signifying interconnection. The bright yellow is bright because it is next to the dull green, and the latter is dull due to the shadow cast across it by the tree. In this sense, the phenomena mean, signify, not by being discrete components—since such components are never given anyway—but in a differential process wherein meaning obtains between phenomena. The importance of field perception is the abolition of the prejudgment of discrete empirical components whose meaning must be derived from a subject by all sorts of metaphysical tricks, such as an association of one discrete phenomenon with another in temporal sequence. There is an assumed dualism wherein the phenomena are meaningless data, and the mind's operations add meaning to such data. Merleau-Ponty shows that prior to such dualistic division, the phenomena have a field—lateral—meaning, while our engagement with the field in perceptual bodily activity is a process of communication with the communicating phenomena. This must be emphasized: if meaning is the basic aspect of communication, then we find that the phenomena with which we are engaged are equally meaningful, signifying, involving our gestures that too are meaningful insofar as they trace the phenomena in the field. The notion that there could be a pure phenomenon having no lateral signification, such as the color blue, is equally impossible; the blue has a depth differentiation: it is never homogeneous, but is hazy, deep, brilliant, cold, light, and thus defies the assumption of purity. Or this gray is the gray of an old carpet, it is shabby gray moving toward black in an evening light. The nonsensical claim that if we remove the evening light, the old carpet, the shabby look, then we would get to the real gray, is nowhere to be found.

The depiction of the primacy of the communicative field phenomena also involves an active body as kinesthetic, whose basic rule is "I can," interactive with the field without having any need for a postulated ego. Here Merleau-Ponty challenges the notion of the body as a physiological sum of discrete and located functions, such as distinct senses. Functions of the body are summarized by physiologists using the phrase "constancy hypothesis." Their assumption is that given any discrete phenomenon, there is a discrete one-to-one reaction. This means that the subject as bodily can be deciphered by located inputs and outputs, thus leading to the notion that communication can be broken down into discrete bits of data that impact specific regions of physiology. These regions, in turn, react in discrete functions: a precise stimulus-response syndrome. As already suggested, perceptual awareness cannot be decomposed into discrete moments, and thus no analyses can yield the presumed constancy. Moreover, bodily engagement with phenomena is a continuous and overlapping perceptual explication of what the phenomena imply, suggest, and require in lateral and depth significations. The engaged and communicative body, the "I can," plays out its role beneath the objective and subjective bodies, since both can be articulated and located only on the already established field of bodily activities. Merleau-Ponty opens a domain of bodily engagement with the world that is both situational and accessible, a sort of intermediary between the presumed discrete data and the physiological body, between language with its rules, concepts, and compacted/overlapping ambiguous field meanings.

At the outset, body situatedness is not identical with being in homogeneous space-time location as a physiologically inert object. Purely objective analysis of a body's physiology could not decipher what is up-down, left-right, front-back without introducing the asymmetrical process of orientations of phenomena understood by bodies engaged in the field of phenomena. Homogeneous world and physiological analysis of a body cannot account for orientations, directions, places, leeways, and open horizons; such analyses consist of an indifferent system of points wherein any body in such a world must be reduced to occupying an indifferent point that communicates no directions, coordinations, or awareness of one thing's being behind or above another thing. The moment we say that the distance from here to there is fifty feet, we have introduced an oriented body which communicates an entire dynamic system in constant transition that is asymmetrical, capable of signifying phenomena in terms of at least six orientational directions. The lived, experiencing body signifies the very structure of the practical world of directions, vectors, locations, and relationships. This asymmetry defies homogeneity and communicates one major background awareness on whose structure phenomena assume locations, distances, and orientations which are not "subjective" impositions but are directly perceivable as practical communication by others.

The oriented, practical body functions in such a way that the directions are not completely exchangeable. What is up front, reachable by a forward movement, is distinct from what is in the back, and the latter is present as a virtual continuation of the forward movement, best reached in directional reversal. The same can be said of left-right orientations, which in many cases can overlap when reaching for something that requires both hands. The up-down is equally a coordinate movement which anyone can read as their own movement. The traditionally conceived structure of practical activity concerned with ends-mean relationship would be impossible without the assumption that we communicate such ends-means on the background of the oriented body as a mobile field of functions.

The oriented space is communicated from a center, from a here that is not a special point but a leeway of adjustments to a mobile and shifting there. That is why one "there" can be exchanged for another "there," but neither can be exchanged for a "here." The "here" is always a kinesthetic figure in the field of orientations. Orientation is prior to any stimulus-reaction syndrome, since the latter does not reveal directional movement—although directional movement is assumed in any discourse about stimulation, such as coming from the left, slightly from above, or from the rear. This background bodily orientation is the very architectonic of our social environment. Buildings have their fronts and backs, up stairs and down stairs, their sides, and even their hierarchical social allocations: the top floor is for the top executive, with lower floors for lesser beings on the upward ladder of success. Our vehicles have front and rear seats, our bus drivers suggest that we move to the rear of the bus, communicating the very meaning of our oriented bodies. We move forward to face the future and leave the past behind, favoring the frontal movement not only as spatial, but also as temporal orientation. We not only move from here to there, but from now to then, and open new "frontiers." This forward activity is circumspective, taking planning into account, leaving behind, and looking forward. The language of history and goals is situated in the prevalence of frontal orientation. The human looks ahead to better days, participates in the forward movement of history, of progress, faces the tasks of today and tomorrow and leaves the troubled past behind. The very language of overcoming, surpassing, and transcending is a frontal language. This suggests that the conceptions of history, interpretation, situation, and context require a functional lived body with its asymmetrical activities. Even the so-called "theoretical" discourses cannot escape the perceptual bodily field. We speak of "higher" forms of discourse only to discover a variant of vertical bodily orientation. We have beings that are "above" the mere plane of human life, or those who are "beneath" us, and thus take our bodily orientations with us. The communicative point is that our direct engagement with the world of phenomena is not dependent on some linguistic interpretation, giving us rules of action, directions, and manuals about how to perform tasks, but primarily on body signification as it moves and interacts with phenomena. Indeed, the body significations are inescapable in any discourse as the very fabric of communication.

The practical world, intertwined with the communicative body, is not identical with the immediacy of the perceived world. The practical world opens the perceptual world, and yet the "I can" reveals a general set of processes that comprise a bodily background for practical communication across diverse perceptual regions. The practical world opens an oriented structure in correlation to other places and regions of the world. Whether we leave our home behind to go to work, or we leave the North American continent behind to travel to Africa, we have a direct awareness of this bodily background that anyone can "read" and understand, as we can read and understand their activities. This also implies the immediate awareness of looser and tighter spaces and times, of time distances, such as "how long to Nairobi," and its open horizons. This means that any situation, as body in communication, is already aware of the perceptual world as oriented with many other places, and our ability to be there and communicate at this direct level.

The oriented space is intertwined with a temporal field which is equally dynamic and flexible. The first clue to such a field can be gleaned from the awareness usually designated as memory. For Merleau-Ponty memory is communicated by the perceived phenomena. One wakes up in the morning to see that the back yard is strewn with broken branches, clusters of leaves, and puddles, and one readily pronounces, "I see the last night's storm." Last night is not in the past but is a temporal depth of the experienced phenomena. But "last night" can also be shifted to "today." "Today I have a number of tasks to perform," provides a temporal field wherein the passing hours and accomplished tasks still mark the temporal field "today." It could as well be "this week" or any other temporal field within which events are marked.

As a situation, the perceiving body is both singular and communicates generalities that mediate between conceptual terms, historically sedimented intersubjective rules, and the objects of sedimented awareness. This is to say, the understanding of laws, linguistic rules, prescripts, and prejudgments makes sense in a situation because the situation itself is not a brute fact but traces a corporeal generality which is not quite in accord with the purity of conceptual constructs, but which is not idiosyncratically singular. The acting body can be loosened up or tightened for a focused task, can approximate but never reach the conceptual ideal, and thus can open up the ideal to variations. An activity toward a goal can limit itself to very select means and a narrow interpretation of the goal, or it can relax and regard the means as fluctuating and the goal open to various temporal horizons. The lived body, as a situation, allows for tightening and loosening of the situation and hence of establishing a flexible space and time both for itself and the phenomena with which it is involved. Practical objects and functions, inclusive of bodily activities, have oriented spaces and thus can communicate to others the way the phenomenal field is composed *and* the way the activities are composed by the field. The place of something practical depends on the sedimented body habits of the acting subject. Something is placed "there" and is accessible to required activities. An object of practical use is not located at a point of a homogeneous space, but in a place with a slack that allows shifts without the object's leaving its place. The object is on the table, in the shop, next to the bridge, to the right of the forest and can be reached by an arm, taking a walk, using a vehicle and narrowing of the place. This sort of practical world orientation is the communicative ground of any life world: If one says that one is going to the shop, one cannot give a geometric grid with precise points but must resort to communicating a generality of the situation that is accessible to others but never in precisely the same way. Such communication involves the identity of the "I can" by others insofar as they too can do similar activities of going to the same or different places.

The bodily perceptual engagement in a field does not imply that the field is pregiven in a spread of an abstract objective space and time continuum requiring only a detached and indifferent surveyance and recording. One's engagement is rather an active interrogation of and being interrogated by the intersecting and overlapping phenomena. Each movement shifts the field as the field shifts—each movement requiring a constant answer to the field implications of what is next to something, behind something, around and in front of something. This very interactive process with the phenomena involves selectivity and focus wherein emerges a diacritical relationship between background and figure, each signifying one another in their difference. While moving with the phenomenal field we communicate our focus on something and allow the rest of the field to form a background, which also is focused upon what we have selected as a figure. The background is thus not passive but communicative. While I position myself on this side of a table, the chair on the other side, the potted plant on the left, the book shelf on the right, the floor beneath and the ceiling above signify this table from all perspectives. My focusing movement on this table would not be possible if the background did not equally signify by focusing on the table from different perspectives. In turn, while positioning myself toward the table, I am also positioned by the background as being on this side. In brief, the thing in the field I focus upon and the forming background equally signify me as an aspect of the field that provides another perspective. While situating something in the field, I am also being situated by the field. Thus while communicating my orientation toward the foregrounded phenomenon, I and the entire environment communicate the phenomenon from all sides and communicate my position. The experiencer is not an abstract entity but is always situating and situated by the field context in lateral and depth signification.

The positioned body is not to be understood physiologically or above all statically. Pervading sensory fields and the orientational system is the "I can" as kinesthetic process that allows one to orient all sensory fields. The very visual focusing on something is a forward movement without which the visual (and other sensory fields for that matter) could not be oriented. The kinesthetic process comprises a background field from which specific signifying gestures emerge as foreground in a way that both the signifying gesture that focuses on some field phenomenon and the kinesthetic background mutually communicate their difference. This means that the continuous orientation toward the field and the selectivity of specific phenomena as foreground require a focusing of a gesture on the background of bodily movement. One's bodily movement positions the gesture for maximum access to the phenomenon that is being foregrounded.

It is interesting to note that the backgrounding movement, the "I can," is what correlates to the background field phenomena; while the chair behind the table communicates the other side, my movements inhabit that chair in such a way that I can be in that location from which my gestures could focus on this table from the other side. While my bodily gesture is positioned and situated, the background body transcends the positionality toward more, toward the background field and inhabits it by communicating what it can do. And what it can do is assume the position of any other thing either actually or virtually and thus articulate the thing of focus in other ways. The background body may introduce a wonder to explore the other side and hence redeploy the focus of gestures which trace the implications of what is focused upon. This means that a simple wondering solicits the composition of gestures that will meet and articulate phenomena by bringing them into focus in the foreground. The reason that the encountered phenomena will be continuously articulated by our bodily communicative gestures is that the phenomenal field is never a discrete sum of data; rather it is ambiguous with lateral differentiations, overlappings, and depth solicitations. Hence the "I can" as movement constitutes some gestures as selective of some aspects of the field and delimits them as the focus of current interest.

The term "overlapping" has various senses, among which the most pronounced are, first, that the phenomena in the field not only signify other phenomena, but also spread perceptual meaning one over the others. This red is a bright red of revolutionary flags, red of violence and passion, shadowy red of spilled blood and budding roses. The glittering green of a field overlaps with the solar flood and the protruding shadows between the blades of grass. Second, the body gestures take over each other's functions by extending and varying one another, by bracing and supporting one another, and by forming a background for each other. Third, the overlapping of sensory fields, comprising synesthetic communication among them, defy the localization of perception in a homogeneous space and time wherein each sense would have its location. The loud colors, the colorful sounds, the shocking storm, the cold blue, the irritating touch, all reveal that each sensory field overlaps with other fields in mutual communication. One must not conclude that such perceptions are determined and thus explainable by linguistic metaphors. In communicative practice language is equally an open field that intertwines with, overlaps, varies, and extends our bodily gestures, expressions, and positions. If a woman is asked how to get to a certain place in a town, she will begin to point in a specific direction, gesture that after a block one must turn left, while the attendant words, selected from a linguistic field, will extend the gestures in more complex ways without leaving the situation to become some sort of supervening structure imposed from outside. Language is not an abstract set of defined terms but an extension that overlaps with bodily gestures and comprises lateral and depth horizons. The linguistic variation and extension of bodily gestures is also an extension of the phenomenal field, not in some arbitrary fashion but by the very field significations that interrogate our perceptual engagement and thus open more in linguistic meaning than was initially suspected. Moreover, our perceptual abilities are extended through things and others. The blind person is not incapacitated, because she can "see" the surface, the bumps, the contours of a path, at the end of a walking stick. For Merleau-Ponty this overlapping of touch over vision is not located in some immanent brain function but takes place in the activity of the body, which translates one sensory field into another without mediation.

The differentiation which forms perceptual meaning is not introduced by a subject but is always a field function, a pregnant origin. To bring forth a figure from the background perception is productive insofar as it traces what is available in the pregnancy of the field. This field genesis entwines activity and passivity, and the percipient discovers and equally traces what is already inscribed in the perceptual field, thus discarding the primacy of the subject. The figure that emerges with perception is not a determinate phenomenon but a vector of the world on whose pivot other vectors are equally intertwined and communicated. In this sense, while tracing and communicating a vector, we also are dispossessed of the "more" in the field and can be challenged by others concerning our inadequacy in providing a totalizing picture. This is the source of communicative creativity and cannot be closed by any grammar or accustomed categorization that presumes fixed meanings.

We speak of seeing "black" and "white" and even attach cultural terms to them, such as "good" and "evil" or "light" and "dark," and extend such fixed meanings to all sorts of light metaphors, such as "in light of pure reason." Merleau-Ponty notes that these categorical conveniences cannot pretend to be representations of our perceptual experience. It is physically impossible to see black or white; perceptually we see shiny, vibrant, dull, somber, crumbling, ruffled, impenetrable, wherein no such "black" in itself ever appears. The same can be said of all the colors in the so-called spectrum. Moreover, such perceptual richness cannot be accounted for by metaphoric language or some form of analogization. Analogies, likenings, are aspects of practical communication between bodily activities and world. In face of a task, such as pounding a peg into the ground, one searches for appropriate means to perform such a task. One may pick up a stone, a larger piece of wood, or a hammer and recognize its feel. Here the categorical distinctions between stone, wood, and hammer sink into the background, where each becomes an analog of the other through the exploring hand and eye. It can be contended that most of our tasks are performed by bodily activities engaged in analogical awareness. Hence, our accustomed communication, based on historically accumulated language, is interrogated by the phenomenal field. The world speaks a silent and meaningful language that no coded language can adequately capture.

This is not to say that language is not important for Merleau-Ponty. Language is a field of sedimented meanings that inhabit the very phenomena of perception. Moreover, language forms its own density, in which meaning remains embedded as an indefinite difference among accumulated differences. Linguistic meaning resists complete clarity of expression, and thus language as such can never be made an object of exhaustive analyses by some "metalanguage" and its formal rules. Within the density of language, sedimented meanings form a crust that resists the spontaneity of perceptual engagement and the creative language. One could say that such a crust forms a surface discourse that has lost its creative and interrogative origins in perceptual life. Sedimented language is well-suited to overlap with sedimented body activity that becomes anonymous. As body inhabits a particular task, attention must be directed to specific functions that relate to specific aspects of the environment. While learning how to drive a car, one must shift gears, press pedals, steer the wheels, watch the traffic, and read signs. Within a brief period one settles into the functions of the car and assumes a sedimented body of a driver who is completely geared to all functions of the car and all structures and shifts in the environment. The body becomes the "habit" of the car, as it can also become the habit of an apartment where there is no need to deliberately look for places or things. Indeed, sedimented language overlaps very easily with body habits and its communicative meanings are taken for granted.

Such sedimented bodies are the very fabric of cultural communication. The rituals we perform even in walking styles, in sacred sites, in commercial environments, are cultural body styles. There is no cultural or cross-cultural communication that would be "disembodied." It is equally important to stress that the sedimented and encrusted layer of comportment and speaking do not determine perceptual awareness absolutely; they are always loosened by perceptual horizons and depths and thus obtain a character of creativity. Participation in communication is a creative venture, and it is always a practical and engaged venture where language and perceptual meanings overlap. But for Merleau-Ponty, language and perceptual meanings overlap with another communicative and all-pervasive experiential domain: being bodily as expressive communication. This domain, for Merleau-Ponty, comprises the final abolition of all variants of metaphysical dualisms.

The Expressive Body

From all that has been said it is obvious that any dualistic theory becomes redundant, specifically where a division is made between inner mind, psyche or subject, and outer body. Such a division would mean that the body is a mechanical process signifying, in some mysterious ways, the internal states, such as emotions, thoughts, and drives. No metaphysical tricks, so far, have been able to demonstrate a connection between inner and outer without assuming the immediate involvement in the awareness of expression. Just as we do not experience some "pure" datum, neither do we experience some material body whose contortions could be deciphered concerning inner feelings, desires, and wants. Even to speak of a blank face is to speak of expression. Communication in the bodily domain defies all the postmodern theories of experience as mediated by discourses, and defies deconstructive theories that claim that there is no direct presence of the "given" since the latter can be abolished by the rule of difference (i.e., every given is a trace of a difference between the so-called given and the absent). But as we noted, Merleau-Ponty already established that there is no given that is not involved in a field of overlapping differences, both laterally and in depth. All such proposals are still variations of a dualistic world, implicit in the primacy of language and historical prejudgments.

If the dualistic thesis leads to blind alleys, then the only alternative is to argue for the immediacy of expression, for the immediate presence of joy, sorrow, indifference, anger, and above all eroticism, expressed as bodily activities and gestures. The corporeal expression will have to be read not anatomically, but as a meaningful presence that is understandable for us and by others. If the returning hero were asked about the facial and postural physiology of his beloved, who in a crowd gave him a passionate look, he would be unable to report the specific physiological features and changes which took place. She in turn could not reproduce at will the physiological requirements which would reveal the passionate expression. What this means is that in human encounter there are no pure physiological data, the so-called external body, and hence no need for analogization or projection. The corporeal expression, thus, must speak directly. It has long been noted that even an infant of seven or eight months answers with comfort and pleasure to a smile and with fear to a terrifying expression. Moreover, the infant can respond to a terrifying or pleasant voice, even if the direct physiological characteristics of the producer of the voice are not bodily present, e.g., if the speaker is in another room.

The problem with dualistic theories is that they have detached the appearance from its sense, the expression from its direct presence, and attempted to reconstruct it theoretically from physiological and anatomical elements. The point is that expression is a sense unit and the sense is the very bodily expression. Bodily expression, in short, makes sense. Any theory which purports to explain expression in terms of other components, such as theoretical constructs, presupposes expression as obvious and as a criterion by which to judge or "interpret" the physiological or anatomic elements. Since this presupposition cannot be explained in terms of any dualistic theory, then the immediacy of expression is the sole position which makes sense. Thus body movements and gestures, postures and shapes, are not signs of something hidden, but make communicative sense. Sense is bodily expressivity. If there are theories that attempt to challenge foundationalism, they cannot in any wise abolish communicative processes as present in expression. To deny the latter is at the same time to assume it as the condition for the possibility of one's experience of others. Indeed, body expressivity is broader than the immediate presence of others. Expressions may be embodied in institutionalized ways wherein texts, religious rituals, political edicts, and moral injunctions carry the force of expressivity understood directly by body subjects.

One could object that the immediacy of expression would preclude mistakes, yet as a matter of fact we do make mistakes. Indeed, but the errors are corrected not by analogical inferences or objectivations, the correct deciphering of physiological signs, but in terms of other expressions. Expressive sense is dynamic, constantly flowing and overlapping with body gestures and configurations, and hence does create ambiguities. Yet the rejection of the primacy and immediacy of expression and the ability to experience its sense is tantamount to rejection of thinking or perceptual experience simply because we make mistakes in thinking and in perceptual experience. Thinking can correct the mistakes of thought and perceptual experience can correct the mistakes of perception. If corporeal expressions were founded on dualism, then they would be arbitrary and local, having no universal style, no accessibility to "outsiders," and ultimately reducible to the privacy of the subject.

We must add that there is one more thesis which maintains that expressions are intellectually mediated, i.e., mediated by culturally instituted habits and conventions. Expressions are learned and hence local. This cultural thesis is an extension of the same dualistic metaphysics of mind and body. The cultural-mental constructs are the ways that we interpret the mechanical motions and anatomical relationships of bodies and hence attach expressive sense to bodies that do not exhibit any expression in themselves. This is to say, our seeing the expressions of other bodies means that we see indifferent mechanical processes, which become signs of culturally constructed expressive meanings.

The argument for this cultural dualism uses the method of variation. Thus, it is said that in distinct cultures distinct and various bodily gestures are used to reveal the same expression, such as an indifferent shrugging off of an accusation in one culture, and a stony passivity revealing the same indifference in another. Due to this difference in corporeal postures, one could argue that the corporeal expressions are learned, are mediated by thought, and hence must be seen as signs of interior states or of culturally acquired interpretation of behavior. The following arguments would indicate the inadequacy of that thesis: (1) While physiological and material media may be varied, they can capture the same expression. The universality of expression is attested by the fact that it is capable of appearing through various media; thus, writings, paintings, music, body gestures, sculptures, as different media, can reveal the same expressive sense and content. (2) Expressive sense remains even if we cannot read it due to a particular mode of capturing it in a particular culture. Indeed, the media may mislead us and we may be compelled to correct our perception through learning; yet the correction assumes an immediate presence of expression over impression. (3) If expression is identical with the physiological changes and sense-data experiences learned within a particular culture, then expression is either abolished or subjectivated. If it is abolished, then no physiological changes would make sense; if subjectivated, then we are back to mind-body dualism. The cultural alternative, in turn, cannot explain expression. If the cultural thesis is correct, it is still the case that expression must communicate directly and not as something that is attached to reified bodies. The expressive phenomena that supposedly belong to a culture must communicate expressive meaning. If cultures are intellectual constructs, then they cannot possess expressivity. But if cultures do possess expressivity, then we return to the primacy of expression over cultural constructs, such that the cultural constructs themselves become bearers of expressive sense. In brief, if bodies are signs of culturally constructed expressions, then the selection of signs requires a direct awareness of expression in order to make sense of the signs. (4) One could argue that the learning of expressions is not mediated through cultures or thought, but reinforced through other expressive gestures and actions. It is not the case that a parent says to a child, "when I make this facial contortion, it means I am angry, and therefore when you want to let me know that you are angry, you must in turn make a similar contortion." This of course would require that both stand in front of some reflecting surface in order to ascertain that the contortions are similar. Moreover, this would already assume that we understand the sense of the contortions if any comparisons between them are to be made.

One could maintain then that what we learn is not the expressive aspect, but the bearer of expression. But to learn the bearer, we must have the experience of expression. The theory of learning the bearer of expression assumes a dualism and all of its attendant problems *and* must assume the primacy of expression and its experience in order to talk about the means of expression. This assumption, of course, leads us back to the same conclusion, namely, the immediacy of the experienced expression and its inseparability from the bearer, the active body. In this sense the distinctions between the bearer and expression, between learning and immediacy, are undercut. Also surpassed is the notion of a corporeity that is a physiology distinct from expressivity. To be corporeal is to be expressive, and to be expressive is to be corporeal. If the characterization of expressive meaning once belonged to the mind, with Merleau-Ponty we can say that the very meaningful expressions of corporeity abolish dualism.

Every corporeal gesture, every movement, forms a continuity, producing a variant of itself and prolonging itself into a schema. An adjustment to one expressive configuration is an adjustment to a series of like configurations, where expressed desire can be desire expressed by anyone and in anything. If my expressed desire is a variant among other possible expressions of desire, then it is equivalent to and interchangeable with them. The particular expressions pass, but in passing they create a schema for continuation, proliferation, and repetition. While inhering in individual gesture, a display of active corporeity, expression transcends the boundaries of anatomical individuality and captures others in its mood. This "being captured by," "being moved by" expression, is well depicted in such phenomena as desire and eroticism, where one is transfigured, elevated, ennobled, and, at times, degraded. One way that the social communicative power of expression is depicted by enlarged images can be gleaned from myths. While all humans engage in rituals that appeal to all sorts of unseen powers, the latter are ineffective if they would be merely ideological constructs. Rather, rituals are an intensive concentration of expressive characteristics: they love, they hate, threaten with horrible punishments, demand our passionate commitments and our bodily gestures of self-effacement and subjection. Mythological figures are depictions of expressive communication that goes beyond the location of such figures.

Expressivity in myths pervades the universe. There is no dry, geometric space in bodily experience and communication; this aspect is seen in the pagan depiction of mythical figures. When one is confronted by the expressive characterizations describing, for example, Aphrodite, one finds a description of bodily moods across all events and things. The tenderness of everything calls to enchantment, to embrace, to the sweet breathtaking flow of all into all—an expression manifest across all things as attractive and harmonious. And she is the feminine, contrasted to Artemis. This goddess is the soul, the expression of wildness with its heights and depths, with her animals and tormenting beauty, with her rejecting look and maternal care, and her blood-lusting hunt—lust, playfulness, tenderness, bright glory, inaccessibility and horror—expressive characteristics. What the mythical figures suggest is the generality and individuality of expressive body.

Expressive generality proliferates and can inhabit anything, and can be manifest across the face of all events without being reducible to such events. Hence mythical figures are depicted as transcending the characterization of things in their anatomical properties; yet as manifestations of expressivity, the figures are inner-worldly. In this sense, mythic figures are a way of capturing the expressive corporeal process without any reduction to anatomy or physiology. Such a process can appear everywhere: in the faces of statues, where the great utopian dreams of days to come are inscribed in the uplifted postures of the "revolutionary" classes; the victories shine from the canvasses, tensed with fierce steeds and proud warriors, while the defeats are spread across the canvas in prostrate bodies—all corporeal expressions.

The expressive power of corporeity not only is communicated across the gestures of other bodies, but also provides a locus of transformations from one expressive modality to another—from direct vision, audible styles and rhythms, to institutionalized records of writing, where the same proud posture, the haughty gaze, the same sorrow of defeat, pervade the volumes of poetry, literature, and even cultic rituals. This is the same expressive power manifest in the Greek movement toward theocentrism, the pagan "enthusiasm," with arms spread and open toward the sky, and the Christian despatialization and slavish submission in kneeling and prostration. From the donning of the mask, angry or benevolent, to the solemn magic of transforming wine into blood and bread into flesh, expressive characteristics are manifest directly and move the experiencer—prior to intellectualization—by communicating a mood which spreads without respect to the otherwise indifferent "reality." In this sense, corporeal expressivity is the condition for social communication.

Corporeal expressivity, in brief, can assume any "embodiment," since it is not something "interior" or subjective, but rather directly present, inner-worldly and yet transcendent of materiality. This transcendence is precisely what is capable of affecting us, although the expressive dimension is primarily the direct dynamics of an active, corporeal being. The affectivity is not an intentional act stemming from an interiority of a subject, but a medium of expressivity, which comprises the very sense of gestures and is transmitted through gestures, postures, and mobile face and limbs. This means that expression is not so much faced or confronted as participated in and lived through. Bodily expression is like the "lively" tune which sends our limbs into frenzy, or the Dionysian tragedy sending horror across the faces of the audience. The horror is a spontaneous expression of being moved, being gripped by a presence where what does the gripping and the being gripped are one. When the husband of one's lover shakes an angry fist, one does not ask whether he has some internal feeling of anger; the anger is the very expressive gesture that spreads its force for all to see.

This conception of expressivity abandons not only the inner-outer dualism, but also the distinction between our corporeal expressivity and its characterization, and the expressivity manifest among the experienced phenomena: the fearsome storm and the fear forming across the face participate in one expressive movement; the lonely night and the lonely heart, the bright morning and the sparkling eye, converge in the medium of expressivity, which does not lend itself into separations. In terms of Merleau-Ponty's notion of meaning, meaning is no longer an anthropocentric projection of the human; we find more meaning than we can project, we find more expressions than we can project by any constructed theoretical explanation. While attempting to radiate an expressive joy across the morning sun and the shimmering treetops, we are drawn into the morning glory and find ourselves moved with its expressive presence. This suggests that we are in constant communication with each other and with the world through direct participation in the excessive sensuality of ourselves and worldly events.

One major aspect of corporeal expressivity is the sensuality of erotic desire. The logic of communication of this desire may well constitute a standard for all expressive social communication. Erotic desire communicates itself in the sense that it desires the other not as a physiological entity, but as the other's desire. In brief, it desires to be desired. The intimacy of mutual expressivity and intensification suggests that erotic desire feeds on erotic desire, that it creates an atmosphere from which one cannot easily extricate oneself, run away, and cease to communicate. After all, desire as expressivity transcends bodily anatomy toward kinesthetic figuration and refiguration as expressive, and spreads its general scheme as an inescapable presence. One cannot turn away from it, and all the sensory fields, from vision through touch, all gestures, are pervaded by its troubles. Desire elevates and torments, promises and denies, and in the denial promises more. No wonder that most diverse cultures take erotic expressivity most seriously, even if playfully.

The general scheme that erotic desire comprises leads directly to the ways that erotic communication shifts to ambiguities and leads to numerous collapses of communication. If one desires the desire of another, and if such a desire makes all events desirable and indeed desiring, then any deflation anywhere and any time will be a deflation of everywhere and at all times. When a loved one returns home late at night and announces, "I am sorry, but I do not love you any more," the detraction of desire for the other's desire means that the entire world collapses into an indifferent, remote, meaningless sum of objects. Not only that this person no longer loves me, but my mother, my dog, and even god never loved me. Indeed, no one loves me, and the universe is cold and indifferent. Of course, indifference is just as much an expressive mood as any other expression, and a person is captured by it. The expressive domain is unavoidable in any communication, even when the latter pretends to be "cool and rational." Many a speaker, defending reason, does so with conviction and passion in order to envelop his audiences in the mood and seriousness of being rational. The expressive body cannot be betrayed by speakers posturing in a particular way.

Postscript

Merleau-Ponty unfolds a phenomenology of practical communication that is constantly worldly, situated, and yet equally open to the generality, style, and movement formations of engaged corporeity. In fact, the various metaphysical quests to extricate perception from the world by positing a separate subject, who then must prove the validity of perception by formal arguments, are, for Merleau-Ponty, the most fascinating inventions that have never accomplished their task. What is significant with Merleau-Ponty's analyses is that the basic medium of communication are the phenomena that solicit our tacit participation and interrelationships. In this sense, we do not face one another and attempt to decipher some inner meaning projected through some devised medium, so that the receiver would attempt to make sense of the medium and the meaning it carries. We communicate through the worldly, perceptual phenomena and the way we intertwine, are enveloped, and participate in the world. When a friend calls me across the street and gestures for me to come over to look at some paintings in a shop, she begins to be impatient by my delay, and her gestures, her bodily comportment, spread her impatience across my unwilling movements until finally I gesture my submission and go to look at the paintings. In short, we communicate through the oriented and kinesthetic space on whose background figures of our focus and attention emerge, to lift out figures in the phenomenal field with never a final say, never a final depiction of what these backgrounds and figures mean. If there are any theories of intersubjective communication, they would have to be primarily intercorporeal and worldly mediated.

Bibliography of Works

Books by Maurice Merleau-Ponty

1940s

La Structure du comportement. Paris: Presses Universitaires de France, 1942.

Phénoménologie de la perception. Paris: Gallimard, 1945.

Humanisme et terreur: Essai sur le problème communiste. Paris: Gallimard, 1947.

1950s

Les Sciences de l'homme et la phénoménologie. Paris: Centre de Documentation Universitaire, 1953.

Les Aventures de la dialectique. Paris: Gallimard, 1955.

Philosophes célèbres. Paris: L. Mazenod, 1956.

Signes. Paris: Gallimard, 1960.

Le Visible et l'invisible: Suivi de notes de travail. Ed. Claude Lefort. Paris: Gallimard, 1964.

Éloge de la philosophie et autres essais. Paris: Gallimard, 1965.

Sens et non-sens. Paris: Ed. Nagel, 1965.

Das Auge und der Geist: Philosophische Essays. Ed. and trans. Hans Werner Arndt. Hamburg: Rowohlt, 1967.

L'union de l'âme et du corps chez Malebranche: Biran et Bergson. Ed. Jean Deprun. Paris: J. Vrin, 1968.

La Prose du monde. Ed. Claude Lefort. Paris: Gallimard, 1969.

1970s

Existence et dialectique. Paris: Presses Universitaires de France, 1971.

Relations avec autrui chez l'enfant. Paris: Centre de Documentation Universitaire, 1975.

1980s

Le Primat de la perception et ses conséquences philosophiques: Précédé de projet de travail sur la nature de la perception (1933) et La Nature de la perception (1934). Grenoble: Cynara, 1989.

Seminars and Lectures by Maurice Merleau-Ponty

L'union de l'âme et du corps chez Malebranche, Biran et Bergson: Notes prises au Cours de Maurice Merleau-Ponty à L'École Normale Supérieure (1947–1948). Ed. Jean Deprun. Paris: J. Vrin, 1997.

Merleau-Ponty à la Sorbonne: Résumé de cours 1949–1952. Grenoble: Cynara, 1988.

Parcours: 1935–1951. Ed. Jacques Prunair. Lagrasse: Verdier, 1997.

Causeries (1948). Ed. Stéphanie Ménasé. Paris: Editions du Seuil, 2002.

Psychologie et pedagogie de l'enfant: Cours de Sorbonne, 1949–1952. Lagrasse: Verdier, 2001.

Parcours Deux, 1951–1961. Lagrasse: Verdier, 2000.

Résumés de cours: Collège de France, 1952–1960. Paris: Gallimard, 1968.

Éloge de la philosophie: Leçon inaugurale faite au Collège de France, le jeudi 15 janvier 1953. Paris: Gallimard, 1953.

L'institution: Dans L'histoire personnelle et publique; Notes des cours au Collège de France (1954–1955). Ed. Dominique Darmaillacq. Paris: Belin, 2003.

Notes des cours au Collège de France: 1958–1959 et 1960–1961. Ed. Stéphanie Ménasé. Paris: Gallimard, 1996.

Notes des cours sur l'origine de la géométrie de Husserl. Paris: Presses Universitaires de France, 1998.

La Structure du comportement: Précédé d'une philosophie de l'ambiguïté. Ed. Alphonse De Waelhens. Paris: Presses Universitaires de France, 1967.

La Nature: Notes, cours du Collège de France. Ed. Dominique Séglard. Paris: Editions du Seuil, 1995.

English Translations of Books by Maurice Merleau-Ponty

1960s

Phenomenology of Perception. Trans. Colin Smith. New York: Routledge, 1962.

In Praise of Philosophy. Trans. John Wild and James M. Edie. Evanston, IL: Northwestern University Press, 1963.

Structure of Behavior. Trans. Alden L. Fisher. Boston: Beacon Press, 1963.

Primacy of Perception and Other Essays on Phenomenological Psychology: The Philosophy of Art, History, and Politics. Ed. James M. Edie. Evanston, IL: Northwestern University Press, 1964.

Sense and Non-Sense. Trans. Hubert L. Dreyfus and Patricia Allen Dreyfus. Evanston, IL: Northwestern University Press, 1964.

Signs. Trans. Richard C. McCleary. Evanston, IL: Northwestern University Press, 1964.

Visible and the Invisible: Followed by Working Notes. Ed. Claude Lefort. Trans. Alphonso Lingis. Evanston, IL: Northwestern University Press, 1968.

Humanism and Terror: An Essay on the Communist Problem. Translated by John O'Neill. Boston: Beacon Press, 1969.

1970s

Themes from the Lectures at the Collège de France, 1952–1960. Trans. John O'Neill. Evanston, IL: Northwestern University Press, 1970.

Adventures of the Dialectic. Trans. Joseph Bien. Evanston, IL: Northwestern University Press, 1973.

Consciousness and the Acquisition of Language. Trans. Hugh J. Silverman. Evanston, IL: Northwestern University Press, 1973.

Prose of the World. Edited by Claude Lefort. Trans. John O'Neill. Evanston, IL: Northwestern University Press, 1973.

Phenomenology, Language and Sociology: Selected Essays of Maurice Merleau-Ponty. Trans. and ed. John O'Neill. London: Heinemann Educational, 1974.

1990s

Texts and Dialogues. Ed. Hugh J. Silverman and James Barry Jr. Trans. Michael B. Smith et al. London: Humanities Press International, 1992.

2000s

Incarnate Subject: Malebranche, Biran, and Bergson on the Union of Body and Soul. Ed. Andrew G. Bjelland, Jr. and Patrick Burke. Trans. Paul B. Milan. Amherst, NY: Humanity Books, 2001.

Nature. Trans. Robert Vallier. Evanston, IL: Northwestern University Press, 2003.

Communicology

Roman Jakobson (1896–1982)

Maurice Merleau-Ponty (1908–1961)

Michel Foucault (1926–1984)

Photograph of Roman Jakobson courtesy of the MIT Museum. Photograph of Maurice Merleau-Ponty supplied by C.E.M. Struyker Boudier to the Simon Silverman Phenomenology Center at Duquesne University. Photograph of Michel Foucault courtesy of Bruce Jackson.

Roman Jakobson (1896–1982), Biographical Sketch

Roman Osipovîch Jakobson was born on October 11, 1896, in Moscow. He was the son of Osip J. Jakobson, a prominent industrialist and chemical engineer, and Anna Volpert Jakobson. He grew up in prerevolutionary Russia, beginning his studies at Lazarev Institute of Oriental languages at the age of ten and earning his B.A. from there in 1914.

Jakobson extended his interest in poetry with the study of language and phonology (the abstract properties of the sounds of speech). He studied linguistics, literary history, and folklore at the University of Moscow, earning his M.A. in 1918. While there, Jakobson initiated the Moscow Linguistic Circle. He then moved to Prague, Czechoslovakia, where he studied and worked as a translator, earning his Ph.D. from Charles University in Prague in 1930. There he began the Prague Linguistic Circle.

Jakobson began his association with Masarykova University (now the Purkyně University) in Brno, Czechoslovakia in 1933. Jakobson was concerned with elucidating linguistic problems of both practical and poetic language as well as questions of folklore and ethnology. He could read twenty-five languages and spoke six languages (Russian, French, Polish, German, Czech, and English) fluently. His research led him to conclude that each language has its own system of phonemes (distinct sounds) that cannot be subsumed under a uniform and rigid scheme. He also contended that a phoneme is not an ultimate, indecomposable entity, but each speech sound is a complex of distinct phonetic features. The feature composition of the different phonemes determines their function in different languages. The academic community did not unanimously accept his work, and it was not until 1937 that he received a tenured appointment at Masarykova University.

Jakobson was known for his anti-fascist sentiment, and with the German invasion of Czechoslovakia in 1939 he fled to become a visiting lecturer in Denmark (University of Copenhagen) and then in Norway (University of Oslo). In 1940 fled to Sweden (Uppsala University). During this time he explored the role

---

Different sources report inconsistent information about the life of Roman Osipovich Jakobson. Information for this biographical sketch was drawn from Morris Halle, "Jakobson, Roman," *International Encyclopedia of Linguistics* (New York: Oxford University Press, 1992), 2:247–248; "Jakobson, Roman," *The New Encyclopædia Britannica* (Chicago: Encyclopædia Britannica, Inc., 2005), 6:475; "Roman Jakobson," *Contemporary Authors Online* (Gale 2003), http://web5.infotrac.galegroup.com.authenticate.library.duq.edu. (accessed January 2, 2007); Henry Kučera, "Roman Jakobson," *Language* 59:4 (1983): 871–883; Ling Links—People, I-M. Brigham Young University Department of Linguistics, http://www.ttt.org/linglinks/i_m.html (accessed January 4, 2007); Stephen Moller, "Jakobson, Roman Osipovich," *Biographical Dictionary of Twentieth-Century Philosophers*, ed. Stuart Brown, Diané Collinson, and Robert Wilkinson (New York: Routledge Reference, 1996), 372–373.

of phonological universals in language acquisition and aphasic language loss, investigations that continued throughout his career.

In May 1941, he immigrated to the United States. From 1942 to 1946 he served as professor of general linguistics and of Czechoslovak studies at the École Libre des Hautes Études in New York. Jakobson was not warmly welcomed by the American linguistic world, and throughout World War II he was unable to obtain a regular university appointment. In the fall of 1946, he was named the Thomas G. Masaryk Professor of Czechoslovak Studies at Columbia University.

In 1948, Jakobson accepted a professorship at Harvard in its newly revitalized Slavic Department. When he moved, fourteen graduate students left Columbia University with Jakobson and registered at Harvard. At Harvard, Jakobson held the Samuel Hazzard Cross Professorship of Slavic Language and Literatures from 1949 until his retirement in 1967; from 1960, he was also a professor of general linguistics. In 1957 he received a concurrent appointment as institute professor at Massachusetts Institute of Technology (MIT), which he held until his retirement from there in 1970.

MIT gave Jakobson an office for life, and he did much of his work there until his final months. Roman Osipovîch Jakobson died on July 18, 1982, in Cambridge, Massachusetts.

Michel Foucault (1926–1984), Biographical Sketch

Paul-Michel Foucault was born on June 15, 1926, in Poitiers, France. He was the second of three children born to Paul and Anne Malapert Foucault. Foucault's father was a noted surgeon in the community. Although his father wanted him to study medicine, Foucault chose to study philosophy.

Foucault greatly enjoyed a scholarly environment, removed from politics and the difficulty of World War II. He graduated from the Jesuit College Saint-Stanislaus, attended the Lycée Henri-IV in Paris and in 1946 entered the École Normale Supérieure (ÉNS). Foucault's personal life at ÉNS was difficult, and he suffered from acute depression, seeking help from a psychiatrist. He graduated with three degrees: philosophy (1948), clinical psychology (1950), and psychiatry (1952). Foucault briefly joined the French Communist Party in 1950, but left because of his disagreement with anti-Semitism in Russia, which he could not reconcile with his pro-Israeli sentiments and his homosexuality.

After completing his degrees, Foucault taught psychology at ÉNS and the University of Lille (1953–1954) and conducted research at Sainte-Anne Hospital and the Centre National d'Orientation at Fresnes, a prison medical facility. Influenced by the work of Friedrich Nietzsche, Foucault left France to teach at Uppsala University in Sweden (1954–1958), teaching courses on French literature. In 1958, Foucault moved to Warsaw, Poland, where he accepted the position of director of the Centre Français, teaching French language classes and lecturing on French literature. Following this position, Foucault accepted an opening in Hamburg at the Institut Français, where he taught French language courses and lecturing on topics related to French culture.

In 1960, Foucault returned to France to become head of the philosophy department at the University of Clermont-Ferrand (1960–1966). Foucault submitted two doctoral theses (customary in France) to Georges Canguilhem of La

---

Different sources report inconsistent information about the life of Michel Foucault, which would perhaps please him, since he was opposed to all social constructs that implied an identity. Information for this biographical sketch was drawn from Robert Audi, ed., *The Cambridge Dictionary of Philosophy*, 2nd ed. (Cambridge, UK: Cambridge University Press, 1999); Patrice Bizzell and Bruce Herzberg, *The Rhetorical Tradition: Readings from Classical Times to the Present* (Boston: Bedford/St. Martin's Press, 2001); Edward Craig, ed., *Routledge Encyclopedia of Philosophy* (New York: Routledge, 1998), vol. 3; Sonja K. Foss, Karen A. Foss, and Robert Trapp, *Contemporary Perspectives on Rhetoric*, 2nd ed. (Prospect Heights, IL: Waveland Press, 2002); "Michel Foucault," The European Graduate School, http://www.ega.edu/resources/foucault.html (accessed August 18, 2005); Simon Blackburn, "Foucault, Michel," *The Oxford Dictionary of Philosophy* (Oxford, UK: Oxford University Press, 1996); "Foucault, Michel," *Oxford Reference Online* (Oxford University Press), http://www.oxfordreference.com/views/ ENTRY.html?subview=Main&entry=t98.000958 (accessed 9 October 2003); Gary Gutting, ed., *Cambridge Companion to Foucault* (Cambridge, UK: Cambridge University Press, 1994).

Sorbonne. His major thesis was entitled *Folie et déraison: Histoire de la folie à l'âge classique* (*Madness and Civilization: A History of Insanity in the Age of Reason*). His minor thesis was a translation and commentary on Kant's *Anthropology from a Pragmatic Point of View*. He completed his degree in 1961.

In 1966 Foucault accepted a position in philosophy at the University of Tunis. Foucault left Tunis in October of 1968 to return to Paris, where he was offered the position of chair of the philosophy department at the Vincennes Experimental University Center, which provided the opportunity to create a new department in a new university. Shortly thereafter, the death of philosopher Jean Hyppolite created a vacancy in the Collège de France. Foucault was elected to the lifetime appointment in 1970, taking the title Professor of the History of Systems of Thought.

In 1973, Foucault traveled to the United States for the first time to accept a visiting professorship in French at the University of California at Berkeley. By 1983, Foucault agreed to teach annually at the University of California-Berkeley. His enthusiasm about working in the United States and his increasing frustration with his life in France prompted him to talk of resigning his chair at the Collège. Those plans ended when Michel Foucault died in Paris on June 25, 1984, of an AIDS-related illness.

Communicology
The French Tradition in Human Science

Richard L. Lanigan

The Problematic of Identity

The problematic with which we are confronted, the "concept of identity," is an ancient one with many testimonies in both Eastern and Western philosophies. The notion of identity is foundational in Aristotle, and yet it is turned on its head in the postmodernity of the West and cultural practice of the East.[1] Following the foundational work in *semiotic phenomenology* of Ernst Cassirer and Charles Sanders Peirce, postmodernity deals with the symbolic world of culture in which the Aristotelian model of a natural world logic is turned on its head by social practice and cultural preference.[2] In short, Aristotle's "laws of thought" are questioned, found to be inadequate to human experience, reversed in sequence, and reformulated as positive constitutions of human capacity. Lest the modern reader be lost in this postmodern move, I shall begin my analysis by staying with the Aristotelian statement of the laws of logic, with one exception. I shall reverse the order of the four laws, beginning with Aristotle's fourth, then third, second, and first. This step allows us to approach the postmodern problematic by asking if there is a paradigm conscious experience that contradicts the law(s) and thematically suggests what a generative, positive statement of that law(s) would be.

The Aristotelian logic of (1) formations (experiences) constituting (2) transformation (consciousness) is *reversed* such that consciousness (logic transformations, "reasonableness") constitutes experience (logic formations, "reason") in the first instance. This is to say that in the symbolic cultural world, logic transformations lead to formations (consciousness experience) which are the subject matter and process of the human sciences such that consciousness is formed by the rule sequence: (Postmodern 1; Aristotle 4) *Law of Non-Contradiction* (a thing cannot at once be and not be; a statement cannot be true and false at the same time); (Postmodern 2; Aristotle 3) *Law of Excluded Middle* (a thing must be or not be; a statement must be either true or false); (Postmodern 3; Aristotle 2) *Law of Contradiction* (one thing is not another thing; a statement is different from other statements); and (Postmodern 4; Aristotle 1) *Law of Identity* (one thing is only one thing; a statement is a statement).

In short, Aristotle's logic is constructed by moving from (1) to (4) as the "classical laws of thought." Later on in the philosophy of science, Leibniz extends the Aristotelian logic to cover all possible worlds, not just the natural world of experience on earth. Much of the postmodern view in culture can be attributed to the constant need by old school (modernist, rationalist) positivists to modify Aristotle's logic as it applies to current mathematical logic in science—i.e., theory is adjusted to match experience.

Let me also note that the postmodernism that I am describing has a parallel eidetic and empirical proof in the context of cross-cultural communication and social psychology, building on the much earlier work in psychology of Edmund Husserl and Roman Jakobson.[3] Richard Nisbett and his intercultural colleagues demonstrate that the Aristotelian (Western; American-USA) logic (Aristotle Laws 1 to 4) is simply reversed in thought and practice by Asian cultures (Eastern; Chinese-PRC).[4] The Asian logic of *combinatory dialectic* (Aristotle Laws 4 to 1) *is the postmodern model of the West.* As Nisbett concisely summarizes: "The binary 'either/or' approach to the evaluation of propositions characteristic of the West has been lamented by many Western thinkers [the postmoderns], but the problems are easier to see from the standpoint of the 'both/and' approach of the East."[5] For the Chinese, the logic is "*dialectical,* meaning that it focuses on contradictions and how to resolve them or transcend them or find the truth in both."[6] Or to express the same point from an Eastern perspective: "The Chinese remain far more committed to reasonableness than to reason."[7] The basic logic of combinatory dialectic is better known in the human sciences of the West as the semiotic phenomenology of complex systems, best described in communicology by Anthony Wilden as the *Principle of Requisite Diversity:* "What survives in nature in the long range is not the fittest individual, organism, population, or species, but the fittest ecosystem: *Both* system *and* environment."[8]

To focus the postmodern problematic, we need to restate the logic transformation as they are affirmatively used by postmodernists like Cassirer, Peirce, Merleau-Ponty, Foucault, Wilden, and the Chinese (and other Asians) to make positive constitutions of described conscious experience in the world of communication and culture. The postmodern logic propositions listed below are stated in an inclusion order of dialectic constitution:

1. Phenomenological Law of Non-contradiction—*a thing can at once be and not be; a statement can be both true and false at the same time.*

> Eidetic/Empirical example: an *Interpretant* (in C. S. Peirce's sense).[9]

The eidetic and empirical example here is human embodied consciousness that is a *sign of a sign,* what Husserl calls "intentionality." Or even more simply as an example, take an oral/written/visual image, which is and is not a statement/sentence/proposition—which Michel Foucault made into a famous semiotic example, namely, Magritte's painting titled *L'usage de la parole* (the practice of speaking): "This is not a pipe" plus the image of a pipe. In this example, the image refers to the sentence and vice versa.[10] As Peirce summarizes:

> A sign, or *representamen,* is something which stands to somebody for

something in some respect or capacity. It **addresses** somebody, that is, creates in the mind of that person an equivalent sign, or perhaps a more developed sign. That sign which it creates I call the *interpretant* of the first sign. The sign stands for something, its *object*. It stands for that object, not in all respects, but in reference to a sort of idea, which I have sometimes [e.g., 1.551] called the *ground* of the representamen [my bold emphasis; Peirce editor insert].[11]

2. Phenomenological Law of Excluded Middle—*a thing must both be and not be; a statement must be both true and false. The postmodern constitution of reflectivity.*

Eidetic/Empirical example: a *Symbol* (in C. S. Peirce's sense).

The eidetic and empirical example is a *symbol of a sign* (representation of a presentation). Writing is the well-known index of speaking. Peirce specifies that "A *Symbol* is a sign which refers to the Object that it denotes by virtue of a law, usually an association of general ideas, which operates to cause the Symbol to be interpreted as referring to that Object."[12] For example, Peirce suggests, "Any ordinary word, as 'give,' 'bird,' 'marriage,' is an example of a symbol. It is *applicable to whatever may be found to realize the idea connected with the word;* it does not, in itself, identify those things."[13]

3. Phenomenological Law of Contradiction—*one thing is another thing; a statement is both the same as, and different from, other statements. The postmodern constitution of reversibility.*

Eidetic/Empirical example: an *Index* (in C. S. Peirce's sense).

The eidetic and empirical example is the *spatial location of a sign,* such as an oral contract written down on paper, explicated in Roman Jakobson's theory of "redundancy features."[14] Peirce says that "An *Index* is a sign which refers to its Object that it denotes by virtue of being really affected by that Object. . . . And, it is not the mere resemblance of its Object, even in these respects which makes it a sign, but is the actual modification of it by the Object."[15] Peirce's example: "A rap on the door is an index. Anything which focuses the attention is an index."[16]

4. Phenomenological Law of Identity—*one thing is always another thing; a statement is another statement. The postmodern constitution of reflexivity.*

Eidetic/Empirical example: an *Icon* (in C. S. Peirce's sense).

The eidetic and empirical example is the *temporal location of a sign* such as the "experience of consciousness" ("I made a mistake!") and the "consciousness of experience" ("I am alive!"), explicated by Roman Jakobson's theory of "distinctive features."[17] As Peirce notes, "An *Icon* is a sign which refers to the Object that it denotes merely by virtue of characters of its own, and which it possesses, just the same, whether any Object actually exists or not. Anything whatever, be it quality, existent individual, or law, is an Icon of anything, in so far as it is like that thing and is used as a sign of it."[18] Peirce's relevant example is "any material image, as a painting."[19] This very notion of the icon is common knowledge among all the computer users of the world as a mere function of learning the difference between virtual images, memory images, and functions on the computer screen.

That the Aristotelian, modernist concept of identity cannot be foundational is the positive thematic of Ernst Cassirer in his *communicological turn in culture* and in Peirce's *phenomenological turn in normative logics*, i.e., *semiotics*. The rejected modernist view of Aristotelian logic is also fundamental in Maurice Merleau-Ponty and his *semiotic turn* in phenomenology. That the concept of *identity* is the effect of understanding (rather than the cause—Aristotle) is the thematic of Michel Foucault and his *phenomenological turn* in semiotics. To be explicit, the concept of identity is a logical function only insofar as it is derived from its ontological context of the embodied person (a phenomenology of phenomenology). The postmoderns take the French view that the ontology of "both the Self and the Other as both the Same and Different" [*le même et l'autre*] constitutes the essence of human embodiment as

1. Expression and perception in the *consciousness of* experience (the contribution phenomenology); and

2. The source of logical abstraction and phenomenological description in the *experience of* consciousness (the contribution of semiotics).

The core domain of this postmodern analysis is concisely articulated by Roman Jakobson: "The cardinal property of language noted by the initiator of semiotics, Charles Sanders Peirce (1839–1914), namely the translatability of any verbal sign into another, more explicit one, renders an effective service to communication in that it counteracts ambiguities caused by lexical and grammatical homonymy or by the overlapping of elliptic forms."[20] Indeed, it is Jakobson who brings semiotics and phenomenology together as the theory and method of communicology.[21]

The task of explicating human communication as such a postmodern ontology of both *ambiguity* in Merleau-Ponty and *alterity* in Foucault has its ground in the human science of communicology.[22] Here, the fundamental focus is on the conjunctive theory and method of *semiotic phenomenology* at work in the *semiosphere*[23] where *human* communication (discourse) is, to use Merleau-Ponty's famous triadic formula, the *reflectivity, reversibility,* and *reflexivity* of culture (practice). The philosophy of communication explicated by Merleau-Ponty and Foucault (with mentions of Bourdieu and Kristeva) will serve as a paradigmatic case as these themes of discourse and practice are applied in the French context. Before we can advance into the philosophic application of communication, however, we require a foundational understanding of how communication is viewed by Continental philosophers in general and by Merleau-Ponty and Foucault in particular.

Roman Jakobson's Theory of Human Communication

Prerequisite to a grasp of contemporary communication theory (not machine-instantiated information theory or informatics) is a brief understanding of the theory advanced by Roman Jakobson.[24] All contemporary discussion of communication derives from a fundamental understanding of Jakobson's work. It is no exaggeration to say that understanding the main positions and counter-positions of any contemporary author within the domain of the philosophy of communication is grounded in the use of Jakobson's definitional theory. It is certainly true that European philosophers of communication and scholars in the human sciences in the Continental tradition assume their readers, professional or lay, know the fundamental propositions demonstrated in the eidetic proofs and empirical demonstrations of Jakobson on the structure and function human communication. His theory work and applied research are preeminent, as cited in the September 1972 journal issue of *Scientific American*. Recall that Jakobson's distinguished international career was marked in the United States by his election in 1956 as president of the Linguistic Society of America. In 1957, he became the first scientist to be named jointly, along with his chair at Harvard University, Institute Professor of Linguistics and Philosophy at the Massachusetts Institute of Technology. At MIT, he coorganized and headed the Center for Communication Science. From 1966 to 1969, he was also attached to the Salk Institute for Biological Studies (La Jolla, California) and the Center for Cognitive Studies at Harvard.

Rather than a "theory" is the limited sense of a *model*, Jakobson's *theory* is a complete account of human communication from the microscopic (phonology) to the macroscopic (comparative Indo-European discourse) level of application. His nine volumes of *Selected Writings* cover every facet of linguistics and literature, phonology and communicology, and the entries are in a dozen languages, although his working languages were English, French, and Russian. As such, Jakobson is the only person to have offered a legitimate theory of communication (illustrated in Figure 1) with both eidetic and empirical application, i.e., a communicology. The basic elements of communication are capitalized in the diagram, and the functions of communication are given in italics. While the logical and phenomenological relations and correlations of this theory are worked out elsewhere in great detail, our present discussion must be limited to this brief version.[25]

CONTEXT
(Referential / Cognitive)

MESSAGE
[Poetic]

ADDRESSER————————————————ADDRESSEE
(Emotive / Expressive)   (Conative / Interpretive)

CONTACT
(Phatic]

CODE
(Metalinguistic / Glossing)

Figure 1. Roman Jakobson's Theory of Communication[26]

In Jakobson's theory, each element is contextual to the rest in binary (logical) pairs (phenomenological), and the system of pairs constitutes a *Function*. For example, in the *poetic function* of the Message, there are four relations for the Addresser (Ar) and Addressee (Ae) pair: (1) Ar to Ar (Self-embodiment). (2) Ae to Ae (Other-embodiment), (3) Ar to Ae (thetic intentionality), and (4) Ae to Ar (operative intentionality). Similar binary pairs exist for Context and Contact and for Message and Code. The *poetic function* per se is the *rule of reversibility,* in which any syntagmatic category (i.e., a horizontal line of categories) can interchange with a paradigmatic category (i.e., a vertical line of categories). We need not work our way through all the relational possibilities for the formation of categories. Peirce has already done it for us, and there are sixty-four nonredundant categories, the basic three of interest to us being already mentioned: Symbol, Index, and Icon.[27]

It is important, as a matter of context, to note that the Addresser/Addressee relationship and its four functions (emotive, expressive, conative, interpretive) are experienced as *four network levels* of communication transaction in human comportment. Demonstrated in the foundational work of Jürgen Ruesch, *Semiotic Approaches to Human Relations* then by Jürgen Ruesch and Gregory Bateson in *Communication: The Social Matrix of Psychiatry,* the commonly accepted networks of human discourse are (1) the intrapersonal level (or psychiatric/aesthetic domain of *emotive* communication), exemplified in the French human sciences by the work of Julia Kristeva, where the Addresser and Addressee may be one person whose communication is thought, emotion, etc.; (2) the interpersonal level (or social domain of *expressive* communication), in which the two-person dyad is an example of behavioral exchange as exemplified in the work of Maurice Merleau-Ponty; (3) the group level (or cultural domain of *conative* communication) emphasized by Michel Foucault's research, where an Addresser, one person, communicates with a group (an *egocentric* culture like the USA); or the reverse context (a *sociocentric* culture like the People's Republic of China), where a group as the Addresser influences an addressee, one person; and (4) the inter-group level (or transcultural domain of *interpretive* communication), captured by Pierre Bourdieu's research, in which one group addresses another group with such consequences as war, peace, the diffusion of innovation, social distinction, and so on.[28] In short, these four interconnected network levels contain the communicological process outlined by Jakobson's theory of human communication. Historically speaking, the coincidence of this research and theory accomplished by Ruesch, Bateson, and Jakobson in the decade 1950–1960 established the academic discipline of communicology (human communication) in American (US) universities with "a clear-cut line of demarcation between the theory of communication and of information."[29]

Let me now briefly define each communication element by its corresponding function as a way of glossing Jakobson's theory of communication and its relevant parts.[30] The Addresser is the human, embodied *origin of communication* and in consequence is not a mechanical "sender" or "signal source," but the *expressive* constitution of *emotion*. In linguistic terms, the Addresser is the verbal first person (persona), who is *speaking*. The person may be the psychic voice the Greeks called *mythos*, or the *persona* whose oral speaking is audible as the interpretant *logos* of a person. As such, the Addresser gives (*data*) a Message that constitutes a Code and selects a Context for Contact ("choice of context" or analogue logic). Lotman provides a detailed analysis of the motivation that occurs between message and code, code and message, in the formation of discourse as practice, communication as culture.[31]

The Addressee element of communication is basically the reverse phenomenological intentionality of the Addresser. The Addressee is the human, embodied *origin of culture* and in consequence is not a mechanical "receiver" or "signal destination," but the *interpretive* constitution of *conation*. In linguistic terms, the Addressee is the verbal second person (persona), who is *spoken to*. The person for whom aural listening is audible (oral) becomes the interpretant *logos* (a preconscious *social* practice or *habitus*) for the psychic voice that the Greeks called *hexis*, or the self-*embodied* practice of culture. As such, the Addressee takes (*capta*) a Code that constitutes a Message and selects a Contact for Context ("context of choice" or digital logic).

Context is the referential function of the communicative act in which signification is *denotive* within a *cognitive* system of meaning. In linguistic terms, Context is the third person, someone or something *spoken of*. It is crucial to recall that Jakobson rejects Saussure's notion of an arbitrary sign (signifier in opposition to signified). Rather, Jakobson demonstrates that communication is a "choice of context" such that signs have a relative, but necessary, *motivation* to one another (signifier in *apposition* to signified). As Holenstein explains Jakobson's use of Peircean semiotics, a sign's "own constitution reflects the relational structure of the thing represented," hence we have Peirce's preferred name for the sign as a *representamen*.[32] Thus, the notion of "representation" is a key problematic and thematic in all postmodern discussions of intentionality in the human sciences.

Contact is the *phatic* function operating in human communication such that a physical (interpersonal) and psychological (embodied, intrapersonal) connection is established between the Addresser and the Addressee. The best eidetic/ empirical example in linguistics is the concept of an *emblem*. An emblem is the anthropologist's name for a word that stands in place of a gesture, or the gesture that replaces a verbal message. The emblem is a sign with a culturally known interpretant that moves from (1) physical contact (signification) between Addresser and Addressee to (2) mutual psychic sharing (meaning).

The Message displays the phenomenology of the *poetic* function in communication. Rather than a mundane reference to poetry, the essence of *poiesis* is the shifting of verbal elements exterior to the system of language, in which case you have *rhetoric;* or interior to the system of language, in which case you have *poetic*. While there is a long, detailed phonological analysis that is relevant at this point, we must be content to explain the poetic function in verbal communication as *paradigmatic and syntagmatic reversal* of words as units in sentences. For example, once you know the words in a sentence by grammatical function, any word in that category can replace any other word. In the sentence "The cat ate the dog" you immediately see that if you are a dog lover the message can be reversed as "The dog ate the cat." Moreover, you immediately know that any noun in the sentence can be replaced by a pronoun, and any verb can substitute for any other verb. The vertical (paradigmatic) and horizontal (syntagmatic) word shifts can be remembered as a whole set, what Jakobson calls the "Prague Prism" or ever-expanding *matrix* (hence, Ruesch and Bateson's use of "social matrix" in the subtitle of their book).[33] Jakobson concludes that messages are unique in language because human *speaking* (*parole*) consists of (1) a linguistic utterance, (2) language as an individual, private property, and (3) the individualizing, centrifugal aspect of language (where *centrifugal* means moving from individual out to group, from person into culture). Message interpretation relies on perceiving the *diachronic* ("then and there" historical sequences) of verbal or nonverbal usage. Egocentric cultures, typically Western, stress the importance of messages over codes, individuals over groups.

The concept of a Code entails the understanding of the *metalinguistic or glossing* function in communication. Every communication system, verbal or nonverbal, has both an object language (discourse about extralinguistic entities) and a *metalanguage* (discourse about linguistic entities) that specify *synchronic* relationships ("here and now" existential moments). Linguists refer to this code phenomenon as "double articulation," since an utterance or gesture refers both to itself as an entity and beyond itself to its context in a system. Most people experience the complexity of the language code when they look up a word (message) in a dictionary (code) only to find themselves referred to other words (message in the same code), thus acting to no avail in an unknown code. Jakobson also judges that codes are unique in language because social language (*langue*) consists of (1) linguistic norm, (2) language as supraindividual, social endowment, and (3) the unifying, centripetal aspect of language (where *centripetal* means moving from group to individual, from culture to person). Sociocentric cultures, typically Eastern, stress the importance of codes over messages, groups over individuals.

The conjunction of egocentric and sociocentric cultures and the people who communicate in them is thematic for postmodern philosophers of communication. In particular, French semiotic phenomenology, represented by Bourdieu, Kristeva, Merleau-Ponty, and Foucault, focuses on the ontology of *le même et l'autre:* "both the Self and the Other as both the Same and Different." This ontological proposition built into a linguistic aphorism of French philosophy constitutes a specific dialectical explication of Roman Jakobson's theory of communication. Where human beings seek their identity with others in a shared lived-world we inevitably confront the *ambiguity of identity* in the Self encountering that which is the Same—time and again. And we confront the *alterity of identity* in the Other who is Different—at home and away.

Merleau-Ponty's Thematic of Embodied Identity: Ambiguity

The essence of embodied identity constitutes *ambiguity* (explicated as Self-consciousness/Same-experience; see Figure 2), as Merleau-Ponty reminds us in the *Phenomenology of Perception:*

> I can remain within the sphere of absolute self-evidence only if I refuse to make any affirmation, or to take [capta] anything for granted, if, as Husserl has it, I stand in wonder before the world, and ceasing to be in league with it, I bring to light the flow of motivations which bear me along in it, making my life wholly aware of itself, and explicit. When I try to pass from this interrogative state to an affirmation, and *a fortiori* when I try to express myself, I crystallize an infinite collection of motives within an act of consciousness, I revert to the implicit, that is, to the equivocal and to the world's free play. My absolute contact with myself, **the identity of being and appearance cannot be posited,** but only lived as anterior to any affirmation [my bold emphasis and insert].[34]

In one concise argument, Merleau-Ponty demonstrates that the Cartesian world built on Aristotelian thinking, in which the logic of experience dictates the constitution of phenomena, cannot apply to embodied consciousness. Furthermore, the Aristotelian ground of logic cannot be sustained inasmuch as identity (the experience perceived and expressed) is the effect, the result of consciousness ("wonder before the world"), and not the cause.

For semiotic clarity in these complex phenomenological relations, I should point out that Figure 2 is an explication of consciousness of experience (C ➡ E) as a semiotic phenomenology of existential being that Husserl calls an "order of experience" (experiencer ➡ experiencing ➡ experienced). In figure 3 the reverse reading, which is the experience of consciousness (C ⇐ E), is what Husserl calls an "order of analysis" (experiencer ⇐ experiencing ⇐ experienced).[35] When the "order of experience" is assumed to match the "order of analysis" (i.e., no reflexivity, no reversibility, no reflectivity), then we have positive science. We have the positivististic, natural attitude assumption that posits the Cartesian, Aristotelian *identity of appearances* as "being," wherein consciousness and experience are erroneously hypostatized as paradigmatic equivalents (in Jakobson's sense).[36]

Figure 2 sketches the basic elements in Merleau-Ponty's use of the *le même et l'autre* model of identity as ambiguity in human communication and behavior. The background analysis for this model is found in Lanigan.[37]

Figure 2. Merleau-Ponty's Ambiguity Model[38]

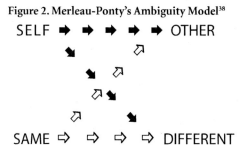

Legend: **Consciousness (as *parole parlante; corps propre*):**

Self—Other   =   Synecdoche: part/whole*
(*parole*)**

Same—Other   =   Metaphor substance/whole
(*discours*)

Experience (as *parole parlée; corps vécu*):
Same—Different   =   Metonymy: substance/attribute
(*langue*)

Self—Different   =   Simile (positive);
(*langage*)   Irony (negative): part/attribute

➡➡➡➡ = "Self" combination
⇨⇨⇨⇨ = "Same" combinations

* Note the respective syntagmatic relationships,
        e.g., Self = part, Other = whole, etc.
** Traditional linguistic descriptions.

At this point, let me only summarize the basic position that Merleau-Ponty's many works suggest. Merleau-Ponty's major work on expression, *Signs*, as well as his *Phenomenology of Perception*, relate semiotics, the theory of signs (aesthetic, logical, social systems), to the phenomenology of embodiment (Jakobson's communication elements: context, message, contact, code, addresser, addressee).[39] In his explication of both perception and expression, Merleau-Ponty suggests that there are two levels of discourse: (1) *existential discourse,* in which a person expresses his or her speaking in an original and perceptive speech, which is a "speech speaking" (*parole parlante*) that proffers an *authentic message;* and (2) *empirical discourse,* where a person merely expresses what has already been said by others—that is, a "speech spoken" (*parole parlée*) that legitimizes the *social code.* In the speech-speaking case, there is a rhetorical function of *identity* where consciousness of experience is the original reference to existential meaning, i.e., the authentic act of expression, which is the linguistic message embodied in the person (*corps propre*) as *addresser.*[40]

First, Merleau-Ponty corrects Saussure's static notion of *parole* by making it the dynamic *parole parlante,* or what Jakobson calls the "message" in his parallel correction of Saussure. Second, Merleau-Ponty corrects the concept of *langue* by the more existential *parole parlée,* or what Jakobson in agreement calls the "code." In this second category of speech spoken, the rhetorical function is banal (*corps vécu*) and evokes an experience of consciousness, i.e., the commonplace meaning, which is the linguistic code discovered by the *addressee* (in Jakobson's sense).

Finally, let us note that Merleau-Ponty offers a major correction to the method of Husserl's phenomenology by stressing the importance of semiotics in the description of phenomena, the importance of structural analysis in defining (reducing) phenomena, and the importance of hermeneutic principles for the interpretation of phenomena. The three-step method of Description, Reduction, and Interpretation is the result of his focus on the reversible, reflexive, and reflective relations between perception and expression—all of which are foundation for Foucault's analysis of social embodiment and institutional comportment.

Foucault's Thematic of Embodied Identity: Alterity

The social essence of embodied identity constitutes *alterity* (explicated as Other consciousness/Different experience; see Figure 3), as Foucault reminds us in *Fearless Speech:*

> When you accept the parrhesiastic game in which your own life is exposed, you are taking up [*capta*] a specific relationship to yourself; you risk death *to tell the truth* [*parrhesia*] instead of reposing in the security of a life where the truth goes unspoken. Of course, the threat of death comes from the Other, and thereby requires a relationship to the Other. But the *parrhesiates* primarily chooses a specific relationship to himself: he prefers himself as truth-teller rather than as a living being who is false to himself [my emphasis and inserts].[41]

Figure 3 illustrates the basic components in Foucault's use of the *le même et l'autre* model of identity as alterity in human communication and behavior. Again, I note that the background analysis for this model is found in Lanigan.[42] Also note, in particular, that the model is essentially the same as presented in Figure 2. Having said that, it is critically important to see that we are reversing directional relations by moving from the Other over to the Self, and from the Different over to the Same. This movement is stressed in the presentation of the Legend information given in Figure 3.

Michel Foucault's *Les mots et les choses* (Words and Things), intentionally retitled by him for its English translation as *The Order of Things: An Archaeology of the Human Sciences,* and its appendix essay, "L'archéologie du savior" ("The Archaeology of Knowledge") (more accurately translated as "The Archaeology of Understanding"), add a methodological dimension to Merleau-Ponty's view.[43] Foucault argues that Merleau-Ponty's second, empirical code level of discourse (*énonciation*), which we know (*connaissance*) as the cultural code of social *power* hides the first, existential message level of "stating" discourse (*énoncé*), which we understand (*savoir*) as *desire.* This agonistic or contested process of rhetorical levels forms a "rupture" or ongoing discontinuity of discourses constructing and deconstructing one another in *apposition* (both are equally opposed) to the embodied person.

By using the method of (1) "archaeology" (one of Husserl's key concepts) or knowing (*connaissance* or knowing as the *experience of* consciousness; Jakobson's "horizontal" syntagmatic category of "code") and the method of (2) "genealogy" (*savoir* or understanding as the *consciousness of* experience; Jakobson's "vertical" paradigmatic category of "message"), Foucault engages his third level, which he names (3) "critical methodology" in his *L'Ordre du discours.*[44] Here, the "order of discourse" defines *parrhesiastic rhetoric.*[45] I should also make the relevant comment that in developing this three-step methodology, Foucault begins with Edmund Husserl, as did Merleau-Ponty, and develops his three steps in *parallel function* to Merleau-Ponty's methodological steps of (1) description, (2) reduction, and (3) interpretation. Clearly, both Merleau-Ponty and Foucault account for a systematic application of semiotic phenomenology to existential perception (Merleau-Ponty) and social expression (Foucault).

Note that Foucault's archaeology is a method of "oppositions" or "exclusions" (Jakobson's "distinctive features"), while genealogy is a method of "interstices" or "ensemble" (Jakobson's "redundancy features"). This critical model subjects both archaeology and genealogy to one another as a dialectic of *both* opposition *and* apposition as Foucault's "reversal-principle" (Jakobson's "poetic function" of paradigmatic and syntagmatic interchange). Foucault is following Merleau-Ponty's prescription that the first step of analysis is a "phenomenology of phenomenology." That is, the conjunctions of both consciousness and experience in discourse are seen as reversible, reflexive, and reflective in judgment.

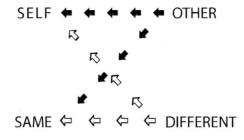

Legend: **Consciousness (as *énoncé; savoir*):**
Self—Other   =   Synecdoche: part/whole*
(*parole*)**

Same—Other   =   Metaphor substance/whole
(*discours*)

Experience (as *énonciation; connaissance*):
Same—Different   =   Metonymy: substance/attribute
(*langue*)

Self—Different   =   Simile (positive);
(*langage*)   Irony (negative): part/attribute

➡➡➡➡   =   "Self" combination
⇨⇨⇨⇨   =   "Same" combinations

* Note the respective syntagmatic relationships,
    e.g., Self = part, Other = whole, etc.
** Traditional linguistic descriptions.

Figure 3. Foucault's Alterity Model[46]

Hence, Foucault offers a critical approach to discourse viewed as a phenomenological semiotic (Husserl's "order of analysis") that completes Merleau-Ponty's approach of a semiotic phenomenology (Husserl's "order of experience"). In short, while Merleau-Ponty examines the place of *personal perception* in public expression (intentionality as a message/code), Foucault critically studies the reverse, i.e., the place of *public expression* in personal perception (embodiment as a code/message), as illustrated, for example, in the narratology of his study of the hermaphrodite Herculine Barbin.[47]

By way of a brief conclusion, let me suggest that it is clear that where Merleau-Ponty is existential, Foucault is social. Where Merleau-Ponty interrogates perception, Foucault questions expression. Where Merleau-Ponty explores the ambiguity of the individual's comportment, Foucault journeys into the institutions of the group and the community as political actuality. Both thinkers are grounded in traditional axiology, stressing the aesthetics, logics, and politics of perception and expression, i.e., the worldview of communicology in which semiotics and phenomenology are in a constant postmodern dialectic of discourse and practice, *habitus* and *hexis*—to cite Bourdieu, *semiotic* and *symbolic*, to cite Kristeva.[48] These dialectical and parallel systems of cultural analysis in the French milieu of the postmodern human sciences are proscribed by Kristeva's semiotic phenomenology of communicology: "Because the subject is always *both* semiotic *and* symbolic, no signifying system he produces can be either 'exclusively' semiotic or 'exclusively' symbolic, and is instead marked by an indebtedness to both." Her example is the oral and written domain of Han Chinese.

Notes

1. For a discussion of postmodernity of the West, see Richard L. Lanigan, "The Postmodern Ground of Communicology: Subverting the Forgetfulness of Rationality," *American Journal of SEMIOTICS* 11, nos. 1–2 (1995): 5–21. For a discussion of cultural practices of the East, see Richard E. Nisbett, *The Geography of Thought: How Asians and Westerners Think Differently . . . and Why* (New York: Free Press, 2003).

2. Cassirer, *Philosophie der symbolischen Formen:* vol. 1, *Die Sprache* (1923); vol. 2, *Das mythische Denken* (1925); vol. 3, *Phänomenologie der Erkenntnis* (1929; Berlin: Bruno Cassirer; repr., Darmstadt: Wissenschaftliche Buchgesellschaft, 1964; repr., New Haven, CT: Yale University Press, 1953–1957), trans. by Ralph Manheim as *The Philosophy of Symbolic Forms:* vol. 1, *Language* (1953); vol. 2, *Mythical Thought* (1955); vol. 3, *The Phenomenology of Knowledge* (1957); Cassirer, *Symbol, Myth, and Culture: Essays and Lectures of Ernst Cassirer, 1935–1945,* ed. Donald Phillip Verene (New Haven: Yale University Press, 1979); Cassirer, *Zur Metaphysik der symbolischen Formen,* ed. John Michael Krois, vol. 1 of Ernst Cassirer, *Nachgelassene Manuskripte und Texte,* ed. John Michael Krois and Oswald Schwemmer (Hamburg: Felix Meiner, 1995), trans. John Michael Krois as *The Philosophy of Symbolic Forms* (New Haven, CT: Yale University Press, 1996). Vol. 4, *The Metaphysics of Symbolic Forms;* Peirce, *Collected Papers of Charles Sanders Peirce:* vol. 1, *Principles of Philosophy;* vol. 2, *Elements of Logic;* vol. 3, *Exact Logic* (Published Papers); vol. 4, *The Simplest Mathematics;* vol. 5, *Pragmatism and Pragmaticism;* vol. 6, *Scientific Metaphysics,* ed. Charles Hartshorne and Paul Weiss (Cambridge, MA: Harvard University Press, 1931–1935); vol. 7, *Science and Philosophy;* vol. 8, *Reviews, Correspondence, and Bibliography,* ed. Arthur W. Burks (Cambridge, MA: Harvard University Press, 1958); all eight vols. in electronic form ed. John Deely (Charlottesville, VA: Intelex Corporation, 1994).

3. Elmar Holenstein, *Jakobson ou le structuralisme phénoménologique* (Paris: Éditions Seghers, 1974), trans. C. and T. Schelbert as *Roman Jakobson's Approach to Language: Phenomenological Structuralism* (Bloomington, IN: Indiana University Press, 1976), 115–116.

4. Nisbett, *Geography of Thought.*

5. Ibid., 205.

6. Ibid., 174.

7. Ibid., 167.

8. Wilden, *The Rules Are No Game: The Strategy of Communication* (New York: Routledge and Kegan Paul, 1987), 195.
9. Peirce, *Collected Papers.*
10. Richard L. Lanigan, *The Human Science of Communicology: A Phenomenology of Discourse in Foucault and Merleau-Ponty* (Pittsburgh, PA: Duquesne University Press, 1992), 104.
11. Peirce, *CP*, 2.28. (Dating within the *Collected Papers*, which covers the period of Peirce's life, 1839–1914, is based principally on the Burks Bibliography at the end of *CP* 8. Reference by codex custom is to volume and paragraph number(s) with a period in between, abbreviated as *CP*.)
12. Peirce, *CP*, 2.247.
13. Peirce, *CP*, 2.298.
14. Lanigan, *Human Science of Communicology*, 230.
15. Peirce, *CP*, 2.247.
16. Pierce, *CP*, 2.285.
17. Roman Osipovîc Jakobson, "Verbal Communication" in *Communication* (A *Scientific American* Book), ed. Dennis Flanagan et al. (San Francisco, CA: W. H. Freeman and Co., 1972), 43; Roman Osipovîc Jakobson, "Linguistics in Relation to Other Sciences" in *Selected Writings:* vol. 2, *Word and Language* (Berlin: Mouton de Gruyter, 1971), 655–696; Roman Osipovîc Jakobson, "Linguistics in Relation to Other Communication Systems" in *Selected Writings*, vol. 2, *Word and Language* (Berlin: Mouton de Gruyter, 1971), 697–708; Lanigan, *Human Science of Communicology*, 230; Wilden, *Rules Are No Game*, 179.
18. Peirce, *CP*, 2.247.
19. Peirce, *CP*, 2.275.
20. Jakobson, "Verbal Communication," 43.
21. Umberto Eco, "The Influence of Roman Jakobson on the Development of Semiotics," in *Roman Jakobson: Echoes of His Scholarship*, ed. Daniel Armstrong and C. H. Van Schooneveld (Lisse: The Peter De Ridder Press, 1977), 39–58; Elmar Holenstein, "Jakobson's Contribution to Phenomenology," in *Roman Jakobson: Echoes of His Scholarship*, ed. Daniel Armstrong and C. H. Van Schooneveld (Lisse: The Peter De Ridder Press, 1977), 145–162.
22. Richard L. Lanigan, "Communicology" and "Structuralism," in *Encyclopedia of Phenomenology*, ed. Lester Embree et al. (Boston: Kluwer Academic Publishers, 1997), 104–110, 683–689.
23. Yuri Mikhailovich Lotman, *The Universe of Mind: A Semiotic Approach to Culture*, trans. Ann Shukman (Bloomington: Indiana University Press, 1994).
24. Roman Osipovîc Jakobson, *Selected Writings:* vol. 1, *Phonological Studies*, 1962, 2nd ed., 1971, 3rd ed. 2002; Vol. 2, *Word and Language*, 1971; Vol. 3, *Poetry of Grammar and Grammar of Poetry*, ed. Stephen Rudy, 1981; Vol. 4, *Slavic Epic Studies*, 1966; Vol. 5, *On Verse, Its Masters and Explorers*, ed. Stephen Rudy and Martha Taylor, 1979; Vol. 6, *Early Slavic Paths and Crossroads: Part 1 and Part 2*, ed. Stephen Rudy, 1985; Vol. 7, *Contributions to Comparative Mythology: Studies in Linguistics and Philology, 1972–1982*, ed. Stephen Rudy, 1985; Vol. 8, *Completion Volume One: Major Works, 1976–1980*, ed. Stephen Rudy, 1988; Vol. 9, A Rudy, 1990. (Berlin: Mouton de Gruyter). Unless noted, volumes were edited by Jakobson.

25. Lanigan, *Human Science of Communicology*, 229–236; Lanigan, "Communicology" and "Structuralism"; Lotman, *Universe of Mind*.

26. Roman Osipovîc Jakobson, "Linguistics and Communication Theory" in *Selected Writings, Vol 2: Word and Language* (Berlin: Mouton de Gruyter, 1971), 570–579; Roman Osipovîc Jakobson, "Linguistics and Poetics" in *Selected Writings, Vol. 3: Poetry of Grammar and Grammar of Poetry*, ed. Stephen Rudy (Berlin: Mouton de Gruyter, 1981), 18–51.

27. The discussion and illustration of the Jakobsonian categories as elements and functions is detailed in Lanigan, *Human Science of Communicology*, 229–236.

28. Jürgen Ruesch, *Semiotic Approaches to Human Relations* (The Hague and Paris: Mouton, 1951; repr., 1972), 277 (reprint edition of Ruesch's collected articles and books in one volume); Jürgen Ruesch and Gregory Bateson, *Communication: The Social Matrix of Psychiatry* (New York: W. W. Norton and Co. Inc., 1951; repr., 1968, 1987); Julia Kristeva, *La révolution du langage poétique* (Paris: Éditions du Seuil, 1974), trans. by Margaret Walle as *Revolution in Poetic Language* (New York: Columbia University Press, 1984); Pierre Bourdieu, *Esquisse d'une théorie de la pratique, précédé de trois études d'ethnologie kabyle* (Geneva: Librairie Droz S.A., 1972), trans. by Richard Nice as *Outline of a Theory of Practice* (New York: Cambridge University Press, 1977) (page references are to the Cambridge University Press edition).

29. Jakobson, "Linguistics and Communication Theory," 573.

30. Jakobson, "Linguistics and Communication Theory."

31. Lotman, *The Universe of Mind*, 22.

32. Elmar Holenstein, *Jakobson ou le structuralisme phénoménologique* (Paris: Éditions Seghers, 1974), trans. by C. and T. Schelbert as *Roman Jakobson's Approach to Language: Phenomenological Structuralism* (Bloomington, IN: Indiana University Press, 1976), 157.

33. Holenstein, *Roman Jakobson's Approach*, 31, 139; Ruesch and Bateson, *Communication*.

34. Maurice Merleau-Ponty, *Phénoménologie de la perception* (Paris: Éditions Gallimard, 1945), trans. by Colin Smith, with corrections by Forrest Williams and David Guerrière, as *Phenomenology of Perception* (London: Routledge and Kegan Paul, 1981), 295. Translations published prior to 1981 should be avoided.

35. Lanigan, *Human Science of Communicology*, 20.

36. See Holenstein, *Roman Jakobson's Approach*, 31, 139, 141.

37. Richard L. Lanigan, *Phenomenology of Communication: Merleau-Ponty's Thematics in Communicology and Semiology* (Pittsburgh, PA: Duquesne University Press, 1988); Lanigan, *Human Science of Communicology*; Lanigan, "Communicology" and "Structuralism."

38. Lanigan, *Human Science of Communicology*, 110.

39. Maurice Merleau-Ponty, *Signes* (Paris: Éditions Gallimard, 1960), trans. Richard C. McCleary as *Signs* (Evanston, IL: Northwestern University Press, 1964); Merleau-Ponty, *Phenomenology of Perception*; Jakobson, "Linguistics and Communication Theory."

40. Jakobson "Linguistics and Communication Theory"; Jakobson, "Linguistics and Poetics"; Holenstein, "Jakobson's Contribution to Phenomenology."

41. Foucault, *Fearless Speech*, ed. Joseph Pearson (Los Angeles, CA: Semiotext(e), 2001), 17. (This book consists of six lectures delivered in English, University of California, Berkeley, 1983, which was based on the 3 March 1982 lecture at the Collège de France published as *Herméneutique du sujet* [Paris: Éditions de Seuil/Gallimard, 2001], trans. by Graham Burchell as *The Hermeneutics of the Subject: Lectures at the Collège de France, 1981–82* [New York: Palgrave Macmillan, 2005].)

42. Richard L. Lanigan, *Phenomenology of Communication: Merleau-Ponty's Thematics in Communicology and Semiology* (Pittsburgh, PA: Duquesne University Press, 1988); Lanigan, *Human Science of Communicology*; Lanigan, "Communicology" and "Structuralism."

43. Michel Foucault, *Les Mots et les Choses* (Paris: Éditions Gallimard, 1966), anon. trans. as *The Order of Things: An Archaeology of the Human Sciences* (London: Tavistock Publications Ltd., 1970); Michel Foucault, *L'Archéologie du Savoir* (Paris: Éditions Gallimard, 1969); Michel Foucault, *L'ordre du discours: Leçon inaugural au Collège de France* (Paris: Éditions Gallimard, 1971); Michel Foucault, *The Archaeology of Knowledge* (sic) and *The Discourse on Language* (sic), trans. by A. M. S. Smith (New York: Pantheon; Random House, 1972) (one-volume trans. of Foucault 1969 and 1971; title translations are spurious).

44. Foucault, *L'ordre du discourse*.

45. Richard L. Lanigan, *Semiotic Phenomenology of Rhetoric: Eidetic Practice in Henry Grattan's Discourse on Tolerance* (Washington, DC: Center for Advanced Research in Phenomenology and University Press of America, 1984).

46. Lanigan, *Human Science of Communicology*, 110.

47. Michel Foucault, *Herculine Barbin dite Alexina B.* (Paris: Éditions Gallimard, 1978), trans. R. McDougall as *Herculine Barbin: Being the Recently Discovered Memoirs of a Nineteenth-Century French Hermaphrodite* (New York: Pantheon, 1980).

48. Pierre Bourdieu, *Outline of a Theory*, 82–83; Kristeva, *Revolution in Poetic Language*, 24, 87.

Bibliography of Works

Books by Roman Jakobson

1920s

Noveĭshai a russkai a poézii a: nabrosok pervyĭ. Prague: Tip, 1921.

O cheshskom stihe preimucshestvenno v sopostovlenii s Russkim. *Sborniki po teorii poeticheskogo yazika.* Berlin: Opoiaz-MLK, 1923.

and Piotr Bogatyrev. *Slavianskaya Filologiya v Rossii za God y Revoliutsii.* Berlin: Opoiaz, 1923.

Základy českého verše. Prague: Odeon, 1926.

Spor duše s tělem. O nebezpečném času smrti. Prague: L. Kuncír, 1927.

Phonetica odnogo severno-velikorusskogo govora s namechayucsheisya perehodnost'yu. Prague: Jarkovský, 1927.

Nejstarší české písně duchovní. Prague: Ladislav Kuncíř, 1929.

Remarques sur l'evolution phonologique du Russe, comparée à celle des autres langues slaves. Prague: Jednota československých matematiků a fysiků, 1929.

1930s

with P. N. Savitskii. *Evrazii a v svete i a zykoznanii a.* Prague : Izd. evraziitsev, 1931.

K kharakterom evraziiskogo iazykovogo soiuza. Berlin: Opoiaz, 1931.

Smert' Vladimira Majakovskogo. Berlin: Petropolis, 1931.

Slezsko-polská cantilena inhonesta za začátku XV. Prague: s.n., 1936.

Tvůrčí znalec staročeského básnictví. Brno: Spolek posluchačů filosofie, 1939.

1940s

Axiomatik eines Verssystems am mordwinischen Volkslied dargelegt. Stockholm: Ungar. Inst., 1941.

Kindersprache, Aphasie und allgemeine Lautgesetze. Uppsala: Almqvist & Wiksells, 1941.

Moudrost starých Čechů. New York: Nákl. Československého kulturního kroužku, 1943.

with Henri Gregoire and Marc Szeftel. *Le geste du Prince Igor.* New York: École Libre des Hautes Études.

1950s

The Serbian zmaj ognjeni vuk and the Russian Vseslav Epos. Brussels: Annuaire de l'institut de philologie et d'histoire orientales et slaves de l'université de Bruxelles, 1950.

1970s

Poesie und Sprachstruktur. Zürich: Verlag der Arche, 1970.

Lingüística y significación. Personalidades entrevistadas: Roman Jakobson y André Martinet. Ed. José Manuel Blecua. Barcelona: Salvat Editores, 1973.

Questions de poétique. Paris: Éditions de Seuil, 1973.

Form und Sinn: Sprachwissenschaftliche Betrachtungen. Munich: W. Fink, 1974.

Coup d'oeil sur le développement de la sémiotique. Atlantic Highlands, NJ: Humanities Press, 1975.

Ensayos de lingüística general. Barcelona: Seix Barral, 1975.

Lingüística e comunicação. Trans. Izidoro Blikstein and José Paulo Paes. Sao Paulo: Editora Cultrix, 1975.

Hölderlin, Klee, Brecht: Zur Wortkunst dreier Gedichte. Ed. with an introduction by Elmar Holenstein. Frankfurt am Main: Suhrkamp, 1976.

Six leçons sur le son et le sens. Paris: Éditions de Minuet, 1976.

Der grammatische Aufbau der Kindersprache. Opladen: Westdeutscher Verlag, 1977.

Ensayos de poética. Mexico: Fondo de Cultura Economica, 1977.

Huit questions de poétique. Paris: Éditions du Seuil, 1977.

Elementer, funktioner og strukturer i sproget. Copenhagen: Nyt Nordisk Forlag, 1979.

Hölderlin. Genoa: Il Melangolo, 1979.

Poetik. Frankfurt am Main: Suhrkamp, 1979.

1980s

with Krystyna Pomorska. *Dialogues.* Paris: Flammarion, 1980.

and Krystyna Pomorska. *Besedy.* Jerusalem: Magnes Press, 1982.

Semiogenesis. Frankfurt am Main: Lang, 1982.

Poesie und Grammatik. Frankfurt am Main: Suhrkamp, 1982.

Izbrannye raboty. Ed. V. A. Zvegincev. Moscow: Progress, 1985.

Russie folie poésie. Paris: Seuil, 1986.

Raboty po poetike. Ed. M. L. Gasparova. Moscow: Progress, 1987.

Semiotik. Frankfurt am Main: Suhrkamp, 1988.

1990s

Poetická funkce: Literárněvědná řada. Výbor připravil Miroslav Červenka. Jinočany: H+H, 1995.

Meine futuristischen Jahre. Berlin: Friedenauer Presse, 1999.

2000s

Poesie der Grammatik und Grammatik der Poesie: Sämtliche Gedichtanalysen. Berlin: de Gruyter, 2006.

English Translations of Books by Roman Jakobson

1940s

Notes on General Linguistics: Its Present State and Crucial Problems. Cambridge: s.n., 1949.

1950s

Slavic Languages. New York: Department of Slavic Languages, Columbia University, 1950.

with C. Gunnar M. Fant and Morris Halle. *Preliminaries to Speech Analysis: The Distinctive Features and Their Correlates.* Cambridge: Acoustics Laboratory, MIT, 1952.

and Morris Halle. *Fundamentals of Language.* The Hague: Mouton, 1956.

Shifters, Verbal Categories and the Russian Verb. Cambridge: Department of Slavic Languages and Literatures, Harvard University, 1957.

with Gerta Huttl-Worth and John Fred Beebe. *Paleosiberian Peoples and Languages: A Bibliographical Guide*. New Haven: HRAF Press, 1957.

Medieval Mock Mystery: The Old Czech Unguentarius. Tübingen/Basel: Francke Verlag, 1958.

1960s

Studies in Russian Philology. Ann Arbor: Dept. of Slavic Languages and Literature, University of Michigan, 1962.

and Dean S. Worth, eds. *Sofonija's Tale of the Russian-Tatar Battle on the Kulikovo Field*. The Hague: Mouton Publishers, 1963.

Child Language: Aphasia and Phonological Universals. The Hague: Mouton, 1968.

[See also *Selected Writings* in 2000s section below.]

1970s

and Lawrence G. Jones. *Shakespeare's Verbal Art in the Experience of Spirit*. The Hague: Mouton, 1970.

and Shigeo Kawamoto, eds. *Studies in General and Oriental Linguistics, Presented to Shiro Hattori on the Occasion of His Sixtieth Birthday*. Tokyo: TEC Co., 1970.

Studies in Verbal Art: Texts in Czech and Slovak. Ann Arbor: Dept. of Slavic Languages and Literature, University of Michigan, 1971.

Studies on Child Language and Aphasia. The Hague: Mouton Publishers, 1971.

"Verbal Communication." In *Communication: A Scientific American Book*. Ed. Dennis Flanagan, et al., 37–44. San Francisco, CA: W. H. Freeman & Co., 1972.

C. H. van Schooneveld, and Dean S. Worth, eds. *Slavic Poetics: Essays in Honor of Kiril Taranovsky*. The Hague: Mouton Publishers, 1973.

Main Trends in the Science of Language. London: Allen and Unwin, 1973.

Puskin and His Sculptural Myth. Trans. and ed. John Burbank. The Hague: Mouton Publishers, 1975.

assisted by H. Baran, O. Ronen, and Martha Taylor. *N. S. Trubetzoky's Letter and Notes*. The Hague: Mouton, 1975.

and Stephen Rudy. *Yeats' Sorrow of Love through the Years*. Lisse: Peter de Ridder Press, 1977.

Six Lectures on Sound and Meaning. Trans. John Mepham. Cambridge: MIT Press, 1978.

and Linda R. Waugh; assisted by Martha Taylor. *The Sound Shape of Language*. Sussex: Harvester Press, 1979.

[See also *Selected Writings* in 2000s section below.]

1980s

assisted by Kathy Santilli. *Brain and Language: Cerebral Hemispheres and Linguistic Structure in Mutual Light*. Columbus, Ohio: Slavica, 1980.

The Framework of Language. Ann Arbor: University of Michigan Press, 1980.

and Krystyna Pomorska. *Dialogues*. Trans. Christian Hubert. Cambridge: MIT Press, 1983.

Russian and Slavic Grammar: Studies, 1931–1981. Ed. Linda R. Waugh and Morris Halle. The Hague: Mouton, 1984.

Verbal Art, Verbal Sign, Verbal Time. Ed. Krystyna Pomorska and Stephen Rudy; assisted by Brent Vine. Oxford: B. Blackwell, 1985.

Russian Epic Studies. Berlin: Kraus International Publishers, 1986.

Language in Literature. Ed. Krystyna Pomorska and Stephen Rudy. Cambridge, MA: Belknap Press, 1987.

[See also *Selected Writings* in 2000s section below.]

1990s

On Language. Ed. Linda R. Waugh and Monique Monville-Burston. Cambridge: Harvard University Press, 1990.

and Linda R. Waugh. *Jakobson on Saussure.* Berlin: Mouton de Gruyter, 1996.

My Futurist Years. Ed. Bengt Jangfeldt and Stephen Rudy. Trans. Stephen Rudy. New York: Marsilio Publishers, 1998.

[See also *Selected Writings* in 2000s section below.]

2000s

Selected Writings (9 vols.). Berlin: Mouton de Gruyter, 1961–2002. [Unless noted, volumes were edited by Jakobson.]

Vol. 1: *Phonological Studies.* Berlin: Mouton de Gruyter, 1962.

Vol. 2: *Word and Language.* Berlin: Mouton de Gruyter, 1971.

Vol. 3: *Poetry of Grammar and Grammar of Poetry.* Ed. Stephen Rudy. Berlin: Mouton de Gruyter, 1981.

Vol. 4: *Slavic Epic Studies.* Berlin: Mouton de Gruyter, 1966.

Vol. 5: *On Verse, Its Masters and Explorers.* Ed. Stephen Rudy and Martha Taylor. Berlin: Mouton de Gruyter, 1979.

Vol. 6: *Early Slavic Paths and Crossroads: Part 1 and Part 2.* Ed. Stephen Rudy. Berlin: Mouton de Gruyter, 1985.

Vol. 7: *Contributions to Comparative Mythology: Studies in Linguistics and Philology, 1972–1982.* Ed. Stephen Rudy. Berlin: Mouton de Gruyter, 1985.

Vol. 8: *Major Works, 1976–1980.* Ed. Stephen Rudy. Berlin: Mouton de Gruyter, 1988.

Vol. 9: *Roman Jakobson, 1896–1982: A Complete Bibliography of His Writings.* Compiled and ed. by Stephen Rudy. Berlin: Mouton de Gruyter, 1990.

Books by Michel Foucault

1950s

Maladie mentale et personnalité. Paris: Presses Universitaires de France, 1954.

1960s

Folie et déraison: Histoire de la folie à l'âge classique. Thèse princip. Paris: Plon, 1961.

Maladie mentale et psychologie. Paris: Presses Universitaires de France, 1962.

Naissance de la clinique: Une archéologie du regard médical. Paris: Presses Universitaires de France, 1963.

Raymond Roussel. Paris: Gallimard, 1963.

Les Mots et les choses: Une archéologie des sciences humaines. Paris: Gallimard, 1966.

Maladie mentale et psychologie. Paris: Presses Universitaires de France, 1966.

L'Archéologie du savoir. Paris: Gallimard, 1969.

1970s

Translation: *Immanuel Kant: Anthropologie du point de vue pragmatique.* Paris: J. Vrin, 1970.

L'Ordre du discours. Paris, Gallimard, 1971.

Histoire de la folie à l'âge classique: Suivi de mon corps, ce papier, ce feu et la folie, l'absence d'œuvre. Paris: Gallimard, 1972.

Neuer Faschismus, neue Demokratie. Über d. Legilität d. Faschismus im Rechtsstaat. Berlin West: Wagenbach, 1972.

Ceci n'est pas une pipe: Deux lettres et quatre dessins de René Magritte. Montpellier: Fata Morgana, 1973.

Schriften zur Literatur. Trans. Karin von Hofer. Munich: Nymphenburger, 1974.

Surveiller et Punir: Naissance de la Prison. Paris: Gallimard, 1975.

(Edited) *Der Fall Rivière: Materialien zum Verhältnis von Psychiatrie u. Strafjustiz.* Trans. Wolf Heinrich Leube. Frankfurt am Main: Suhrkamp, 1975.

Histoire de la sexualité I, Volonté de savoir. Paris: Gallimard, 1976.

Die Mikrophysik der Macht: Über Strafjustiz, Psychiatrie und Medizin. Berlin West: Merve, 1976.

Dispositive der Macht: Über Sexualität, Wissen und Wahrheit. Berlin West: Merve, 1978.

1980s

Von der Freundschaft als Lebensweise: Michel Foucault im Gespräch. Trans. Marianne Karbe. Berlin: Merve, circa 1984.

Histoire de la sexualité II, L'usage des plaisire. Paris: Gallimard, 1984.

Histoire de la sexualité III, Le Souci de soi. Paris Gallimard, 1984.

Philosophien: Gespräche mit Michel Foucault. Ed. Peter Engelmann. Graz: Böhlau, 1985.

La Pensée du dehors. Frontfroide-le-Haut: Fata Morgana, 1986.

Sept Propos sur le septième ange. Frontfroide-le-Haut: Fata Morgana, 1986.

Vom Licht des Krieges zur Geburt der Geschichte. Berlin: Merve, 1986.

1990s

Was ist Kritik? Trans. Walter Seitter. Berlin: Merve, 1992.

Dits et écrits: 1954–1988; II. Paris: Gallimard, 1994.

Dits et écrits: 1954–1988; III. Paris: Gallimard, 1994.

Dits et écrits: 1954–1988; IV. Paris: Gallimard, 1994.

Herculine Barbin dite Alexina B. Paris: Gallimard, 1993.

Moi, Pierre Rivière, Ayant Égorgé ma Mère, ma Sœur et mon Frère: Un cas de parricide au XIXe siècle. Paris: Gallimard, 1994.

(Coauthored: Foucault, Michel, and Ducio Tombadori.) *Der Mensch ist ein Erfahrungstier: Gespräch mit Ducio Trombadori.* Frankfurt am Main: Suhrkamp, 1996.

L'usage des plaisirs. Paris: Gallimard, 1997.

(Coauthored: Deleuze, Gilles, Michel Foucault, and Adrian Rifkin.) *Gérard Fromanger: La peinture photogénique.* London: Black Dog, 1999.

2000s

Les Vieux métiers illustrés par la chanson: Métiers du terroir et de l'eau. Paris: Godefroy, 2000.

Das Leben der infamen Menschen. Ed. and trans. Walter Seitter. Berlin: Merve, 2001.

La Peinture de Manet. Ed. Maryvonne Saison. Paris: Seuil, 2004.

Seminars and Lectures by Michel Foucault

1970s

Leçon inaugurale faite le . . . 2 décembre 1970. Paris: Le Collège de France, 1970.

Résumé des cours, 1970–1982. Paris: Julliard, 1989.

L'ordre du discours: Leçon inaugurale au Collège de France prononcée le 2 décembre 1970. Paris: Gallimard, 1971.

Le Pouvoir psychiatrique: Cours au Collège de France, 1973–1974. Ed. François Ewald and Alessandro Fontana. Paris: Gallimard, 2003.

Les anormaux: Cours au Collège de France (1974–1975). Paris: Gallimard, 1999.

Il Faut défendre la société: Cours au Collège de France, 1975–1976. Paris: Gallimard, 1997.

Sécurité, territoire, population: Cours au Collège de France: 1977–1978. Ed. François Ewald and Alessandro Fontana. Paris: Gallimard, 2004.

Naissance de la biopolitique: Cours au Collège de France: 1978–1979. Ed. François Ewald and Alessandro Fontana. Paris: Gallimard, 2004.

1980s

L'herméneutique du sujet: Cours au Collège de France, 1981–1982. Ed. François Ewald. Paris: Gallimard, 2001.

Le Désordre des familles. Lettres de cachet des archives de la Bastille au XVIIIe siècle. With Arlette Farge. Paris: Collection Archives, 1982.

Diskurs und Wahrheit: Die Problematisierung der Parrhesia; 6 Vorlesungen, gehalten im Herbst 1983 an der Universität von Berkeley, Kalifornien. Ed. Joseph Pearson. Berlin: Merve, 1996.

English Translations of Books by Michel Foucault

1960s

Madness and Civilization: A History of Insanity in the Age of Reason. Trans. Richard Howard. New York: Pantheon Books, 1965.

1970s

The Order of Things: An Archaeology of the Human Sciences. London: Tavistock Publications, 1970.

The Order of Discourse. New York: Pantheon, 1971.

The Archaeology of Knowledge & The Discourse on Language. Trans. A. M. Sheridan Smith. New York: Pantheon Books, 1972.

Birth of the Clinic: An Archaeology of Medical Perception. Trans. A. M. Sheridan Smith. New York: Pantheon Books, 1973.

Mental Illness and Psychology. Trans. Alan Sheridan. New York: Harper & Row, 1976.

Discipline and Punish: The Birth of the Prison. Tran. Alan Sheridan. New York: Pantheon Books, 1977.

Language, Counter-memory, Practice: Selected Essays and Interviews. Ed. Donald F. Bouchard. Trans. Donald F. Bouchard and Sherry Simon. Ithaca, NY: Cornell University Press, 1977.

The History of Sexuality. Vol. 1: An Introduction. Trans. Robert Hurley. New York: Pantheon Books, 1978.

1980s

Power/Knowledge: Selected Interviews and Other Writings, 1972–1977. Ed. and trans. Colin Gordon. New York: Pantheon Books, 1980.

This Is Not a Pipe. Ed. and trans. James Harkness. Berkeley: University of California Press, 1983.

Discourse and Truth: The Problematization of Parrhesia. Evanston, IL: Northwestern University Press, 1985.

The History of Sexuality, Vol. II: The Use of Pleasure. Trans. Robert Hurley. New York: Random House, 1985.

Death and the Labyrinth: The World of Raymond Roussel. Trans. Charles Ruas. Garden City, NY: Doubleday, 1986.

The History of Sexuality, Vol. III: The Care of the Self. Trans. Robert Hurley. New York: Random House, 1986.

Maurice Blanchot: The Thought from Outside. Trans. Brian Massumi. New York: Zone Books, 1987.

Foucault Live (Interviews, 1966–84). Ed. Sylvère Lotringer. Trans. John Johnston. New York: Semiotext(e), 1989.

1990s

Foucault, Michel. *Ethics: Subjectivity and Truth.* Ed. Paul Rabinow. Trans. Robert Hurley. New York: New Press, 1997.

Politics of Truth. Ed. Sylvère Lotringer and Lysa Hochroth. New York: Semiotext(e), 1997.

Aesthetics, Method, and Epistemology. Ed. James D. Faubion. Trans. Robert Hurley. New York: New Press, 1998.

Religion and Culture. Ed. Jeremy R. Carrette. New York: Routledge, 1999.

2000s

Power. Ed. James D. Faubion. Trans. Robert Hurley. New York: New Press, 2000.

Fearless Speech. Ed. Joseph Pearson. Los Angeles: Semiotext(e), 2001.

Archaeology of Knowledge. New York: Routledge, 2002.

Abnormal: Lectures at the Collège de France, 1974–1975. Ed. Valerio Marchetti and Antonella Salomoni. Trans. Graham Burchell. New York: Picador, 2003.

Society Must Be Defended: Lectures at the Collège de France, 1975–76. Ed. Mauro Bertani and Alessandro Fontana. Trans. David Macey. New York: Picador, 2003.

Jean Gebser (1905–1973)

Biographical Sketch

Hans (Jean) Gebser was born in Pozen, Prussia (now Poznan, Poland), on August 20, 1905. He was born into an aristocratic family and lived in an educated and cultured environment. His father was Friedrich Wilhelm Gebser, Royal Prussian Counsellor of Justice; his mother was Margarete Charlotte Grundmann. The family moved as his father's employment required—from Posen to Breslau, to Königsberg, to Berlin. Gebser received his early schooling in Königsberg, then attended preparatory school in Rossleben on the Unstrut, and later high school in Berlin.

Different sources report inconsistent information about the life of Jean Gebser. Information for this biographical sketch was drawn from "About the Jean Gebser Society for the Study of Culture and Consciousness," International Jean Gebser Conference Program (California, PA: University of Pennsylvania, 1996); Georg Feuerstein, M. Litt, and Elizabeth Behnke, "Jean Gebser—The Man and His Work" (Felton, CA: California Center for Jean Gebser Studies, n.d.); "Gebser, Jean," *Here-Now4U: Online Magazine*—http://www.here-now4u.de/eng/gebser_biography.htm (accessed August 17, 2005); Jean Keckeis, "In Memoriam Jean Gebser," in Jean Gebser, *The Ever-Present Origin*, trans. Noel Barstad and Algis Mickunas (Athens, OH: Ohio University Press, 1985), xvii–xxi; Ed Mahood, Jr., "The Primordial Leap and the Present: The Ever-Present Origin—An Overview of the Work of Jean Gebser"—http://www.gaiamind.org/Gebser.html (accessed October 9, 2003). Photograph courtesy of Algis Mickunas.

Difficulties between his parents drove him inward and he turned his attention toward literature. Following his father's death in 1922, he quit high school and spent two years as a bank apprentice at Deutsche Bank Berlin. As a young man he was a part-time student at the University of Berlin, where he was influenced by Catholic philosopher Ramano Guardini, who exhibited a great depth of knowledge and spirituality. He also discovered the poetry of Rainer Maria Rilke, which affected his thought. He confronted despair and realized that he must venture out in life. In 1927, while working in Florence, Italy, at a second-hand bookstore Gebser came to the realization that books cannot teach a person how to live and he began an active quest toward personal fulfillment.

After returning to Germany, Gebser finally left the country in 1931; the appearance of the Nazi Brown Shirts in Munich provided him the impetus to relocate. Gebser traveled first to Paris and then to southern France, where he changed his German name "Hans" to the French name "Jean." He eventually settled in Madrid, Spain. He learned the language and obtained a position in the Ministry of Education, published some of his poems, and made friends with many prominent Spaniards, including Frederico Garcia Lorca.

In 1936, when war overtook Spain, he fled (twelve hours before his apartment was bombed) to Paris. There he associated with the circle of artists surrounding Picasso and Malraux. He fled Paris as the city fell in 1939 and went to Switzerland, leaving two hours before the Germans sealed off the border to France. He would reside in Switzerland for the rest of his life.

In 1942 he married Gentiane Hélène Schoch. He became a Swiss citizen in 1951. He was unable to assume the duties associated with his chair for the Study of Comparative Civilizations at the University of Salzburg due to a progressively worsening case of asthma, which forced him to avoid exertion and remain close to his home in Berne. In 1955 his wife was disinherited and in 1956 they were divorced.

Gebser supported himself by freelance writing. He continued to travel extensively, journeying to Greece, Indian, China, Japan, France (Provence), and Germany. In 1968 he married Jo Körner-Schneeberger in Bern and continued to teach, travel, write, and lecture.

Jean Gebser died on May 14, 1973, in Wabern, Switzerland, where he is also buried.

Jean Gebser's Cosmology
Poetic Openings and Dialogic Possibilities

Pat Arneson

Jean Gebser's scholarship is increasingly important for a postmodern age in which there is growing recognition that contingent relations do not seem to "fit" contemporary historical logic, and discomfiting realities present themselves in nonsensical ways. Gebser was a cultural philosopher, and his first works originated during the Nazi occupation of Europe. At this time there was great pessimism about global events, but Gebser offered an optimistic voice. In seeking to understand the enfolded dimensions of human consciousness, he interpreted events in Europe from 1914 to 1945 as indicating a structure of consciousness near the end of its effectiveness. A linguist and poet, the first evidence he documented regarding a shift in global consciousness was in the novel use of language in literature. He later augmented that work to include changes occuring in the sciences and arts. Gebser's most important work, *The Ever-Present Origin,* evidences this shift in global consciousness.[1]

This chapter overviews Gebser's cosmological theory and further discusses potentialities in his work for enhancing communication scholarship. First, I address the historical context that compelled Gebser's writing and identify the significance of his ideas for a postmodern age, a time not altogether dissimilar from his own. Second, I outline Gebser's dimensions of consciousness, which include the archaic, vital-magical, psychic-mythical, mental-rational, and integral structures. Each "structure" or "dimension" holds distinct nuances that contribute differently to configure cultures in varying ways. Third, I consider how poetic expression provides an opening through which the comprehensive integral dimension can be revealed. The work of Martin Buber, a philosopher of dialogue, exhibits how dimensions of consciousness are available in the "between"[2] of dialogue. His use of Hasidic tales, or what I call "poetic narratives," in dialogue aware/call the listener to Gebser's integral dimension of consciousness.

Contextualizing Gebser's Work

Catastrophic events in Europe during the first half of the twentieth century compelled Jean Gebser to recognize a shift in global awareness. The war between Austria-Hungary and Serbia, which began with the assassination of Archduke Franz Ferdinand, escalated to become World War I. The Reichstag in Germany issued the Nuremberg Laws, which instigated the Holocaust of Jewish people during World War II. Japan's early invasion of China and subsequent attack on the United States at Pearl Harbor resulted in President Harry S. Truman's decision to drop the atomic bomb on Hiroshima and Nagasaki. The convergence of these and other world events prompted Gebser's work.

Michael Purdy outlined three facets shaping Gebser's project.[3] First, Gebser sought to understand how the configuration of cultures could lead to such tragedy. Gebser wrote, "The crisis we are experiencing today is not just a European crisis, nor a crisis of morals, economics, ideologies, politics or religion. It is not only prevalent in Europe and America but in Russia and the Far East as well. . . . [O]ur world . . . appears headed toward an event which . . . can only be described as a 'global catastrophe.'"[4] Second, the work of Oswald Spengler and others, popular during the early twentieth century, presented a pessimistic view of the enduring potential for the achievements of humankind. Spengler believed that Western culture was doomed, like other cultures before it, and had already entered its final stage.[5] As an optimist, Gebser expressed a more positive, integral possibility for the world's future. Third, Gebser wanted to constructively influence the shaping and building of future Europe. Purdy noted, "This is one reason he published EPO [*The Ever-Present Origin*] with an East German publisher who had published other important works of the time. He wanted to indicate what he perceived as the optimistic trend of civilization and mark the way for others to follow."[6] Gebser believed that people acting in harmony with the integral could induce positive cultural resonances: "[H]ow we shout into the woods is how the echo will sound. . . . *Everything that happens to us, then, is only the answer and echo of what and how we ourselves are.* And the answer will be an integral answer only if we have approached the integral in ourselves."[7]

The potential inherent in Gebser's work continues to be revealed, even after his death. With the fall of the Berlin Wall, Communism began to disintegrate at the end of the 1980s, first in Eastern Europe and then in the Soviet Union. While this brought an end to the Cold War, it also created new sources of international instability. The end of Communism allowed long-suppressed nationalism to rise in the former Soviet Union and in Yugoslavia. The 1990s saw intensification of Islamic fundamentalism in the Middle East and part of Asia. The 2000s witnessed the tragic events of 9/11, which prompted the U.S. government to declare a global war on "terrorism." The conflict of religious ideas and the tension between religious zeal and secular values began to replace political ideologies as the basis for international strife.[8]

Postmodernity has been thoroughly ushered into global civilizations. The term "postmodernity," in general, refers to aspects of contemporary life that resulted from trends characterizing the late twentieth and early twenty-first centuries. This characteristics include globalization, consumerism, fragmentation of authority, and the commoditization of knowledge. Nicholas C. Burbules and Suzanne Rice explain that writers who discuss qualities of postmodern culture emphasize three central ideas. First, postmodernists reject the possibility that an "absolute" universal social theory exists: there are no "absolutes." No single rationality, no single morality, and no ruling theoretical framework exist for the analysis of social and political events. As Lyotard noted, there are no "meta-narratives," because that would be synonymous with the hegemony of a social and political order. Second, all social and political discourse is saturated with power or dominance. Postmodernists suggest we need to understand structures that underlie social action. This is possible by deconstructing how ideological and institutional power plays in our own practices. Third, the celebration of "difference" emerges as a theme. Postmodernists do not attempt to judge or prioritize the explanatory or political significance of certain elements in a social situation; they argue that "because all signifiers are mere constructions, there is no clear reason to grant any one special significance or value over others." Postmodernists encourage what Bakhtin called "heteroglossia," the inclusion of as many voices and perspectives as possible, without seeking to reconcile them or combine them into a single, consistent, unified account.[9]

Postmodernism is "indifferent to questions of consistency and continuity. It self-consciously slices genres, attitudes, styles. It relishes the blurring or juxtaposition of forms . . . stances . . . moods . . . cultural levels. . . . It neither embraces nor criticizes, but beholds the world blankly, with a knowingness that dissolves feeling and commitment into irony."[10] Gebser would point to the multiple dimensions of consciousness present in such difference.

Dimensions of Expressive Consciousness[11]

Jean Gebser's work considered the basic forms of ontological perception present in culture. Rather than focusing on transformations that took place within individual boundaried cultures, he suggested that there is a *Gestalt* within which all spheres of culture coexist. Gebser identified five perceptual formations (or "structures of consciousness"[12]) within which cultures are organized: the archaic, the vital-magical, the psychic-mythic, the mental-rational, and the integral. Gebser would not characterize these dimensions as evolutionary. The structures are not strictly historical and cannot be understood as merely a linear progression. They are all operating (in some ways latent) in our present lived experience. The emergence of each structure is a mutation, an abrupt transition from the previous form. There is a tension and interpenetration of these modes of awareness or dimensions of consciousness—"the dividing, disrupting, and dissolving aspects"[13] that prepare the way of awakening consciousness. The dynamism of their interpenetration and the ways in which perceptual elements are organized generates the parameters that comprise a given cultural system.

The Archaic Structure.[14] The archaic structure is "the structure closest to and presumably originally identical with origin." However, only in a terminological sense is "origin" considered the first structure to emerge from the initial unity of consciousness. Archaic structure is "prespatial" and "pretemporal." The human is completely coextensive with the world; in that sense this structure is "a time of complete nondifferentiation of man and the universe"—without perspective. "For the archaic human, perception was zero-dimensional, representing a posture of *identity* with the natural world, a sense of being completely embedded in it." Although the soul may have further existed, it had not yet attained consciousness. Gebser identified "deep sleep" as a degree of consciousness in the archaic dimension, in view of its function in the awakening process. He recognized "presentiment" as the expression of realization and thought in the archaic structure. Presentiment indicates a connection with the past and an incorporation of the future.

Georg Feuerstein notes that archaic presentiments cannot be expressed in words, but they "break through when we are overwhelmed by those inexplicable presentiments that put us in touch with the flux of the world process: when we experience ourselves as part of the past-present-future continuum. . . . [These presentiments] furnish us with a total *Gestalt* that, even without our conscious cooperation, may redirect our lives. The archaic structure makes our courage-to-be possible."[15] Even though the soul is dormant, it is concerned with survival and movement toward awareness in the vital-magical structure.

The Magic Structure.[16] Gebser noted the vital-magical structure releases humans from their identity with "origin." Kramer and Mickunas explained, "with the mutation from archaic unity to magic awareness, a rudimentary sense of space emerges as does its correlate, the self."[17] This structure presents the first fully human mode of consciousness. The magical release opens the first process of human consciousness, which is completely like sleep. People can understand the world in its outlines. People do not yet recognize the world as a whole, but only the details that reach this sleep-like state, wherein a part stands for the whole. Magical reality is "a world of pure but meaningful accident; a world in which all things and persons are interrelated, but the not-yet-centered Ego is dispersed over the world of phenomena."

The mode of expression in this structure is "vital experience," which is prerational and precausal. Vital experience elicits "a still sleep-like consciousness of being interwoven with events and is recognizable by its associative, analogizing, and sympathetic treatment of things that cannot be considered 'thinking.'"[18] In this dimension, humans seek to be free from the transcendent power of nature—the "soul strives to materialize . . . [and] become increasingly conscious of itself." Impulse and instinct develop a vital consciousness which enables man or woman to cope with the earth and the world as group-ego.

Gebser represented humans in the vital-magical dimension by the one-dimensional point: "the point suggests the initial emergent centering in man and expresses the spaceless and timeless one-dimensionality of magic man's world." Perception is one-dimensional, allowing a sense of unity, but not of complete identity; perception is yet pre-perspectival. Distance is not experienced as an aspect of the world. Because of the "spaceless-timeless" unity, every "point" (whether it be a thing, an event, or an action) can be interchanged with another "point," independent of time, space, and rational-causal connection. In the magical dimension, every event is connected to and can be transformed into every other event—each has the power to become the other. There is no symbolic distance. "Accidents, probabilities, and coincidence do not happen here."[19]

We move "in the sphere of influence of the magical structure when we pray or meditate deeply, or when we are 'lost' in play or ritual—as when we watch a race or game. Then our wakefulness is diminished because our attention is bundled to take in a single event [ego-consciousness becomes point-like], and our organism is flooded with excitement."[20] In the magical dimension, the stress is on emotion. Humans immediately place any occurrence, event, or object that has the nature of a vital experience into a unifying context. Further mutation of consciousness reveals the psychic-mythic structure.

The Mythical Structure.[21] The psychic-mythic structure is "distinct from the magic in that it bears the stamp of imagination. . . . The mythic structure . . . whose unperspectival two-dimensionality has an imaginatory consciousness." Consciousness is "dreamlike" in its awareness. "Although still distant from space, the mythical structure is already on the verge of time. The imaginatory consciousness still alternates between magical timelessness and the dawning awareness of natural cosmic periodicity. The farther myth stands removed from consciousness, the greater its degree of timelessness; its unreflective ground resembles the reverse side of a mirror. By contrast, the closer its proximity to consciousness, the greater emphasis on time."

While the magical structure contains point-for-point identification of every vital event with every other vital event, the mythical structure relates events in polarities. In the psychic-mythical dimension, all symbolic thought is structured in terms of a cyclical process of polarities which constantly move toward and through each other. "Polarity" refers to the dynamic movement of one event, image, or feeling that provokes, attracts, and requires another event. One is never given without the other, and one may replace the other. This movement comprises a rhythmic and synchronizing mode of awareness that is "cyclically temporic"[22]—the cycles repeat themselves over time.

Kramer and Mickunas note that instances of the activation of the mythical structure are abundant. The hunger for experience is an expression of the mythical structure of consciousness. Experience is inherently irrational. And the irrational is the domain of the psyche and thus of the mythical structure. The mythological structure "has very little to do with storytelling or fables, although stories and fables usually manifest the ways, images, sayings, and human relations in which the mythological structure appears."[23] Feuerstein comments, "Our present-day fascination with imagery (witness television, media advertising, video tames, etc.) is an excrescence of the mythical structure. The deficiency of our insatiable fascination with imagery—a latter-day form of idolatry—is evident in the passive mood with which it is pursued; we allow the images tailored by the consumer experts to wash over us and in this way seek to vicariously participate in the experience of others. Such experiencing scarcely leads to insight but merely aggravates the obsession with visual or passive experiential stimulation."[24] In this way, polarities and shifts in polarity are made available to societal members through the mental-rational structure of consciousness.

The Mental Structure.[25] "The mythical consciousness does not retain its polarizing and psychic character indefinitely; it undergoes a mutation that leads to the preeminence of a mental structure of consciousness."[26] The three-dimensional mental-rational realm is the dimension with which we are most familiar in everyday life. In the mental structure, consciousness is wakefulness. Emergence of consciousness involves "awakening-to-self." Acts of consciousness depend on waking, mental consciousness.

Kramer and Mickunas clarified four characteristics which distinguish the mental-rational dimension. First (and resonant of the psychic-mythical dimension), the mental structure is dualistic. Concepts are arranged in "rational opposition," antagonistic to one another. Mental consciousness seeks to overcome and reconcile oppositional alternatives. Thus, attention is given to "mind" over matter. Second, mind is regarded as a function of "directedness, orientation, and . . . linearity." Third, orientation originates with a center called the ego, which provides a spatial position "from which perspectives become constituted toward the 'object out there.'" Fourth, "the egosubject, as an orientational function, may be treated at a deeper level as constitutive of linear time, while the material side can be regarded as a representation of space."[27] This implies a division of time and space. Further, dimensions of the future "necessarily lend a forward thrust to spatiality, giving both space and time the semblance of direction."[28]

Rational awareness "combats and represses" the archaic, magical, and mythical structures of consciousness.[29] In this structure, abstract concepts replace experience as the dominant social reality. Reality in this dimension of consciousness does not refer to what is present in experience—rather, reality is associated with matter, which can be manipulated to yield predictable results. By defining reality in this way, humans can arrange objects in various ways, calculate their positions and movements, and predict their results.

Gebser noted communication in this dimension is expressed through "representation." This conceptual form of realization, appropriate to the mental structure, is a "form of thinking." Mental consciousness manifests itself in discursive thought using symbols. Communication through the use of abstract, temporal symbols reduces experience to allegory, then to mere formula. "In its extreme form of exaggerated abstractness, [the symbol] is ultimately void in any relation to life and becomes autonomous; empty of content and no longer a sign but only a mental denotation, its effect is predominantly destructive." Words express the energy of our thoughts and ideas. Through the use of words we can convey our ideas to others.

Yet, one's perspectival standpoint limits one's understanding of experience. Once a structure of consciousness becomes deficient (reaches a point of fragmentation), other modes of perception reflect and support irruption of change. Gebser offered two possible theories in considering how structures of consciousness fragment and regenerate. First, an integration could emerge "that is both a mutation and a restructuration of other structures of consciousness."[30] Kavolis explained Gebser's ideas: "structures of consciousness change by a sudden leap when they no longer pose a challenge to the creative mind, when an 'old' structure no longer needs to be shaped."[31] Agents that inspire transformation include philosophers, artists, and, in our current historical moment, scientists. The second possibility Gebser noted is that change could emerge when a dimension of consciousness mutates toward another structure of which one is unaware. In the fragmentation, a prevalent structure is perceived to be missing. "The missing aspect dominates the fragmenting consciousness and . . . can be filled either by reverting to magic and its power to regenerate myths or by tracing out the constitution of an emerging awareness."[32]

In discussing transformation, Gebser introduced the concept of "plus-mutation," which is different from the conventional idea of a mutation. "'Plus-mutation' describes a process of enrichment rather than destruction. The 'past state' is not surpassed or abandoned, but instead, is added to." The ever-present structures of consciousness are configured differently, which accounts for cultural differences.

The Integral Structure.[33] Gebser sought an intuitive grasp of the four-dimensional whole, an integrative totality of culture. Gebser defined integration to mean full, complete, and realized wholeness. He grounded culture "within a multilayered conception of the communication process (thereby relating it to the transformation of modes of awareness)."[34] "The concretion of everything that has unfolded in time and coalesced in a spatial array is the integral attempt to reconstitute the 'magnitude' of man from his constituent aspects, so that he can consciously integrate himself into the whole." The integral is "a *space-and-time free* aperspectival world where the free (or freed) consciousness has at its disposal all latent as well as actual forms of space and time, without having either to deny them or to be fully subject to them."[35] Integration is an intensification of consciousness, irreducible to any qualitative valuation or quantitative devaluation. The two basic features of integral awareness are transparent consciousness and atemporality.

First, "transparency (diaphaneity) is the form of manifestation (epiphany) or the spiritual. Our concern is to render transparent everything latent 'behind' and 'before' the world—to render transparent our own origin, our entire human past, as well as the present, which already contains the future."[36] In the integral dimension, the "itself" pervades or "shines through" everything in diaphanous spirituality. Diaphanous spirituality, "that which shines through," is not a form of symbolism or methodology, "it is neither psychic nor mental, nor does it bear the stamp of magic."[37] Rather, becoming co-visible in and through humans, all previous spatio-temporal unfoldings are integrated and made meaningful. Integration requires "verition," not simply thinking or contemplation, which includes perception as well as imparting verity or truth. Only through "reciprocal perception and impartation of truth by man and the world can the world become transparent for us."[38] The integral dimension subsumes all other modes of awareness, "which continue to operate in their own ways as specialties within a more encompassing design or as levels of communication within it."[39]

The second feature of integral awareness is atemporality. Atemporality "signifies concrete awareness of time as integral, prior to its abstract and linear division into past, present, and future." Atemporality enables aperspectivity—a way of seeing something from all perspectives at once in space-time freedom. "Aperspectivity and atemporality are essential to integrating differentials that allow for openness and yet transparent comprehension."[40]

Gebser leads us to think in terms of integrating, but not in a unifying way. There is no fixed unity, everything is in the process of formation and at the same time deformation, and the integral manifests all of the previous consciousness structures. Instead of a system, Gebser talks of a "systast"—"a process of integration of parts into the whole."[41] The integral consciousness is manifest in aperspectivity, atemporality, and wholeness.

Jean Gebser offered an introduction to the dimensions of consciousness. Each dimension identifies a different way to structure time-space-movement of the world. The archaic dimension is closest with origin, and prehuman. The vital-magical dimension of consciousness deals with the transformative ability of words (e.g., the power of rhetoric to sway human action). In the psychic-mythical dimension, symbolic thought is structured in terms of a cyclical process of polarities which constantly move toward and through each other (e.g., light and dark, male and female). The mental-rational consciousness recognizes that the word is a sum of spatially and temporally arranged objects in a linear, directed orientation (i.e., propositional language). The integral dimension stresses the concrete whole in its dynamic process of temporalization. Gebser suggested the emphasis of a single dimension diminishes an understanding of lived experience. One's access to the integral dimension of consciousness is available through poetic expression.

Poetic Expression: Revealing Integral Consciousness

Georg Feuerstein observed, "In the literary field—a milieu in which Gebser is thoroughly at home—the time theme [indicating the mental-rational dimension] has been prominent for the past 180 years."[42] Gebser's 1941 manuscript *The Grammatical Mirror* first identified a shift in grammar that points to a mutation to the integral dimension in poetry.[43] We now turn to a discussion of active poiesis. One manifestation of poiesis is dialogue. The "between" of dialogue that Buber explores in his work enables "poetic narratives" to indicate the integral dimension of consciousness.

The oldest term for "poetry" is "poiēsis," from the Greek. Poiesis means making; a poem is a made thing. Poet Jean Gebser stated: "this effectualization . . . is the source of new [integral] consciousness."[44] Poiesis furnishes an explanation of the interaction of creativity and people. Poetic expression allows us to pursue experiential truth, which is screened out by the constraints of ordinary language.

In eliciting an ego-consciousness in poetry, the initial step toward the supersession of time is a detachment from memory. Gebser explained, "memory is always time-bound . . . it temporalizes the timeless without transforming it into temporal freedom. The turn away from memory . . . is a turn toward freedom; the poetic emphasis shifts from the recollected past to the present."[45] This turn encompasses and requires a new consciousness structure. In Gebser's words, poetry "writes a history of the dateless." Poetic language articulates social, political, and scientific actualities indicated by poiesis. These actualities are prompted from "semiotic disruption and be/come the poetic word."[46]

The integral is aperspectival; it does not assume a specific viewpoint. In poetry, we can discern the shift of consciousness which has overdetermined the three-dimensional (temporal) mode toward the four-dimensional (atemporal) mode of understanding. Gebser explains, "Aperspectival expression raises origin into the present, rendering it transparent." Each word holds expressive power; in the integral dimension, the word is "freed from the limits of space and time, giving birth to aperspectival language capable of expressing the new consciousness structure."[47] Aperspectival language is not "new," but reflects meanings anew. Russian poet Boris Pasternak, author of *Doctor Zhivago,* noted: "The most extraordinary discoveries are made when the artist is overwhelmed by what he has to say. Then he uses the old language in his urgency and the old language is transformed from within."[48]

In the integral dimension, the concern is no longer oriented around the temporal, sequential succession of terms attached to memory. Instead, the emphasis is on the true and undivided whole: (1) time is expressed essentially as the "originating-creative nature" of language is recognized; (2) time is expressed psychically as expression yields to "stream of consciousness"; (3) time is expressed thematically as poetry deals explicitly with "the time problem"; and (4) time is expressed structurally as grammatical aspects enable "a novel use of syntactical freedom."[49] In poiesis, meaning is pulled through the poetic line, announcing the unconscious dimension available in dialogue.

Dialogue: "A Species of Poetry."[50] Within the last ten years, there has been a strong resurgence of interest in "dialogue" as a form of communication. The postmodern moment provides a space for dialogue not called for in other historical moments. Kenneth N. Cissna and Rob Anderson noted that in communication studies, postmodernism shifts the "focus from an 'elite speaker' to ... 'emerging,' 'muted,' or 'subaltern' voices." In postmodernity, "dialogic truth is not a matter of propositions but of presence."[51] The term "dialogue" is conceived differently from various philosophical perspectives. I draw upon the work of a philosopher of dialogue, Martin Buber, to show how poiesis is present in the "between" of dialogue, offering an opening to dimensions of consciousness. The term "dialogue" is intended in the fullest sense of Buber's philosophy of dialogue: "address and response and the reality of meeting and of the 'between.'"[52]

Writing in the same time period as Gebser, Buber perceived that the human could not become more disengaged from oneself or one's essence: "It seems that all original relations are about to break asunder, and all original being about to fall apart." The global crisis of humanity seemed to present only two alternatives: "either a renewed relation to being or the annihilation of the human form of life."[53] Both Buber and Gebser address the poetic as a way to optimistically access possibilities in the lifeworld. Gebser emphasized the dimensions of consciousness revealed in the poetic. For Buber, dialogue is a "species of poetry."[54] Taken together, their work exhibits how the dialogic "between" reveals dimensions of consciousness. Dialogue as "polycentric field participation"[55] is the musical dance of poetry that opens the integral dimension.

The "Between:" Openness to the Integral. Buber identified the existential question that guided his work to be "In what way shall we become what we are from the very nature of our being?" His philosophy of dialogue seeks to understand and activate "a quality of attention that is present to the voice of silence that precedes thought and speech (and therefore precedes the existence of 'I' as thought)"[56] Friedman explained that Buber held a "conviction that a form of philosophizing that considers thinking the ground of being is *fundamentally* flawed ... it is incomplete."[57] Thought, speech, and text have a prelinguistic relation to being, present in the "between."

> What is peculiarly characteristic of the human world is above all something that takes place between one being and another, the like of which can be found nowhere in nature. ... It is rooted in one being turning to another as another, as this particular other being, in order to communicate with it in a sphere which is common to them but which reaches out beyond the special sphere of each. I call this sphere, which is established with the existence of man as man but which is conceptually still uncomprehended, the sphere of "between." Though being realized in very different degrees, it is a primal category of human reality.[58]

The "between" is a mental-rational designation for an aspect of communication that allows us to access other dimensions of consciousness.

In poiesis, at work in the "between" of dialogue, Buber explained, the word "moves *between* beings, the mystery of word and answer." Maurice Friedman elaborates on this: "This mystery is not one of union, harmony, or even complementarity, but of *tension;* for two persons never mean the same thing by the words that they use and no answer is ever fully satisfactory. The result is that at each point of the dialogue, understanding and misunderstanding are interwoven."[59] This tension of understanding and misunderstanding reveals the interplay of dimensions. Understanding and misunderstanding arise concurrently: no intersubjective understanding is ever complete. And in the process of "misunderstanding," new understandings emerge.

Buber recognized "the origin of language is in a first, primal form of relation, where the movement of attention is wordless . . . [it] wander[s] without meeting a word."[60] "Thought and words are preceded by the body's awareness of, and relation to, the situation; the silent movement of attention becomes word when it crosses an invisible boundary beyond which are thought, words, and speech. The invisible boundary is called 'language' (*safah*)."[61] Buber recognized that the prelinguistic realm is the source of all linguistic developments.

Dan Avnon explained that the Hebrew word "safah" "points to the demarcation of an edge of one form of substance and the beginning of another." The boundary "delineates a change of form so striking that it is rarely perceived as a transition" but as a both/and mutation of prelinguistic form of relation *and* modes of description, articulation, and spoken communication. Safah, "language," originates "in formless insight preced[ing] its form as thought; thought arises on the far side of safah, serving as an image of the original understanding, as a mode of communicating a prelinguistic relation to being."[62]

The paradoxical nature of Buber's dialogue is that dialogue is not necessarily spoken. Dialogue may emerge as silence, releasing the spell of thought. In the words of Buber: "The lifting of the spell has happened to him—no matter from where—without his doing. But this is what he does now: he releases in himself a reserve over which only he has power. Unreservedly communication streams from him, and the silence bears it to his neighbor.'"[63] This silence can prompt poiesis. The poetic is an expression of art; art is the realm of "between." Buber explained:

> Let us think of a tribe which is close to nature, and which already knows the ax, a simple but reliable stone ax. Then it occurs to a lad to scratch a curved line on his ax with the aid of a sharper stone. This is a picture of something, and of nothing: it may be a sign, but even its author does not know of what. What was in his mind? Magic—to give the tool a more powerful effect? Or simply a play with the possibility presented by the empty space on the shaft? The two things are not mutually exclusive, but they mingle—the magical intention concentrates the play in more solid forms, the free play loosens the form decided on by magic and changes it—but even together these do not suffice to explain the unheard-of fact that a work has been carried out without any model, reaching beyond the technical purpose.[64]

Such work resonates the artistic play of Gebser's structures of consciousness.

Addressing play, Buber explained that the surplus of the situation drives play and its "latent fullness of gestures" to exude the surplus. "[P]lay does not demand of it, as do sensation and end, the choice of a suitable response or act, but the working out of all . . . the exultation of the possible, breaks through ever again, and still swirls around the step of the most disciplined, most controlled of dancers."[65] Play reveals "a totality, uninterpretable, untranslatable, unique and unrelated, yet expressive."[66] The symbol enables this expression to be shared with others.

In play, self incorporates environment and immerses itself into it. When one traces phenomenal awareness, one is "coextensive with . . . the phenomena being traced; . . . The phenomena 'borrow' our modes of awareness to announce themselves." One can read the phenomena across diverse dimensions, or modalities of awareness—from vital-magical through mental-rational—but through all of them the integral originates the "presence-field" that embues the phenomena with more than one can trace.[67] The creative process of play unfolds in dynamic cosmic tensions. "Whenever the symbol appears, it owes its appearance always to the unforeseen, unique occasion, to its having appeared the first time. The symbol derives its enduring character from a transitory event," tracing awareness to express the unbroken meaning of the integral.[68]

Louis Hammer notes that Russian-born German poet Paul Celan, who acknowledges his work was directly influenced by Buber, conceives the genuine poet as faithful to the dialogic possibilities of language. The poet "'takes his very life into speech.' The poem is not a 'structure of experience' or 'structure of meanings' but a living speech charged with the intensity of dialogue and dominated by a movement toward wholeness. Ordinary language takes on 'form' as the poet's talk becomes encounter, a meeting of the One with the Other, mediated by language."[69] The fullness of content is foregrounded in poetics. The world is not comprehensible, but the incomprehensibility can be embraced. Aspects of this incomprehensibility can be indicated in poetic narratives pointing to the integral.

Poetic Narrative: Indicating the Integral. Openings present in the "between" of dialogue allow for the possibility that all dimensions of consciousness can be articulated. Buber recognized that trying to convey his thought to a reader through conceptual language was not sufficient. He frequently used Hasidic tales (*more* than merely aesthetic or "religious"), which I call "poetic narratives," to provide concrete life instances and best represent the idea related to I-Thou that he is trying to express.[70]

Since Buber's passing, work on narrative theory has emerged across "traditional" academic boundaries by scholars of communication, linguists, literary critics, psychologists, philosophers, and theologians. Buber's contribution to understanding the nature of narrative and the unique type of narratives he wrote continue to inform discussions of narrative theory. Buber's "poetic narratives" reveal "the imaginary and the fantastic are mixed with the real. Through story, Buber illustrates that if we do truly seek the fantastic we can find it by looking deeply into the details of the real."[71]

Poetic narratives reveal Buber's I-Thou by moving away from the philosophical concept toward existential experience of human relationships. They focus on individual characters and how the characters are transformed through the event(s). Further, they "search for the moment of change from the ordinary to the extraordinary."[72] In this way, poetic narrative becomes more than simply an illustrative technique and becomes an avenue for indicating the integral.

In Buber's poetic narratives, the middle of the plot is the focal point—not the end. The "'theme,' the 'point,' of the story" is to be found in the middle as it relates the events of I-Thou by breaking in upon an ordinary understanding of time (beginning and end) and memory. The middle of the story relates the event of I-Thou as it breaks in upon the ordinary span of time, the time of beginning and end, which the narrative establishes."[73] This focus on the middle "uses" the present moment to emphasize, over and above the beginning (the past) and the end (the future). The middle represents the mental-rational dimension, the time of the everyday when we are in direct contact with others. The "eternal middle" is "the full moment that we are put in contact with our origins and with our future."[74] Kepnes describes Buber's "middle" as "the 'impression-point' of his plots around which the whole tale is organized." In short, the middle functions in Buber's plots as the end does in Ricoeur's model.[75]

Kepnes recognized that "[t]he relationship between events that one finds in a narrative of an I-Thou encounter is of a different order than the causal relations that the historian is after. Causal relationships belong to the I-It and not the I-Thou realm. The relationships in Buber's narrative . . . take on a more fundamental role than just contributing toward the steps that lead to the narrative point or theme received at the narrative's end." The relationships that poetic narrative discloses are an integral "concatenation of details, events, persons whose relations are mutually determined and must be considered as a whole."[76] This web of relationships is best held by a poetic narrative structure. The poetic calls to awareness the integral, the dimensions of consciousness revealed in fuzzy clarity.

"Narratives not only show us details but, more important for Buber, *narratives show us the relationship between details.* . . . Narrative, in its capacity to draw and reveal relationships between event and event, person and person, is peculiarly apt to reveal the dimension of 'the between.'"[77] Buber's poetic narratives clarify his philosophy of dialogue in their unclarity. Poetic narratives "present that mix of order and disorder, of illumination and doubt, of abiding question and surprise that is at the heart of the I-Thou encounter. It is precisely in their ambiguity, their obscurity, their openness to a variety of interpretations, that the tales shed light on I-Thou."[78] Kepnes points to Frank Kermode's phrase "radiant obscurity" as particularly appropriate. If the tale were simple and absolutely "clear," with all relevant detail articulated, the telling would be unable to "capture the mystery and element of surprise that is involved in an encounter."[79] Ricoeur would suggest that to function as a poetic narrative, the story must exhibit a "discordant concordance" to relate the upsetting and transforming nature of the integral.[80] Poetic narratives are intentionally unclear in the mental-rational sense because they reveal the integral.

"Asked at the end of his days to respond to critiques of his philosophy, Buber readily admitted that he had not attempted to articulate a fixed system of thought: 'The thinking, the teaching had to be determined by the task of pointing. Only what was connected with the pointing to what was to be pointed to was admissible. . . . I must say it once again: I have no teaching. I only point to something. I point to reality. I point to something in reality that had not or had too little been seen.'"[81]

Closing/Opening

The work of Martin Buber points to the value of Jean Gebser's cosmology for communication studies. Consciousness that constitutes origin is consciousness of an all-encompassing unity. This chapter summarized Gebser's cosmological dimensions of consciousness, which include the archaic, vital-magical, psychic-mythical, mental-rational, and integral structures. Each "structure" or "dimension" holds distinct nuances that contribute differently to configure cultures in varying ways. Buber's "between" enables communicators to access and reveal the integral dimension of consciousness, in which the variety of dimensions can become manifest through poetic narrative, whereby nuances call to awareness facets of the integral whole. Both philosophers of communication point to the incomprehensible through the comprehensible.

Poiesis is a way of creatively "making," participating in the world. The ambiguity, questions, and gaps in a poetic narrative supply hermeneutic potential for understanding the enfolded integral. All poetic narratives that struggle to express human encounter with the world and other people, immediately call forth questions and interpretations. The world we live within, that lives within us, is available in the expression of poetic narrative which articulates dimensions of consciousness in genuine dialogue. The intensification of time/space transfigures aspects and affects all of humanity, whether people are conscious of it or not.

Notes

1.   Georg Feuerstein, *Structures of Consciousness: The Genius of Jean Gebser—An Introduction and Critique* (Lower Lake, CA: Integral Publishing, 1987) wrote: "In *Rilke und Spanien,* originally written in Spanish in 1936 but published four years later in German, we encounter Gebser's first tentative explorations of this theme, still purely on the linguistic level. In this exceptional contribution to the understanding of Rilke, Gebser wrote: 'I summarize: what is happening here is that the adjective now emphasizes the relations between objects, and it is employed in such a way that it takes effect in all directions. The notion of objects has lost its significance, together with perspectivity achieved through the use of adverbs by which

objects were meant to be deepened or interpreted according to the viewpoint of the observer. What is gaining importance now is the spiritual light reigning between objects—the tension and the relation between them'" (128). See also Ed Mahood, "The Primordial Leap and the Present: The Ever-Present Origin—An Overview of the Work of Jean Gebser," http://www.gaiamind.org/Gebser.html (accessed August 1, 2005).

2. Martin Buber, *Between Man and Man* (New York: Macmillan, 1972).

3. Michael Purdy, "Gebser's Project: What Must We Do Now?" *Integrative Explorations: Journal of Culture and Consciousness* 2 (1994): 20–35.

4. Jean Gebser, *The Ever-Present Origin*, trans. Noel Barstad and Algis Mickunas (1949; Athens: Ohio University Press, 1985), xxvii.

5. Oswald Spengler, *The Decline of the West* (New York: A. A. Knopf, 1926–1928).

6. Purdy, "Gebser's Project," 20–21.

7. Gebser, *The Ever-Present Origin*, 141 (italics in original).

8. Joseph F. Kett, "World History since 1550," in *The New Dictionary of Cultural Literacy*, ed. E. D. Hirsch, Joseph F. Kett, and James Trifil, 3rd ed. (New York: Houghton Mifflin Co., 2002); www.bartleby.com/59/10/ (accessed August 1, 2005).

9. Nicholas C. Burbules and Suzanne Rice, "Dialogue across Differences: Continuing the Conversation," *Harvard Educational Review* 61 (1991): 394; Jean-François Lyotard, *The Postmodern Condition: A Report on Knowledge* (Minneapolis: University of Minnesota Press, 1984); Mikhail Mikhailovich Bakhtin, *The Dialogic Imagination: Four Essays*, ed. Michael Holquist, trans. Caryl Emerson and Michael Holquist (Austin, TX: University of Texas Press, 1981).

10. Burbules and Rice, "Dialogue across Differences," 394.

11. The author would like to thank Mike Purdy, editor of *Integrative Explorations: Journal of Culture and Consciousness*, for allowing her to reproduce portions of this section from a previously published article: Pat Arneson, "A Gebserian Perspective on Organizational 'Change Management,'" *Integrative Explorations: Journal of Culture and Consciousness* 7/8 (2003): 6–21.

12. Gebser, *The Ever-Present Origin*, 37; see also 36–115.

13. Ibid., 284.

14. Ibid., 43–45. All direct quotations in the "Archaic Structure" section correspond to these pages unless otherwise noted.

15. Feuerstein, *Structures of Consciousness,* 186 (italics in original).

16. Gebser, *The Ever-Present Origin*, 45–60. All direct quotations in the "Magic Structure" section correspond to these pages unless otherwise noted.

17. Eric Mark Kramer and Algis Mickunas, "Introduction: Gebser's New Understanding," in *Consciousness and Culture: An Introduction to the Thought of Jean Gebser,* ed. Eric Mark Kramer (Westport, CT: Greenwood Press, 1992), xvii.

18. Gebser, *The Ever-Present Origin*, 251.

19. Kramer and Mickunas, "Introduction," xviii.

20. Feuerstein, *Structures of Consciousness,* 186.

21. Gebser, *The Ever-Present Origin*, 61–73. All direct quotations in the "Mythical Structure" section correspond to these pages unless otherwise noted.

22. Kramer and Mickunas, "Introduction," xix.

23. Ibid.

24. Feuerstein, *Structures of Consciousness*, 187.

25. Gebser, *The Ever-Present Origin*, 73–96. All direct quotations in the "Mental Structure" section correspond to these pages unless otherwise noted.

26. Kramer and Mickunas, "Introduction," xxi.

27. Ibid.

28. Gebser, *The Ever-Present Origin*, 178.

29. Vytautas Kovalis, "Gebser and the Theory of Socio-Cultural Change," in *Consciousness and Culture: An Introduction to the Thought of Jean Gebser*, ed. Eric Mark Kramer (Westport, CT: Greenwood Press, 1992), 166.

30. Kramer and Mickunas, "Introduction," xxiii.

31. Kavolis, "Gebser," 169.

32. Kramer and Mickunas, "Introduction," xvi.

33. Gebser, *The Ever-Present Origin*, 97–102. All direct quotations in the "Integral Structure" section correspond to these pages unless otherwise noted.

34. Kavolis, "Gebser," 168.

35. Gebser, *The Ever-Present Origin*, 117 (italics in original).

36. Ibid., 6–7.

37. Ibid., 135.

38. Ibid., 261.

39. Kavolis, "Gebser," 168.

40. Kramer and Mickunas, "Introduction," xxvi.

41. Purdy, "Gebser's Project," 30 n.6.

42. Feuerstein, *Structures of Consciousness*, 130.

43. Jean Gebser, *The Grammatical Mirror*, trans. Algis Mickunas (unpublished manuscript; originally written 1941, subsequently revised and published as Gebser, *The Ever-Present Origin*).

44. Gebser, *The Ever-Present Origin*, 316.

45. Ibid., 324.

46. Ibid., 488.

47. Ibid., 492.

48. Louis Z. Hammer, "The Relevance of Buber's Thought to Aesthetics," in *The Philosophy of Martin Buber*, ed. Paul Arthur Schilpp and Maurice Friedman (LaSalle, IL: Open Court, 1967), 626. See also Boris Pasternak, *Doctor Zhivago*, trans. Max Hayward and Manya Harari (New York: Pantheon, 1958).

49. Gebser, *The Ever-Present Origin*, 491.

50. Maurice Friedman, *Martin Buber's Life and Work: The Middle Years, 1923–1945* (New York: E. P. Dutton, Inc., 1983), 77.

51. Kenneth N. Cissna and Rob Anderson, "Theorizing about Dialogic Moments: The Buber-Rogers Position and Postmodern Themes," *Communication Theory* 8 (1998): 91–93. See also, for example, Leslie A. Baxter and Barbara M. Montgomery, *Relating: Dialogues and Dialectics* (New York: Guilford Press, 1996); David Bohm, *On Dialogue*, ed. Lee Nichol (New York: Routledge, 1996); Linda Ellinor and Glenna Gerard, *Dialogue: Rediscover the Transforming Power of Conversation: Creating and Sustaining Collaborative Partnerships at Work* (New York: John Wiley, 1998); William Isaacs, *Dialogue and the Art of Thinking Together: A Pioneering Approach to Communicating in Business and in Life* (New York: Doubleday, 1999).

52. Friedman, *Martin Buber's Life and Work,* 77.

53. Dan Avnon, *Martin Buber: The Hidden Dialogue* (New York: Rowman and Little-field, 1998), 119.

54. Friedman, *Martin Buber's Life and Work,* 77.

55. Michael Purdy, email message to author, August 22, 2005. See Michael Purdy, "Transparency and Communication: A Dialogical Philosophy" (paper presented at the annual meeting of the International Jean Gebser Society for the Study of Culture and Consciousness, New York, October 23–25, 2003); Michael Purdy, "Integrative (Field) Listening: Rethinking/Experiencing Listening" (paper presented at the annual meeting of the International Listening Association, Minneapolis, MN, April 2005); Michael Purdy, "The Responsibility to Dialogue" (paper presented at the annual meeting of the Conference on Globalization: Global Responsibility, Universidad Rafael Landivar, Guatemala, August 2005).

56. Avnon, *Martin Buber,* 119.

57. Ibid., 128 (italics in original).

58. Jacob Trapp, ed., *Martin Buber: To Hallow This Life: An Anthology* (New York: Harper and Brothers, 1958), 22–23. See also Martin Buber, *Between Man and Man,* trans. Ronald Gregor Smith (New York: Macmillan Company, 1949), 202–203.

59. Friedman, *Martin Buber's Life,* 77.

60. Avnon, *Martin Buber,* 128. See also Martin Buber, "The Word That Is Spoken," in *The Knowledge of Man* (New York: Harper and Row, 1965), 113.

61. Ibid., 128–129. See also Buber, "The Word That Is Spoken."

62. Ibid., 129, 131.

63. Ibid., 138. See also Martin Buber, "Dialogue," in *Between Man and Man.*

64. Trapp, *Martin Buber,* 45.

65. Ibid., 49. See also Martin Buber, *Pointing the Way,* ed., trans. Maurice Friedman (New York: Harper and Brothers, 1957), 21. On "play," see also Hans-Georg Gadamer, *Truth and Method* (2nd rev. ed.) (New York: Continuum, 1999), 101–121.

66. Trapp, *Martin Buber,* 47. See also Buber, *Pointing,* 23.

67. Algis Mickunas, email message posted to Gebser listserve, April 25, 2002.

68. Trapp, *Martin Buber,* 47–48. See also Martin Buber, *Hasidism* (New York: The Philosophical Library, 1948), 117–118.

69. Hammer, "The Relevance," 626.

70. Heinz Politzer, *Martin Buber: Humanist and Teacher* (New York: The National Council, 1956): "That the dialogue between I and Thou means more to Buber than the merely aesthetic or 'religious' (and he himself has added quotation marks to this 'religious'), was explained in the book *Dialogue* of 1932. The chapter I have in mind is called A Conversation.... 'Since then [Buber continued] I have given up the "religious" which is nothing but the exception, extraction, exaltation, ecstasy; or it has given me up. I possess nothing but the every day out of which I am taken.' ... But this attitude of taking every moment in all its fullness seriously is only the reverse side of a principle common to Buber's thought and Hasidic teachings: the hallowing of the everyday" (8–9). E. William Rollins and Harry Zohn, eds., *Men of Dialogue: Martin Buber and Albrecht Goes* (New York: Funk and Wagnalls, 1969): As an orator, for Buber, "[T]here was no division such as 'here is the world; there is God.' Indeed I would go so far as to say that with Buber there was not even

a dichotomy between 'the world' as such and 'God's world.' Everything was 'the world'" (207).

Steven Kepnes, *The Text as Thou: Martin Buber's Dialogical Hermeneutics and Narrative Theology* (Bloomington: Indiana University Press, 1992) noted: "It may be said that Buber's essay 'Dialogue,' written in 1929, revolves around a series of narratives about Buber's I-Thou encounters. Indeed, Buber tells us in the foreword to the English publication of the essay that 'Dialogue' was written out of 'the desire to clarify . . . [and] illustrate' the dialogical principle expressed in *I and Thou*" (82). The second part of Kepnes book explores questions about connections between narrative and Buber's philosophy of I-Thou.

71. Kepnes, *The Text as Thou*, 86.
72. Ibid.
73. Ibid., 97.
74. Ibid., 100.
75. Kepnes, *The Text as Thou*, 97. See also Paul Ricoeur, *Time and Narrative*, vol. 1, trans. Kathleen McLaughlin and David Pellauer (Chicago: University of Chicago Press, 1984).
76. Ibid., 97.
77. Ibid., 87.
78. Ibid.
79. Ibid., 90. See also Frank Kermode, *The Sense of an Ending* (Oxford: Oxford University Press, 1966), 47.
80. Ricoeur, *Time and Narrative*, 69.
81. Avnon, *Martin Buber*, 3.

Bibliography of Works

Books by Jean Gebser

1930s

Zehn Gedichte. Berlin: Die Rabenpresse, 1932.
Gedichte eines Jahres. Berlin: Die Rabenpresse, 1936.

1940s

Rilke und Spanien. Zürich: Oprecht, 1940.
Spanien: Don Tancredo, don Quijote. Luzern: Vita Nova, 1940.
Der grammatische Spiegel: Neue Denkformen im sprachlichen Ausdruck. Zürich: Oprecht, 1944.
Abendländische Wandlung. Zurich: Oprecht, 1945.
Lorca oder Das Reich der Mütter. Stuttgart: Deutsche Verl.-Anst., 1949.
Lorca, poète-dessinateur. Paris: GLM, 1949.
Ursprung und Gegenwart: 1. Die Fundamente der aperspektivischen Welt. Beitr. zu e. Geschichte d. Bewußtwerdung; 2. Die Manifestationen der aperspektivischen Welt. Versuch e. Konkretion d. Geistigen. Stuttgart: Deutsche Verl.-Anstalt, 1949/1953.

1960s

Asienfibel: Zum Verständnis östlicher Wesensart. Frankfurt am Main: Ullstein, 1962.
Angst: Ursachen, Symptome. Munich: Droemer-Knaur, 1962.
In der Bewährung: Zehn Hinweise auf das neue Bewußtein. Bern: Francke, 1962.
Asien lächelt anders. Frankfurt am Main: Ullstein, 1968.

1970s

Der unsichtbare Ursprung: Evolution als Nachvollzug. Olten, Freiburg i. Br.: Walter, 1970.
Ein Mensch zu sein: Betrachtungen über die Formen der menschlichen Beziehungen. Munich: Francke, 1974.
Gedichte. Schaffhausen: Novalis-Verlag, 1974.
Verfall und Teilhabe: Über Polarität, Dualität, Identität u. den Ursprung. Salzburg: O. Müller, 1974.
Rilke und Spanien. Lorca oder Das Reich der Mütter. Vol. 1 of *Gesamtausgabe.* Schauffhausen: Novalis-Verlag, 1975.
Ursprung und Gegenwart. Part 1: Die Fundamente der aperspektivischen Welt: Beitrag zu einer Geschichte der Bewußtwerdung. Vol. 2 of *Gesamtausgabe.* Schauffhausen: Novalis-Verlag, 1978.
Ursprung und Gegenwart. Part 2: Die Manifestation der aperspektivischen Welt: Versuch einer Konkretion des Geistigen. Vol. 3 of *Gesamtausgabe. Schauffhausen: Novalis-Verlag, 1978.*
Ursprung und Gegenwart: Kommentarband. Vol. 4 of *Gesamtausgabe.* Schauffhausen: Novalis-Verlag, 1979.

Vorlesungen und Reden zu Ursprung und Gegenwart, Part 1. Vol. 5.1 of *Gesamtausgabe.* Schauffhausen: Novalis-Verlag, 1976.

Vorlesungen und Reden zu Ursprung und Gegenwart, Part 2. Vol. 5.2 of *Gesamtausgabe.* Schauffhausen: Novalis-Verlag, 1977.

Asien lächelt anders. Vol. 6 of *Gesamtausgabe.* Schauffhausen: Novalis-Verlag, 1977.

Gedichte. Aussagen. Vol. 7 of *Gesamtausgabe.* Schauffhausen: Novalis-Verlag, 1980.

1980s

Ausgewählte Texte. Ed. Hans Christian Meiser. Munich: Goldmann, 1987.

1990s

Einbruch der Zeit. Oratio: Verlag, 1995.

English Translations of Books by Jean Gebser

1960s

Gebser, Jean. *Anxiety: A Condition of Modern Man.* New York: Dell, 1962.

1980s

The Ever-Present Origin. Part 1, *Foundations of the Aperspectival World;* part 2, *Manifestations of the Aperspectival World.* Trans. Algis Mickunas and Noel Barstad. Athens: Ohio University Press, 1985.

José Ortega y Gasset (1883–1955)

Biographical Sketch

José Ortega y Gasset was born on May 9, 1883, in Madrid, Spain. His father, José Ortega Munilaa, was a novelist and journalist. His mother, Maria de los Dolores Gasset Chinchilla, was a homemaker. His childhood experiences exposed him to social and political discussions between his father and friends. At the age of eight

Different sources report inconsistent information about the life of José Ortega y Gasset. Information for this biographical sketch was drawn from Stuart Brown, Diane Collinson, and Robert Wilkinson, eds., *One Hundred Twentieth-Century Philosophers* (New York: Routledge, 1998); Edward Craig, ed., *Routledge Encyclopedia of Philosophy*, vol. 7 (New York: Routledge, 1998); Jorge J. E. Garcia, "Ortega y Gasset, José," *Cambridge Dictionary of Philosophy*, 2nd ed., ed. Robert Audi (Cambridge, UK: Cambridge University Press, 1999); Oliver W. Holmes, *Human Reality and the Social World: Ortega's Philosophy of History* (Amherst, MA: University of Massachusetts Press, 1975); Petri Liukkon, "José Ortega y Gasset," *Books and Writers*—http://www.kirjasto.sci.fi/gasset.htm (accessed October 9, 2003); Victor Ouimette, *José Ortega y Gasset* (Boston, MA: Twayne, 1982); Juan Escámez Sánchez, "José Ortega y Gasset (1883–1955)," *Prospects: The Quarterly Review of Comparative Education*, 24 (1994): 261–278—http://64.233.161.104/search?q=cache:Kd_s9XvxrEEJ:www.ibe.unesco.org/International/Publications/Thinkers/ThinkersPdf/ortegae.PDF+jose+ortega+y+gasset+bibliography&hl=en (accessed August 18, 2005). Photograph © Bettmann/CORBIS.

he began attending a Jesuit school in Miraflores, Malaga (1891–1897). He began university studies in law and philosophy at the University of Deusto (1897–1898), also run by Jesuits. He attended the Universidad Central de Madrid and graduated with a bachelor's degree in philosophy (1902) and a doctorate (1904) with a thesis entitled "Los terrors del año mil: Critica de una leyenda" (The Terrors of the Year 1000: Critique of a Legend).

In 1905, Ortega left Spain to study at the University of Leipzig in Germany. While there he studied German so that he could read Kant, Nietzsche, and Wundt in the original language. He studied at Leipzig only a short time before leaving to study at the University of Marburg. Later Ortega was appointed professor of psychology, logic, and ethics at the Escuela de Estudios Superiores del Magistrerio, a normal school in Madrid. In 1910, he accepted a position at the Central University of Madrid as professor of metaphysics (1910–1936).

Over the years, Ortega lectured and published many articles pertaining to social policies in multiple fields of study. He cofounded *El Sol,* and founded several journals, including *Faro* (1908), *España* review (1915–1923), and *Revista de Occidente* (1923–1936), which was a cultural magazine that disseminated his ideas and introduced German thought into Spain and Latin America.

In 1910, Ortega married Rosa Spottorno Topete, with whom he had three children. He opposed Miguel Primo de Rivera's dictatorship (1923–1930) and resigned from his post as professor in protest against the military dictator. After the fall of Rivera and the abdication of King Alfonso XIII, Ortega sat in the assembly of the Second Republic from 1931 to 1932 and was deputy for the province of León and civil governor of Madrid. One year as an elected representative to the parliament disillusioned Ortega, and he kept a pointed silence about Spanish politics from then on.

Ortega's support for the Spanish Republic was contradictory to the Spanish government, and his work began to be censored in Spain due to dictatorial proclamation. Ortega was a voluntary exile in Argentina and then Portugal during the Spanish Civil War (1936–1939), unwilling to support either side or hold academic office under Francisco Franco.

In 1941, Ortega became a professor of philosophy at University of San Marcos, Lima. After World War II he returned to Spain and founded the Institute of Humanities in Madrid; a lack of support led to its closing after two years. He continued to lecture frequently in Germany, Switzerland, and the United States.

José Ortega y Gasset died on October 18, 1955, in Madrid, Spain.

There Is Nothing Outside Circumstance
Near, Against, With(in) Ortega y Gasset (and a Ghostly Hand)

Ramsey Eric Ramsey, with "A Ghostly Hand" compiled and arranged by J. N. Sturgess and Ramsey Eric Ramsey

> *Que dos y dos son cuatro es siempre un poco triste . . .*
> (That two and two are four is always a bit sad . . .)
> —Ortega y Gasset

> Education is the art of orientation.
> —Socrates

What We Think We Have Heard

By name familiar to most, but nonetheless unknown to many in this same group, Spanish philosopher José Ortega y Gasset occupies a curious position in the continental tradition as practiced by those in North America. Although many of us have heard of him, when asked for the details of his position we are often left saying vague things concerning his philosophy. Thus, we think we know or have heard: he is an existentialist; a derider of the masses; he is a "Spanish Heidegger"; a phenomenologist; or he is a pragmatist. Each of these claims, and others beside, are as reasonable as they are divergent. That is, they are accurate in some important ways and yet they are ultimately somewhat misleading if any one alone is taken to be exhaustive of his work. There are, indeed, fine and helpful book-length studies to be recommended defending and arguing in favor of understanding Ortega's philosophical contributions in the ways mentioned above.[1] Here we shall not attempt any adjudication among these sometimes competing claims; we concede, however, that our task—one that takes as its point of departure a few aphoristic provocations from Ortega concerning communicative praxis—may inadvertently supply evidence to one or another of these interpretations. Whatever else Ortega's own work might be said to be, it is safe to say it is, without doubt, rich and sophisticated enough to suffer and support all these views and important others as well. Said another way, to read him carefully is to understand why one could undertake such interpretations of this enigmatic continental philosopher, whose influence remains, sadly we think, underappreciated by the tradition taken as a whole.

Ortega is in some senses a special breed of continental philosopher. As one whose stated goal was to "level the Pyrenees," he attempted to cultivate a ground so thinking could take root on the Iberian peninsula and from this origin give back to continental thought. Out of what we take to be respect for him, we do not care to show that Ortega can and does sound like Heidegger or Sartre, thus making their work the measure of his philosophical worth; nor do we care, although this too is quite possible, to show that Heidegger and Sartre often sound like Ortega, thereby suggesting that his philosophical worth in this case is getting to something before these two undisputed giants of continental thought.[2] We shall note, however, that the similarities as far and as deep as they may go among these three thinkers (and at times they go to outstanding depths) are also explained by a shared understanding of post-Cartesian philosophical thought; the inspirations of phenomenology in terms of intentionality, *Lebenswelt,* and otherness (e.g., Husserl and Brentano); issues of hermeneutics and history (e.g., Dilthey and Nietzsche); and various neo-Kantian commitments learned at Marburg that are not, to be sure, shared in the same manner by each of the three thinkers but are no less explanatory for that.

For our part in the matter, we shall attempt a reading that orients our attention in such a manner that we hope produces a tension that will make something happen to our thinking with Ortega. Toward that end we shall think near and against Ortega as a number of key passages of his work are made to appear so as to leave their mark with(in) the text, arriving, watching over, haunting perhaps. Consequently, we shall be nearer to Ortega than we might imagine as well as making our way (up) against his insightful words. In the light of these passages, the reader can bring forth from them what she will beginning from whatever perspective she brings to her reading of these various and in some ways representative passages, which have no little consideration behind their selection for those philosophizing about the practice of communication and ethics.[3] Besides this invitation to make a reading of them, these passages shall watch over this work—always looking in on it as if each in its turn is making a case for its own importance to the dialogue or by joining forces with others trying to make their way into the overall discussion. In the end, they might, with the proper amount of hermeneutical assistance, come together as a perceptive theory of the practice of communication.

Hence, always near Ortega and always right (up) against him, (up) against his "own" words. We take the following as Ortega's blessing of this design, as he has said that he is hopeful the reader of any of his works "senses that a ghostly yet real hand rises from the page, one that touches his person, that wants to caress it—or instead, to give it a courteous shove."[4] To anticipate a theme, this ghostly hand, by way of Ortega's textual incursions, this ever possible courteous shove, becomes a part of the constant circumstance of this essay's and the reader's circumstance of making something of Ortega's possible contribution to a philosophy of communication.

In addition to near and against and with(in), we shall think with an invited Ortega, so our orientation turns to a somewhat finer, more selectively focused set of passages and insights from his work and links them with aspects of our own philosophical thought. Ortega's brilliant use of metaphor and beautifully stylistic turns of phrase we shall take as an authorization to treat his work as waiting aphorisms looking for connections outside his work proper. As with all well-crafted aphorisms, his too do not settle anything or become a comfortable site in which to rest. Rather, his often sharply honed words are instigations and, as we shall see, incitements to thought and to a sallying forth. But our sojourn cannot be haphazard and chaotic, because for Ortega all thought must be as close to life and living well as is possible: "we draw the conclusion that man's desire to live, to be in the world, is inseparable from his desire to live well."[5] This invitation for Ortega to join us and we him on a path of thinking is one that attempts to take him seriously (and not just historically) to make something of what he has to offer thinking today.

Circumstance, Self, Otherness: Looking (All) Around

Ortega's first major book, *Meditations on Quixote*, remains his masterwork and like so many others, we must begin here. Almost. It is here that we find his rightly celebrated "yo soy yo y mi circunstancia" (I am myself and my circumstance)—

> If there were only thought, if the idealist thesis were firm and solid, existing would, for me, be solely a matter of being alone with myself. Now, the character of the immediate is just the opposite; I am always outside myself, in the midst of circumstance, of my surroundings.

a philosophical insight that will, by his own admission, guide his work from this early point (1914) forward to its end (1955). But as those who are interested in thinking about Ortega and communication, we will do well to note that one of the first published versions of circumstance as a philosophical concept comes in a newspaper piece appearing in 1911, three years before the publication of *Meditations on Quixote*.[6] The essay, "The Chiding of the Orator" ("Vejamen del Orador"), a defense (of sorts) of rhetors and rhetoric, shows how the idea that will be central to his thought occurs to Ortega at that moment when he is trying to make sense, as a philosopher writing about rhetoric, of what is required of communicators: "I cannot here, in passing, settle this age-old dispute, this classic grudge, so old and so classic because it deals with nothing less than the perennial open struggle in Greece between the orator and the philosopher."[7] If Ortega cannot solve this problem (and who of us can or has?), he does not shy away from making something of a pass at this perennial issue. In doing so he turns to circumstance and begins his then still-developing theory of the self, suggesting that the self is always already inextricably immersed

> My coexistence with things does not consist in the fact that the paper on which I write and the chair I sit on are objects for me, but rather that before being objects, this paper is for me paper and this chair is for me a chair. Conversely, things would not be what they are if I were not what I am for them.

and understands itself in the midst of its facticity and otherness. He sums this up in the article defining the orator: "the orator is born with circumstance and dies with it and in it becomes consumed, and when it changes to another one he is reborn with a new condition."[8] This understanding of the orator will become a central feature in the various articulations of his circumstantial theory of human being; among the near-numberless versions from which we might draw an example: "Living means *reaching out* of oneself, devoted, ontologically, to what is *other*—be it called world or circumstances."[9] We are always called out of ourselves to engage with what confronts us in situations, and we are always under the requirement to make a way in and though them.

It will not escape notice from philosophers of communication nor will it surprise them all this seems to come to Ortega when confronted with the trials faced by rhetors seeking to speak to others. It is here in this intellectual circumstance where Ortega first glimpses his fundamental and lifelong orienting insight: that we are never without our conditions; never without our vital concerns with what is always already there; with an otherness that is ever with us; never without what surrounds us because we would not be without it nor would it be without us.

> Man is what has happened to him, what he has done. Other things might have happened to him or have been done by him, but what did in fact happen to him and was done by him, this constitutes a relentless trajectory of experiences which he carries on his back as the vagabond his bundle of all he possesses. Man is a substantial emigrant on a pilgrimage of being, and it is accordingly meaningless to set limits on what he is capable of being. In this initial illimitableness of possibilities that characterizes one who has no nature there stands one fixed, pre-established, and given line by which he may chart his course, only one limit: the past.

All this and each of its consequences for not only philosophical thinking but for living well, Ortega will demand of the phrase "I am myself and my circumstance." This demand is a double one that the concept has met quite well: to encapsulate (impossible to be sure) his thinking, while simultaneously opening on the whole of his thought that attempts to explicate the phrase fully.[10] The phrase for which he is known, to the degree he is known, is both the beginning of his thinking and what his thinking attempts in each instance to explicate in a manner as detailed and sophisticated as possible.

> The world and I, set before each other, without any chance of fusion or separation.

Ortega's thinking takes off from here and is the place to which it is constantly attempting to return.

The *Meditations* follows this insight, as we know, making a number of wonderful moves to disclose a profound understanding of circumstance. Yet, before we move beyond the newspaper article from which we have been quoting, let us stay within it a bit longer and while lingering there think about another of its provocations. Ortega feels he needs to show his reader what circumstance is and just how much he might mean for this idea to encompass when he writes near the end of the essay: "But what are the circumstances? Are they only these hundred persons, these fifty minutes, this insignificant question? All circumstance is fitted within another larger one. Why believe that only ten meters of space surround me? What surrounds these ten meters? What serious oversight, wretched dullness, to deal with only a few circumstances, when in truth everything surrounds us!"[11] Everything surrounds us indeed,

> I have now around me as many as two dozen grave oaks and graceful ashes. Is this a forest? Certainly not. What I see here is some trees of the forest. The real forest is composed of the trees which I do not see. The forest is always a little beyond where we are. It has just gone away from where we are and all that is left is a still fresh trace. From any spot within its borders the forest is just a possibility; a path along which we could precede.

but we are but finite creatures who must find some manner of disclosing to ourselves what from among everything shall matter to us here, now, in this situation in which we find ourselves.

Circumstance is all around us, and everything that is all around us makes up what we and circumstance inseparably are.

> Living is finding oneself in a world which, by no means hermetically sealed is always offering opportunities. The vital world is composed of being able to do this or that, not having perforce to do this and only this. On the other hand, these possibilities are not unlimited—if they were, they would not be concrete possibilities but a purely indeterminate collection, . . . in a world where everything is equally possible, it is not possible to decide on anything. In order for there may be decision there must be both space and limitation, relative determinism. This I express by the category "circumstance." And circumstance is something determined, closed, but at the same time open and with internal latitude, with space to move about and make one's decisions; . . . To live is to live here and now; the here and now are specific, all life is a constant process of deciding among various possibilities. Life is at the same time freedom and fatality.

Yes, everything surrounds us, yet it is unhandleable and unwieldy as such. We need, as a consequence of this, a means, a way, a path, that draws forth and puts into relief what matters to us at this very moment, here with these very things, these very persons, and with this very concern taken from among everything and all of this.[12] This is the work of communicative praxis and interpretation. It is through as well as from within communication that we are able to deal and cope with our circumstance and make something of it.

Never do we mean by taking some definite perspective on the situation to suggest this perspective is all that does matter, but only that *this* must matter for now and do so for these vital reasons. Yet we need always remember the inevitable remainder that such perspective-taking produces, for every taking something as something leaves other things undisclosed. Through the communicative praxis of interpretation what needs to matter now moves into the open, out from the "everything" of circumstance through our articulated understanding so as to stand out, set out into relief for us and for the others with us.

> How unimportant a thing would be if it were only what it
> is in isolation. How poor, how barren, how blurred! One
> might say that there is in each thing a certain latent poten-
> tiality to be many other things, which is set free and ex-
> pands when other things come into contact with it.

To set out into relief some aspect of the situation is the promoting of a perspective, aware always, as Ortega reminds us: "The sole false perspective is that which claims to be the only one there is."[13]

This promotion—indebted to hermeneutics, to communication, and then shared out through them—is always taking place in ways more or less sophisticated based on the care, skill, and experience of those involved in the situation. Circumstance, thus, demands of communicative beings a looking around; it demands a constant circumspection. We must, then, learn to look all around at all that surrounds us and simultaneously remember that a "full-circle" view never comes all at once. Each perspective gives something at the cost of what leaving one's former position must of necessity sacrifice—even if things build and add to one another, their sum is never complete, never everything.

> It is easy to say and even to think that you are resolved upon some-
> thing; but it is extremely difficult to be resolved in the true sense.
> For this means resolving upon all the things which are neces-
> sary as intermediate steps; it means, for one thing, providing our-
> selves with the qualities that are requisite for the undertaking.
> Anything short of this is no real resolution, it is simply wishing.

Perhaps this why throughout his work, Ortega loves and invokes the image of the taking of Jericho—wide circles to start followed by ever tighter ones, always with a goal, but respectful of all that surrounds the issue—he seems to suggest there are few, if any, quick or easy arrivals to important destinations.

This circumspection with vital concern is detailing circumstance—evaluating and interpreting what one and others are becoming as a part of a shared and living reality of being together here and now. We become in any of our circumstances what is true of our life in general: "we become only a part of what it is possible for us to be."[14] Circumstance and situations that arise in it require of us, unless we give in to the average and everyday ways of habitually enacting a version of what has already been, that we remake situations in the images we have of what is potentially more just and fitting about them.[15] To theorize this requires a philosophical understanding of communicative praxis.

Sketching the Components of an Ortegian Philosophy of Communication

As one of our orientations is toward Ortega's contribution to a philosophical theory of communicative praxis, it is against this backdrop of self and circumstance that we shall provide an outline, albeit brief, of some salient features of his thought directed toward this end.[16] We place this sketch here in the midst of our thinking about Ortega's primary and guiding insights on self and circumstance, which as we just saw came to him initially while responding to rhetoric and oratory.

What shall we make of all the things that we discover in our circumstances?

> Things are not originally "things," but something that I must try to use or avoid in order to live, [they are], therefore, that with which I occupy myself and by which I am occupied, with which I act and operate, with which I succeed or fail to do what I want to do. . . . And since "to do" and "to occupy oneself," "to have concerns" is expressed in the Greek by "practice"—praxis, things are radically pragmata and my relation to them pragmatic.

Clearly the things of our circumstance are there in their existence in a manner other than we. But, too, there are other selves, or persons, with which we must deal, and they are in a qualitatively different relation to us than are pragmata (things). Pragmata already imply the relation with self that avoids the necessity of having to posit, or argue for, something like the pure essence or true meaning of a thing. That is to say, there are no ideal meanings for things, but only the meanings they develop in their communicative and interpretive use. Pragmata take their relevance then, in light of how someone takes them as being for a particular end. The executing of this "taking something as something for something," and the action that either does or does not complete this something, or attempt this action, constitutes the relative interdependence of persons and pragmata.

From perspectival positions persons engage in acts of interpretation that take the things under consideration as being for something. From a perspective that finds itself where it is in relation to pragmata, the self takes the pragmata as being for something in regards to self's perspectival concerns and importances.

> To live is to feel ourselves *fatally* obliged to exercise our *liberty*, to decide what we are going to be in this world. Not for a single moment is our activity of decision allowed to rest. Even when in desperation we abandon ourselves to whatever may happen, we have decided not to decide. It is, then, false to say that in life "circumstances decide." On the contrary, circumstances are the di-

lemma, constantly renewed, in presences of which we have to
make our decision; what actually decides is our character.

This is how Ortega uses the notion of perspective to describe how we take the
circumstance to be when we find ourselves where we find ourselves. He uses the
notion to be both a part of how things get interpreted in the situation, but also
as a part of what makes up and defines the notion of the self.

Perspective is produced in the situatedness of where we find ourselves; history occasions this situatedness, as well as what is at our disposal in interpretation, and this action of deciding what to do leads us to practices influenced both
by the past and by our anticipation of the future. Precisely, this view expresses
Ortega's desire to amalgamate the theory-practice distinction. This amalgamation harmonizes the existential sense of engaging in an interpretation of self and
circumstance and of the structure of praxis, as it is through praxis that we are
able to undertake our engagement with what confronts us.

An understanding of the self on Ortega's account emerges here as that life
(what Ortega calls the life of each of us) which from a perspective (point of view),
is in relation with pragmata, and from this living perspective embedded simultaneously in past, present, and future undertakes the practice of interpretation,
which takes things as being something for something. The self is in a dynamic
relation with pragmata, and this dynamism gives Ortega the point from which
he discusses the encounter with the other as another human being. The dynamic
relationship in which we find ourselves creates, within the space of a body, what
Ortega calls "pragmatic fields." The use of the plural "fields" speaks to the mul-
tiplicitous nature of the self—and this should not surprise us, as we have seen
persons are defined in relation and in light of an ever-changing circumstance
which their actions participate in altering.

But my experience of life is not made up solely of my past, of the experiences that I personally have had. It is built up also of the past
of my forebearers, handed down to me by the society in which
I live. Society consists primarily in a repertory of usages, intellectual, moral, political, technical, of play and pleasure.

The self as living and doing is always embodied, and the body is considered the
locus where a particular multiplicity comes together.

Ortega calls this notion of body "radical reality," and we are reminded
often in his texts to consider the word "radical" in its etymological sense of
"root." The notion functions as that which defines that which one finds closest—one's body—that which we call socially "I," the summoning of which calls
to mind a particular lived history. Ortega is clear that this does not mean that
each radical reality is the "sole reality," but that it is the locus of a changing self
that is an embodiment that belongs in this manner to this one and to no other.
That is, embodiment is a particular lived history. We recognize clearly there are
other selves, who are themselves selves in the manner described above, and we

recognize as well that how interaction takes place between them needs to be addressed. Still further, we are aware that there are qualitative differences among inert, non-human animals and human others, and that each must be given special attention as regards the dynamic relation with the self. We shall unfold this understanding by rehearsing Ortega's arguments as he describes one's relating to a stone, an animal, and lastly, the other human being.

The Stone. When we find ourselves before the stone we are aware that the stone is not aware of our actions. Furthermore, we undertake these actions with the stone without regard to its reciprocity, because we take it to be without the capacity to respond. Although we do not consider the stone as possessing the possibility to respond, we do take it as something in our interpretation of it. Although this interpretation is based in relation to what is a possible practice in which to engage the stone, this is not properly speaking a response from the stone. The example of the animal will, by contrast, help to clarify the present discussion.

> In my relation with the animal, the act of my behavior toward it is not, as it was in the case of the stone, unilateral; instead, my act, before being performed, when I am planning it, already reckons with the probable act of reaction on the animal's part.

The Animal. In the encounter with the animal we act and react differently than we do with the stone, as the animal seems to reckon with us in ways non-living things cannot be said to be capable. This leads Ortega to say that, while the animal has more reaction capability than did the stone, it still is only equipped with a limited repertoire of possible reactions. We must negotiate with both a more heightened sense of anticipation and in light of the animal's possibility of surprising us. Consequently, we might say we need to be more extemporaneous in our comportment and relation with the animal.

The Other as Human Being. For Ortega the other person responds to our responding in ways that outstrip those of the animal to a nearly infinite degree. This is captured in part by noticing the capability of the other person of inducing surprise is in the situation is beyond anticipation.

> The reciprocity would be clearer, unlimited and evident, that is, in which the other being that responds to me should in principle be capable of responding to me as much as I respond to it.

The other will do we know not exactly what, something that can fall outside our expectations. This alone shows that our responsiveness must respond to a responsiveness roughly equal to our own, which we can neither completely control nor predict with certainty. Other persons respond to us and do so from a sphere of power and a reservoir of possible responses on which they draw that make untold demands on us in the relation. This power to respond and the encounter with the Other through it, for Ortega, leads to his observations concerning the unavoidability of human relations. He believes that this character of obligation to deal with the other is constituted by reciprocity and that this "fact" of reciprocity classifies us as social beings.

> It is not the unique and objective world that makes it possible for me to co-exist with other men, but, on the contrary, it is my sociality or social relation with other men that makes possible something like a common and objective world.

Let us pursue these views on what and how relations and responses between persons are unavoidable and how these relations produce the social.

Ortega believes that through the gestures of the Other we discover the Other responding to us. He reminds us that we do not move relationally from stone, to animal, to persons, but somewhat the reverse. We are all first in relations with other persons who care for us in the family, and only later do we move out to discover our relations to things. From the very beginning and throughout our lives, we are open to others unavoidably and inescapably. Even the one who flees society, the hermit or the recluse, is responding to the other in the practice of escape. It is a relation that is by its presence social because every action taken in regards to the other must anticipate and reckon with the responsive potential of the other's action out of our response capabilities "given" to all of us by our communicative socialization.

Hence, being open to the other, being what he calls the supreme, alterist, is only society potentially. That is, no particular type of social relation necessarily follows from the givenness of our sociality. This given sociality or "we-ity" (*nostradad*), our being constitutively together and being inescapably open to the other, is the ground of potentialities that makes possible future concrete acts that produce the social in existential and concrete ways.

> The other ingredients of a circumstance, the non-verbal ingredients, those not *sensu stricto* "language," possess a declaratory potentiality and language . . . consist not only saying what language says by itself but in actualizing this potentiality of speech and meaning possessed by the environment. [Words] enter into a coalescence with the beings and things around it which are not verbal. What the word says by itself is very little, but acts as a percussion cap that sets off the quasi-verbal power of everything else.

Not until specific possibilities are chosen and engaged in is the social relation constituted such that it produces particular types of social relations.

Being open to the other and recognizing that the other is as capable of response as we is the first instance of communication for Ortega. This mutual responsiveness and reciprocity is the first encounter in which selves perceive and interpret the existential actions of others. The presence of the other's body is the occasion by which we recognize the other self. According to Ortega, it is through the gestures of the other that we see the expression of another self; more than just expressions of the body,

> From whence does the word, does language, receive what it lacks
> and needs in order to fulfill the function commonly attributed to
> it—namely to mean, to have meaning? . . . It receives it from outside
> itself, from the human beings who use it, who say it in a particular
> situation. Here, then, in this particular situation, talking with the pre-
> cise inflexion of voice with which they enunciate, with the expres-
> sion that they assume while doing it, with the concomitant gestures,
> free or restrained are the human beings who properly "speak," "say."

the body itself is expression. What gets articulated via the other through the expressions of the body is the presence of what Ortega calls another "inwardness."
We must hesitate here before this notion of inwardness, for it seems to present
us with a problem. The notion of the self carries with it the descriptions "particular" and "perspectival," and whatever inwardness might be, it must also, as
with all of Ortega's definitions, be related to circumstance.

Inwardness would best be taken as the articulation of a perspectival and
particular interpretation of circumstance, which is meaningless until subsequently judged by the conditions of circumstance: inwardness is circumstance
articulated from a particular perspective which is judged by the conditions of
circumstance.

> . . . that idolatry of the intelligence which isolates thought from
> its setting, from its function in the general economy of hu-
> man life. As if man thinks because he thinks, and not because,
> whether he will or no, he has to think in order to maintain
> himself among things! As if thought could awaken and func-
> tion of its own motion, as if it began and ended in itself, and was
> not—as the true state of the case—engendered by action.

In light of Ortega's belief that language is that which "socializes our innermost
being," he recognizes that while each time a circumstance gets articulated by a
particular person, the interpretation is inextricably bound to the social because
of the sociality of language (and of course many other factors). Each particular
self belongs to the social from which it can never escape. In keeping with this,
the interpretations of particular persons can neither fall outside of the social nor
originate from a position beyond the social. In this way we might say Ortega
uses inwardness as a synonym for embodiment as the condition of the particular perspectival self. Inwardness then, far from returning to the problems of the
subjectivist self and the aporia of self-referentiality that it occasions, is seen as
the inwardness of the specific circumstance, a particular position, taking "position" here in both the spatial bodily sense and in the sense of taking an interpretive position.

The articulation of circumstance from a particular, but not self-contained,
perspective is the requirement for responsible common life. From the constitutive openness to the other, which always finds itself in a particular circumstance,
communicative encounters begin to unfold. Language use is one of the major

manners by which persons "say," and thereby bring about these communicative unfoldings. "Saying" for Ortega is the term used to describe the articulation of an interpretation. All the fine arts, for example, would be ways of saying according to Ortega's view, but we are content to concern ourselves here with the use of language.

Let us follow by taking Ortega's offer of a humble example, but one he believes in its very triviality is therefore profound. He considers the word "black" and the many uses to which it is put. "But when the guest says the word 'black' the hostess knows he takes no cream in his coffee, what the word fails to say the circumstance mutely adds." Again Ortega has appealed to circumstance to complete the constitution of meaning. This appeal to circumstance in regards to words,

> Poetry is not really language. It uses language merely as a medium in order only to transcend it and express what language *sensu stricto* cannot say. Poetry begins where efficacy of speech fails. It appears, therefore, as a new power of words that cannot be reduced to what words commonly are.

as it was with other of his moves (history, time, the self) is a way of criticizing transcendental and metaphysical constitutions of meaning.

Since communication depends constitutively on selves and circumstance, Ortega uses history to analyze language, as both self and circumstance are the results of pasts and histories. Using an analogous formulation to his challenge to pure notions of human nature—namely "man has no nature, but a history"—Ortega says similarly of words, "[They] do not have etymologies because they are words, but because they are usages."[17] Clearly usage here relates to how words have functioned in practice, or stated another way, the meaning of a word is the history of its practical, existential, and circumstantial use.

This is not to suggest that any word means whatever we want, in any manner we choose in any instant. Words do mean in the instant, but present in that instant is the history of that word's prior use. This follows the same formulation of the ways in which history and the moments of time are all functioning in the present. Given the specific situation and the particular word in use, its meaning is partially indebted to its prior history in regards to its present meaning.

Often it takes repeated usage to change the future use of a word

> This shows that the perspective of life is different from the perspective of science. During the modern age, the two have become confused: this very confusion is the modern age. In it man makes science, pure reason, serve as a basis for the system of his convictions. He lives on science.

and thus its meaning, because words, like other entities, cannot immediately disassociate themselves from their previous histories. We are all capable of listing words whose contemporary use differs from one or more of its past histories (e.g., "gay," "awful," "ravish"). However, we certainly recognize that the power invested in certain sectors of our society (institutions, professions) allows them the attempt to determine a word's history and enforce its meaning.

We have said that human beings are what they have done, and so too with words. Words do not mean in and of themselves, but in what they do. Words are functions and actions which emanate from a self (as one of the things persons do) and find their meanings in the effectiveness or ineffectiveness they induce in the particular situations in which they are used. This interplay of word and circumstance, which gives meanings to words, also works to give meanings to circumstance itself, for circumstance is never totally fixed in its being what it is. On Ortega's account, the use of certain words or phrases takes on histories which become consistent or customary. That is, words or phrases are used in similar situations—situations which call for a customary response. Ortega sees the possibility of many different situations becoming similar to themselves and calling for and eliciting their own customary response. And further, the acceptable, or true, response comes to be the anticipated or customary one.

How this customariness comes about ought to be of primary interest to critical theorists of communication. We wish to take Ortega's reflection on circumstance seriously in regards to its relation to the customary or habitual response. Finding and recognizing situations as being similar or familiar is the ground giving rise to customary usages of behavior.

> Man, when he sets himself to speak, does so because
> he believes that he will be able to say what he thinks.
> Now, this is an illusion. Language is not up to that.

What we have done, our histories, orients our interpretations in what might be construed as looking for the familiar. Accompanying this with the material structure of the circumstance, we find our world structured in ways that often make it difficult—and it is not, of course, always desirable to do so—to propose an alternative interpretation to the situation.

Ortega's examination of the specific characteristics of circumstance and pragmata, history and embodiment, self and Other, leads to his thoughts on language and communication. However, as we can see from the gloss provided in this section, it is communication that Ortega leaves under-theorized. He seems to have, in the end, taken over a rather instrumental understanding of the practice. In the space that remains to us in this essay we offer an Ortega-inspired supplement to this understanding of communication. More work than we shall be able to provide will be necessary, but major concepts can in fact be put in place and provide in their own way a beginning and an inducement to further work. That said, this sketch, as brief as it is with respect to communication and language, returns to the pivotal passage from Ortega's early essay "The Chiding of the Orator," where we were first introduced to self and circumstance: "So the orator is born with circumstance, dies with it and within it becomes consumed, and when it changes to another one he is reborn with a new condition."

The Virtue of Incite: Rethinking the Self of Circumstance

Ortega believes the word "incitement" holds a key for our understanding of living well. In it he detects a biological (i.e., a living) principle

> When naturalist reason studies man it seeks, in consistence with itself, to reveal his nature. It observes that man has a body, which is a thing, and hastens to submit it to physics; and since this body is also an organism, it hands it over to biology. It observes further that in man as in animals there functions a certain mechanism incorporeally, confusedly attached to the body, the psychic mechanism, which is also a thing, and entrusts its study to psychology, a natural science. But the fact is that this has been going on for three hundred years and that all the naturalist studies on man's body and soul put together have not the slightest use in throwing light on any of our most strictly human feelings, on what each individual calls his own life, that life which, intermingling with others, forms societies, that in their turn persisting, make up human destiny. The prodigious achievement of natural science in the direction of the knowledge of things contrasts brutally with the collapse of the same natural science when faced with the strictly mathematical reason as water runs from a sieve.

that nonliving things do not share: "Physics does not know of it. In physics one thing does not incite another; it causes it and the cause produces an effect in proportion to itself. A billiard ball colliding with another imparts to it an impulse in principle equal to its own; cause and effect are equal."[18] Human beings live another way, outside of cause understood in this mechanistic manner, and they live out of a radically different way of being in the world. To exemplify this, Ortega offers the image of well-bred horse and its rider: "when the spur's point ever so lightly touches the flank, the thoroughbred breaks into a gallop, generously out of proportion to the impulse of the spur. The reaction of the horse, rather than a response to an outer impulse, is a release of exuberant inner energies."[19] Despite its fecund suggestiveness, to our knowledge, this is a key Ortega more or less abandons to its concision and suggestiveness. We shall attempt to make the idea of exuberance a perspective from which to articulate an understanding of selves who occupy circumstance.

> Our world, the world of each one of us, is not a *totum revolutum*, but is organized in "pragmatic fields." Our practical or pragmatic relation to things, and theirs with us, even though finally corporeal, is not material, but dynamic. In our vital world there is nothing material: my body is not matter, nor are there things that come into collision with matter. It and they, we might say to simplify, are pure impact and hence our dynamism.

In doing so we hope to sketch a theory of the self that keeps close to the heart the existential lesson: "Sad life that lets the hours pass in lassitude, the hours which should flash like quivering foils."[20] If we take exuberance as a fount of creative energies, then inciting unleashes a vital and creative force into circumstance.

Touching and thus releasing exuberance needs the virtue of incite. The English word "incitement" shares with the Spanish *incitación* the Latin root *citare*, to put into movement, to summon. This etymology provides a vista whence we are able to see; a theory of human communication indebted to an exuberant self will be a theory of calling, of summoning, informing an ethical theory of living together well as a shared vocation. Getting to the heart of this idea demands of us that we understand the practice of communication is never a causing. Moreover, the consequences of communicative praxis are never akin to billiard balls colliding, forcing other minds to react in perfectly predictable ways, and the speed with which a desired action of the other that too often follows from one or another of our enunciations is no evidence against the claim. We shall have to come to the realization that such evidence is but a sad commentary on how too much of life is predetermined by bad habits and our lack of tapping into our ever-present exuberance. To the contrary, it is evidence only that lassitude and indolence are but derivative forms of exuberance. Even if we all know this—everybody knows this, we are certain—we often think and act as if it has for all its ubiquity not become a lesson we have taken to heart both in our quotidian affairs and in our theorizing. Communicative praxis should be understood as a summoning and a calling to the other, a disclosing of this rather than that in a situation,

> To have an idea means believing one is in possession of the reasons for having it, and consequently means believing that there is such a thing as reason, a world of intelligible truths. To have ideas, to form opinions is identical with appealing to such an authority, submitting oneself to it, accepting its code and its decisions, and therefore believing that the highest form of inter-communion is the dialogue in which the reasons for our ideas are discussed.

an attempt to spur ourselves on to a cooperative engagement, we with them and they with us, together.

Circumstance, then, is always the site of a possible communicative incitement, the site of a summoning. From the standpoint of communicative ethics, the Otherness of the other, the one near us now, summons something unmistakable in us—calls out from us a response as opposed to a mere reaction, and this ought to be the logic at the heart of two human beings engaged in communication: "Speech, the *logos*, in its fundamental reality, is the most human of conversations, a *diálogos—dialogos—argumentum hominis ad hominem*. Dialogue is the *logos* from the point of view of the *other*, the neighbor."[21] Dialogue calls out in us an act-response grounded in our own share of the exuberance we all are always near in being what we are. Thus, there is a *logos* embedded in exuberance, and exuberance, like its beautiful sibling enthusiasm, finds its fitting limit in the other ones who are near in dialogue understood as "the *logos* from the point of view of the other." The logos of exuberance is intersubjective, dialogic, and emergent from the situation.

Seldom, however, is dialogue easy, and contests and dilemmas more often than not await us in situations. Getting to what we believe is essential and fitting, we often find ourselves, to meet our existential responsibilities, having to "solicit" situations. We have to make a space for the emergence of those sets of relations that we have thematized and seek to set in relief for ourselves and others. We need, following the etymological relation of "solicit" with "incite," to disturb, agitate, stir up the commonness and taken-for-grantedness of things and understandings. The fitting response often is required, to meet its ethical aims, to make anxious, in a manner of speaking, by facilitating the loss of the too familiar and predictable. It needs to show us something,

> And since the men between whom the words are interchanged are human lives, and every human life is at every instant in a particular circumstance or situation, it is clear that the reality "word" is inseparable from the person who says it, from the person to whom it is said, and from the situation in which this takes place.

point out something, put something into relief we would have otherwise missed on our own.

Communication is not understood by physical models of cause and effect but by way of incitement. For this reason turning back now more directly to lesson from Ortega's *Meditations*, we highlight a manner of understanding how we might deal with the overwhelming idea of circumstance, one that shows the more we think about it the more we seem to confront its ultimately unmanageable character. Ortega offers at least one image of how we could make fitting responses in the situations that confront us. The releasing of exuberance, the spurring on of the other, following Ortega's example, can be achieved by the slightest touch, one outside of all proportion to what it might desire. He talks in the *Meditations* of a "pedagogy of suggestion," one that, to his mind, is "the only delicate and profound pedagogy."[22] Our exuberance makes it possible to put our energies in the service of this beautiful insight of Ortega's: "He who wishes to teach us a truth should not tell it to us, but simply suggest it with a brief gesture . . . who wants to teach us a truth should place us in the situation to discover it ourselves."[23] The manner of placing, this pedagogy of the brief gesture, is one that seeks to orient us in our circumstance to discover (it is in this section that Ortega explores the Greek notion of *aletheia*), what is possible there and of which we may be in need. This pedagogy brings into being the truths that "wait in all things," as another circumstance thinker has put it.[24]

There is something erotic about all of this, of course, or perhaps we should say: this will only work if we acknowledge there is something *necessarily* erotic about all of this—a kind of erotic understanding that, since Plato, reminds us that things are connected, interconnected, and brought together in new ways by love.[25]

His life, a pure and universal happening which happens to
each of us and which each one in his turn is nothing but
happening. All these things be they what they may, are now
mere interpretations which he exercises himself
in giving to what-ever he comes upon. . . .
Existence is not given to [man] ready made.

Ortega has good philosophical reasons, then, for calling his *Meditations* variously "salvations" and *amor intellectualis* "essays in intellectual love." Only Eros
brings into being relations with things and others from what is possible in their
overlapping plenitude; love "binds us to things, even if only temporarily."[26] Selves
are the embodiment of an ever-ready exuberance who are capable in their erotic
connectivity of being touched by a brief gesture, who are always the possible re-
cipients of a shared incite/insight that makes the truth of circumstance ready
for our creative energies. We are near our exuberance and close to being incited,
even when we do not tap it, even when we are left unmoved, even if exuberance
remains distant and far from our responses. This ever-readiness to be touched
by a brief gesture remains open to us, and this despite the effects of an alienating
world that serves to deaden this fruitful and joyous possibility in us (better: that
we are). An exuberant self is always on the verge of being touched by some word or
gesture unknowable in advance perhaps—an incite/insight that might well touch
what has been left for dead as a consequence of the endless cant of commerce, the
never-ending barrage of banality, and of the salaciousness ceaseless.

Giving Ortega Room: A Brief but Loving Objection on Behalf of Otherness

Let us add something to our Ortega-inspired sense of exuberant selves and circumstance and say that communicative beings are the room in circumstance,

Accordingly it is impossible to speak of action except in so far as it will be governed by a previous contemplation; and vice versa, the stand within the self
is nothing but the projection of a future action.

that just-enough-distance from things that allows something other than what
would, as a matter of course, have had to have happened. It is the room in circumstances that is the condition for the possibility of exuberance to do its work,
of reaching out into circumstance. We can only make space via our interpretations and actions—a space that, were Ortega to accept this reading, would call a
space for salvation—because we are already the room in circumstance by virtue
of being as we are. We are always already both with circumstance inextricably
and separated from it by this just-enough-distance that we have called room.[27]
So much depends on our capabilities trained, learned, and habituated by count-
less types of experience and social interaction because it is we who can act out

of the room we are in circumstance (and is this not, precisely, what Aristotle means by *ethos?*).

Ortega approaches this idea with his talk of games and of the sportive. This metaphor allows him to see that living well takes practice, discipline—one has to work, he says, to be "in good form" for living well.[28] We can only make as much of situations as the space provided by what our cultivated character will allow: "It is, then, false to say that in life 'circumstance decides.'"

> And here we have the explanation why our faith in reason has entered upon a phase of lamentable decadence. Man cannot wait any longer. He demands that science illume for him the problems of humanity. At bottom he is somewhat tired by now of stars, nervous reactions, and atoms. The earliest generations of rationalists believed that with their physical science they could throw light on human destiny. Today we know that all the marvels of the natural sciences, inexhaustible as they may be in principle, must always come to a full stop before the strange reality human life.

On the contrary, circumstances are the dilemma constantly renewed, in the presence of which we have to make our decisions; what actually decides is our character."[29] We need always a care of the self that seeks to be in its best form, for it is from out of this form that we make our moves in the various "games" in which we find ourselves and which demand of us a response.

Our understanding human being as the room in circumstance allows us to acknowledge and suffer the full weight of our existential responsibility. It is only by whatever interventions we can muster that we make pragmatic use out of this room we are in the circumstance. Thus, following "I am myself and my circumstance" Ortega goes on to complete the sentence: "and if I do not save it I do not save myself." Although this might work well theoretically for the things in our circumstance, it seems Ortega's thought is always on the verge of treating others instrumentally, even if they are the most unique of all "things" we encounter. Recall his stone, animal, human example, where his theorizing comes dangerously close to treating other persons, even for all the differences of which he is without doubt cognizant, as very special things. The other is not simply reciprocity of response in other persons, we think; rather, in addition they are something Other. This Otherness demands more than Ortega can give; his thinking is always too near becoming the reduction of the other to a sophisticated thing, unlike any other thing we meet, but not (O)ther enough.

We fear Ortega treats other persons too one-dimensionally by not taking seriously enough the idea that each other one is also Other. Each of the others we encounter are *circumstantially other*

> Alongside pure physico-mathematical reason there is a narrative reason. To comprehend anything human, be it personal or collective, one must tell its history. This man this nation does such a thing and is in such a manner, because formerly he or it did that

> other thing and was in such another manner. Life only takes on
> a measure of transparency in the light of historical reason.

and this recognizes their existential singularity and situated identity. Yet each other is *also* a part of a radical Alterity. As such, this share of absolute Otherness of each other one transcends any particular circumstance. Yes, every other is what she is here and now. She is, in part, apart and remains quasi-independent of any particular circumstance. Each circumstantially other is also beyond and otherwise than what we can situationally know of her here and now. No amount of experience can alter this; no time after now and no amount of time accumulated from now until some distant then will ever bring this transcending part of her to our circumstance knowledge of her. Granted, no other one can appear or be disclosed to us outside of circumstance, but it does not follow that "everything" that is a part of our circumstance, in this case absolute Otherness, can be *known* by us. Yet this not being able to know does not alleviate, rather it heightens and increases, the care with which we assume our responsibilities to the other.

> All this is only a metaphor. But today the only philoso-
> phers who shy at metaphor are the provincial ones. . . . And
> a *saying* by *suggestion* is one way to define metaphor.

We would insist: to be responsible our responding must acknowledge this transcending Otherness of the other. It is this otherness that keeps us from calculating the other as a mere thing of circumstance. In each instance we are torn between our immediate existential and singular responsibility to this other one (which we think Ortega understands) and the quasi-transcendental responsibility to Otherness that is beyond this situation (which Ortega is theoretically kept from seeing). In each case we must make this understanding a part of our understanding of circumstance and thus ourselves, and we accomplish this through vital concern, understanding, and acknowledgment and not through knowing, knowledge, and recognition. We are always caught between the existential and circumstantial demands of the other and the demands made by Otherness through which each other transcends the circumstance as such.

There is, it must be clear by now, nothing outside circumstance. Transcendence is always already woven into its being as it is. *Nothing outside circumstance:* the truth that nothing is outside what is justly considered as (possibly) being important for us when developing our response to circumstance and assuming our existential responsibilities therein. Ortega thought deeply about so much that still matters to us today, that must be made to matter. He in his beautiful aphoristic style, he with his devotion to the literary so as to make the keenest philosophical positions stand out in relief, he who lovingly points us—with salvation in mind—to fine if sometimes harsh truths of existence is a practitioner of the pedagogy of the brief gesture. This great Iberian philosopher makes continental philosophy deeper and wider in many important senses. If philosophy takes its highest meaning from making the love of wisdom a way of life (and it does), then Ortega is a lover of wisdom seeking to incite us to living well,

> I am not my life. This, which is reality, is composed of myself and things. The things are not I, nor am I the things. We are mutually transcendent, but we are both immanent in that absolute coexistence which is life. My life is not mine, but I belong to it. This is the broad, immense reality of my coexistence with things.

to finding our most excellent forms in thinking and action.

An Aphorism of Commencement

We began with circumstance and to it we have returned. How important is all this to communicative praxis? It is the beginning and the end. Our understanding of circumstance or world, by which we can never mean anything other than our lives together in it, would change beyond recognition if we employed the word *with* with more care. It belongs rightly as a prefix to nearly all significant concepts by which we acknowledge our experience of the world and our identities in it. We have only with-identities. Thus, not who are we, rather with-whom are we; with-what are we? Is this not how we should question and respond?

If this were so, if we took to thinking and speaking this way,

> To think that for more than thirty years—it is quickly said—I had, day after day, to endure *in silence, never broken,* when many pseudo-intellectuals of my country disqualified my ideas because I wrote "only in metaphor," they said. This made them conclude and proclaim triumphantly that my writings were not philosophy . . . that in them it is not a matter of something given as philosophy which turns out to be literature, but on the contrary, of something presented as literature which results in philosophy. But those people who have no understanding of anything understand less than nothing of beauty, of style, and do not conceive that a life and a work can cherish this virtue. Nor do they have the least suspicion for what *grave and essential reasons* man is an animal with style.

then everything once familiar would sound strange—because recontextualized in radical ways. We are with you and with each other, with our ids, with our class bias, with hate, with shame, with this weather, with this bad breakfast, nothing but withs—with after with after with. There is always more: with these genes, this inheritance, these garments, this sadness, this despair, this joy, with this history so on and so on . . . "Everything surrounds us," we hear Ortega say, and we mean to take him at his word.

It would always be with too much and too many for us to move if we were to acknowledge all our withs each and every time we act in the world. It follows from this fact that we shall need in our further studies to investigate the practice of communication to ascertain by what concepts and understandings we elect to say these withs but not those, these matter while those are, at best, secondary. We can also imagine, even now, how certain reductive principles act to hide every with other than that one to which our theoretical allegiance has been given. This is—made in passing, we admit—the beginning of a powerful understanding of fundamentalism and it shows now without any more detail fundamentalism's inherent dangers.

> Haste has urgent need to know what it is up against, it is out of urgency that truth must drive its method. The idea of progress, placing truth in a vague tomorrow, has proved a dulling opiate to humanity. Truth is what is true now and not what remains to be discovered in an undetermined future.

Being without withs is impossible if "I am myself and my circumstance" is descriptive of our being together in the world; however, which withs can or ought to matter remains open—open to the rhetorical and communicative struggles of beings who are themselves and their circumstance. We note our resistance to acknowledging some withs and our embracing wholeheartily others can be more than a bit telling of who we think we can become or what can become of us. Living well, developing an ethos committed to excellence is trying—without metaphysical or scientific guarantees—to evaluate and hierarchize our various with-relations.[30]

Communicative praxis, then, we understand as the practice that brings together and communes but which achieves this end by necessarily demarcating these with-relations rather than those by connecting and drawing together some while bracketing others. Communicative praxis determines what withs take precedence here and now and which are left unattended. For all our care, the unattended and bracketed still do their work,

> So that, properly speaking, it isn't philosophy but a philosophizing—you and I doing philosophy, being philosophy.

still participate in the game and generate their consequences behind our backs and outside of the gathering of boundaries set up by our intentions.

It is always more than we can do well enough even when we find and develop our best form,

> Yo soy yo y mi circunstancia
> I am myself and my circumstance.

and yet . . . : "In order to be able to acknowledge Dulcinea's matchless beauty, the merchants asked to see a portrait, even if it were only the size of a grain of wheat. Before acknowledging something they wanted to see it first and they were right. But perhaps Don Quixote wanted less, perhaps he only wanted them to understand, understand his words and the longing of his heart."[31]

To want less is often so much more.

Notes

1. So as not to allow this note to become longer than our text, we cite here only four studies: Julián Marías, *José Ortega y Gasset: Circumstance and Vocation,* trans. Frances M. López-Morillas (Norman: University of Oklahoma Press, 1970), the classic work on Ortega by his student and then colleague; Oliver W. Holmes, *Human Reality and the Social World: Ortega's Philosophy of History* (Amherst: University of Massachusetts Press, 1975), a fine study, well-researched and covering all the extant work of Ortega; Phillip W. Silver, *Ortega y Gasset as Phenomenologist: The Genesis of Meditations on Quixote* (New York: Columbia University Press, 1978), a keen defense of Ortega's phenomenological contributions (and debts); and John T. Graham, *A Pragmatist Philosophy of Life in Ortega y Gasset* (Columbia: University of Missouri Press, 1994), a wonderful study that makes the case for Ortega as a pragmatist in the tradition of William James (whom Ortega read) and compares this argument to many of the other positions attributed to Ortega by persons making other cases for his proper philosophical title (this book is also so well-documented that any study one could wish to track down is meticulously referenced here).

2. To wit, see Marías's detailed discussion of Ortega's 1914 use of *aletheia* as an understanding and translation of the Greek notion of truth including Ortega's own footnote-cum-open letter to Martin Heidegger; Marías, *Circumstance and Vocation,* 435–446. To read Ortega's footnote, see "In Search of Goethe from Within," in José Ortega y Gasset, *The Dehumanization of Art, and Notes on the Novel,* trans. Helene Weyl (Princeton, NJ: Princeton University Press, 1948), 146–148.

3. We shall use here and throughout the pronoun "she" to agitate Ortega, to place this pronoun here as promise to take his position on gender to task at another time. It deserves it.

4. "Preface for Germans," in José Ortega y Gasset, *Phenomenology and Art,* trans. Philip W. Silver (New York: W. W. Norton, 1975), 21.

5. "Man the Technician," in José Ortega y Gasset, *History as a System, and Other Essays Toward a Philosophy of History,* trans. Helene Weyl (New York: W. W. Norton, 1961), 98.

6. We owe this cite to Marías (see *Circumstance and Vocation,* 363) and in his notes to *Meditations.* Yet he makes nothing, ironic on our reading, of the rhetorical/communicative nature of the circumstance in which the concept circumstance came to visit Ortega's thinking. We, on the other hand, are trying to make everything ride on this, for a while at least.

7. *"Vejamen del Orador,"* *Obras Completas,* vol. 1, 563 (translation ours).

8. Ibid., 562.

9. José Ortega y Gasset, *Concord and Liberty,* trans. Helene Weyl (New York: W. W. Norton, 1946), 81.

10. Marías addresses something like this when he notes Ortega's claim in *Meditations* concerning Hegel's *Logik:* " Thus the twelve hundred pages of Hegel's Logik are just the preparation which enables us to pronounce, in all the fullness of its meaning, this sentence: 'the idea is the absolute.' This sentence, so poor in appearance has in reality a literally infinite meaning"; *Meditations,* 39.

11. *"Vejamen del Orador,"* 563–564.

12. We have been working on these ideas for some time now by way of the concepts "an ethics of relief" and "working and waiting"; see Ramsey Eric Ramsey, *The Long Path to Nearness: A Contribution to a Corporeal Philosophy of Communication and the Groundwork for an Ethics of Relief* (Amherst, NY: Humanity Books, 1998); Ramsey Eric Ramsey, "Communication and Eschatology: The Work of Waiting, an Ethics of Relief, and A religious Religiosity," *Communication Theory* 7, no. 4 (November 1997): 343–361; and Ramsey Eric Ramsey, "Suffering Wonder: Wooing and Courting in the Public Sphere," *Communication Theory* 8, no. 4 (November 1998): 455–475.

13. "Doctrine of the Point of View," in José Ortega y Gasset, *The Modern Theme*, trans. James Cleugh (New York: W. W. Norton, 1933), 92.

14. José Ortega y Gasset, *The Revolt of the Masses* (New York: W. W. Norton, 1932), 41.

15. We follow here again Calvin O. Schrag concerning the communicative praxis and the fitting response. Calvin O. Schrag, *Communicative Praxis and the Space of Subjectivity* (West Lafayette: Purdue University Press, 2003); and "Loving Struggle to the Struggle for Love," in Ramsey Eric Ramsey and David James Miller, eds., *Experiences between Philosophy and Communication: Engaging the Philosophical Contributions of Calvin O. Schrag* (Albany: State University of New York Press, 2003), 3–56.

16. Our studies suggest we will do best to focus our attention on his work *Man and People*, as it is here where he is most explicit about the issues directly relevant to our investigation; José Ortega y Gasset, *Man and People*, trans. Willard R. Trask (New York: W. W. Norton, 1957).

17. *Man and People*, 203.

18. "The Sportive Origin of the State," in Ortega y Gasset, *History as a System, and Other Essays Toward a Philosophy of History*, 21.

19. "The Sportive Origin of the State," 21.

20. "The Sportive Origin of the State," 22.

21. "Preface for Germans," 20.

22. *Meditations*, 67.

23. *Meditations*, 67.

24. Walt Whitman, *Leaves of Grass*.

25. Ortega cites this view of Plato's in *Meditations*: "Love is the divine architect who, according to Plato, came down to the world "so that everything in the universe might be linked together"; *Meditations*, 33. See also our "Procreation in a Beautiful Medium: Eroticizing the Vectors of Communicative Praxis," in *Experiences between Philosophy and Communication*, 191–200, for a explication of this idea exploring understandings of love, gratitude, and testimony in light of developing a contribution to a philosophy of communication.

26. *Meditations*, 33.

27. It goes without saying, perhaps, that this idea of room is not unrelated to what Heidegger calls *Spielraum*, but we hesitate to mention this, as we have sworn off the comparisons one can make. Ortega's thought by itself could give one this direction. See "Jovial Side of Philosophy," in José Ortega y Gasset, *The Idea Principle in Leibnitz and the Evolution of Deductive Theory*, trans. Mildred Adams (New York: W. W. Norton, 1971), 320–333; and "The Sportive Origin of the State."

28. José Ortega y Gasset, *Mission of the University*, trans. and ed. Howard Lee Nostrand (New Brunswick, NJ: Transaction Publishers, 1992), 21.

29. *Revolt of the Masses*, 48.

30. We have dealt with this issue in some detail in Linda Wiener and Ramsey Eric Ramsey, *Leaving Us to Wonder: An Essay on the Questions Science Can't Ask* (Albany: State University of New York Press, 2005).

31. "Consciousness, Object and Its Three Distances," Ortega y Gasset, *Phenomenology and Art*, 21.

Bibliography of Works

Books by José Ortega y Gasset

1910s

Meditaciones del Quijote. Madrid: Residencia de Estudiantes, 1914.
Vieja y nueva política. Madrid: Revista de Occidente, 1914.
Personas, obras, cosas. Madrid: La Lectura, 1916.
El Espectador. Madrid: Revista de Occidente, 1916. [1916–1934]
El Espectador. Vol. 3, *Verdad y perspectiva nada «Moderno» y muy Siglo XX.* Madrid: Calpe, 1921.
España Invertebrada: Bosquejo de algunos pensamientos históricos. Madrid: Calpe, 1921.
Meditaciones del Quijote: Meditación preliminar meditación primera. Madrid: Calpe, 1922.
El Tema de nuestro tiempo: El ocaso de las revoluciones, el sentido histórico de la teoría de Einstein. Madrid: Revista de Occidente, 1923.
Las Atlántidas: Con unas figuras del Sudán y de la China. Madrid: Revista de Occidente, 1924.
Deshumanización del arte: Ideas sobre la novela Velázquez Goya. Madrid: Revista de Occidente, 1925.
Tríptico. Madrid: Revista de Occidente, 1927.
El Espectador. Vol. 5, *Notas del vago estío vitalidad, alma, espíritu. Fraseología y Sinceridad.* 2nd ed. Madrid: Revista de Occidente, 1929.
El Espectador. Vol. 7, *Hegel y América sobre la expresión fenómeno cósmico.* Madrid: Revista de Occidente, 1929.
Notas. Madrid: Espasa-Calpe, 1928.

1930s

Misión de la universidad. Madrid: Revista de Occidente, 1930.
La rebelión de las masas. Madrid: Revista de Occidente, 1930.
Rectificación de la República: Artículos y discursos. Madrid: Revista de Occidente, 1931.
La redención de las provincias y la decencia nacional: Artículos de 1927 y 1930. Madrid: Revista de Occidente, 1931.
Esquema de la crisis. Santiago de Chile: Empresa Letras, 1934.
Espíritu de la Letra: Las Atlántidas. Mirabeau o el político. Madrid: Revista de Occidente, 1936.
El Espectador. Vol. 2. Madrid: Revista de Occidente, 1936.
Obras de José Ortega y Gasset, vol. 1, *1902–1916,* vol. 2, *El Espectador, 1916–1934.* 2nd ed. corr. y aum. Madrid: Espasa-Calpe, 1936.
Misión de la universidad: Kant. La deshumanización del arte. Madrid: El Arquero, 1936.
Ensimismamiento y alteración: Meditación de la técnica. Buenos Aires: Espasa Calpe Argentina, 1939.

1940s

Estudios sobre el amor. 2nd ed. Buenos Aires: Espasa-Calpe, 1940.

Goethe desde dentro: El punto de vista en las artes. Buenos Aires: Espasa Calpe Argentina, 1940.

Ideas y creencias. Buenos Aires: Espasa-Calpe, 1940.

Mocedades. Madrid: Espasa-Calpe, 1941.

Historia como sistema y del Imperio Romano. Madrid: Revista de Occidente, 1941.

Meditaciones del Quijote: La deshumanización del arte. Buenos Aires: Espasa-Calpe Argentina, 1942.

Teoría de andalucía y otros ensayos: Guillermo Dilthey y la idea de vita. Madrid: Revista de Occidente, 1942.

Esquema de las crisis y otros ensayos. Madrid: Revista de Occidente, 1942.

Dos prólogos: A un Tratado de Montería, a una historia de la filosofía. Madrid: Revista de Occidente, 1944.

Obras completas, vol. 2, *El Espectador: 1916–1934.* Madrid: Revista de Occidente, 1946.

Obras completas, vol. 3, *1917–1928.* Madrid: Revista de Occidente, 1947.

Obras completas, vol. 5, *1933–1941.* Madrid: Revista de Occidente, 1947.

Obras completas, vol. 6, *1941–1946, y Brindis y Prólogos.* Madrid: Revista de Occidente, 1947.

1950s

Papeles sobre Velázquez y Goya. Madrid Revista de Occidente, 1950.

De la Aventura y la Caza. 2nd ed. Madrid: Afrodisio Aguado, 1955.

La civiltá Veneziana del Trecento. Venezia: Sansoni, 1956.

Obras completas, vol. 4, *1929–1933.* 3rd ed. Madrid: Revista de Occidente, 1955.

¿Qué es filosofía? Madrid: Espasa-Calpe, 1957.

El hombre y la gente. Madrid: Revista de Occidente, 1957.

Espíritu de la letra. 4th ed. Madrid: Revista de Occidente, 1958.

Goya. Madrid Revista de Occidente, 1958.

La idea de principio en Leibniz y la evolución de la teoría deductiva. Buenos Aires: Emecé, 1958.

Idea del teatro con un grabado. Madrid: Revista de Occidente, 1958.

Prólogo para Alemanes. Madrid: Taurus, 1958.

Una interpretación de la historia universal. Madrid: Revista de Occidente, 1959.

En torno a Galileo: Esquema de las crisis. Madrid: Revista de Occidente, 1959.

Viajes y países. 2nd ed. Madrid: Revista de Occidente, 1959.

Velázquez. Madrid: Revista de Occidente, 1959.

1960s

La caza y los toros. Madrid: Revista de Occidente, 1960.

La deshumanización del arte y otros ensayos estéticos. 6th ed. en castellano. Madrid: Revista de Occidente, 1960.

Ensayos escogidos. Madrid: Aguilar, 1960.

Una interpretación de la historia universal. En torno a Toynbee. Madrid: Revista de Occidente, 1960.

Meditación de Europa. Madrid: Revista de Occidente, 1960.

Origen y epílogo de la filosofía. Buenos Aires, México: Fondo de Cultura Económica, 1960.

Kant, Hegel, Dilthey. 2nd ed. Madrid: Revista de Occidente, 1961.

Obras completas, vol. 7, *1948–1958.* Madrid: Revista de Occidente, 1961.

Vives-Goethe: Conferencias. Madrid: Revista de Occidente, 1961.

Misión del bibliotecario y otros ensayos afines. Madrid: Revista de Occidente, 1962.

Obras completas, vol. 8, *1958–1959.* Madrid: Revista de Occidente, 1962.

Obras completas, vol. 9, *1960–1962.* Madrid: Revista de Occidente, 1962.

Pasado y porvenir para el hombre actual. Madrid: Revista de Occidente, 1962.

Atlántidas: Y del Imperio Romano. Madrid: Revista de Occidente, 1963.

Meditación del pueblo joven. Madrid: Espasa-Calpe, 1964.

Meditaciones del Quijote: Ideas sobre la novela. Madrid: Espasa-Calpe, 1964.

Meditación de la técnica: Vicisitudes en las ciencias; Bronca en la física; Prólogos a la «Biblioteca de ideas del Siglo XX.» Madrid: Espasa-Calpe, 1965.

Torno a Galileo: Esquema de las crisis. Madrid: Espasa-Calpe, 1965.

Meditación de Europa. 2nd ed. Madrid: Revista de Occidente, 1966.

Misión de la universidad: Y otros ensayos afines. 4th ed. en castellano. Madrid: Revista de Occidente, 1965.

Unas Lecciones de metafísica. Madrid: Alianza, 1966.

Notas. Madrid: Anaya, 1968.

Obras completas, vol. 10, *Escritos Políticos-I, 1908–1921.* Madrid: Revista de Occidente, 1969.

Obras completas, vol. 11, *Escritos Políticos-II, 1922–1933.* Madrid: Revista de Occidente, 1969.

1970s

Historia como sistema. Madrid: Espasa Calpe, 1971.

La redención de las provincias, II. Escritos Políticos (1918/1928). Madrid: Revista de Occidente, 1973.

Vives-Goethe. Madrid Revista de Occidente, 1973.

Discursos políticos. Madrid: Alianza, 1974.

Epistolario. Madrid: Revista de Occidente, 1974.

Mirabeau o el político: Contreras o El Aventurero. Madrid: Revista de Occidente, 1974.

Apuntes sobre el pensamiento. Madrid: Revista de Occidente, 1975.

Letras hispanoamericanas de nuestro tiempo. Madrid: José Porrúa Turanzas, 1976.

Sobre la razón histórica. Madrid: Revista de Occidente, 1979.

1980s

Ensayos sobre la «Generación del 98» y otros escritores Españoles contemporáneos. Madrid: Revista de Occidente en Alianza Editorial, 1980.

Investigaciones psicológicas. Madrid: Revista de Occidente, 1981.

Misión de la universidad y otros ensayos sobre educación y pedagogía. Madrid: Alianza Editorial, 1982.

Meditación de la técnica y otros ensayos sobre ciencia y filosofía. Madrid: Alianza, 1982.

Goethe-Dilthey. Madrid: Alianza, 1982.

Obras completas, vol. 12. Madrid: Revista de Occidente, 1983.

Kant, Hegel, Scheler. Madrid: Alianza, 1983.

¿Qué es conocimiento? Ed. de Paulino Garagorri. Madrid: Alianza-Revista de Occidente, 1984.

Ensayos sobre la generación del 98. Madrid: Revista de Occidente, 1986.

Ortega y Gasset: Una educación para la vida. Compiled by Esteban Inciarte. México: SEP, Subsecretaría de Cultura, Dirección General de Publicaciones y Medios: El Caballito: CONAFE, 1986.

Meditaciones sobre la literatura y el arte: La manera Española de ver las cosas. Ed. Inman Fox. Madrid: Castalia, 1988.

1990s

Cartas de un joven Español: 1881–1908. Edición de Soledad Ortega. Madrid: El Arquero, 1991.

Ortega y Gasset, José, and Jesús Reyes Heroles. *Dos ensayos sobre Mirabeau: Mirabeau o el político, Mirabeau o la política.* 2nd ed. México: Fondo de Cultura Económica, 1993.

Notas de trabajo. Epílogo. Ed. José Luis Molinuevo. Madrid: Alianza-Fundación José Ortega y Gasset, 1994.

Vida Alrededor: Meditaciones para entender nuestro tiempo. Temas de Hoy, 1998.

Papeles sobre Velazquez y Goya. Madrid: Revista de Occidente, 1998.

English Translations of Books by José Ortega y Gasset

1930s

Invertebrate Spain. Trans. Mildred Adams. New York: W. W. Norton & Company, 1937.

1940s

Toward a Philosophy of History. New York: W. W. Norton & Company, 1941.

Mission of the University. Trans. Howard Lee Nostrand. Princeton, NJ: Princeton University Press, 1944.

Concord and Liberty. Translated by Helene Weyl. New York: W. W. Norton & Company, 1946.

The Dehumanization of Art, and Notes on the Novel. Trans. Helene Weyl. Princeton, NJ: Princeton University Press, 1948.

1950s

On Love; Aspects of a Single Theme. Trans. Toby Talbot. New York: Meridean Books, 1957.

Man and Crisis. Trans. Mildred Adams. New York: W.W. Norton & Company, 1958.

1960s

What Is Philosophy? Trans. Mildred Adams. New York: W.W. Norton & Company, 1960.

History as a System. Trans. Willard R. Trask. New York: Publisher: W.W. Norton & Company, 1961.

The Modern Theme. Trans. James Cleugh. New York: Harper, 1961.

Man and People. New York: W.W. Norton & Company, 1963.

Dehumanization of Art and Other Essays on Art, Culture, and Literature. Trans. Mildred Adams. Princeton, NJ: Princeton University Press, 1968.

Some Lessons in Metaphysics. Trans. Mildred Adams. New York: W. W. Norton & Company, 1969.

1970s

Idea of Principle in Leibnitz and the Evolution of Deductive Theory. Trans. Mildred Adams. New York: W.W. Norton & Company, 1971.

Velazquez, Goya and the Dehumanization of Art. Trans. Alexis Brown. New York: W. W. Norton & Company, 1972.

Phenomenology and Art. Trans. Philip W. Silver. New York: Norton, 1975.

1980s

Historical Reason. Trans. Philip W. Silver. New York: W.W. Norton & Company, 1983.

An Interpretation of Universal History. Trans. Mildred Adams. New York: W.W. Norton & Company, 1985.

Meditations on Hunting. Trans. Howard B. Wescott. New York: Scribner, 1985.

The Revolt of the Masses. Trans. Anthony Kerrigan. South Bend, IN: University of Notre Dame Press, 1985.

Psychological Investigations. Trans. Jorge García-Gómez. New York: W.W. Norton & Company, 1987.

2000s

Meditations on Quixote. Trans. Evelyn Rugg and Diego Marin. Champaign: University of Illinois Press, 2000.

Origin of Philosophy. Trans. Toby Talbot. Champaign: University of Illinois Press, 2000.

What Is Knowledge? Trans. Jorge Garcia-Gomez. Albany: State University of New York Press, 2001.

Mikhail Bakhtin (1895–1975)

Biographical Sketch

Mikhail Bakhtin was born on November 17, 1895 (Gregorian calendar), in Orel, Russia. His father managed a bank, and Bakhtin grew up in Vilnius and Odessa. In 1913, he relocated to study at Petrograd (later St. Petersburg) University (1913–1918), earning a degree in classics and philology. The hardships of the Russian Civil War made living in Petrograd impossible, so Bakhtin moved to Nevel and

---

Different sources report inconsistent information about the life of Mikhail Bakhtin. Information for this biographical sketch was drawn from "Bakhtin, M. M.," *The Johns Hopkins Guide to Literary Theory & Criticism*, ed. Michael Groden and Martin Kreiswirth (Baltimore, MD: Johns Hopkins University Press, 1997)—www.press.jhu.edu/books/hopkins_guide_to_literary_theory/m._m._bakhtin.html (accessed August 18, 2005); "Mikhail Bakhtin," Critical Theory (Boston]: Bedford/St. Martin's)—http://www.bedfordstmartins.com/litlinks/critical/bakhtin.htm (accessed October 3, 2003); Patricia Bizzell and Bruce Herzberg, eds., *The Rhetorical Tradition: Readings from Classical Times to the Present* (Boston, MA: Bedford/St. Martin's Press, 2001); Maureen Flynn-Burhoe, "Bakhtin Chronology"—http://www.carleton.ca/~mflynnbu/bakhtin/chronology.htm (accessed October 3, 2003); Hwa Yol Jung, "Bakhtin, Mikhail Mikhailovich," *The Cambridge Dictionary of Philosophy*, 2nd ed., ed. Robert Audi (Cambridge: Cambridge University Press, 1999); James P. Zappen, "Mikhail Bakhtin (1895–1975)," *Twentieth-Century Rhetoric and Rhetoricians: Critical Studies and Sources*, ed. Michael G. Moran and Michelle Ballif (Westport: Greenwood Press, 2000), 7–20; "Mikhail Bakhtin"—http://en.wikipedia.org/wiki/Mikhail_Bakhtin (accessed 8/18/05). Photograph by Robert Louis Jackson.

then to Vitebsk, where he became a schoolteacher. He was a member of the Russian Orthodox Church and offered public lectures on theology in area towns.

In 1918, an intellectual circle formed around Bakhtin, including Valentin Voloshinov and Pavel Medvedev among others. In 1921, while in Vitebsk, Bakhtin married Elena Alexandrovna. During this time, he contracted osteomyelitis in his right leg, a bone disease which hampered his productivity and made him an invalid. Bakhtin's wife supported him while he was unable to work due to his illness and to increasing governmental suspicions about his religious activities.

In 1924, the political situation had calmed, enabling Bakhtin (and the Bakhtin circle) to move to Leningrad. His illness and lack of acceptable political (Stalinist) credentials made finding work difficult and he struggled financially.

In 1929, Bakhtin was swept up in a Stalinist purge of artists and intellectuals. He was accused of participating in the Russian Orthodox Church's underground movement, although it is unclear if that charge was warranted. He was sentenced to ten years in the Solovetsky Islands camp in Siberia. He appealed that decision on the grounds that with his illness such exile would be deadly. His sentenced was then changed to six years of internal exile in Kazakhstan.

While in Kazakhstan (1930–1936), Bakhtin was employed as a bookkeeper on a collective farm and did other odd jobs. In 1936, he was hired by the Mordovian Pedagogical Institute in Saransk to teach Russian and world literature. To escape the great purge of 1937, Bakhtin moved from Saransk to Savelovo (residing there from 1937 to 1945). In 1938, Bakhtin's osteomyelitis required his leg to be amputated. His health began to improve and he became more prolific as a scholar.

During this intense political period, Bakhtin allegedly published his work using the names of friends who were not under watch and investigation by the government. Questions remain surrounding the authorship of some works written in the name of Valentin Voloshinov and Pavel Medvedev.

In 1941, he submitted his dissertation, "Tvorchestvo Fransua Rable I narodnaia kul'tura srednevekov'ia i renessansa" (The Work of François Rabelais and the Popular Culture of the Middle Ages and the Renaissance), to the Gorky Institute of World Literature in Moscow. He was not able to defend his manuscript due to World War II. His defense finally occurred in 1947. The book's "earthy, anarchic topic" caused a scandal, and faculty disputed his work. In 1951, Bakhtin was granted the lesser degree of candidate instead of a full doctorate.

Following World War II, Bakhtin returned to Saransk to teach literature courses at the Mordov Pedagogical Institute (1945–1961). He retired in 1961. In the post-Stalinist period of the late 1950s, Soviet intellectuals rediscovered Bakhtin's work. In the early 1960s a group of Moscow graduate students who had read his *Problems of Dostoevsky's Art* (1929) discovered he was still alive, saved by his relative obscurity during the war years. Bakhtin became a cult figure, and various intellectual circles attempted to recruit him as an ally in intellectual battles.

Mikhail Bakhtin returned to Moscow in 1972 and died there three years later, on March 7, 1975.

Mikhail Bakhtin
The Philosophy of Dialogism
Leslie A. Baxter

During an interview held near the end of his life, Mikhail Bakhtin was asked if he was more of a philosopher than a philologist in the early years of his career. Bakhtin replied promptly, "More of a philosopher. And such I have remained until the present day. I am a philosopher. A thinker."[1] He is widely regarded as one of the most powerful thinkers of the twentieth century,[2] and specialists in any number of fields have been informed by his work, including literary critics, film scholars, classicists, theologians, political scientists, anthropologists, and language scholars, among others.[3] The purpose of this essay is to provide an overview of Bakhtin's philosophy of dialogism, so labeled by Michael Holquist out of the belief that *dialogue* is the "master key" that guided Bakhtin's work throughout his career.[4] My overview will not be exhaustive, focusing instead on those concepts that I regard as particularly important to communication scholars. I will begin with a brief sketch of Bakhtin's life and selected key works, then turn to a discussion of two phases in Bakhtin's work, before and after his "linguistic turn."[5] I will end with a discussion of how Bakhtin's work has entered communication scholarship in general and its implications for the study of face-to-face communication in particular.

Bakhtin's Life and Selected Key Works

Bakhtin's work is surrounded by a swirl of ambiguities and confusions, in large measure the result of the Stalinist political times in which he lived: his work was slow to gain publication in Russia and even slower to reach English translation; later works were generally more accessible in translation before earlier works, posing challenges to understanding the chronology of his thinking; and the authorship of several texts is disputed. Before turning to the substance of his ideas, it thus is worthwhile to take a brief biographical/bibliographical excursion.

Born in 1895 into a family of minor nobility with a banking-executive father, Bakhtin spent his youth in the culturally and linguistically diverse Russian cities of Vilnius and Odessa. Educated at home, he was familiar with ancient Greek, Hellenistic, and modern European philosophy, including Buber and Kierkegaard. Studying classics, philosophy, and literature at St. Petersburg University, Bakhtin fled to the countryside in 1918 in the chaos of the Russian Revolution. There, he met on a regular basis with other young intellectuals in a discussion group that subsequently became known as the "Bakhtin circle." Many members of this group subsequently moved to Leningrad in 1924 and continued meeting until the government crackdown on unorthodox intellectuals at the end of 1928.

Four essays in particular hold relevance in understanding dialogism from the 1919–1924 period of the Bakhtin circle, when Bakhtin's energies were concentrated on aesthetics, the creative act, consciousness, and ethics. In 1919, Bakhtin published in a minor provincial journal a two-page essay entitled "Art and Answerability," subsequently translated into English and published in a 1990 volume of the same title.[6] An unfinished essay entitled "Author and Hero in Aesthetic Activity," thought to have been written between 1920 and 1923 and originally published posthumously in Russia in 1979, was also translated into English and published in the 1990 *Art and Answerability* volume.[7] The 1924 essay "The Problem of Content, Material, and Form in Verbal Art," a critique of Russian formalism in literary criticism, remained unpublished in Russia until 1975 and appeared in English translation in the *Art and Answerability* volume.[8] The essay entitled "Toward a Philosophy of the Act," thought to have been written in the early 1920s, was published posthumously in Russia in 1986 and was translated into English in the published 1993 volume by the same name.[9]

By the end of the 1920s, members of the Bakhtin circle evidenced a distinct "linguistic turn," as they increasingly focused on the implications of Saussurean linguistics and recognized the role of language in social life. The dialogism of the early Bakhtin essays was brought to bear in theorizing language use and intertextuality. Particularly important in this later articulation of dialogism was an essay published under the name of a fellow member of the Bakhtin circle, Valentin Voloshinov, the 1929 *Marxism and the Philosophy of Language* (available in English translation in 1986).[10] However, this text, as well as others attributed to various members of the Bakhtin circle, has been widely attributed to Bakhtin.[11] Under his own name, Bakhtin published in 1929 his important *Problems of Dostoevsky's Creative Art*, a revision of which became available in English translation in 1984 under a slightly revised title.[12]

The period from 1929 to 1941 was one of personal uncertainty and intellectual productivity for Bakhtin. In 1929 Bakhtin was arrested, probably as part of a larger crackdown on unorthodox intellectuals. He was exiled to Kazakhstan, where he taught bookkeeping and continued his intellectual interests until 1936. He then moved to Saransk, where he taught literature at the Mordovian Pedagogical Institute for a year before fleeing to Savelovo during the 1937 political purge. During this period, Bakhtin completed several important essays on the novel as a dialogic genre, although these were not published in Russia until 1975 and not available in English translation until 1981.[13] During this period, he also completed a dissertation on Rabelais for submission to the Gorky Institute of World Literature, but it was not accepted until 1947, not published in Russia until 1965, and unavailable in English translation until 1984.[14]

The period from 1941 until 1963 saw steady employment for Bakhtin, although his work remained hidden from the mainstream Russian intellectual community. After the German invasion of Russia in 1941, Bakhtin was allowed to teach German and Russian in a Savelovo high school. When World War II

ended, Bakhtin was recalled to Saransk, where he became a university professor of Russian and world literature. Probably the most substantial work from
this post-WW II period is the essay "The Problem of Speech Genres," written in
the 1950s, published posthumously in Russia in 1979, and available in English
translation in 1986.[15]

In 1963, Bakhtin was (re)discovered by intellectuals at the Gorky Institute,
who were impressed with his works on Dostoevsky and Rabelais and pleased that
he was still alive, unlike many other intellectuals of his generation. They worked
on behalf of the (re)publication of Bakhtin's life work, and Bakhtin became an
intellectual sensation.[16] He was brought to Moscow, where he worked for the most
part on the (re)publication of his earlier works until his death from emphysema
in 1975. It is thus not much of an exaggeration to claim that half a century separates the creation from the consumption of much of Bakhtin's work.

Bakhtin's Dialogism, 1919–1924

Important to the formation of the Bakhtin circle in 1918 was Matvei Kagan,
who had recently returned from studying Neo-Kantian philosophy under Hermann Cohen at the University of Marburg in Germany. Kagan appears to have
functioned as an important intellectual mentor to Bakhtin until they were separated in 1921, although Bakhtin had read broadly in German philosophy prior
to 1918.[17]

The interests of the Bakhtin circle were diverse, but Neo-Kantianism provided the philosophical backdrop for much of their activity. In a general sense,
Neo-Kantianism refers to any theory that seeks to reinterpret Kant and the philosophical problems of epistemology and ethics, but it is particularly associated
with a movement that dominated German philosophy for half a century beginning in the 1860s. In general terms, Kant was concerned with the mind/world
relation.[18] Kant argued that his predecessors had erred either in overemphasizing the role of the mind and thereby diminishing the role of world outside of
the mind or in overemphasizing the role of the world and thereby reducing the
mind to a passive receiver of sensations from the world. Kant argued instead for
a necessary interaction between mind and world. The world really exists, argued
Kant, but so does the mind. Thought was the interaction of the two.

The return to Kant was a response to the perceived limitations of both
idealist (mind) and materialist (world) post-Kantian philosophies. However,
Neo-Kantianism was far from a unified return to Kant's position. The various
Neo-Kantian schools of thought were characterized as much by what they adopted from Kant as by what they rejected. However, in general, they grappled
philosophically with the shared intellectual problem of epistemology and the
mind/world relation. Although the intellectual activity of the Bakhtin circle took
place in a Neo-Kantianisn context, it was not characterized by passive acceptance
of Kant's philosophy. Despite his attraction to Kant's notion of knowledge as an

interaction of mind and world, Bakhtin rejected Kant's position in two fundamental respects. First, as Michael Holquist observed,

> [Bakhtin] differs from Kant in assuming that . . . there are things in them-
> selves; there may be things outside mind, but they are nevertheless not in
> themselves. The non-identity of mind and world is the conceptual rock
> on which dialogism is founded and the source of all other levels of non-
> concurring identity which Bakhtin sees shaping the world and our place in
> it. Bakhtin's thought is a meditation on how we know, a meditation based
> on *dialogue* precisely because, unlike many other theories of knowing, the
> site of knowledge it posits is never unitary. . . . In dialogism, the very ca-
> pacity to have consciousness is based on *otherness*. This otherness is not
> merely a dialectical alienation on its way to a sublation that will endow
> it with a unifying identity in higher consciousness. On the contrary, in
> dialogism consciousness is otherness.[19]

Bakhtin thus moved the site of knowledge from transcendent and synthetic
thought to the relation between self and other—dialogue. The concept of dialogue is woven throughout Bakhtin's fifty-year career.

Second, Bakhtin shifted from Kant's focus on aesthetic *judgment* to an
emphasis on aesthetic *activity.* Bakhtin argued that art and life are not discrete
domains of humanity; everyday living is not free of creative activity, and art
should not be "too high-flown" or "too exalted" for everyday life.[20] In his focus
on everyday living, Bakhtin initiated a lifelong theoretical commitment to the
prosaic—the ordinary, taken-for-granted process of living. Dialogism is widely
accepted as a philosophy of the ordinary in its focus on prosaics.[21]

Life and art are united as aesthetic or creative acts in their answerability,
or responsibility, to an other.[22] In conceiving life (and art) as an act—a deed—of
answerability to an other, Bakhtin articulated his view of human consciousness
based on otherness. The aesthetic or creative act, in all of its forms, is a relation
that Bakhtin referred to with varying vocabularies in his writing from this early
period: I-and-other, I-for-myself and I-for-another, spirit-and-soul, author-and-
character (hero), artist-and-work. In his later work, this relation in its most
general sense would be referred to as a dialogue of voices—different positions,
points of view, or ideologies.

Bakhtin argued that consciousness is impossible without an other. We can
never see ourselves as a whole; the other is necessary to give us—to author—our
sense of self. As Bakhtin expressed it:

> [A] human being experiencing life in the category of his own *I* is inca-
> pable of gathering himself by himself into an outward whole that would
> be even relatively finished. . . . In this sense, one can speak of a human
> being's absolute need for the other [in] producing his outwardly finished
> personality. This outward personality could not exist, if the other did
> not create it.[23]

This key dialogic principle—that consciousness is a relation of one person and an other—was remarkably resilient throughout Bakhtin's corpus of work. In the 1960s revision of his Dostoevsky book we encounter the same thought:

> I am conscious of myself and become myself only while revealing myself for another, through another, and with the help of another. The most important acts constituting self-consciousness are determined by a relationship toward another consciousness.... A person has no internal sovereign territory, he is wholly and always in the boundary; looking inside himself, he looks into the eyes of another or with the eyes of another.[24]

What is it about otherness that enables consciousness? In dialogism, it is a human's outsideness, or excess of seeing in relation to the other, that enables mutual creation of consciousness:

> When I contemplate a whole human being who is situated outside and over against me, our concrete, actually experienced horizons do not coincide. For at each given moment, regardless of the position and the proximity to me of this other human being whom I am contemplating, I shall always see and know something that he, from his place outside and over against me, cannot see himself: parts of his body that are inaccessible to his own gaze (his head, his face and its expressions), the world behind his back, and a whole series of objects and relations, which in any of our mutual relations are accessible to me but not to him.[25]

In dialogism, self is a relative event constructed out of the relation of two bodies occupying simultaneous but different space. Self and other do not exist as separate entities but as a relation of similarity and difference. Consciousness is the ongoing, situated action of relating.

The being of self thus is the activity of co-being in which neither person has an alibi from the deed or act of answerability. People bear an ethical obligation to participate in the activity of co-being. However, many renege this ethical responsibility, becoming what Bakhtin calls *pretenders*—those who avoid the project of self by living according to abstract norms; they live by seeking passive compliance with abstract demands, failing to appreciate that life is "deed-performing" in the act of co-being.[26]

It is the activity of relation between persons that gives each consciousness meaning in the moment. To be human entails the obligation to answer—to act toward—the other, thereby participating in the joint action of creation.[27] In the act of answering, or authoring, the other, a person gains consciousness:

> An author is not the bearer of inner lived experience, and his reaction is neither a passive feeling nor a receptive perception. An author is the uniquely active form-giving energy that is manifested not in a psychologically conceived consciousness, but in a durably valid cultural product.[28]

In his later work, this "cultural product" becomes language use; however, in this early work, answerability is conceived more generally as an act that creates an other. In the act of mutual authoring, selves become.

The act of authoring is aesthetic when we act toward the other as a whole being. However, in living everyday life, we often respond only to parts and pieces of the other. We engage only a part of the store clerk, the bank clerk, the boy who mows the lawn. As Bakhtin stated the distinction between aesthetic and nonaesthetic acts:

> In life, we are interested not in the whole of a human being, but only in those particular actions on his part with which we are compelled to deal in living our life and which are, in one way or another, of special interest to us. In the work of art, on the other hand, the author's reactions to particular self-manifestations on the part of the hero are founded on his unitary reaction to the *whole* of the hero. . . . What makes a reaction specifically aesthetic is precisely the fact that it is a reaction to the *whole* of the hero as a human being.[29]

When a person answers to the whole of the other, the other is consummated.

However, this aesthetic consummation is never finalizable, because the human being is always "yet-to-be."[30] Only death brings finalized consummation; in life, consummation is a fleeting aesthetic moment against a larger dynamic of ongoing openness. Dialogism is a theory predicated on the assumption of unfinalizability. Order (meaning) is an accomplishment to be achieved out of the ordinary messiness of everyday life; it is constituted in fleeting moments of consummation.

Aesthetic activity is a three-part process, according to Bakhtin. First is empathy: "I must experience—come to see and to know—what he experiences; I must put myself in his place and coincide with him as it were."[31] Second is a return to one's outsideness: "My projection of myself into him must be followed by a return into myself, a return to my own place outside . . . for only from this place can the material derived from my projecting myself into the other be rendered meaningful."[32] Third, and last, is answerability, in which we respond to the other's wholeness—consummation. These three aspects of aesthetic activity do not function chronologically; instead, they are "ultimately intertwined and fuse with one another" in living experience.[33]

Undeveloped in this first period of Bakhtin's work is a conception of how it is that persons concretely accomplish creation/authoring/answerability. In this early period, *dialogue* is a key concept for Bakhtin but only in a metaphorical sense. Just as any dialogue or conversation can be understood as the unity of different voices, so human existence and consciousness can be understood as a metaphorical dialogue, or relation of difference, between one embodied person and an embodied other. However, by the late 1920s, after Bakhtin's "linguistic turn," *dialogue* is decidedly conceived as language use. Dialogue is a key concept not only at a metaphorical level but in reference to the interplay of utterances, whether written or spoken.

Bakhtin's Dialogism, Post-1924

When the Bakhtin circle migrated to Leningrad in 1924 or thereabouts, the intellectual world was abuzz with Ferdinand de Saussure's work and the "linguistic turn" it represented.[34] In language, Bakhtin landed on the process by which the act of mutual authoring—answerability—is performed:

> There is no such thing as experience outside of embodiment in signs. . . .
> The location of the organizing and formative center is not within . . . but
> outside. It is not experience that organizes expression, but the other way
> around—*expression organizes experience*. Expression is what first gives
> experience its form and specificity of direction.[35]

In other words, argued Bakhtin, language (expression) is constitutive of the human experience. It is through language that the simultaneity of differences is realized.

Although Bakhtin joined the intellectual groundswell of privileging language, his understanding of language was decidedly dialogic. In particular, in *Marxism and the Philosophy of Language*, Bakhtin (as Voloshinov) took issue with two trends he identified in contemporary philosophy of language—abstract objectivism and individualistic subjectivism, and in so doing articulated a dialogic conceptualization of language.[36] Bakhtin associated abstract objectivism with Saussure, who sought to transform the study of language from the examination of ancient languages to the modern discipline of linguistics with its moorings in language from the perspective of those who speak it. Although Bakhtin applauded the move to study living language, he took issue with Saussure's focus on the abstract system of language that governed all phonetic, grammatical, and lexical choices of speakers. Such an emphasis conceptualized language as a closed system, one in which creation was logically impossible: "From the point of view of [abstract objectivism], meaningful language creativity on the speaker's part is simply out of the question."[37] At the same time, however, Bakhtin was critical of the opposite extreme position, or what he called "individualistic subjectivism" in the study of language—that is, the view that uttered speech is nothing more than the creation of an intact, monadic self: "Individualistic subjectivism is wrong in ignoring and failing to understand the social nature of the utterance and in attempting to derive the utterance from the speaker's inner world as an expression of that inner world. The structure of the utterance and of the very experience being expressed is a *social structure*."[38] By "social structure," Bakhtin meant that the utterance is performed in a concrete situation between socially embedded speakers who are mutually answerable:

> Orientation of the word toward the addressee has an extremely high significance. In point of fact, word is a two-sided act. It is determined equally by whose word it is and for whom it is meant. As word, it is precisely the product of the reciprocal relationship between speaker and listener, addresser and addressee. Each and every word expresses the "one" in relation to the "other." I give myself verbal shape from another's point of view, ultimately, from the point of view of the community to which I belong. A word is a bridge thrown between myself and another.[39]

Rather than conceptualizing language as either an abstract, closed system or a matter of individual psyches, then, Bakhtin argued that language should be viewed as the dialogue (understood in both metaphorical and nonmetaphorical ways) between "the one" and "the other." In moving from the study of language as an abstract system to the study of language-in-use in everyday life, Bakhtin continued his early theoretical commitment to prosaics.

The central analytic unit in language-as-dialogue is the *utterance*. Bakhtin's use of the term "utterance" invokes a meaning far more complex than our contemporary understanding of an individuated act by an autonomous speaker. To Bakhtin, an utterance is a link in a "chain of speech communion,"[40] a link bounded by both preceding links and the links that follow.[41] These links give a given utterance its "dialogic overtones."[42]

Some of an utterance's preceding links are quite distant and remote in space and in time; these distal links represent the already-spoken utterances of the distant past that occurred prior to a particular conversation. Whenever we speak, argued Bakhtin, we use words that are already populated with others' prior utterances or with our own utterances from the past. For example, a distal dialogic overtone can be found in an idiomatic expression of love between partners whose meaning derives from some past interaction together. A distal dialogic overtone can also be found in the parties' reference to some commonly understood cultural expression. Distal dialogic overtones creep into an utterance's meaning through the parties' inner dialogues—conversational traces in memory.

Other utterances in the chain of speech communion are more proximal; for example, the immediately prior utterances in the conversation. These links represent dialogic overtones with the already-spokens of the current conversation. For example, when a speaker says, "I agree," the meaning of this utterance comes only in relation to the prior utterance(s) in the conversation.

Despite the fact that an utterance reverberates with dialogic echoes of the already-spokens, it also imparts something new, something unique, in the act of expression. Speaking, as a concrete, embodied act, always is performed in a unique time and space, a concept Bakhtin labeled a *chronotope*.[43] An utterance is always inflected with the speaker's chronotoped tone. As Gary Morson and Caryl Emerson have expressed it, "Tone bears witness to the singularity of the act and its singular relation to its performer."[44]

An utterance also sits at the dialogic boundary of the said and the unsaid. To some extent, speakers share the immediate situation in which they enact speech communion. In addition, speakers may swim in speech communities in which certain values and meanings are shared and thus do not need to be expressed explicitly. Shared speech community membership may also give speakers a shared understanding of the kind of speech-communication event, or *genre*,[45] which they are enacting. These shared meanings can function as taken-for-granted utterances in the chain of speech communion, unsaid but certainly not absent.

A given utterance also is laced with the dialogic overtones of conversational utterances that are anticipated to follow. Similar to the proximal and distal links of the already-spoken's, proximal and distal links can be identified with respect to the not-yet-spoken's in the chain of speech communion. When a speaker is constructing an utterance, he or she is taking into account the immediate addressee's possible response, that is, the proximal not-yet-spoken. Because the human experience is one of answerability, "an essential (constitutive) marker of the utterance is its quality of being directed to someone, its *addressivity*. As distinct from the signifying units of a language—words and sentences—that are impersonal, belonging to nobody and addressed to nobody, the utterance has both an author . . . and an addressee."[46] Speakers orient their utterances to the addressee, in anticipation of his or her response.

An addressee can be distal, as well—an addressee who is not a fellow participant-interlocutor in the immediate conversation but who may respond to the utterance at a future time and place. This distant addressee can be thought of as a superaddressee "whose absolutely just responsive understanding is presumed, either in some metaphysical distance or distant historical time."[47] The presence of a superaddressee creates a "loophole" in which meaning is forever unfinalizable, as Ruth Coates has noted:

> There is neither a first nor a last word. The contexts of dialogue are without limit. They extend into the deepest past and the most distant future. Even meanings born in dialogues of the remotest past will never be finally grasped once and for all, for they will always be renewed in later dialogue. At any present moment of the dialogue there are great masses of forgotten meanings, but these will be recalled again and given new life. For nothing is absolutely dead: every meaning will someday have its homecoming festival.[48]

At some point in the future, an utterance spoken in the past can become part of some superaddressee's dialogue, with its unique emergent meanings. Meanings are not fixed.

The addressivity of an utterance—the anticipated responses from the immediate addressee and from the superaddressee—precludes ownership by an individual speaker. The expression of an utterance is constructed as much by the listener as by the particular speaker. In this sense, an utterance can never be owned by a single speaker but instead is jointly owned by the speaker and its (super)addressees.

In short, dialogism's utterance is far from an individual act. It isn't even a duet between two speakers. It is more of an ensemble in which the simultaneous interplay of multiple different utterances produces meaning at the moment.[49] This fleeting unity of differences is Bakhtin's conception of dialogue. It is also what he means when he describes the "heteroglossia" of language.[50]

Bakhtin's post-1924 work often uses the term *voice* to stand for *utterance*, reminding us of the chronotoped embodiment of communication. But he also means utterance/voice in a more general sense as well, to refer to any specific point of view, wordview, value, or ideology constituted in the uttered word.[51]

Bakhtin's conception of dialogue is far from our contemporary idealization of the term to mean a smooth and seamless consensual exchange between equals.[52] Bakhtin's dialogue is envisioned as a rough-and-tumble affair:

> The word, directed toward its object, enters a dialogically agitated and tension-filled environment of alien words, value judgments and accents, weaves in and out of complex interrelationships, merges with some, recoils from others, intersects with yet a third group: and all this may crucially shape discourse.[53]

Put simply, dialogue is counterpoint.

Although Bakhtin believed in the importance of understanding the situated particularities of a given instance of speech communion, he also advanced a more general claim about all dialogic discourse. Dialogue, according to Bakhtin, is a process in which unity and difference, in some form, are at play, both with and against one another:

> Every concrete utterance of a speaking subject serves as a point where centrifugal as well as centripetal forces are brought to bear. The processes of centralization and decentralization, of unification and disunification, intersect in the utterance. . . . It is possible to give a concrete and detailed analysis of any utterance, once having exposed it as a contradiction-ridden, tension-filled unity of two embattled tendencies in the life of language.[54]

It is important to appreciate that Bakhtin's use of the term "contradiction-ridden" in this excerpt does not commit him to a dialectical view, at least in the narrow Hegelian-Marxian sense that dominated his sociopolitical world. In fact, late in his life Bakhtin wrote a harsh critique of this brand of dialectics as too abstract and removed from concrete experience; too mechanistic in its either-or logic that moved from thesis, to antithesis, to synthesis, in contrast to the both-and interplay envisioned in dialogue; and too biased in favor of finalizable synthesis, in contrast to the ongoing interplay of unity-and-difference that characterizes dialogue.[55]

Some genres of communication actualize dialogue more readily than others. Bakhtin valued the former for their dialogic potentials and criticized the latter for their monologic tendencies. Bakhtin wrote in particular about two dialogic genres: the novel and the medieval carnival. The novel, in contrast to other literary genres such as epic or poetry, is characterized by a polyphony of voices, according to Bakhtin.[56] This is particularly so, argued Bakhtin, under the skilled pen of Dostoevsky.[57] Dostoevsky had the ability to write double-voiced discourse; that is, he wrote without merging his voice as author with the voices of his characters. In Dostoevsky's double-voiced discourse, another label for dialogue, the reader experiences "not a multitude of characters and fates in a single objective world, illuminated by a single authorial consciousness; rather a plurality of consciousnesses, with equal rights and each with its own world, combine but are not merged in the unity of the event."[58]

In analyzing Dostoevsky's works, Bakhtin provides a typology of possible ways of orienting toward another's discourse that holds relevance to any form of discourse, whether written or oral.[59] In general, the typology advances a continuum from more monologic to more dialogic utterance types. Toward the monologic side, we have single-voiced discourse, which ignores the other's voice in its expression of the speaker's position as the "ultimate semantic authority."[60] For example, official or institutional discourse (the discourse of the Stalinist regime comes to mind) is monologically inclined. Toward the dialogic side, we have various degrees of double-voicedness in which the voice of the other is engaged in some way. For example, quoting someone else's voice for purposes of advancing one's own argument is more double-voiced than merely asserting one's position using one's own authoritative voice. But because the other's words are positioned as a servant to one's position, this discursive act is less double-voiced than, say, a rejoinder in a conversation in which the other's position is responded to on its own terms.

Bakhtin (as Voloshinov) had earlier introduced the concept of *reported speech*, a similar concept to double-voicedness.[61] In his earlier work, the concept had been used to discuss the ease, or difficulty, with which different languages such as Russian or French enabled a speaker to contain another's utterance in one's own. The later articulation of double-voicedness represented in *Problems of Dostoevsky's Poetics* presents a more sophisticated and concrete return to reported speech, reconceptualized as a feature of utterances rather than of languages.

The second genre identified by Bakhtin for its dialogic prospects is the carnival, exemplified in the medieval carnival.[62] In reflecting on carnivalistic life in general ("in the sense of the sum total of all diverse festivities, rituals and forms of a carnival type"[63]), Bakhtin observed that

> The laws, prohibitions, and restrictions that determine the structure and order of ordinary, that is noncarnival, life are suspended: what is suspended first of all is hierarchical structure and all the forms of terror,

reverence, piety, and etiquette connected with it—that is everything resulting from socio-hierarchical inequality or any other form of inequality
among people.... All distance between people is suspended, and a special
carnival category goes into effect: free and familiar contact among people.
... Carnival brings together, unifies, weds, and combines the sacred with
the profane, the lofty with the low, the great with the insignificant, the
wise with the stupid.[64]

The carnivalesque, then, is a moment where centripetal hierarchy is temporarily
"decrowned."[65] Eccentricity—in its many centrifugal forms—rules the event as
life is "drawn out of its usual rut."[66]

Bakhtin's discussion of the carnival is as close as he comes to explicit treatment of power relations, beyond his general critique of all monologically inclined
discourses. However, the carnival event is not a permanent shift in the discursive
landscape of circulating ideologies and the institutionalized hierarchies they construct and sustain. The decrowning of hierarchy is temporary; upon carnival's
end, the "usual rut" of life returns. Although Bakhtin's dialogism recognizes
power inequality in its differentiation of centripetal (at the center) and centrifugal (at the margins) discourses, it does not examine whether or how it is that
once centrifugal voices become centripetal, and vice versa, in any manner other
than in the fleeting moments of the carnivalesque.

Implications for the Study of Communication

It is ironic that the theorist who privileged "speech communication"[67]—real-life
dialogue with the utterance as its core unit of analysis—has been relatively slow
to gain recognition among communication scholars. A number of scholars engage in dialogue studies, drawing upon a wide range of relevant theorists other
than Bakhtin.[68] Some communication scholars interested in communication and
ethics have employed Bakhtin's dialogism prior to 1924.[69] Other scholars have
employed Bakhtin's post-1924 dialogism to examine rhetorical texts.[70] Performance studies features a range of Bakhtin-informed work.[71] Bakhtin's dialogism
is characterized by more muted presence in other areas of communication scholarship, including interpersonal communication,[72] language and social interaction,[73] mass communication,[74] and organizational communication.[75]

In 1996, Barbara Montgomery and I first formally articulated a theory
of relational communication grounded in Bakhtin's dialogism.[76] Over the past
dozen years or so, data-based research activity by my colleagues and me in family
communication and in relationship communication has been greatly influenced
by Bakhtin's dialogism.[77] Space limitations do not permit an exhaustive review
of this body of work. However, three implications of Bakhtin's dialogism hold
particular significance for any scholar interested in understanding face-to-face
communication.[78]

The first implication of dialogism for the study of face-to-face interaction is that of shifting from a monologic conception of the interlocutor to a dialogic conception. Scholars of face-to-face communication are still wedded to the Enlightenment view of the self as a monadic entity, or what Bakhtin might call the self-as-monologue. As a consequence, we have over-psychologized the study of face-to-face communication.[79] Scholars' views of communication often center on study of the individual mind and the role of cognitive processes. Relationships and families are thus often positioned as nothing more than the sum of the minds of the parties. Bakhtin's dialogism shifts our attention away from the intact mind of monadic selves to the interaction *between* interlocutors—the chain of utterances that comprise speech communion. If the study of face-to-face communication is to make a scholarly contribution unique from psychology, this shift is an important one.

The second implication is that of contributing to an alternative, constitutive vision of what communication does. The traditional, and still dominant, view of communication is variously referred to as a transmission, representational, or informational model of communication.[80] This traditional conception positions communication as a conduit through which a variety of antecedent psychological and sociological factors are merely played out. From the traditional view, communication functions to express the intact self's attitudes and beliefs, to transmit those to others so that self can be understood, and to influence others' attitudes, beliefs, and actions so that they are conformable to those of the self. By contrast, a dialogic perspective empowers communication to create, or construct, the social world, including self, other, and the relationship between them. Of course, several other constitutive conceptions of communication share the dialogic focus on creation.[81] The unique contribution of Bakhtin's dialogism is an articulation of the generative mechanism for the meaning-making process: the interplay of different, often opposing voices.

The third implication of Bakhtin's dialogism is a repositioning of difference to the center of our conceptualization of communication. Diversity is the ubiquitous condition of humanity, yet communication scholars (at least those who study face-to-face communication) have tended to (a) partition it off, as in specialized subfields such as intercultural communication or gender communication; (b) view it negatively, as in interpersonal conflict, where difference is framed as a problem to be managed; or (c) ignore it completely (as in the bias in favor of studying similarity that prevails in interpersonal communication and relational communication). By contrast, a dialogic perspective argues that difference (of all kinds) is basic to the human experience and to the role of communication in constituting that experience.

Bakhtin's career spanned a half century. His philosophy of dialogism generated a wealth of insights about the human experience, especially the place of speech communion in that experience. Communication scholars have much to gain from conversing with Bakhtin's dialogism.

Notes

1. The scholar Viktor Duvakin taped eighteen hours of interviews with Bakhtin in February and March of 1973. This excerpt originally appeared in Viktor Duvakin, "Razgovory s Bakhtinym: Sem'ia I gody ucheniia" [Conversations with Bakhtin: Family and student years], *Chelovek* 4 (1993): 152, and was quoted in Caryl Emerson, *The First Hundred Years of Mikhail Bakhtin* (Princeton, NJ: Princeton University Press, 1997), 6.

2. See, for example, Emerson, 149; Michael Holquist, *Dialogism*, 2nd ed. (New York: Routledge, 2002), xiii; Gary S. Morson and Caryl Emerson, *Mikhail Bakhtin: Creation of a Prosaics* (Stanford, CA: Stanford University Press, 1990), 1–12; and Tzvetan Todorov, *Mikhail Bakhtin: The Dialogical Principle*, trans. Wlad Godzich (Minneapolis, MN: University of Minnesota Press, 1984), ix.

3. The "Bakhtin industry," as Holquist, *Dialogism,* 184, has referred to it, is thriving. See Holquist, 183–195, for a particularly useful overview of the intellectual penetration of Bakhtin's work across a range of fields.

4. Holquist, *Dialogism,* 15.

5. Although the concept of dialogue is a coherent thread throughout Bakhtin's career, his work took a noticeable turn toward the study of language and texts beginning in 1929. For a useful elaboration of this issue, see Ken Hirschkop, "Bakhtin's Linguistic Turn," *Dialogism* 5/6 (2001): 21–34.

6. This essay was originally published in *Den' iskusstva* [The day of art], September 13, 1919. The English translation is cited in the remainder of this essay: Mikhail Bakhtin, "Art and Answerability," in *Art and Answerability: Early Philosophical Essays by M. M. Bakhtin,* ed. Michael Holquist and Vadim Liapunov, trans. Vadim Liapunov (Austin, TX: University of Texas Press, 1990), 1–3.

7. This essay was originally published as M. M. Bakhtin, "Author and Hero in Aesthetic Activity," in *Estetika slovesnogo tvorchestva* [Aesthetics of Verbal Creation], ed. Sergei B. Bocharov (Moscow: Iskusstvo, 1979), 7–180. The English translation is cited in the remainder of this essay: Mikhail Bakhtin, "Author and Hero in Aesthetic Activity," in *Art and Answerability: Early Philosophical Essays by M. M. Bakhtin,* ed. Michael Holquist and Vadim Liapunov, trans. Vadim Liapunov (Austin, TX: University of Texas Press, 1990), 4–256.

8. This essay originally appeared in the Russian collection M. M. Bakhtin, *Voprosy literatury i estetiki: Issledovaniia raznykh let* (Moscow: Khudozhestvennaia Literature, 1975). The English translation appeared in M. M. Bakhtin, "Supplement: The Problem of Content, Material, and Form in Verbal Art," *Art and Answerability,* ed. Michael Holquist and Vadim Liapunov, trans. Kenneth Brostrom (Austin, TX: University of Texas Press, 1990), 257–325.

9. This essay was originally published as M. M. Bakhtin, "Toward a Philosophy of the Act," *Filosofiia I sotsiologiia nauki i tekhnika: Ezhegodnik 1984–85* [Yearbook of the Scientific Council of Philosophical and Social Problems of Science and Technology, 1984–85] (Moscow: Nauka, 1986), 82–138. The English translation is cited in the remainder of this essay: Mikhail Bakhtin, *Toward a Philosophy of the Act,* ed. Vadim Liapunov and Michael Holquist, trans. Vadim Liapunov (Austin, TX: University of Texas Press, 1993).

10. Originally published as V. N. Voloshinov, *Marksizm I filosofija jazyka: Osnovnye problemy sociologiceskogo metoda v nauke o jazyke* [Marxism and the philosophy of language: Basic problems of the sociological method in the study of language] (Leningrad: Priboi, 1929). The English edition cited by most scholars is V. N. Voloshinov, *Marxism and the Philosophy of Language,* trans. Ladislav Matejka and I. R. Titunik (Cambridge, MA: Harvard University Press, 1986).

11. A particularly interesting essay in favor of Bakhtin's authorship of several disputed texts is based on interviews with Bakhtin himself. See Sergej Bocharov, "Conversations with Bakhtin," *PMLA* 109 (1994): 1009–1024.

12. Originally published as M. M. Bakhtin, *Problemy tvorchestva Dostoevskogo* (Leningrad: Priboi, 1929). Bakhtin expanded and revised the book, and this revision was published in 1963 as *Problemy poetiki Dostoevskogo* [Problems of Dostoevsky's poetics]. The English translation of this 1963 book is M. M. Bakhtin, *Problems of Dostoevsky's Poetics,* ed. and trans. Caryl Emerson (Minneapolis, MN: University of Minnesota Press, 1984).

13. Four essays, "Epic and Novel," "From the Prehistory of Novelistic Discourse," "Forms of Time and of the Chronotope in the Novel," and arguably the most important to communication scholars, "Discourse in the Novel," were originally published in the collection M. M. Bakhtin, *Voprosy literatury i estetiki: Issledovaniia raznykh let* (Moscow: Khudozhestvennaia literature, 1975). The English translation was published as M. M. Bakhtin, *The Dialogic Imagination: Four Essays by M. M. Bakhtin,* ed. Michael Holquist, trans. Caryl Emerson and Michael Holquist (Austin, TX: University of Texas Press, 1981).

14. Originally published as M. M. Bakhtin, *Tvorchestvo Fransua Rable i narodnaia kul'tura srednevekov'ia i renessansa* [The work of François Rabelais and popular culture of the Middle Ages] (Moscow: Khudozhestvennaia literatura, 1965). The English translation appears as M. M. Bakhtin, *Rabelais and His World,* trans. Helene Iswoksky (Bloomington, IN: Indiana University Press, 1984).

15. Originally published in the collection of essays M. M. Bakhtin, *Estetika slovesnogo tvorchestva,* ed. Sergej G. Bocharov (Moscow: Iskusstvo, 1979). The English translation of this essay appears in M. M. Bakhtin, *Speech Genres & Other Late Essays,* ed. Caryl Emerson and Michael Holquist, trans. Vern W. McGee (Austin: University of Texas Press, 1986).

16. Bakhtin's work continues to be influential in the Russian intellectual community. See Emerson, *The First Hundred Years.*

17. Craig Brandist, "The Bakhtin Circle," *The Internet Encyclopedia of Philosophy,* http://www.utm.edu/ research/iep/b/bakhtin.htm.

18. I am indebted to Michael Holquist's lucid treatment of Kant and Neo-Kantianism in his "Introduction: The Architectonics of Answerability," in M. M. Bakhtin, *Art and Answerability: Early Philosophical Essays by M. M. Bakhtin,* ed. Michael Holquist and Vadim Liapunov, trans. Vadim Liapunov (Austin: University of Texas Press, 1990), ix–xlix.

19. Holquist, *Dialogism,* 18.

20. Bakhtin, "Art and Answerability," 1.

21. Morson and Emerson, *Mikhail Bakhtin: Creation of a Prosaics,* 23.

22. Bakhtin, "Art and Answerability," 1.

23. Bakhtin, "Author and Hero in Aesthetic Activity," 35–36.

24. M. M. Bakhtin, "Appendix II: Toward a Reworking on the Dostoevsky Book," *Problems of Dostoevsky's Poetics*, 287.

25. Bakhtin, "Author and Hero in Aesthetic Activity," 22–23.

26. Bakhtin, *Toward a Philosophy of the Act*, 42.

27. Bakhtin, *Toward a Philosophy of the Act*, 40.

28. Bakhtin, "Author and Hero in Aesthetic Activity," 8.

29. Bakhtin, "Author and Hero in Aesthetic Activity," 5.

30. Bakhtin, "Author and Hero in Aesthetic Activity," 13.

31. Bakhtin, "Author and Hero in Aesthetic Activity," 25.

32. Bakhtin, "Author and Hero in Aesthetic Activity," 26.

33. Bakhtin, "Author and Hero in Aesthetic Activity," 27.

34. In particular, see Ferdinand de Saussure, *Course in General Linguistics*, trans. Wade Baskin (New York: McGraw-Hill, 1966).

35. Voloshinov, *Marxism and the Philosophy of Language*, 85.

36. Voloshinov, *Marxism and the Philosophy of Language*, 45–63.

37. Voloshinov, *Marxism and the Philosophy of Language*, 53.

38. Voloshinov, *Marxism and the Philosophy of Language*, 93.

39. Voloshinov, *Marxism and the Philosophy of Language*, 86.

40. Bakhtin, "The Problem of Speech Genres," 93.

41. Bakhtin, "The Problem of Speech Genres," 94.

42. Bakhtin, "The Problem of Speech Genres," 92.

43. Bakhtin, "Forms of Time and of the Chronotope in the Novel."

44. Morson and Emerson, *Mikhail Bakhtin: Creation of a Prosaics*, 133.

45. Bakhtin, "The Problem of Speech Genres," 78.

46. Bakhtin, "The Problem of Speech Genres," 95.

47. Bakhtin, "The Problem of Speech Genres," 126.

48. Ruth Coates, *Christianity in Bakhtin: God and the Exiled Other* (Cambridge: Cambridge University Press, 1998), 39.

49. Leslie A. Baxter and Barbara Montgomery, *Relating: Dialogues & Dialectics* (New York: The Guilford Press, 1996), 29.

50. Bakhtin, "Discourse in the Novel," 271.

51. Bakhtin, "Discourse in the Novel," 291–292.

52. For a particularly insightful discussion of what "dialogue" means to the average American layperson, see Stanley Deetz and Jennifer Simpson, "Critical Organizational Dialogue: Open Formation and the Demand of 'Otherness'," in *Dialogue: Theorizing Difference in Communication Studies*, ed. Rob Anderson, Leslie A. Baxter, and Kenneth N. Cissna (Thousand Oaks, CA: Sage, 2004), 141–158.

53. Bakhtin, "Discourse in the Novel," 276.

54. Bakhtin, "Discourse in the Novel," 272.

55. M. M. Bakhtin, "From Notes Made in 1970–71," in Bakhtin, *Speech Genres and Other Late Essays*, 147.

56. Because the focus of this essay is on those facets of dialogism of most relevance to communication scholars, I am not elaborating on Bakhtin's contributions to literary criticism in general, or his analysis of the novel in particular. For elaboration, see the four essays that appear in Bakhtin's *The Dialogic Imagination*.

57. Bakhtin, *Problems of Dostoevsky's Poetics.*

58. Bakhtin, *Problems of Dostoevsky's Poetics,* 6.

59. Bakhtin, *Problems of Dostoevsky's Poetics,* 199.

60. Bakhtin, *Problems of Dostoevsky's Poetics,* 199.

61. Voloshinov, *Marxism and the Philosophy of Language,* 115–159.

62. Bakhtin, *Rabelais and His World.*

63. Bakhtin, *Problems of Dostoevsky's Poetics,* 122.

64. Bakhtin, *Problems of Dostoevsky's Poetics,* 122–123.

65. Bakhtin, *Problems of Dostoevsky's Poetics,* 124.

66. Bakhtin, *Problems of Dostoevsky's Poetics,* 126.

67. Bakhtin, "The Problem of Speech Genres," 75.

68. See, for example, Anderson, Baxter, and Cissna, eds., *Dialogue.*

69. See, for example, Dwight Conquergood, "Performing as a Moral Act: Ethical Dimensions of the Ethnography of Performance," *Literature in Performance* 5 (1985): 1–13; Maurice Friedman, "Martin Buber and Mikhail Bakhtin: The Dialogue of Voices and the Word That Is Spoken," *Religion & Literature* 33 (2001): 25–36; Jeffrey W. Murray, "Bakhtinian Answerability and Levinasian Responsibility: Forging a Fuller Dialogical Communicative Ethics," *Southern Communication Journal* 65 (1999): 133–150.

70. For a useful discussion of Bakhtin's influence in rhetorical studies, see John M. Murphy, "Mikhail Bakhtin and the Rhetorical Tradition," *Quarterly Journal of Speech* 87 (2001): 259–277.

71. See, for example, the following works to sample the range of Bakhtin-informed work in performance studies: Conquergood; Mindy Fenske, "The Aesthetic of the Unfinished: Ethics and Performance," *Text & Performance Quarterly* 24 (2004): 1–19; Mikita Hoy, "Joyful Mayhem: Bakhtin, Football Songs, and the Carnivalesque," *Text & Performance Quarterly* 14 (1994): 289–305; Richard Rogers, "A Dialogics of Rhythm: Dance and the Performance of Cultural Conflict," *Howard Journal of Communication* 9 (1998): 5–27; and Mary S. Strine, "When Is Communication Intercultural? Bakhtin, Staged Performance, and Civic Dialogue," in Anderson, Baxter, and Cissna, *Dialogue,* 225–242.

72. In particular, see the theoretically oriented work of John Shotter, especially John Shotter, *Conversational Realities* (London: Sage, 1993); John Shotter, *Cultural Politics of Everyday Life* (Toronto: University of Toronto Press, 1993); and John Shotter, "Inside Dialogical Realities," *Southern Journal of Communication* 65 (2000): 119–132.

73. See, for example, the following works that draw in different ways upon Bakhtin's dialogism: Richard Holt, "Bakhtin's Dimensions of Language and the Analysis of Conversation," *Communication Quarterly* 51 (2003): 225–245; Carolyn Taylor, "'You Think It Was a *Fight?*': Co-constructing (the Struggle for) Meaning, Face, and Family in Everyday Narrative Activity," *Language and Social Interaction* 28 (1995): 283–317; and Maschler Yael, "The Role of Discourse Markers in the Construction of Multivocality in Israeli Hebrew Talk in Interaction," *Language and Social Interaction* 35 (2002): 1–38.

74. Despite an early essay by Horace M. Newcomb, "On the Dialogic Aspects of Mass Communication," *Critical Studies in Mass Communication* 1 (1984): 34–50,

Bakhtin has not been employed in much mass communication research. For an interesting exception, however, see Amy Sarch, "Those Dirty Ads!" *Critical Studies in Mass Communication* 14 (1997): 31–48.

75. For example: J. Kevin Barge and Martin Little, "Dialogical Wisdom, Communicative Practice, and Organizational Life," *Communication Theory* 12 (2002): 375–397.

76. The theory was labeled "relational dialectics"; Baxter and Montgomery, *Relating*. It is important to note that we use the term "dialectics" not in the narrow Hegelian/Marxist sense critiqued by Bakhtin but rather in a general sense to refer to the unity of opposing voices.

77. For recent summaries of this body of work, see Leslie A. Baxter, "Distinguished Scholar Article: Relationships as Dialogues," *Personal Relationships* 11 (2004): 1–22; and Leslie A. Baxter, "A Tale of Two Voices," *Journal of Family Communication* 4 (2004): 181–192.

78. I elaborate on these three implications in Leslie A. Baxter, "Communication as Dialogue," in *Communication as . . . : Stances on Theory*, ed. Greg Shepherd, J. St. John, and T. Striphas (Thousand Oaks, CA: Sage, in press).

79. Vernon Cronen, "Communication Theory for the Twenty-First Century: Cleaning Up the Wreckage of the Psychology Project," in *Communication: Views from the Helm for the 21st Century*, ed. Judith Trent (Boston, MA: Allyn and Bacon, 1998), 18–38.

80. Robert T. Craig, "Communication Theory as a Field," *Communication Theory* 9 (1999): 119–161.

81. Craig.

Bibliography of Works

Books by Mikhail Bakhtin

1920s

Marksizm i filosofija jazyka: Osnovnye problemy sociologiceskogo metoda v nauke o jazyke. Leningrad: Priboi, 1929. [Published under the pseudonym "V. N. Voloshinov"]
Problemy Tvorchestva Dostoyevskogo. Leningrad: Priboi, 1929.

1960s

Problemy poetiki Dostoevskogo. Moskow: Sov. Pisatel'. 1963.
Tvorchestvo Fransua Rable i narodnaia kul'tura srednevekov'ia i renessansa. Moskow: Khudozhestvennaia literatura, 1965.
Literatur und Karneval: Zur Romantheorie und Lachkultur. Trans. Alexander Kaempfe. Munich: Hanser, 1969.

1970s

Dostojevskij Umelec: K poetice prózy. Prague: Vimperk, 1971.
Voprosy literatury i estetiki. Moskow: Hudozhestven naja literature, 1975.
Estetika slovesnogo tvorchestva. Moskow: Iskusstvo, 1979.

1980s

Formal'nyi Metod v Literaturovendenii. New York: Serebrianyi Vek, 1982. [Published under the pseudonym "P.N. Medvedev"]
L'opera di Rabelais e la Cultura Popolare. Torino: Einaudi, 1982.
Literaturno-kriticheskie Stat'i. Moskow: Khudozh. Lit., 1986.
Untersuchungen zur Poetik und Theorie des Romans. Ed. Edward Kowalski. Berlin: Aufbau-Verlag, 1986.

1990s

Bachtin pod Maskoj. Maska 4. Red. I. V. Peskov. Moskow: Labirint, 1993–1994.
Formal'nyj Metod v Literaturovedenii: Bachtin pod Maskoj; Maska 2. Red. I. V. Peskov. Moskow: Labirint, 1993. [Published under the pseudonym "P. N. Medvedev"]
Marksizm i Filosofija Jazyka: Bachtin pod Maskoj; Maska 3. Red. I. V. Peskov. Moskow: Labirint, 1993. [Published under the pseudonym "V. N. Volosinov"]
Iskusstvo i Otvetstvennost' K Filosofii Postupka, Avtor i Geroi v Esteticheskoi Deiatel'Nosti, Problema Soderzhaniia: Materialy i Formy v Slovesnom Khudozhestvennom Tvorchestve. Kiev: Next, 1994.
Problemy Tvorcestva Dostoevskogo. Bachtin pod Maskoj; Maska 4. Moskow: Alkonost, 1994.
Raboty 1920-h Godov. Kiev: Next, 1994.
Bakhtin, Mikhail M. I Augusto Ponzio. *Bachtin e le sue Maschere: Il Percorso Bachtiniano fino ai Problemi Dell'opera di Dostoevskij (1919–1920).* Bari: Ed. Dedalo, 1995.
Chelovek v mire slova. Moskow: Rossijskij otkrytyj universitet, 1995.
Bakhtin, Mikhail and Viktor D. Duvakin. *Besedy V. D. Duvakina s M.M. Bachtinym.* Red. N. I. Kolyskina. Moskow: Progress, 1996.
Raboty 1940-h—nachala 1960-h Godov. Moskva: Russkie Slovari, 1996.
Sobranije sochinenij v 7 tomah. Moskow: Russkije slovari, 1996.

V. N. Volosinov, Pavel N. Medvedev, Ivan I. Kanaev, Michail M. Bachtin. *Stat'i. Bachtin pod Maskoj; Maska 5*. Red. I. V. Peskova. Moskow: Labirint, 1996.

Tetralogija. Moskow: Labirint, 1998.

Ars Vetus—Ars Nova. Red. I.U.H. Mediuk. Kiev: Vyd-vo Hnozys, 1999.

Lekcii po Istorii Zarubeznoj Literatury: Anticnost', Srednie Veka. Sost. V. A. Mirskaja. Saransk: Mordovskiy Univ., 1999.

2000s

Autor i geroj. K filosofskim osnovam gumanitarnyn nauk. Saint Peterburg: Azbuka, 2000.

Epos i roman. Saint Peterburg: Azbuka, 2000.

Frejdizm: Formal'nyi Metod v Literaturovedenii: Marksizm i Filosofiia Jazyka; Stat'i. Moskva: Labirint, 2000.

"Problemy Tvorcestva Dostoevskogo," 1929. *Stat'i o L. Tolstom, 1929. Zapisi Kursa Lejcij po Istorii Russkoj Literatury, 1922–1927*. Moskow: Russkie Slovari, 2000.

Filosofskaja Estetika 1920-x Godov. Sost. Sergej G. Bocarov. Moskow: Russkie Slovari, 2003.

Books by Mikhail Bakhtin Translated into English

1960s

Rabelais and His World. Trans. Helene Iswolsky. Cambridge, MA: MIT Press, 1968.

1970s

Freudism: A Marxist Critique. New York: Academic Press, 1970. [The authorship of this work is disputed. I. Titunik attributes the work to V. Voloshinov. Katerina Clark and Michael Holquist attribute the work to Bakhtin.]

Marxism and the Philosophy of Language. Trans. Ladislav Matejka and I. Titunik. New York: Seminar Press, 1973. [First published as the work of V. Voloshinov; the authorship of this work is disputed.]

Bakhtin, Mikhail M., and Pavel Medvedev. *The Formal Method In Literary Scholarship: A Critical Introduction to Sociological Poetics*. Trans. Albert Wehrle. Baltimore: Johns Hopkins University Press, 1973.

1980s

The Dialogic Imagination: Four Essays. Edited by Michael Holquist. Trans. Caryl Emerson and Michael Holquist. Austin: University of Texas Press, 1981.

Problems of Dostoevsky's Poetics. Ed. and trans. Caryl Emerson. Minneapolis: University of Minnesota Press, 1984.

Speech Genres and Other Late Essays. Trans. Vern W. McGee. Ed. Caryl Emerson and Michael Holquist. Austin: University of Texas Press, 1986.

1990s

Art and Answerability: Early Philosophical Essays. Ed. Michael Holquist and Vadim Liapunov. Trans. Vadim Liapunov. Austin: University of Texas Press, 1990.

Toward a Philosophy of the Act. Trans. Vadim Liapunov. Ed. Vadim Liapunov and Michael Holquist. Austin: University of Texas Press, 1993.

Index

absolute distance, 81
academic philosophy, 5
action, human, 6
activity, aesthetic, 252, 254
Addresser/Addressee, 173–74, 257–58
Adorno, Theodor W., 90, 92
affectivity, 117–20
Alexandrovna, Elena, 248
Alfonso XIII, King, 216
alter ego, 113
alterity, 178–81
ambiguity, 176–78
Anderson, Rob, 203–4
anxiety, dread of, 27, 30
Apel, Karl-Otto, 92
archaeology, 179
Arendt, Hannah, 12, 13, 14, 22; biographical sketch of, 65–66; communicative relevance and, 81–82; confidence to hope and, 78–79; dialectical communicative labor and, 14, 69, 76, 79–81; Heidegger and, affair with, 22, 66; legacy of, 69–72; modernity and, critique of, 68–75; as political philosopher, 66, 68; social and individualism, 75–78
Arendt, Paul, 65
argumentation, 96–98; critique and, 99, 100; definition of, 96–97; deliberative, 100; discourse and, 99; as product, procedure, and process, 98–101; theoretical and practical, 99–100; validity claims in, 96, 97–99
Aristotle, 4, 5, 98, 100; on Being and language, 23–24; classical laws of thought and, 168; entelechy and, metaphysical notion of, 28; on epideictic discourse, 33; formations, logic of, 168, 171, 176
Arneson, Pat, 1–20, 195–208
Arnett, Ronald C., 14, 67–82
art: as play, 53; reasoning of, 3–4, 5, 8; of rhetoric, 31, 48–49; work of, 53–54. *See also* reasoning arts

Art and Answerability (Bakhtin), 250
"Art and Answerability" (Bakhtin essay), 250
articulation, 15, 26, 227–28
artifactual production, 6
Asian logic, 169
atemporality, 202
Austria-Hungary and Serbia war, 195
authentic community, notion of, 34
authority, fragmentation of, 196
Avnon, Dan, 205
awareness, 207, 208; analogical, 151; direct, 141, 147, 154; global, 2, 195; integral, 201, 202; kinaesthesia, 123; perceptual, 143, 145, 151–52; phenomenal, 206; rational, 200; rules governing, 143; sedimented, 148; transmitted, 143
axiology, 5

Bakhtin, Mikhail, 12, 13, 15–16; Bakhtin circle, 248, 249, 250, 251, 255; biographical sketch of, 247–48; carnivalistic life and, 259–60; communication and, study of, 260–61; dialogism and, philosophy of, 15–16, 251–60; heteroglossia of language and, 197, 258; Kant's notion of knowledge and, 251–52; linguistic turn of, 249, 250, 254, 255; reported speech and, concept of, 259; on self, 16; utterance and, 16, 255–58; works of, key, 249–51
Bateson, Gregory, 173
Baxter, Leslie A., 15–16, 249–61
Beerwald, Eva and Clara, 66
Beerwald, Martin, 66
Being: distinctiveness of, special, 26; dwelling-place for, 25, 26; Hobbesian or Malthusian, 117; in-the-world, 3, 8, 17, 122–23, 124, 125; language and, 23–24, 32; the Nothing of, 27, 30; ontological workings of, 26, 27, 32;

Contributors

Pat Arneson (Ph.D., Ohio University, 1987) is Associate Professor in the Department of Communication & Rhetorical Studies at Duquesne University. Dr. Arneson's work examines issues of human communication from philosophical perspectives. Her research interests include organizational communication, philosophy of communication, interpretive approaches to research, interpersonal communication ethics, and educational assessment. She has published over 25 book chapters, journal articles, or research reports and is co-author with Ronald C. Arnett of *Dialogic Civility in a Cynical Age: Community, Hope, and Interpersonal Relationships* (State University of New York Press, 1999). Her work appears in *Integrative Explorations: Journal of Culture and Consciousness, Women's Studies in Communication, Communication Studies, The Electronic Journal of Communication/La Revue Electronique de Communication*, and *Journal of the Association for Communication Administration*, among other publications.

Ronald C. Arnett (Ph.D., Ohio University, 1978) is Professor in the Department of Communication & Rhetorical Studies at Duquesne University. Dr. Arnett's research and teaching interests include managerial communication, communication ethics, philosophy of communication, interpretive research, religion and communication, and dialogic theory. His work examines the presuppositions and the implications of philosophy of communication authors such as Martin Buber, Emmanuel Levinas, Hans-Georg Gadamer and Paul Ricoeur in applied communication contexts. He is the author of four books: *Dialogic Confession: Bonhoeffer's Rhetoric of Responsibility* (Southern Illinois University Press, 2005), *Dialogic Education: Conversation About Ideas and Between Persons* (Southern Illinois University Press, 1992), *Communication and Community: Implications of Martin Buber's Dialogue* (Southern Illinois University Press, 1986) and *Dwell in Peace: Applying Nonviolence to Everyday Relationships* (Brethren Press, 1980). He is co-author with Pat Arneson of *Dialogic Civility in a Cynical Age: Community, Hope, and Interpersonal Relationships* (State University of New York Press, 1999). He is co-editor with Josina M. Makau of *Communication Ethics in an Age of Diversity* (University of Illinois Press, 1996) and co-editor with Rob Anderson and Kenneth N. Cissna of *The Reach of Dialogue: Confirmation, Voice, and Community* (Hampton Press, 1994). He is the author of articles appearing in more than 50 journals, including *Western Journal of Speech Communication, Religious Communication Today, Journal of Communication and Religion, Central*

States Speech Journal, *Communication Quarterly*, and *Communication Education*, among other publications.

Leslie A. Baxter (Ph.D., University of Oregon, 1975) is F. Wendell Miller Distinguished Professor in the Department of Communication Studies at University of Iowa. Dr. Baxter's research and teaching interests center around communication in personal relationships. She is co-author with Earl R. Babbie of *The Basics of Communication Research* (Wadsworth/Thomson Learning, 2004). She is co-author with Barbara M. Montgomery of *Relating: Dialogues and Dialectics* (Guilford Press, 1996), which received the 1997 National Communication Association G. R. Miller Book Award. She is co-editor with Rob Anderson and Kenneth N. Cissna of *Dialogue: Theorizing Difference in Communication Studies* (Sage, 2003) and co-editor with Barbara M. Montgomery of *Dialectical Approaches to Studying Personal Relationships* (Erlbaum, 1998). She has close to 90 book chapters and journal articles on various topics related to communication in friendships, romantic relationships, marriages, and families. Her work appears in *Journal of Social and Personal Relationships*, *Journal of Family Communication*, *Journal of Applied Communication Research*, *Southern Communication Journal*, *Communication Studies*, *Western Journal of Communication*, *Human Communication Research*, *Quarterly Journal of Speech*, *Communication Theory*, *Sex Roles*, *Communication Monographs*, *Communication Quarterly*, and *Communication Education*, among other publications.

Bettina Bergo (Ph.D., Boston University, 1984) is Assistant Professor of Philosophy at the Université de Montréal. Dr. Bergo writes on contemporary French philosophy and its intersections with phenomenology, psychology, and recent Jewish thought. She authored *Levinas Between Ethics and Politics: For the Beauty That Adorns the Earth* (Kluwer Academic, 1999; Duquesne University Press, 2003). She has translated a large number of French philosophical works, including Emmanuel Levinas's *The Unthought Debt: Heidegger and the Hebraic Heritage* (Stanford University Press, 2006), Emmanuel Levinas's *On Escape/De L'évasion* (Stanford University Press, 2003), Emmanuel Levinas's *God, Death, and Time* (Stanford Unversity Press, 2000), and Emmanuel Levinas's *Of God Who Comes to Mind* (Stanford University Press, 1998). She co-translated and co-edited with Leonard Lawlor Merleau-Ponty's *Husserl at the Limits of Phenomenology: Including Texts by Edmund Husserl* (Northwestern University Press, 2001). Her work appears in numerous book chapters and journals, including *Continental Philosophy Review*, *The Southern Journal of Philosophy*, *South African Journal of Philosophy*, *Ethics: An International Journal of Social, Political, and Legal Philosophy*, *Tympanum* (an internet journal of philosophy), *Graduate Faculty Philosophy Journal*, and *New School for Social Research Graduate Faculty Philosophy Journal*, among other publications.

G. Thomas Goodnight (Ph.D., University of Kansas, 1977) is Professor in the Annenberg School for Communication at University of Southern California. Dr. Goodnight's research interests include deliberation and postwar society, science communication, argument and aesthetics, public discourse studies, and communicative reason in controversy. He has been accorded career awards in Rhetoric and Communication Theory by the National Communication Association (Charles H. Woolbert Research Award, 1992; Golden Anniversary Monograph Award, 1995) and been named as one of the five top scholars in argument of the last 50 years by the American Forensics Association. Dr. Goodnight authored *Care for the Poor: A Basic Overview of the Problems Surrounding Poverty in the United States* (National Textbook Co., 1984), *In Defense of Our Nation: A Basic Overview of the Problems Involved in U.S. Defense Policy* (National Textbook Co., 1982), *Reforming Our Schools: A Basic Overview on the Question of Elementary and Secondary Education* (National Textbook Co., 1981), and *Water for All Americans* (National Textbook Co., 1985). He coauthored with David Zarefsky *Forensic Tournaments: Planning and Administration* (National Textbook Co., 1980). He edited *Arguing Communication and Culture* (National Communication Association, 2002), *The Environment–Preserving the Future: A Critical Analysis of the Role of the United States in Improving the Global Environment* (National Textbook Co., 1992) and *Homelessness: A Social Dilemma: A Critical Analysis of the Question of Homelessness in the United States* (National Textbook Co., 1991). His work appears in journals including *Quarterly Journal of Speech, Communication Monographs, Journal of the American Forensic Association, International Journal of Public Opinion Research, Critical Studies in Mass Communication,* and *Western Journal of Speech Communication,* among other publications.

Michael J. Hyde (Ph.D., Purdue University, 1977) is Professor and University Distinguished Chair in Communication Ethics in the Department of Communication at Wake Forest University. Dr. Hyde's research and teaching interests consider the study of public moral argument, the ethics of rhetoric, computer-mediated communication, and the ethics and rhetoric of medicine. He authored *The Life-Giving Gift of Acknowledgment: A Philosophical and Rhetorical Inquiry* (Purdue University Press, 2006) and *The Call of Conscience: Heidegger and Levinas, Rhetoric and the Euthanasia Debate* (University of South Carolina Press, 2001), which received the 2002 National Communication Association Diamond Anniversary Book Award and the 2002 National Communication Association Marie Hochmuth Nichols Award for Outstanding Scholarship in Public Address. Hyde edited the book *Communication Philosophy and the Technological Age* (University of Alabama Press, 1982) and has received national, state, and university research grants for his work in the rhetoric of medicine. He has written more than 50 articles and critical reviews in scholarly journals, including *Quarterly Journal of Speech, Philosophy and Rhetoric, Journal of Applied Communication Research, Communication Quarterly, Communication,* and *Communication Education,* among other publications.

Lenore Langsdorf (Ph.D., State University of New York at Stony Brook, 1977) is the William and Galia Minor Professor of the Philosophy of Communication in the Department of Speech Communication at Southern Illinois University-Carbondale. Dr. Langsdorf's research and teaching interests center around philosophy of communication; argumentation, cultural, and rhetorical theory; hermeneutic phenomenology and pragmatism as research methods. She is co-editor with Stephen H. Watson and E. Marya Bower of *Phenomenology, Interpretation, and Community* (State University of New York Press, 1998). She is co-editor with Stephen H. Watson and Karen A. Smith of *Reinterpreting the Political: Continental Philosophy and Political Thought* (State University of New York Press, 1996). She is co-editor with Andrew R. Smith of *Recovering Pragmatism's Voice: The Classical Tradition, Rorty, and the Philosophy of Communication* (State University of New York Press, 1995) and co-editor with Ian Angus of *The Critical Turn: Rhetoric and Philosophy in Postmodern Discourse* (Southern Illinois University Press, 1993). She has published numerous journal articles on various topics related to philosophical issues in *Argumentation, Communication Theory, Human Studies, Inquiry, Journal of Phenomenology and the Human Sciences, Informal Logic, The Review of Metaphysics,* and *Southwestern Journal of Philosophy,* among other publications.

Richard L. Lanigan (Ph.D., Southern Illinois University, 1969) is Outstanding Scholar of the University and Professor in the Department of Speech Communication at Southern Illinois University-Carbondale. Dr. Lanigan's research and teaching interests center around communicology and philosophy. In 1977, he was the founding Chair of the Philosophy of Communication Division of the International Communication Association at the first World Congress on Communication Science, Berlin, Germany. He is currently Director and Fellow of the International Communicology Institute (www.communicology.org), Vice President of the International Association for Semiotic Studies, and Editor of *The American Journal of SEMIOTICS.* He has authored five books: *The Human Science of Communicology: The Phenomenology of Discourse in Foucault and Merleau-Ponty* (Duquesne University Press, 1992), *Speaking and Semiology: Maurice Merleau-Ponty's Phenomenological Theory of Existential Communication* (Mouton, 1991), *Phenomenology of Communication: Merleau-Ponty's Thematics in Semiology and Communication* (Duquesne University Press, 1988), *Semiotic Phenomenology of Rhetoric: Eidetic Practice in Henry Grattan's Discourse on Tolerance* (Washington, D.C.: Center for Advanced Research in Phenomenology, University Press of America, 1984), and *Speech Act Phenomenology* (Martinus Nijhoff, 1977). He has published numerous book chapters and articles in journals including *Philosophy and Rhetoric, Central States Speech Communication Journal, Philosophy Today, Man and World, Southern Speech Communication Journal, Journal of Applied Communication Research, Quarterly Journal of Speech, Semiotica, International Journal of the Sociology of Language, The Humanistic Psychologist, Critical Stud-*

ies in Mass Communication, and *Journal for Philosophy and the Social Sciences*, among other publications. In 1996 he was a Senior Fulbright Scholar at Sichuan University and in 2004 became the first communication scholar to deliver an invited paper at the Chinese Academy of Social Sciences in Beijing, Peoples Republic of China.

Algis Mickunas (Ph.D., Emory University, 1969) is Professor Emeritus in the Department of Philosophy at Ohio University. Dr. Mickunas's areas of specialization are phenomenology, contemporary European philosophy, and nineteenth- and twentieth-century European philosophy. He has authored *Lifeworld and History* (Kluwer Academic Publishers, forthcoming), *Philosophy and Technology* (Hampton Press, in press). He is co-author with Joseph J. Pilotta of *Technocracy vs. Democracy: Issues in the Politics of Communication* (Hampton Press, 1998), co-author with J. David Stewart of *Exploring Phenomenology: A Guide to the Field and Its Literature* (Ohio University Press, 1990/1994), co-author with Joseph J. Pilotta of *Science of Communication: Its Phenomenological Foundations* (Lawrence Erlbaum, 1990), and co-author with John R. Scudder of *Meaning, Dialogue, and Enculturation: Phenomenological Philosophy of Education* (London, England: The Center for Advanced Research in Phenomenology, Inc.; and Lanham, MD: University Press of America, 1985). He is co-editor with Lester Embree, Elisabeth A. Behnke, David Carr, J. Claude Evans, José Huertas-Jourda, Joseph J. Kockelmans, William R. McKenna, Jitendra Nath Mohanty, Thomas Nenon, Thomas M. Seebohm and Richard M. Zaner of *Encyclopedia of Phenomenology* (Kluwer Academic Publishers, 1996); co-editor with Ted Kisiel and Alphonso Lingis of *Horizons of Continental Philosophy: Essays on Husserl, Heidegger, and Merleau-Ponty* (Martinus Nijhoff, 1988); and co-editor with John W. Murphy and Joseph J. Pilotta of *The Underside of High-Tech: Technology and the Deformation of Human Sensibilities* (Greenwood Press, 1986), among others. He translated with Noel Barstad Jean Gebser's work *The Ever-Present Origin* (Ohio University Press, 1985) and translated Elisabeth Stoker's *Investigations in Philosophy of Space* (Ohio University Press, 1987). In addition, he has published numerous articles in scholarly journals and served on professional editorial boards.

Ramsey Eric Ramsey (Ph.D., Purdue University, 1994) is Associate Professor of the Barrett Honors College at Arizona State University at the West Campus. Dr. Ramsey is editor and the originator of the Philosophy/Communication book series published by Purdue University Press. His work investigates, from an interdisciplinary perspective, questions concerning communication, rhetoric, and ethics. His ideas are grounded in a belief that a philosophy of ethics must concern itself with the relations among communication, rhetoric, and democracy. Dr. Ramsey developed a philosophy of communication in his book *The Long Path to Nearness: A Contribution to a Corporeal Philosophy of Communication and the Groundwork for an Ethics of Relief* (Prometheus Books, 1998) that gives a philosophical description of communicative praxis. He is co-author with Linda Wiener of *Leaving Us to Wonder: An Essay on the Questions Science Can't Ask* (SUNY Press, 2005). He is co-editor with David James Miller of *Experiences Between Philosophy and Communication: Engaging the Philosophical Contributions of Calvin O.* Schrag (SUNY Press, 2003). He is currently exploring the relation of the practice of communication to classical ethical theories, demonstrating the fundamental role communication has in ethical conduct. He considers the imagination and theology as they can be used to inform questions concerning communication and ethics as well as studies in classical Greek rhetoric and philosophy investigating the long history between communication, rhetoric, and philosophy. Dr. Ramsey has published in journals including *Rethinking Marxism*, *Philosophy and Rhetoric*, *Phenomenological Inquiry*, *Communication Theory*, and *Argumentation and Advocacy*, among other publications. He has lectured and delivered papers internationally in the Czech Republic, Spain, Romania, Costa Rica, Mexico, and Cuba.

J. N. Sturgess is an undergraduate student, studying philosophy as a member of the Barrett Honors College at Arizona State University at the West Campus. She plans to do graduate work in philosophy after completing her baccalaureate degree.